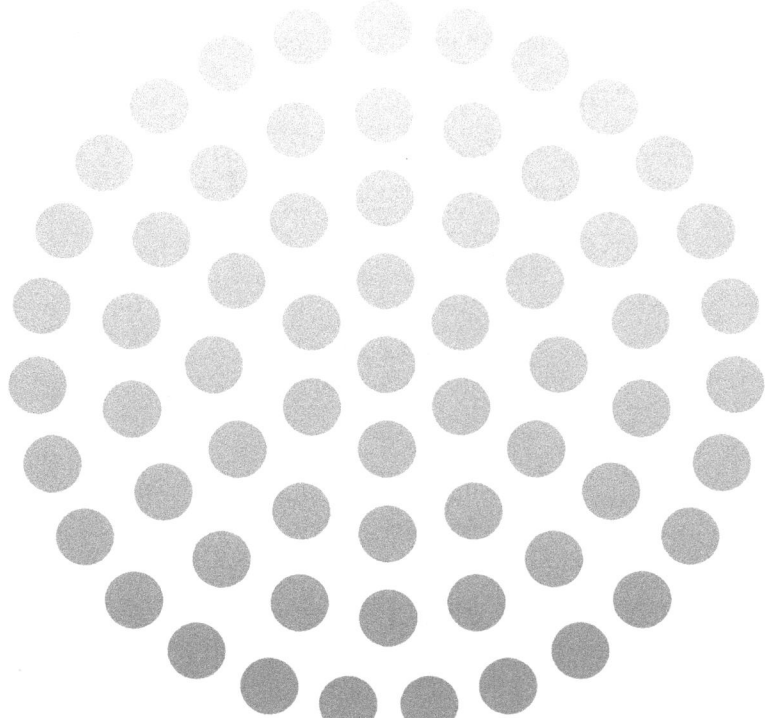

GENE KEYS

This 2nd edition published in Great Britain and USA 2020
by Gene Keys Publishing Ltd
13 Freeland Park, Wareham Road, Poole BH16 6FA

Copyright © Richard Rudd 2018, 2020

All rights reserved. No part of this book may be reproduced
or utilised in any form or by any means, electronic or mechanical,
without prior permission in writing from the publishers.

Richard Rudd

THE 64 WAYS
Personal Contemplations on the Gene Keys

ISBN 978-1-913820-00-8

Transcribed and edited by Richard Rudd and Pam Deleo.

The content in this book is purely inspirational which you may choose to use on a personal journey of investigation and exploration. This should not be entered into lightly. It is to be used with the understanding that neither the publisher nor author is engaged to render any type of psychological or other professional advice in any way, shape or form. The content of the course is the sole expression and opinion of its author, and not necessarily that of the publisher. No warranties or guarantees are expressed or implied. The publishers take no responsibly for how you use the content.

genekeys.com

About the Author

A teacher, mystic and poet, Richard Rudd attended Edinburgh University where he gained a Master's degree in literature and metaphysics. A born explorer, he has studied with great teachers in the East, traveled through the Himalayas, the Pacific, the Americas and the Arctic. He worked in the film industry in Australia, trained as a teacher of Chi Kung and meditation in Thailand and sailed across the Atlantic Ocean on a small yacht. Throughout his adventures Richard has explored his love of writing and in 2006 he won the FISH International Poetry Award in Ireland. Richard's mystical journey began early in life as he experienced strange energies rushing throughout his body. This catalysed his spiritual search. All his studies became synthesised in 2002 when he began to write and receive the Gene Keys. It took 7 years to write the book and understand its teachings and applications. Today Richard continues to study and teach the profound lessons contained in the Gene Keys.

Table of Contents

Gene Key 1 - The Way of Freshness.....................1

Gene Key 2 - The Way of Orientation..................11

Gene Key 3 - The Way of Innovation...................19

Gene Key 4 - The Way of Understanding.............31

Gene Key 5 - The Way of Patience......................41

Gene Key 6 - The Way of Diplomacy...................51

Gene Key 7 - The Way of Guidance.....................61

Gene Key 8 - The Way of Style..........................69

Gene Key 9 - The Way of Determination.............79

Gene Key 10 - The Way of Naturalness.............87

Gene Key 11 - The Way of Idealism....................95

Gene Key 12 - The Way of Discrimination.........105

Gene Key 13 - The Way of Discernment............113

Gene Key 14 - The Way of Competence.............123

Gene Key 15 - The Way of Magnetism...............135

Gene Key 16 - The Way of Versatility..............143

Gene Key 17 - The Way of Far-sightedness........151

Gene Key 18 - The Way of Integrity.................161

Gene Key 19 - The Way of Sensitivity..............173

Gene Key 20 - The Way of Self-assurance........181

Gene Key 21 - The Way of Authority...............189

Gene Key 22 - The Way of Graciousness..........199

Gene Key 23 - The Way of Simplicity...............209

Gene Key 24 - The Way of Invention................225

Gene Key 25 - The Way of Acceptance.............233

Gene Key 26 - The Way of Artfulness.............243

Gene Key 27 - The Way of Altruism.................253

Gene Key 28 - The Way of Totality.................263

Gene Key 29 - The Way of Commitment............271

Gene Key 30 - The Way of Lightness................281

Gene Key 31 - The Way of Leadership..............291

Gene Key 32 - The Way of Preservation...........303

Gene Key 33 - The Way of Mindfulnes............313

Gene Key 34 - The Way of Strength................321

Gene Key 35 - The Way of Adventure.............331

Gene Key 36 - The Way of Humanity.............341

Gene Key 37 - The Way of Equality.................349

Gene Key 38 - The Way of Perseverance..........359

Gene Key 39 - The Way of Dynamism...............367

Gene Key 40 - The Way of Resolve..................377

Gene Key 41 - The Way of Anticipation.............387

Gene Key 42 - The Way of Detachment............397

Gene Key 43 - The Way of Insight...................405

Gene Key 44 - The Way of Teamwork...............413

Gene Key 45 - The Way of Synergy.................423

Gene Key 46 - The Way of Delight..................431

Gene Key 47 - The Way of Transmutation........441

Gene Key 48 - The Way of Resourcefulness.....449

Gene Key 49 - The Way of Revolution.............459

Gene Key 50 - The Way of Equilibrium............471

Gene Key 51 - The Way of Initiative.................481

Gene Key 52 - The Way of Restraint...............493

Gene Key 53 - The Way of Expansion...............501

Gene Key 54 - The Way of Aspiration...............511

Gene Key 55 - The Way of Freedom.................521

Gene Key 56 - The Way of Enrichment.............529

Gene Key 57 - The Way of Intuition.................539

Gene Key 58 - The Way of Vitality....................547

Gene Key 59 - The Way of Intimacy.................555

Gene Key 60 - The Way of Realism..................565

Gene Key 61 - The Way of Inspiration..............575

Gene Key 62 - The Way of Precision................585

Gene Key 63 - The Way of Inquiry..................597

Gene Key 64 - The Way of Imagination.............607

Dilemmas of the Gene Keys.............................616

The text of this book has been transcribed from the author's original oral contemplations on the 64 Gene Keys. Although slight changes have been made to the text, we have endeavoured to retain the informal flow, style and cadence of the original oral transmission.

Foreword

The book in your hands has been a great labour of love. These personal contemplations on the 64 Gene Keys are my oral exploration of this vast wisdom transmission. It has taken me over three years to record and transcribe them. Coming as they have, after the main Gene Keys book, the 64 Ways are very different in style from the original. Being an oral transmission they have a more subjective flavour and I believe they make an illuminating complimentary companion to the original work.

When we speak aloud we activate a different part of the brain from when we write. Therefore as I have contemplated the wisdom of each of the 64 Ways, you will find that I often revert to stories or recite pieces of poetry to help bring the wisdom alive. I have used images and examples from my personal life and have also gone in more depth into the original imagery of the I Ching, upon which the Gene Keys are based. These are my deepest inner contemplations on the 64 Gene Keys and the Spectrum of Consciousness that underpins them.

The Art of Contemplation is a subjective path towards truth. As you learn to wrap your imagination and your intuition around the subject of your choice, so the natural wisdom within you springs to life. In this sense contemplation is always a journey of unravelling in which the layers of the great mystery are progressively revealed within your heart. It is thus my hope that these contemplations, both in their original oral form and through these transcriptions, will be inspiring and useful to all voyagers of the Gene Keys.

The 64 Ways are indicators that point towards the great mystery. As you realise through listening to them or reading them, there always comes a moment when the limits of language are reached. As the great sages have always said truth cannot be spoken, only pointed at. That said, if you have been drawn to the Gene Keys, these contemplations may be one of the most accessible ways into the wisdom. I hope they will bolster your own practice of contemplation and illuminate your journey through the labyrinth.

Richard Rudd

THE 1ST WAY

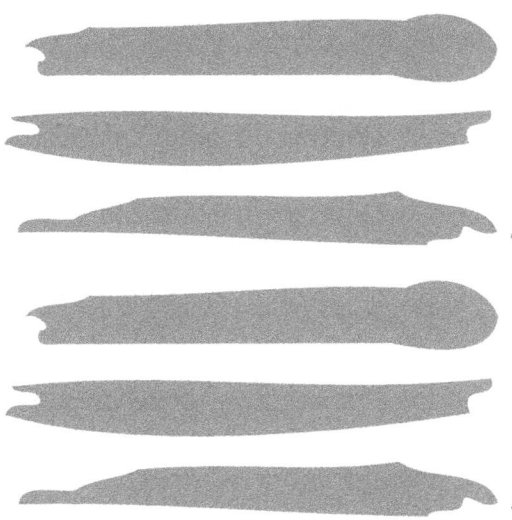

Gene Key 1

THE WAY OF FRESHNESS

The Transformational Way of the 1st Gene Key moves from Entropy to Beauty, and it's the Way of Freshness.

The Dilemma of this Gene Key is a feeling we all know, although we don't always recognise it when we're in it - it's numbness. Contrary to what we might think, numbness is in fact a feeling. Therefore to realise that we're numb is a huge insight. For many of us this realisation is just the beginning of our journey into the human heart. Because of the layers of our wounding, whether from our childhood or through inherited ancestral memories, the state of numbness is one of the most widespread human Shadow states.

Rare is the human who knows that they're numb. We will try anything to avert the realisation that we're feeling numb. We keep ourselves busy or we go through one of the many doors of distraction that the world offers. We spend entire days doing things without ever realising that we're actually doing them, like a zombie. Entropy, the Shadow of this Gene Key, represents the loss or depletion of energy within any system. It's why we sometimes get to the end of a day and feel exhausted but not fulfilled. Many things about our lives can be entropic. Our relationships can leak energy because we don't pay them enough attention. Our jobs can be entropic if we don't draw inspiration from them. Our environments can be draining - the places we work, the streets where we live or the media we take in through our senses. They all conspire to maintain the numbness and the entropy, and they leave us in survival mode.

In this contemplation I want to draw our attention over and over again into the numbness. Put your hand on your chest. How does it feel? Do you feel open there? Do you feel joy stirring? Or do you feel tired, empty or nothing? It's perfectly normal to feel nothing; it's

Shadow: Entropy   **Gift**: Freshness   **Programming Partner:** Gene Key 2
Dilemma: Numbness   **Siddhi**: Beauty   **Codon Ring:** The Ring of Fire

the starting block for transformation. Once we realise our numbness then our awareness goes to work. We begin to breathe into the numbness, just softly at first, ever so softly. We tell the numbness that it's ok, it's allowed. We can trust the numbness and let it in deeper. It's important to see how deeply we avoid this feeling. It's important to see how it makes us want to go and do something or eat something, or call someone, or send a text, whatever it is, we would rather do anything but feel the numbness.

There's this new phenomenon in the world today. We see it particularly on public transport - people are looking down at their mobile phones all the time. Have you noticed? Are you one of them? You know, the grey faces staring down at those tiny screens. How often do we see someone simply staring into space or looking around? It's the numbness, this Dilemma and it's all - pervasive. We don't allow our children to just be bored anymore. If we don't know the bored state, the blank state, we're missing one of the great lessons in life - the fertile state of emptiness that precedes creativity.

My kids sometimes come to me (all parents know this), and say 'I'm bored'. Most parents then offer a list of options, but I don't think that's what they are wanting. They always say no to everything on our list anyway. I think they're simply wanting to have the blank state acknowledged. That's what we all need. We need to be comfortable with the numbness, comfortably numb, as the song goes. Having said that, it isn't comfortable. It isn't meant to be. It's the gap, and life needs gaps. Everything needs pauses. Pauses are healthy.

We can be okay being uncomfortable. That's the secret of transforming the 1st Shadow into the 1st Gift, and it's the great secret of creativity that's in this Gene Key. This is the Ring of Fire, the great yang hexagram - the beginning of the entire I Ching.

Fire emerges from water. Yang arises from yin. Something comes from nothing. Joy comes from numbness. The numbness is the kindling, our awareness is the breath fanning the first sparks and then the joy emerges as the fire catches. The process takes as long as it takes and it's a magical process. Sometimes our lives hit one of these numb patches. Sometimes it's a few hours, sometimes days, months or even years. There are cycles of success and cycles of decline in everything. Life is a dance between the poles. We have to keep opening to the numbness in our breast and trust it, with no pressure for it to change. We just have to let it remain for as long as it wants. Only our deep trust will show us the magic. And we can begin this right now, right where we are. We can make a practice of it. It's our numbness vipassana meditation. Here we are just trusting the numbness, just being with it. The 1st Siddhi is Beauty and one day we'll even come to see the numbness as part of that beauty.

The 1st Gift - Freshness

Do you know what the foundation of creativity really is? Which quality do you think is most central to the creative process? I would say this: to be unafraid of making mistakes. To be original we must stretch our limbs out into deep space and take an untrodden path. As the poet Antonio Machado famously said: 'Caminante, no hay camino, se hace camino al andar.' 'Wanderer, there is no path, we make the path by walking.'

This is the meaning of this wonderful word 'freshness'. It means to be original, to be a pioneer, to be a fool. Like in the old Tarot system - the most magical card, the alpha card, the first card in the pack, was always the Fool. And here we are with the 1st Gene Key in the pack. There are 63 Gene Keys to come. What a journey lies ahead! And it all begins here with the Fool - the step that no one else has ever taken. And guess where that step leads us? It leads out of the numbness, out of the stasis, out of the void and into life. Even if it's a disaster. Even if our attempt at novelty or success crashes and burns in a spectacular way, we've made it out of our box. What a feeling that is. We've begun to live. That's what the French mean by that wonderful expression la joie de vivre, the joy of life, the elan vital. With the 1st Gift that's what we have - élan, panache - all these beautiful French words to launch our lives out of the cinders, to reach for the sky, to burn with love for the new.

This is the 1st Gift, the very ground of human genius. And genius is built upon mistakes, hundreds and hundreds of them. There are so many dead - end paths. How do we think the great inventions got here, through lucky guesses? Never. Through endless trial and error. Through toil and patience and dogged craziness. That's what it takes to break new ground. It's like my new courses. Every time I teach a new course I first come up with a name. I know that a whole mystery lies behind that name. Maybe I sketch a few words around the name and then I advertise the course. Do you think I have any idea whatsoever what that course consists of? I have no idea! And I love that thrill. For me it's the not - knowing that's the real reason I do this. Not for the knowing, but for the not - knowing. I do it for the mystery and the magic of the emergent. And the closer I get to the course the more it arrives. It comes at me from all directions. The whole universe conspires with me. It's as though the universe loves my devilish risk - taking and it responds by rewarding me with a living transmission of wisdom that falls together before my eyes. People often ask me where or how I come up with all these things. They think I'm some kind of a channel, but it's not like that. I don't have a gift of knowing. I'm no more special than anyone else. If I have a gift at all, it's that I know I don't know anything. I said of a friend recently, 'you know, when it comes to the Gene Keys he knows everything I know but he doesn't know what I don't know'!

Creativity is God at play. Once we get hooked by it we can begin to use it in many ways though our communication, our work, our family, through all kinds of areas. Creative freshness is our inheritance. We just have to stretch for it. Every human alive has hidden abilities; we all come from the other side trailing clouds of glory. Our purpose is to rekindle those abilities that we felt as children and to keep those same fires alive in our children as they grow. It may sound powerful and awe - inspiring from my fiery diction, but in the child the fire is often so delicate. It's a tiny flame so easily extinguished and it's extinguished so often, by homogenised education, by a processed diet, by institutional isolation.

For most of us the flame of creativity fades during our school years. It's deeply sad that we have created such a spirit - quashing system. That's why the Gene Keys came alive in me, because the flame arose again. The phoenix is rising. You can't hold the human spirit down. Now here I am sharing it and building a forest fire. A harmony of creative rebels, that's the communal vision of the Gene Keys. That's the potential of this Ring of Fire, to reconnect people to their hearts, to their real professions. To have people think outside the box, to live outside the box. To blow the bloody box to smithereens! That's the Gift of Freshness. Some Gene Keys, we just can't explain them. We don't have to. We just have to let them sing out inside us. We just have to let the transmission into our cells. There is nothing numb about this Gene Key. We have to become the fire.

Creativity means making mistakes. It means flexibility and letting go. An idea moves one way and then it moves another. When ideas begin to become real and move into the world of form they encounter resistance and friction from unforeseen complexities and contact with human emotion and drama. We have to be so yielding to see a creative impulse through all the way and it will have a life of its own. Every endeavour, book, play, business has its own destiny. We have to be midwives, and we can't control the outcome. We only think we're in control. Creativity, the Gift of Freshness, is less about having great ideas (which let's face it, anyone can do), and more about letting go and gentling that idea into form. This is a Gift of knowing how to work with the delicacy of fire, and we need to treat fire with respect. If we go in with a lot of ego we'll get burned.

Everyone can contemplate this Gift of Freshness no matter what our Profile looks like. We all have this Gift. It's the Gift of giving birth, of bringing the unknown into the known. It's the midwife's Gift, to be there when it happens.

A friend of mine wrote this awesome song recently and I asked how it came through for him. His response was simply: 'I was just there when it happened'. The really creative people are humble, not fixed. They're open rather than rigid. They're soft rather than hard. They're dull rather than shiny. To be close to the mystery we must be like the mystery. We must be vulnerable, fallible, naked, pliant. To really understand fire, to shape it with our fingers, we must be just like water.

If we do happen to have this in our Profile then we're one of humanity's pioneers. We are here to bring the void into form. We are here to dance with fire and to be a risk-taker in life but not necessarily on the outside. It is on the inner planes where we must risk our ego, our fixedness, our very identity, because when we engage fully with the creative process it will reshape us. That's the beauty we find in this Siddhi; that creativity changes us and beautifies us and that's a real mystery.

The 1st Siddhi - Beauty

What does it mean to be beautified? To let go so completely into a creative process that it transforms, purifies, cleanses and puts us in touch with our soul, with our essence. This is the true meaning of creativity - to move into the heart of life's mystery.

This 1st Siddhi is one of the four great pillars of the I Ching along with its programming partner the 2nd Gene Key, the 63rd and the 64th. Beauty, Unity, Truth and Illumination, the four great principles of the cosmos. Beauty and unity are a dance, a couplet. They're soul mates. These two principles can't be separated. If we want to know what beauty is we can only know it through unity. To see where everything is connected, to see the perfection of the whole shimmering in its myriad ways, this is beauty. Beauty is quintessentially human. It's the crystallisation of our perception. Yet it's beyond the senses. Our senses reach for beauty but they can't encapsulate it; it lives beyond the fringe of their world. Our longing stretches itself towards beauty as well. We yearn for an experience of beauty. We chase it our whole lives.

Where is beauty? What is it? How do we find it? The fact is that it lies beyond us. This is why we will always yearn for it. Beauty is an experience of the divine. It's to see the face of God. How many people are given that? We may believe we know what that is, but we don't. I am reminded of this wonderful story about Lao Tzu. One of his old friends, another master, one day sent one of his young disciples to Lao Tzu. He thought he showed promise, that he might one day reach the unreachable. Lao Tzu lived alone in nature as a hermit and wasn't accustomed to receiving visitors but he graciously received this young man into his hut. The young man came in, bowed in great humility and surrendered himself entirely to the great sage. They went everywhere together; they slept, ate, walked together and neither spoke a word to the other.

This went on for some weeks until one morning very early before dawn Lao Tzu arose and together they climbed the mountain above his little hut. It was a long trek and they arrived at the summit just before the sun rose. They sat together and witnessed the most exquisite dawn as the sun rose over the mountains. The whole world felt like it still had dew on it, as though Eden was everywhere. Overcome by the beauty of the scene and the experience the young man spoke for the first time. He spoke only a single word choked with his emotion: 'Beautiful'. Lao Tzu said nothing and they silently returned to their hermit's hut. They continued living together in silence for several months until the time came for the young man to return to his other master. They bade each other farewell in silence with warmth and reverence. Several weeks later, the old master visited Lao Tzu, and they had tea together and chatted about things. Lao Tzu was a lover of meaningful conversation. The subject of the young apprentice came up as you might expect; 'What did you make of him?' asked the old master. Lao Tzu took a sip of his tea, drew a deep breath and pondered the question for a few minutes in silence. 'Rather a noisy fellow', said Lao Tzu and smiled one of his deep beautiful smiles.

That's what beauty is. It's so delicate that a single word can crack it. It's so subtle that we will never experience it unless we have cultivated a great inner quietness - a quiescence. It's the haven of nature. Beauty is fostered by nature. It's cradled by silence. It's nurtured by mystery. Forget trying to find beauty on the outside. That's a wild goose chase, a fool's game. Beauty is a lens provided by love. It's a jewel hanging in the immensity of space and a poetic way of living. It's an unseen, unsung moment that never ends - a moment of crystal, a shaft of eternity, a gust of wind inside the god, as Rilke might have put it. Yes to dance with beauty, true beauty, we have to be a dissolver, a softener, a lover of the subtle and the silent. There can be no showiness in this; there isn't a way to show another. Lao Tzu gave this man the chance but the young man wasn't ready. Our silence must be total, not 99%. It's that 1% that makes all the difference.

Let us ask ourselves, can we let go of everything? Can we let the moment cradle us in its arms? Can we court the subtle? Can we be that yin? It's a strange thing to be that yin. We talk about the mystery of the feminine but most of us don't really know what it is. It's actually quite rare to meet a woman who is pure yin. In fact, sometimes the man is more yin. This statement might get some hackles up, perhaps because it's hit the yang inside us. To be utterly yin is to be unconcerned with such things. It's to be unprovocable. It's to surrender utterly. Here we find the great paradoxes. Within the deep yang, the pure fire of the 1st Gene Key, we find the pure yin, the deep yin. It's the same within the yin; there we find the yang, the pure yang. When yin or yang is absolutely pure it actually becomes something quite magical; it becomes neutral. How can this be?

If we read Lao Tzu, we will find this same truth written over and over, that the soft contains the hard, that the sharp contains the blunt. It's what happens when truth and illumination penetrate us to the core, unity, the unity of the opposites. Then we know beauty for what it is. It's beyond such definitions; it's beyond opposites and sides and male and female. It doesn't give a damn about our agendas. It's penetrated to the core and it's come to the subtlest truth, that beauty is all there is. When that is present in a pair of human eyes we're looking into the eyes of a true master, a rare and precious thing.

Let's distinguish then between beauty as a divine principle and things that are considered beautiful. As Lao Tzu himself said, 'the truth is not always beautiful'. At the same time, beauty is truth. As always, the words are getting in the way of what I wish to convey, so let us lapse once again into silence and let the words dissolve…

The 2nd Way

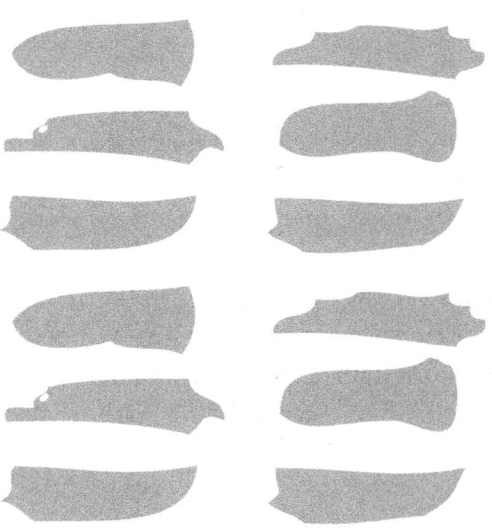

Gene Key 2

THE WAY OF ORIENTATION

The Transformational Way of the 2nd Gene Key moves from Dislocation to Unity, and it's the Way of Orientation.

In the original I Ching, in the halls of antiquity, a great injustice occurred. It is part of the primal human wound. We were gifted great and marvellous treasures, secret knowledge, pure transmissions direct from the source. As soon as we left the Garden of Eden, our unfallen state as a single undivided consciousness, the treasures began arriving. Such is the compassionate nature of the universe that no consciousness can forget what it is for long. Humanity has always received the echoes of truth, the truth of our true nature. The I Ching is one of these ancient transmissions, but it's been tampered with down the aeons. Its pages are weathered and here at its beginning lies the greatest lie of all. It doesn't begin with the number 1! It can't begin with the masculine. All things emerge from the female and return to the female. This 2nd Gene Key represents this primal female. It is the ultimate yin - the receptive.

This is why its Shadow is Dislocation, because it's been dislocated by human consciousness. It's in the wrong place. It's been put into second place. It's been superseded by the masculine, by evolution. The feminine is being, the masculine is becoming. We have to understand that there is nothing wrong here. No one need be concerned. It's a perfect mistake! Evolution has an agenda. Evolution is an agenda. Everything about the Dilemma of this 2nd Shadow of Dislocation is about agenda. It's all about having an agenda.

It's our perception that dislocates us from the truth. We can't be separate from the truth even if we try. We are the truth, every step of the way. It's not possible for a human being to make a mistake, but at the Shadow frequency we believe that mistakes exist. We believe

Shadow: Dislocation **Gift**: Orientation **Programming Partner:** Gene Key 1
Dilemma: Agenda **Siddhi**: Unity **Codon Ring:** The Ring of Water

---

that we know better than life. We believe we're in control. We take the whole world on our shoulders. In fact, we're a part of life. Life is growing through us. Life is dreaming through us. Life is us. Yet we feel separate. It's not our fault. We're in a phase of our evolution in which our perception is limited by our biology and our biology is limited by our perception.

Every one of us has this Gene Key in our DNA. We contain them all. The Programming Partner is the 1st Gene Key with its Shadow of Entropy. This configuration is what makes us feel lost. It's this 2nd Shadow that implants this yearning inside us for home. Our home is our unity. Yet every story we live–every myth, movie, novel, soap opera–every drama in our lives has the fundamental theme of our longing for happiness–for home. We're lost children yearning for our mummy. Our sadness is so deep inside us because everywhere in the outer world we're desperately seeking this unity, this home, and yet it always eludes us. This hollow ache is inside every human being until we've faced into it and been transformed by it.

The 2nd Shadow is the Shadow of our busyness. It drives us out into the world, into busyness. We've forgotten how to receive, how to simply be and how to trust. We're already home. It's inside each one of us. It lies at a higher frequency and it can only be discovered through love. That's why we seek love. This is the Codon Ring of Water. There's so much sadness in water. Here we find the great sadness of our civilisation. There is no civilisation unless the feminine is honoured above all, and I don't mean women. I mean the feminine in us all. The home inside us - the sense of unity. When that's lost, we're lost. Our world is lost. It will have to decay and crumble. How sad that makes us feel–that we've failed because we didn't place love above all else.

Agenda is all about gender. Words all contain jokes. With the 2nd Shadow we think we're important. We think we have to help the world. We think there's something we can do to help. All agendas emerge from distrust in life. It doesn't mean we don't act to help, but we help as a response from our love. We don't help because we feel lost and we need something to fill the void. It's so rare to find a truly loving heart in this life - a heart that doesn't want to help us, a heart with no agenda. In fact, the heart has no agenda. Only the mind and the emotions have agendas. We're cursed by evolution. It's true! It's our curse. Our true being doesn't evolve. The yin, the void, can't evolve. Only the yang carries that agenda. So each of us has to face this deep fear of the void inside us. There is no other way to get back home.

The 2nd Gift — Orientation

In the Tao Te Ching, simple words lay out this journey of transformation through the 2nd Gene Key. How do we find our way in life? How do we know what to do in life? How do we know what's right? The very questions are so revealing. They presuppose that we've totally lost our way. The rest of nature doesn't ask these questions. The answers are always the same, but they're always going to sound nebulous, watery. Thus we hear phrases such as: be like water, follow the water, seek the low, act by not-doing. The Taoists call this wu wei, the art of not doing, the watercourse way. We orient ourselves as we become aware of the Shadow frequencies. When we feel lost we need to surrender to the feeling and allow it to soak into our bones. When we feel sad, dislocated, angry, hopeless, afraid, excited, joyous, blissful, enthusiastic, we can allow the feeling to become utterly infused into our DNA. All we need do is receive, receive that which comes our way, receive and trust in everything that comes our way. We must give ourself to it, listen to it and let it all in. The 2nd Gift is the Gift of Orientation. It means we begin to open our heart up to life. We begin to allow life to resonate inside us at a higher frequency. We begin to love it. We let it crush us, we let it drown us, we let the water in.

Slowly, slowly, we begin to relax. Trust is the by-product of a host of chemicals that our DNA releases into our chemistry as we evolve. The agenda of the Shadow isn't wrong. It drives us into our suffering eventually. Every human being one day reaches a stage in which they get so tired of looking outside for home, they get so disappointed by the outer world, that finally they begin to turn inwards and seek the true source of their suffering. We have to follow the river back towards its source. As we do so, we go through a transformation, a healing. Nature returns our energies to us. We open to receive the currents of life and love once again. It also works the other way around–our acceptance of the present moment, of the way we think and feel, sends a signal into our DNA, which then releases chemicals and hormones which make us feel better.

The more we surrender to everything, to every moment as perfect, the more oriented we become. The more we drop our agendas, our trying, our incessant concerns about our lives and those around us, the more we radiate the presence inside us. Then the magic occurs. Our aura, our vibration, animates our environment. It opens up the currents of the quantum field; it catalyses transformation. We become a force of orientation for all life forms. Simply by doing nothing we become a field of transformational forces.

The Gift of Orientation is so profound that it creates a torus around us. That is what our trust does, we trust the suffering of another. We open our hearts to them without agenda, and they receive our trust at a cellular level. Energetically, we let others know that fear is safe. Fear is safe. That's the key sentence to this Gift. Let it sink into us deeply. Fear is safe.

If this is our gift, then this is our genius, to bring others out of the shadows and begin to turn them inwards towards the source inside them. To orient another person correctly, and I mean truly correctly, is to not give them advice. Advice we can get anywhere. To orient someone is to love them. It's to be with them. It's to be ourself with them. It's to let them see our weakness as well as our strength. It's to be empty like water, and yet to be full. It's to be intuitive, to trust, to soften, to yield, to flow. People don't need help. People need love. They need to be reminded of what it feels like to be in the presence of love. It's as simple as that. No agendas. Just love.

The 2nd Siddhi — Unity

When we're home, we know we're home. All seeking comes to an end. We remember. Life is for living. Life is love. Love is life. All life has an innate urge to complete a story. This is evolution. This is the outer journey–it's the Odyssey. We all eventually return home to Ithaca, to Eden, to the Isle of Avalon. It's a state, a frequency band within our DNA that allows us to experience it, but it isn't the state. When we die the state ends, but not the consciousness that the state allows us to access. The consciousness is so light, so delicate, so feminine. It's the subtlest breeze. It's indescribable. It's why the poets look to the clouds, the trees, the leaves, the midnight fires, the sweeping swallows. One of my favourites, Rainer Maria Rilke, asks: 'But if the endlessly dead could awake a symbol in us, perhaps they would point to the catkins hanging from the empty hazel-trees...' It's always something ephemeral but lasting that we point towards when we need to understand unity. The trees appear to die every year, but then there they are again the following year, and those catkins have dropped their seeds to ensure there will always be new trees...

But unity will not yield to understanding. It is our unbending essence. It is leafless. It is everlasting. It is unfeasibly beautiful. It is our home. All our metaphors lead here to this experience of awakening, enlightenment, realisation. In fact it is really normalcy. It is our ordinariness, but inside, it contains everythingness. This 2nd Siddhi is the Siddhi of Unity. It is the Siddhi of Oneness. It is our original innocence. All life leads here. In human beings it leads us beyond our perception, beyond our senses, into the vibrations within our cells, within our DNA. Enlightenment, Unity, is a physical phenomenon. It's not something outside the body. It requires the body, it celebrates the body.

When we look at these two first Gene Keys, these Programming Partners, the prime yin and yang, we're looking at spirit and form, at energy and matter. Yet they're so inside each other that we can't tell which is which. In the tradition of the Hindu school of Advaita Vedanta, this is why they don't refer to it as Oneness, but rather 'not two'. There aren't two things anymore. There is no separation. Everything is entangled with everything else. Everything is locked in a dance with itself. It's easy to get metaphysical here, but the 2nd Siddhi is so far from philosophy. It's the Divine Feminine, and the Divine Feminine is a mystery.

It contains the masculine, so we can no longer call it feminine.

Let's end on a practical note since we're talking about the Divine Feminine. What does all this mean for us at home in our lives? It means we can't make a mistake. Let that truth penetrate deep into the cells of our bodies. Every Gene Key is saying this. It's inviting us to receive the universe through our daily lives. It's inviting us to trust, to remember the feeling of trust. We don't need to add anything to our life. We don't need to learn anything to get this. There's nothing to get. The answer is so simple, it's too simple for words. We have to learn to forgive ourselves, to realise that we don't need to try. Life is always delivering exactly what we need. Every experience is perfect. Every experience is suffused with Grace when we're able to hear it. Transformation is life. To be transformed is to be completely relaxed, like water. It's to trust in the timing of everything. It's even to trust in fear. This is what these transformational keys show us; trust the Shadow, it contains a Gift. Trust everything, and go on trusting everything. Trust everyone. Trust our disappointments, trust our sexuality, trust our longing, trust our boredom, trust our sadness, trust corruption, trust conspiracy, trust the world. Trust the whole shebang. Know that we can never be lost and we can never be wrong because we are life itself.

The only way to find unity is to dissolve. This is why the symbol is water. We have to allow all our boundaries and attachments to dissolve into life. Our life offers us this every day, in every way. We only have to melt into our own life to become one with it. The universe and all its mysteries are hanging in the air before us every day and in every way. Melt into the dream that's life. Let our heart flow out into the sea of creation. Just surrender ourself to life. Become soft, become like water.

THE 3RD WAY

Gene Key 3

THE WAY OF INNOVATION

The Transformational Way of the 3rd Gene Key moves from Chaos to Innocence, and it's the Way of Innovation.

The essence of the whole I Ching is the nature of change itself. It's usually translated as the 'Book of Changes'; yet because we humans find change so difficult, this hexagram is translated as 'Difficulty at the Beginning'.

No matter who or what we are, we're subject to constant change. It's been said, by the Buddha in fact, that the only constant is change, impermanence. When we let that truth in, it's very uncomfortable, at least at the beginning. This Gene Key is all about the process of letting change in. We have to let it into our heart, body, and soul. This is a contemplation on change. We can see here that the Dilemma is clinging. We naturally cling to the structures around us when change comes. Structure gives us the illusion of security. This is what most people do; we try to cling to our relationships, our marriages, our possessions, our habits, our routines. It sort of works, for a bit, but the big spoiler is death.

I mean death really screws everything up. It's the biggest reminder of the Truth. For years we can be humming along in our own little world, absorbed with our lives, lost in our suffering, shuttling between pain and pleasure, until sooner or later, along comes death.

It reminds me of a story. I was with a very wise old man, and we had taken a substance together, a mind-altering substance. We were sitting there together gazing at this wonderful view. We had been talking sporadically, and then every now and again, a silence just descended on us, and each time it happened, we gave ourselves up to it. In the middle of one of these sweeping silences, suddenly out of the blue came the words:

Shadow: Chaos   **Gift:** Innovation   **Programming Partner:** Gene Key 50
Dilemma: Clinging   **Siddhi:** Innocence   **Codon Ring:** The Ring of Life and Death

---

'all roads lead to death'. My friend had spoken them, and after a moment of recoil, we just started laughing. We laughed and laughed, you know, a deep belly laugh.

I'm still laughing many years later, and that feels like a healthy and authentic response to the nature of change. We have to let it in deeply. It has to get past some resistance, some clinging. There's a lot of clinging in us. Our lives are surrounded by anchor points. Some of our greatest anchor points are our relationships. My greatest anchor points are undoubtedly my children. But can we love those who are closest to us and not cling to them? That is a great challenge. We tend to have clinging with the things we love the most. The clinging actually creates interference. When we cling it's because we haven't quite moved into unconditional love. We create chaos. This is the Shadow of Chaos. It's chaos because the love is tainted by fear.

When we contemplate this Gene Key, we can look at our anchor points - our jobs, relationships, homes, clothes, bodies. All these things give us the illusion of stability. When we're threatened with losing one of our anchor points it shows us our clinging. It shows us the hidden chaos. It doesn't create the chaos. It shows us that it's already there. We often think of chaos as a hurricane or a tempest or something awful, but it's often very subtle. It's an undercurrent. It's an anxiety, a nervousness, a deep and hidden fear inside. Just seeing our anchor points begins to change our relationship to the world around us. We'll begin to release them. We'll begin to pull up those anchors and it won't feel safe - not in the beginning. It's difficult. It's terrifying. We'll feel a deep discomfort in our stomach, our belly. It's the chaos. It's the vibration of our attachment, our clinging.

Let us imagine ourselves without any anchor points. Who are we? What are we? Do we have a name? Can we let that one go as well? That's the question of this Gene Key. It cuts deep inside us. We can see how it's connected to its Programming Partner the 50th Gene Key, Corruption. We're corrupted. We aren't who we really are. We're clinging to all these illusory anchors. At the other end of the spectrum is Harmony, the 50th Siddhi. Harmony and chaos. Chaos is the process of coming back into harmony. We have to enter deeply into the chaos inside. We have to dig into the cellular memories, the false belief systems, the mind maps, the emotional fixations, the desires. I recommend we go deeply into this Gene Key and contemplate our anchor points. Let your awareness dig out the roots. There's something magical in this Gene Key, and it's love.

Clinging is just incomplete love. It's love that hasn't quite gone the whole way yet. Just love a bit more, a bit more deeply. Unconditional love vaporises the anchor points; it love dissolves them. Love releases the clinging and it emerges as we see the clinging. It's a two-way street. As we feel the chaos, so the love emerges from behind it, from inside it. If we have this Gene Key prominent in our Profile, then our whole life's lesson is to love more and not run away, which is the Shadow pattern. The 3rd Shadow wants to change the outer in order not to feel unsafe. It tries to create another anchor before the old one gives way. What a thankless task that is! We're projecting our inner chaos onto our outer life, which is awful.

Contact the places within where the tremor of chaos comes to the fore. Cultivate that habit. It feels unpleasant, but after a while, more love grows as we root out the weeds. And remember, we needn't run away. Changing the circumstances on the outside isn't going to help. It will just be a distraction. We need to be courageous and uproot the fears. They're right inside us. We'll find a new life emerging, a new Gift, a sense of spaciousness and laughter. There's so much laughter within this Gene Key. We just need a little courage to go within, through contemplation, meditation, intuition. Take heart, the difficulty is only in the beginning, but most people never begin this work. It's not surprising. Who willingly goes into chaos and discomfort? Be the one who does. It's there anyway. It just needs to come to the surface, and then everything becomes easier.

The 3rd Gift - Innovation

The essence of the evolutionary impulse is this - in order to survive, life must embrace change. It must adapt and innovate. Everything in the Universe is spinning. All the spheres, all the stars, every photon, every cell, every atom, they all have a whirlpool at their core. Life breathes change into its lungs and exhales innovation. This is a beautiful subject to contemplate. Think about nature. There's this truth we've all heard that nature abhors a vacuum and yet this is the origin of innovation. Out in my garden, if I cut down a small bush then immediately something else starts growing there, something adapts itself and springs into that space. It's a miracle.

I sometimes do this experiment in my house. We have this beautiful big kitchen where almost everything goes on in our house, and in the middle is this big table, like most kitchens. My aesthetic sense really enjoys coming into that room and seeing a clear table. Just the beauty of the wood and the cleanness of the space. You know what I mean? But I have 3 children, and the moment they see an empty table, some gene inside them just goes - Quick! get something on that table! This isn't right! This is my experiment and you'd be amazed at the amount of stuff that comes pouring out of the cupboards onto that empty table! And then of course, they forget to put it away…but that's another story.

Now this may not be how we normally think of innovation, but it is how it works. Life constantly needs to expand, experiment, and then maybe make a breakthrough, or not. Think of all the innovations that fail. You know, when I was a boy I had this book of innovations that had failed. It's hilarious, flying machines with flapping wings and things like that. The very nature of innovation is to keep failing until there's success. Hence the passing-through chaos phase. The first thing about this 3rd Gift is that we have to be okay with chaos. We can't be freaked out by chaos. If we don't embrace chaos, then we'll have a very difficult life. It's why this Gene Key has a lot to do with the inner child and with children, because children embrace chaos so effortlessly. We adults, we all have children inside us somewhere.

This 3rd Gift is about reawakening that spirit of youthful play inside. It really helps to spend some time around children if we have this Gift or are contemplating it. The way a young child plays is so exquisite, especially on their own. My young daughter was upstairs this morning with all her beads and counters and buttons, and she was sorting them into boxes and bags, and her toy panda was buying them - they had become sweets and lollies and things like that. She was just lost in this world. It's captivating. She's just innovating unconsciously. What innovation often does is take something it's seen like that and then repeats it but in a new way, and as it's repeating it, it stumbles spontaneously onto a new idea. That's exactly how DNA replication works. Mutations are innovations. Some might say they're mistakes but that's adding a judgment. They're simply changes. What then makes a successful innovation as opposed to an unsuccessful one? Well, think about our bodies. Innovation is going on there all the time. The miracle of our body has come about because of innovation - cells dividing, sub-dividing, splitting, replicating, trying out new patterns and on and on. We are an evolutionary machine. Sometimes the innovations don't work. That's what cancer is; it's the cutting edge of the innovation. It can eventually kill the organism. If we give life enough time, it will eventually work out how to create an immortal body. Individual bodies are its experimental ground. If some die along the way that's part of the price evolution has to pay to perfect itself.

We have to realise that this is what evolution is doing. We may think it's random, but most people who have studied anything in depth will tell you that's impossible. It's as though life has a goal in mind and it will relentlessly pursue that goal. It's the same with the acorn. The acorn has a goal. It has a pattern that it works towards and it innovates and innovates and if the conditions are right, it will eventually become an oak tree. Life itself is that acorn; it has a hidden plan and that plan is to perfect itself, to attain physical immortality. That's something to ponder. And you know what? the only way to get there is by coordination, by working in harmony. That's the problem with those cancer cells; they go against the whole. Or do they? In the bigger picture, maybe they actually provide the key.

Life needs to know how not to do it, so that it can then succeed and have a breakthrough. We humans are in the midst of this game. We're a part of life's plan. Life has to engineer its own spontaneous breakthroughs and we're one of those, and we'll go so much further. If this current race of humans doesn't manage it, then another race of creatures will spring up in our place in a few billion years. Life can't be stopped. It will stop short of nothing but God.

The secret of innovation is coherence. We have to create a pocket of coherence in the chaos. When we do that we bring order to the chaos and the more coherence we create, the more organised the cosmos becomes. The order actually exists already within the chaos, just as the Siddhi exists inside the Shadow, or the oak within the acorn. It's all just enfolded and innovation is the unfolding mechanism. It looks random but it isn't. It all follows a pattern and a timing.

How do we apply this in our life? How can we create this coherence around us? One of the best ways is to get in touch with the ideal inside us. The ideal is where we're heading. Contemplate the Siddhis. Contemplate them over and over, just as the acorn contemplates the oak tree through its every tiny innovation. Let our whole life be a passage of perfection towards that Siddhi, without ever needing to leave the present moment. We're allowed to be an unfolding. We can still be in the now and be in a state of unfolding. Bring our awareness over and over to the oak tree. It won't be the same oak tree that we'll become, because ours is just an echo, a future memory still to come. But the impulse is true. Let our joyous unfolding be creative. When we contemplate the Siddhis, we'll feel a great upsurge of creativity. We'll naturally begin innovating as our energy transforms the raw material of the Shadow state into a higher coherence.

Innovation feels so good. It's so delightful. It's a good addiction and this Gene Key does have a bit of an addictive character to it, in common with the 24th Gene Key that is part of the same Codon Ring. This is good addiction, especially when it's put into the service of a high ideal. Innovation without that ideal can easily become a cancer, as we see so often in the world around us. We see how many of our scientific innovations, brilliant though they are, are actually destroying the world we love. That's because they're not rooted in a high ideal. Use the tremendous creative energy of this Gene Key, and pour it into an ideal, because that's the only way it won't drive us mad!

The 3rd Siddhi - Innocence

I was listening to a physicist the other day, and he was postulating how a Universe like ours might come to be created. He said that this Universe most likely came out of another Universe, which made me chuckle in itself. He said that all it would take is for a single proton to escape the event horizon of one Universe and enter into the deep void. That single proton, when faced with the immensity of that nothingness, would just delight in its own expansion, and give birth to another Universe.

It's like my kitchen table you see? Life is unstoppable. I live in the beautiful, rich, rolling countryside of South Devon in England. A greener place it's hard to imagine. Devon is famous for its farm products, in particular its dairy products, cream, milk, butter. These fields full of cows are such a bucolic sight, like Eden. The cows with their tails swishing and they lazily drift from field to field. It's very peaceful. Every now and again the farmer opens up a new field when they've eaten all the grass in the old one. I don't know if you've ever seen this, but it's an incredible sight! These cows, they just go crazy with excitement. You know, a lush, untouched new pasture, green and inviting. It's their idea of heaven, and these huge and usually placid creatures turn into great huge puppies. They rush, prance and climb on each other and jump and kick in the air. They're a lesson in ecstasy! That's the 3rd Gene Key. That's the 3rd Siddhi - the unutterable joy of play, of filling the void with our dance, our voice, our presence.

While we're on England's green pastures, I want to tell you about William Blake, a wonderful English painter and poet. He was an early English ecstatic, a deep, deep mystic. He wrote these poem cycles called the Songs of Innocence and the Songs of Experience. They're wonderful, short pastiches of rural and urban life with this motif running underneath. It's all about innocence and the loss of innocence, but then the final regaining of innocence through the search for the Divine. That final innocence is even more exquisite than the firstborn innocence, if you know what I mean. Read these poems if you get the chance.

So there are two kinds of innocence - ignorant innocence that's like a newborn baby, the creature that just expresses its beauty without awareness of itself. Then there's the wise innocence, like the old man or lady whose mind and heart has opened up again after a long search with much pain and travail. This wise innocence and this ignorant innocence; they're the same - the same field. The Siddhi is in the Shadow. The only difference is awareness. Wise innocence has come full circle. It's why grandparents and grandchildren have such a strong bond. It's why little babies look like old people, and why old people often become very childlike again.

What about the rest of us in the middle I hear you say?! Well, we're the journey. We're Blake's poems. We're that passage. We don't have to wait until we're old to be wise. Wisdom isn't dependent on age. Wisdom is dependent on love. How deeply can we love? How far can we expand our love into the green meadows of life? Life is an unravelling. It's already complete, even though it's still in the process of unravelling. Can we be both? Can we be both its beginning and its end? Can we be awake in the dream that's the middle? The ancients called life a Leela, a play. It's a good translation of the word, because the word play means both a piece in theatre, a drama, and also playfulness; they're both needed. We can't make a joke about everything in the middle. There's so much suffering, so much tragedy, so much injustice. It's hard to be playful in the face of most of what goes on on this planet. But the playfulness, the innocence, is of the inner awareness. That's where the dance is. We may be grieving on the outside, but on the inside there's an awareness of the play unfolding.

This is the Ring of Living and Dying. These 6 Gene Keys are the Gene Keys of the drama of life. The 24th is our addiction to the drama and the eternal recreation of the drama. The 23rd is the evolutionary impulse towards complexity and then finally coming back to simplicity and finding its essence once again. The 27th is the human story of that, as we move from Selfishness to Selflessness, and the 42nd is the ending just as the 3rd is the beginning. We have to let go of expectation along the way. We know the ending, but we also don't know how it's going to get there! That's the mystery part. That's the beauty. That's the play, 'the play's the thing wherein I'll catch the conscience of the King.' I love that line from Hamlet when he puts on a play within the play to trick his father into giving away his guilt. It's beautiful, because of course we're watching this play within the play with the rising sense that it's a tragedy! And in this Ring of Living and Dying, who's watching us?

GENE KEY 3

The 20th Gene Key, Divine Presence, when it awakens, when it's time. When the curtain comes down and the audience becomes aware of itself once again, presence arises. It's like that feeling in the theatre when the lights go back on; we kind of rub our eyes, look around, and remember where we are. Through this Ring of Living and Dying, the lights will come on one day. One day the innocence of everything will reawaken to itself. It happens in the individual and the individual realises it's all an illusion. One day it will also happen to the whole. In the meantime we're in the Maya, the Leela, the Divine Play.

As our awareness begins to grow inside, we surrender our attachment to the outcome. We know the grand outcome anyway. We know the curtain will go up. Why worry about the twists and turns of the sub-plots? It's all the twists and turns of the serpentine 3rd Siddhi, as it spontaneously explores the cosmic meadow. This is why it's about death, because that's what we're here to transcend. We are even here to transcend our awareness. Only consciousness is deathless. Only consciousness is outside the movie. When it remembers that, it giggles. It inwardly giggles, and then it falls into silence. That's the 24th Siddhi, what the hell am I going to say? I'm not going to stand up in the middle of the play and shout out to everyone 'It's just a play!'

So the 3rd Siddhi just says: maybe I'd better be quiet, maybe I'd better just play along. So we let the Tao unfold. We let nature go on exploring itself, and we come to deep innocence and deep surrender. The game is over but the play still goes on. What a mystery. What a wonder - to be love. That's the thing. To be love. Every Siddhi ends the same way - without ending! The mind says, 'but there must be an ending, everything needs to end at some point', and the heart says 'how can there be an ending, there's no such thing?'. We're not very familiar with the eternal, because it lies beyond the lower mind. It's the domain of the higher mind, the heart-mind, the domain of pure essential being.

This is the Harmony of the Spheres, the Programming Partner here, that even chaos, even tragedy is part of the harmony and part of the innocence. Everything is part of the everything. Ok, enough now. Let's enjoy the silence.

THE 64 WAYS

THE 4TH WAY

Gene Key 4

THE WAY OF UNDERSTANDING

The Transformational Way of the 4th Gene Key moves from Intolerance to Forgiveness, and it's the Way of Understanding.

This 4th Gene Key is a real lynchpin in our genome. In the future, this Gene Key is going to cause mutations in our DNA, and it is already in the early stages of that process. We can see from its related physiology that it has to do with the neocortex and the way humans think and reflect. The Shadow field of this Gene Key is Intolerance. These Shadow words often contain worlds. We may not think of ourselves as intolerant, but humans really don't live in a field of tolerance. Even in our closest relationships, we often react in anger and irritation. We're easily provoked; note the Programming Partner here - the Shadow of Reaction in the 49th Gene Key. The closer we are with someone, the easier it is to be provoked, and often by the most insignificant things.

At the Shadow frequencies we live in a world of judgment, comparison, good and bad, right and wrong, all generated by our neocortex. We live inside a mental construct and we have no idea how deeply embedded we are in it. We barely tolerate our neighbours. We certainly don't love them. This mental world we live in is made up of thousands and thousands of reasons. Our modern, logical mind is so adept at finding reasons, and reasons is the Dilemma of this Gene Key. But there are truths that won't be detected by reasons; for that, we must look elsewhere. It all begins with language. If we look through the eyes of someone who's autistic, we'll see a world without its reasons. Everything is experienced as pure, undivided, unfiltered. If the consciousness is not ready for that, then the person will have great difficulty living safely in the world. The awakened state also filters life without reasons, without even morals. We have to prepare ourselves for that.

Shadow: Intolerance   **Gift:** Understanding   **Programming Partner:** Gene Key 49
Dilemma: Reasons   **Siddhi:** Forgiveness   **Codon Ring:** The Ring of Union

---

Most of us are governed by reasons, but a world without reasons seems to be an ungovernable, amoral world. It's a terrifying prospect to us. Think about this – a man kills a woman. Why did he do it? There must be a reason. In his childhood something must have happened, or perhaps she just drove him mad. There may be substance to those things, but what if there were no reason? What if it was meant to happen just because that's what life chose? The 4th Shadow is obsessed with knowing why things are the way they are. It's endlessly hungry for answers. It drives us to look for answers. It's the mental expression of our unconscious distrust in life, because out of reasons come blame, justification and guilt.

We usually think of intolerance as directed at others, but we can understand it at a far deeper level if we look within. If we close our eyes and sit in a room for an hour doing nothing, we will soon discover intolerance. Most of us can't even tolerate our own minds. They recently did a psychological test where they put men in a room with no stimulus, and then put an electric shock machine in the room. 70% of the men preferred to give themselves electric shocks, rather than be alone with their thoughts. The Shadow can't tolerate silence, truth, or any kind of discomfort. This Gene Key is in the Codon Ring of Union, the part of our collective DNA that governs relationships. If this Gene Key didn't exist, we would see relationships without reasons, without expectations and without blame. We would have a very different planet. This is going to happen eventually, and this 4th Siddhi will play a big part in it's manifestation.

All Shadows have their games. This Gene Key may drive us all mad but it also drives us to question the world, and as we do so, we discover all manner of things. We've gone to the moon, split the atom, manipulated DNA, and all this is an ongoing game.

When this 4th Shadow does mutate, it will bring an end to science as we know it. The yearning that drives it will end. The desperation to have reasonable answers will end, and then a new kind of science can begin. We'll no longer question in the ways we have for the last 500 years. We'll simply see the world as it is. Because our awareness will have developed to handle that, we'll be comfortable in the world. We won't stop thinking, but we'll stop asking. The questions will simply not be there anymore. It's almost unthinkable. We might like to contemplate this, especially in our relationships – that there are no reasons. If we try it, we are sure to get a glimpse of our collective future.

The 4th Gift — Understanding

It's here in the 4th Gift that the world as we know it is gradually, slowly beginning to change. The Gifts are about genius; the genius that cracks us open from the inside, rather than something we learn from the outside. This is a light cracking through from within our cellular structure.

When I contemplate the depths of this Gene Key and where it's going, I feel how deeply it's going to one day change our world. All this mental, intellectual energy that we're using across our planet never quite resolves the big questions. We've discovered so much; our physicists have created so many grand theories, but there's still that big piece that eludes us. It's because we are standing in our own way. It's not our time yet. We don't understand how the universe works at a fundamental level. We don't understand because we're still looking for reasons. We're looking for knowledge, and that isn't enough. One day however, we will realise beyond a doubt that the universe is eternal and that time has no beginning and no end. When we realise that, it will literally short-circuit our thinking. We will finally come into understanding. It will flood our bodies as light. Everything is light. Consciousness is everywhere, in all things, breaking forth like a wave. This kind of understanding opens up our hearts.

The answer we seek is staring us right in the face. It's the simplest one. It kills the question. It stops the mind. Life is sacred, and free energy can be harnessed from anywhere. That will be the end of intolerance! It's all about energy and food, and they're both free when we reach understanding. The world will then take a completely different direction. If we have this 4th Gift in our profile, or are drawn to activating it in our DNA, then we have to look no further than our relationships. We're never going to understand anything until we understand love.

Most people won't believe what I'm saying! We've evolved to be a predominantly thinking race. Our western world has essentially grown out of the scientific view, and left the magic behind in faery tales, since there seems to be no empirical evidence for it. But understanding comes from the causal plane, the higher plane at the farthest reaches of our minds, where the heart and mind combine. When we truly open up our hearts, our mind sees so much further than when our hearts are closed. Our minds reach the holographic union of truth. We see, feel and know the truth. We don't need to prove or question it. How can we question love? If we've ever been in love, do we really think our minds have any power to question that feeling? The truth is indisputable. Only if the love fades, do the questions return.

The Chinese called this hexagram Youthful Folly. It's an apt description of human beings during our current state of awareness, pre-mutation. We can barely tolerate each other. Whoever we are, no matter what Gifts we're here to bring into the world, this 4th Gene Key is going to have a huge impact on our life. The Gift of Understanding occurs as we let go of our mind's many tricks of trying to understand and control our life and the daily decisions we make. Our mind can't give us the answers we're seeking. It can't tell us what to eat, where to live, whom to love, what to do, anything. It can only see and play with the polarities of mind itself. It can't judge. It can only measure. Only our spirit can understand life. Only our spirit can let another person live in our heart.

We've all been fools. Fools for love. We seek the answers outside, when all along they're inside us. The light we seek is in our own body, locked away in the DNA. It's so simple to unlock it. Just input the right code. Just see through our own Shadows. Watch our mind, laugh at its antics, as it stumbles and trips its youthful way through the world. When we have cellular understanding, only then does our mind rise up to see through the great questions and paradoxes, and only then does it stop taking sides.

If we have this Gene Key prominently in our profile, we probably know all the answers to everything, but can't stop needing to know more. One day our genius is going to emerge out of the mists, and guess what? We're going to stop needing to know, and finally understand. Happiness never comes through answers. It comes only when we're so tired of answers, that we just decide to live the questions fully. Our life radiates the answers and finally we can relax and be of the deepest service to the world.

The 4th Siddhi — Forgiveness

It's a huge word – Forgiveness. What is Forgiveness? Who can understand its mystery? And how is it connected to our mind, since so much of this Gene Key seems to be about our mind? Forgiveness seems to be in the emotional realm, but really it's about understanding. Only when we understand fully, can we forgive. Understanding is not on an intellectual level; this Gift of Understanding is of the full being – mind and heart together. Who is it we're forgiving? When we understand Forgiveness, we usually think of forgiving a person or an injustice. We see it on a personal level. This 4th Siddhi is about a universal type of forgiveness, and personal forgiveness is but a tiny echo of that. The Programming Partner of the 4th Gene Key is the 49th Gene Key, which is reaction/Revolution/Rebirth. When we put these two keys alongside each other we have intolerance causing reaction at the Shadow level, moving into Revolution in understanding, and culminating in Rebirth through Forgiveness. Aren't the Gene Keys easy to understand?

To really understand this 4th Siddhi, we'll have to dive into the esoteric field of the Corpus Christi, the science of the subtle bodies that underpins the Gene Keys. The glossary in the Gene Keys book describes the way in which higher consciousness emerges into the world of form. At a certain phase in our evolution, as our hearts begin to open more consistently to life, the subtle body known as the buddhic body begins to dominate our inner consciousness. The 4th Siddhi is key in this. In the mystical teaching known as the Opening of the Seven Seals, there are seven specific Gene Keys and their Siddhis that have special significance in global awakening. One of these Seven is the 4th Siddhi of Forgiveness.

Forgiveness isn't personal; it's the realisation that nothing is personal. The 4th Siddhi is such an alien concept to human beings at the moment. That is why it will take a Rebirth. It involves the death of a whole part of our old mind – the part that needs and looks for answers and reasons. It will move us into an acausal world, a world without blame or guilt. Forgiveness is the only antidote to guilt, and guilt is not always what it seems. It's an ancient force carried through the DNA that is passed on at conception. Guilt is one of the 6 core human wounds. We humans carry guilt because we feel responsible at a deep unconscious level. We carry the guilt of our ancestors, and that guilt is triggered inside us at various stages in our lives by the karmic events playing out around us.

Guilt is a karmic debt that we all carry, and collectively it's held by whole gene pools that are literally at war with each other. We can see these debts played out on the stage of the world economy. Debt and guilt are tightly interwoven. Forgiveness then is a force that descends upon us. It comes when something inside us lets go of the drama that's controlling us. At one level we might say that Forgiveness is given, as its etymology suggests. But we also claim it. We forgive ourselves. We are forgiven by ourselves. It happens when it happens. We cannot do Forgiveness. No technique can bring it about. It comes when we're so tired of the drama that we spontaneously surrender. We then see how deeply we've trapped ourselves in our belief structures, our resentments, our ambitions, and our broken dreams.

The Gift of Understanding comes out of the process of utter self responsibility. We realise that the resentments, disappointments, and hurts in our relationships ultimately stem from our own incomplete self love. This leads to self-forgiveness. Only when we forgive ourselves fully can we begin to return non-love with love. Remember this Key is in the Codon Ring of Union, whose cosmic realm is the transformation of all human relationships. This Siddhi also has a very obvious archetypal resonance to the teachings and embodiment of Christ. Christ's teaching of peace on earth and goodwill to all contains the full transmission of this 4th Siddhi. We forgive each other our trespasses and debts. We return non-love with love. This is the power of the buddhic body coming into incarnation.

These Siddhis contain some astounding stories, and the 4th Siddhi is going to bring an end to war. It's going to bring an end to war through the releasing of all ancestral, karmic debt. One day it will bring about world peace, this mutation in the 4th Gene Key. It's going to change the way our brains operate. As we saw with the Shadow, it's going to stop us asking questions. It's going to settle us down. It's going to propel us into a deep natural morality that at the same time is rooted in an amoral understanding of life. It may be far away in the future, but it's also here now and programmed in us. Assuming we're allowed to complete our natural evolution, we will one day live in the field of this cosmic Forgiveness. Even though it may sound boring to our drama-addicted minds, the truth is it's actually going to feel really, really nice!

THE 64 WAYS

THE 5TH WAY

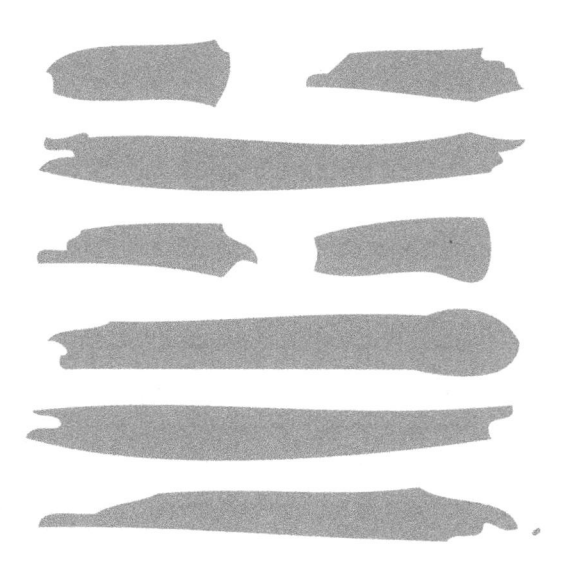

Gene Key 5

THE WAY OF PATIENCE

The Transformational Way of the 5th Gene Key moves from Impatience to Timelessness, and it's the Way of Patience.

The Shadow of Impatience is an interesting one. It's also very contemporary. We're becoming a more and more impatient species. Part of this is due to our pace of life and the technology we have in place that makes everything so fast. There's not much we have to wait for these days. If we want something, it's generally there at the click of a button. If we go to a culture where things are more primitive, or more simple I should say, then we can have a deep realisation about impatience.

Take meals for example. When we're hungry, we generally just eat. A lot of the time we even eat when we aren't hungry. In simpler cultures, many people eat only once a day. Another thing we may see is people sitting around doing nothing. It's not that they're lazy, but that their rhythm is different. The drive to earn money really changes a culture. I'm not saying one thing is good or bad, and I'm not wanting to romanticise the poorer nations and cultures either. However, there are things we can learn from each other.

Generally, the more time we have to pause and look around us, the more we appreciate life, and the kinder we are. Kindness is linked to patience. Impatience is linked to intolerance, the Shadow of the 4th Gene Key, one back in the sequence. If we go one forward in the sequence, we come to the 6th Gene Key and the Shadow of Conflict. Impatience is sandwiched between Intolerance and Conflict, which already tells us a lot. Impatience is even seen as a good thing by some. Some speak of it with a kind of pride, but that's mixing impatience with enthusiasm. Enthusiasm is unbridled, optimistic, positive energy, and it has an innocence and freedom to it. The moment it becomes impatient, the water

Shadow: Impatience **Gift**: Patience **Programming Partner:** Gene Key 35
Dilemma: Surrender **Siddhi**: Timelessness **Codon Ring:** The Ring of Light

---

is muddied. Think about it - we have a big job ahead of us, and our working partner is full of enthusiasm. That's going to be a fun job. Now imagine the same person full of impatience. Not a fun job, so impatience has created a drop in frequency. It puts tension and nervousness in the air. It's an uncomfortable energy to be around. It'll also ensure that whatever job is undertaken, it will neither go smoothly nor be fulfilling. In fact it may even fail. The timing will be out. The rhythm will be unstable and erratic. There'll be stress.

The Programming Partner of the 5th Gene Key is the 35th Gene Key, the Shadow of Hunger. This hunger isn't just physical; it's emotional and intellectual. It's insatiable. Let's look at our own impatience and any situation when it gets triggered. My greatest test of patience is being a parent. Children really push our impatience buttons, especially when we have several children. They start getting at each other, which as far as I can tell, all children do from time to time. They drive us to distraction. That's my personal edge of impatience. Sometimes I lose it, I just lose my composure. I forget all my grand teachings and just lose it.

Every parent knows exactly what I mean. We all have our edges. Impatience is an undercurrent in our society, and it's now part of our culture. Therefore to transmute this Shadow in our life, we have to go directly against the grain of the culture. When I was younger I lived in New York for a while. I somehow, god knows how, because I was a bearded madman at the time, ended up going out with this beautiful woman, a successful model. We were like beauty and the beast. Anyway, she loved me, and I was pretty footloose, so she invited me to her modelling sessions. I was in a deep meditative phase of my life. How blissful it was. In those kind of professions, just like in the movie business, there's a huge amount of waiting. I'd just sit there on a chair, watching the whole scene.

I'd literally be there for hours. Just sitting. Sometimes I'd close my eyes. Sometimes I'd open them. And you know, I created this huge stir. It's weird really. Everyone was talking about me. They all chilled out. Things went more smoothly around the sets. I was just happy being there. That's what we covet now as a society. The more affluent we become, the more we wish to get back to the simple truths. The Dilemma here is surrender. This is what impatience is teaching us - to surrender. Impatience teaches us patience. It's a marvellous thing in that respect.

We have to let go and realise that we're mad, that our mind has gone mad, that life will flow in the way it wishes to, and that if we fight it, we'll only create problems and ill health for ourself. So please look at your life and see how deep your impatience is. How much do we let it run our life? Do we feel the joy of surrender? Our awareness of impatience will ultimately help us let go and surrender into the core of ourself, so that we breathe again in depth. Then our life will start to become simple once again, all on its own.

The 5th Gift - Patience

This Gift is my Life Purpose. In my Profile, the 5th Gene Key is my Purpose. I've often joked that if our Life Purpose is Patience then we can be sure we're going to need it. It's the same with all our Gifts. So I've had to learn patience. I'm still learning it. To me there are two types of patience. There is surface patience, and then there's deep patience.

Surface patience is a good start. It's a technique we can employ. It's really all about learning to wait. We witness our own impatience, stop the action that was coming out of that impatience, and simply wait. The impatience probably continues beneath the surface, so we still feel uneasy, tetchy, and anxious. But we stop the activity that recreates the loop and learn to wait. We have to learn to pause, be still, breathe. Over time surface patience goes deeper inside; we begin to spontaneously relax, and then surrender happens. We can't do a surrender technique. It's just something that happens in our body. Then deep patience begins. It's like a kind of cooling mist that rises up and calms our aggravated system. It stills the hungry flames. It moistens our dryness. It settles our spirit. It's watery rather than fiery. When we learn to contemplate, this is the state that we'll discover hiding inside - this deep patience. It's actually fathomless. The more we catch our impatient, clinging mind, the more we'll find this inner space. It'll begin to open in us, and we'll find that we can just sit for hours.

The other thing about patience is that it's the underlying foundation of love. Patience is the way in which the Shadow transforms into the Gift, so it's fundamental to every aspect of the Gene Keys. It's the field - the spaciousness - the cauldron - in which the dynamic change, the alchemy of life occurs. In the words of Beinsa Douno, the great world teacher, the secret of patience is this: 'When someone offends you, you should find the good aspect of the offence and make use of it. An offence is a very hard walnut that someone has given you. You need to break the shell, remove the nut and eat it. If you can feed yourself in this way you will be completely healthy. When people speak bad of you, when they blame you for something, they are providing you with food. If you know how to use this food correctly, you will be most satisfied. Patience creates the conditions for love's manifestation. It is the first fundamental quality of love's arrival, its vanguard.' Patience is love's vanguard. That's a beautiful concept. This is the whole work we're each here to do, to transform this suffering that our fate brings us, to accept it gladly into an opening heart, and use that heart to open to deeper love. Patience is absolutely key in this. It isn't just a nice side plate. It's the main course. So let's treasure patience, and measure our progress by how patient we are.

Patience is needed more than ever in times of interpersonal conflict. We have to continue to treat others with respect, forgiveness, and patience, and then we leave the rest up to God, or the universal flow. The most we can do is love someone, send them good thoughts and feelings, and then wait and trust that destiny will shape the correct course over time. Some difficulties take years, even lifetimes to resolve, but if we've cultivated deep patience, this won't matter to us. We can just accept people as they are. This is what we learn in the Venus Sequence, in Part 2 of the Golden Path. We learn the art of returning non-love with love and that's another way of saying we learn the great art of patience.

The 5th Siddhi - Timelessness

In our spiritual path, patience rules supreme. I can't think of a single quality that's more needed on a spiritual path. Love of course, but then we have just seen that patience is the foundation of love. Why patience? Well for one thing, it's not what people want or seek, so that tells us a lot! In the Tao Te Ching, a well known verse says of the qualities of the true sage:

> *Sages thus seek what no one else seeks*
> *They don't prize hard-to-get goods*
> *They study what no one else studies*
> *they turn to what others pass by*
> *to help all things remain natural*
> *they dare not act.*

Patience doesn't look that exciting does it? But a person with deep patience is capable of everything. The other reason we need patience with ourselves is because we constantly fall off the horse. In spiritual practise, our focus wavers from time to time, as the world pulls at us, tests us, pushes us. We also make mistakes, although from the point of view of deep patience, there aren't any mistakes. There's only just learning, so patience gives us the long term perspective and dissolves time. This is when we begin to move towards the Siddhi, the Siddhi of Timelessness.

Time is the great lynchpin of awakening. We live like fish submerged in time. We live, eat, and breathe time. We don't know anything other than time. Consciously or unconsciously, we're the product of our past thoughts, beliefs, and actions, and our future is being formed in every present moment. We're forming our own future right now, as we listen to or read these very words. What kind of future will we form? This is why the mystics have always pointed us towards the present, because they know that the present creates the future, and the future always holds the promise of awakening. I've come to an impasse in words with this paradox - while the future holds that promise, we still awaken in the present, and we have to build that present.

My teaching differs slightly from the traditional model of mindfulness that calls us over and over to come into the present and observe all passing away. Contemplation is different from meditation. It sometimes uses the higher mental body, the causal plane, to attune to that which is coming into form. For example, we hold a vision for the future manifestation of the kingdom of heaven coming to earth. I'm being realistic here. We can see that heaven is not yet here on earth, but one day it will be. We attune to that future certainty, and over time as we do this, we bring that certainty into the cells of our body, and then carry it into the present moment. I find this a beautiful paradox. To carry the future in the present. We also carry the past in the present. We carry the memory of our loved ones, our ancestors. We carry all that is best in them. We transmute all the Shadow that they left by remembering only that which was fine and beautiful about them. We carry that too in the present. You see, there really only is the present. Past and future are gathered here in this moment.

The great masters and initiates have always visited this plane. They are our future, and they were here at the beginning. We began with a Golden Age, we fell from Grace, and we shall return again to a Golden Age. The masters, or I should say, the Master, incarnates from Timelessness into time - coming from outside the water, diving into time, and teaching us about life above the water.

As we die, we return into the timeless realm. We return into the boundless. It isn't somewhere else far away. It's right here within. No one ever dies. Nothing ever dies. Life is nothing but eternity. Ideas change shape. Humans change shape. It's the same thing; the essence is the same. The essence remains always. The one we love who has died hasn't died. Their essence is within us. They haven't gone to the stars far away. A part of them has, but those stars are also within us. They're closer than breath, closer than heartbeat. That which is best in them beats in our heart.

When the Master descends into form, he or she does so to play a pivotal role within the game of time. Life is like one of those addictive tv series that continues to unfold. That's evolution, and the Master represents our future. It is our future right now. In the game as it stands today, we're at a threshold moment. A new Age is opening up - a new epoch, a new Aquarian epoch. The symbol of Aquarius is interesting. Symbols are the ways the gods communicate. They're like the chapter headings of evolution, these signs. Aquarius is the water bearer. It captures the idea of abundance, of water being poured from a vessel, but at the same time it's an air sign. Like the dragonfly of the Gene Keys, the coming epoch is a movement from water into air. The fish will sprout wings and fly into the air. We are those fish. We are those dragonflies emerging from the waters of the Piscean Age.

Any astrologer will tell you that Aquarius is ruled by Uranus, the father of time. Uranus is the unpredictable, the changeable, the changeless, the dervish. That which will come after will bear little resemblance to that which we see now. The causal plane is that plane of being that lies beyond logic, beyond science and beyond the objective mind. All that we hold so dear now - our empirical view of the world - will fall away. It must. We don't see the causes at present. We don't realise that we're powerful beyond measure, not as materialists, but as spiritual beings. Can we imagine what the world might be like if time starts to break down? Can we imagine the chaos? This is what Uranus is bringing. Time has been our crutch for so long. When we begin to see through the veil of time into the eternal, then all our taboos will crack, and the greatest taboo of all is death. One day, in the now, we will remember all our incarnations. We will see the future as the Master does. The Master can't disclose the future, at least not ordinarily. He or she can indicate it in big gestures, and sometimes in specific cases, but otherwise it's a secret. The time is coming when time will melt, and therefore along with it, space. Time and space are two sides of the same spinning coin. I love that the secret of time in physics is held by the image of the black hole. Many times I've spoken of the black hole and its relationship to the white hole. The black hole dissolves time and leads through the wormhole into the white hole, which is eternity. We're eternal. Contemplate that. Sometimes I contemplate eternity. I just take the word, and roll it around inside myself until it softens me and diffuses my boundaries. I become all syrupy. I begin to merge with the higher bodies.

Tune into that cellular certainty of the end of time. Our consciousness will know it when we die, not very long from now. Contemplate it often. Smother yourself in it. Smooth your passage towards it, and see your role in the evolutionary saga. See your current role, your current incarnation within time, and play it to the hilt. One day this game will come to an end, and we'll all be unified, so bring that certainty into the now. Don't get caught in worrying about the details of the plan. Don't worry about the maya. We can help when and where we can, but we needn't worry. I'm going to finish with a beautiful prayer I often do as I meet the sunrise. Listen particularly to the last line. I repeat that line over and over until I'm immersed in its truth. I always see the paradox of knowing it, and yet still being at a stage in the drama where it hasn't come about yet. Paradoxes such as this are to be enjoyed…

HOLY INCANTATION OF SOLACE

Let love flow through my soul
Let light flower in my heart
Let warmth radiate my belly
Let purity shimmer in my bones
Let kindness resound in my voice
Let clarity shine through my mind
Let solace abound in my life
Touching all who I meet
Let solace abound in the world,
bringing all beings into perfect union.

The 6th Way

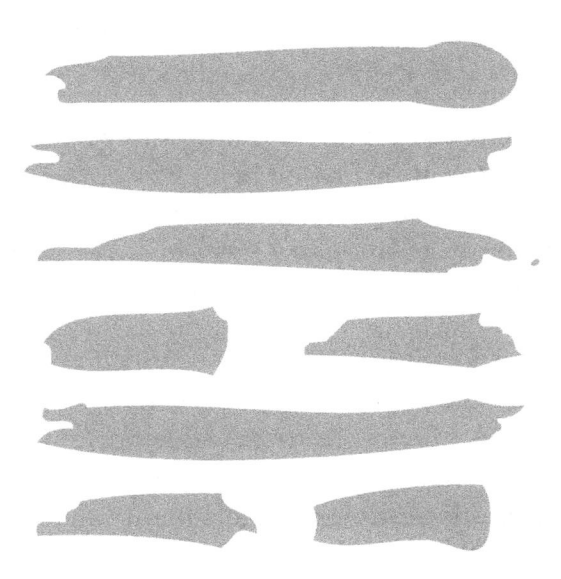

Gene Key 6

THE WAY OF DIPLOMACY

The Transformational Way of the 6th Gene Key moves from Conflict to Peace, and it's the Way of Diplomacy.

This is really the great emotional master key, this 6th Gene Key. It contains the secret to peace, the elusive grail sought by human beings since the beginning of time. Inner peace, outer peace, how do we find peace? This is the question of this Transformational Way. Peace is the very purpose of evolution. Only when we have finally found peace, can evolution really end. Then evolution ends and being begins.

What is conflict, and where does it come from? Every Shadow is rooted in a frequency of conflict. It's the friction created by duality, by the sexes, by life and death. It's why we're here, this edge of creation, Conflict. Let's see how this works in our lives. This Gene Key governs our emotions, and at the Shadow frequency we completely identify with our emotions. The Dilemma of this Shadow is protection. It's all about the fear that another person can hurt us, or that they can take something from us. It's the deep unconscious fear that we can be a victim and taken advantage of by another. At its most horrific level this is the fear that another can take our life away. That's a deep fear, that another can harm us. It drives all human beings at the Shadow frequency. It's in all of us. Think of the most challenging relationship in your life right now and ask yourself what is the essence of that conflict? It is that we have an unconscious belief or fear that the other person has some control over us, over our freedom and over our emotions. They seem to have the ability to ruin our peace, and we therefore believe that we have to protect ourselves from that. Thus we harden our heart, and make internal or external judgments about them, or we just plain avoid them. The bottom line is that we don't like the part of ourselves that they seem to bring out.

Shadow: Conflict **Gift**: Diplomacy **Programming Partner:** Gene Key 36
Dilemma: Protection **Siddhi:** Peace **Codon Ring:** The Ring of Alchemy

When we look deeply and honestly into these relationships, we see something else. We see that this person is allowing us access to an inner conflict inside ourselves, a conflict that runs very, very deep. It's the conflict we have with the unconscious fear in our DNA. It's a part of our ancestral legacy, an older part of our brain. It takes a big person to admit they have deep fears inside them. Once we begin to realise that these fears are inside and not outside, we break out of the patterns that are holding that relationship at the Shadow frequency. This is when we begin to let go of our protection mechanisms, the defence strategies we learned in our early childhood, and we begin to become vulnerable again. We go into our wound and feel, share, accept, and transform it. Every human being is emotionally vulnerable until they drop their protective defences. The defences form around our hearts, and as long as our hearts remain defended and closed, they can't heal. The hurt can't be felt, expressed, and released. Conflict is the prima materia of our evolutionary journey. It's where we most need to focus our attention. We have to own it.

Let's look at these relationships in our lives; they're the gold dust. They contain the seeds of inner peace. Let's not shy away from them but take courage and move towards them with an open mind and heart. We can allow ourselves to be vulnerable and hurt, except for physically, of course. When the hurt comes, we can own it, listen to it, learn from it, and learn to parent ourselves. The other person is not responsible for our feelings in response to the hurt; we are.

We need to look after our own heart and learn to bring it back to life. It's not that we have to keep putting ourselves in the firing line, but we have to see that these relationships, these conflicts, are always here. They're where the transformation occurs. Once we begin to heal ourselves inwardly then these relationships no longer have such a hold over us.

In fact, the dynamic has no choice but to change. The other person either begins to also be transformed, or they move out of our life in some way. A huge amount of energy is wasted on protection, on defence. Collectively, let's look at this Shadow. We humans are obsessed with protecting ourselves from each other. This is just an outer manifestation of the inner truth. We defend our principles, our opinions, our territory, our resources, our hearts. From what?

Conflict is propagated by our false belief that another person or entity can take something away from us. There is a radical teaching in this Gene Key, and when embraced, it will shatter the greatest illusion we have - that there's anything or anyone outside ourselves in the first place.

The 6th Gift — Diplomacy

The Gift of Diplomacy begins as soon as we drop our defences and open our hearts. To be diplomatic in this sense has nothing to do with strategy. The heart is not strategic, at least not in any studied sense. It is however, completely tactful; it senses empathically where another person's heart is and the degree of their openness. Each Gift carries a genius inside it and people with the 6th Gift really know how to commune with others. Not just communicate, mind you, they know how to commune. They understand defences because they themselves are willing to be vulnerable. They're the most vulnerable; they're right there with us, with their hearts on their sleeves.

This ability to be with oneself, to take care of oneself internally and to be safe even in the midst of fear, is a hallmark of the 6th Gift. It's what happens when we no longer fear fear itself. Only then do we stop being a victim of fear. Only then do we stop allowing ourselves to be unconsciously manipulated by other people's fears. This internal ability to be responsible for ourselves changes everything in our lives. It begins to open our lives up onto a whole other frequency, another dimension, and in this new dimension, the heart can breathe again and love begins to pour through us.

Every Gift is the junction for the forces of evolution and involution. Evolution moves from the Shadow state upwards and involution moves from the Siddhi state downwards. In other words, Peace is always there, every step of the way. It's like Michaelangelo's block of marble, just waiting to be chipped away. The Gift state releases all the trapped creative energy from the Shadow, the kundalini. This energy lifts us up and opens up so many possibilities. Only one who has had the courage to take the journey knows the truth about love. Love requires we expose everything about ourselves. It requires that we open our hearts up to another, risking rejection, anger, whatever emotional energy life throws at us. With diplomacy, we sense when to speak and when to listen, when to leap and when to pause.

With the Gift of Diplomacy, we can unlock any human being who comes within our aura, and it's also all karmic. Those who we're designed to unlock and who unlock us, always keep coming into our life. As we rise up on the wings of the Gift, more and more people come to us for this love, and we open up more in them, and this opens up more inside us. We can see how the people of this Gift have the power to change the world. It's placed inside them. It's in all of us, but those with this genius have a specific karmic task of creating the conditions of Peace. It's through this Gift that the borders will begin to come down, that balance will return to human relationships, and that people and nations will stop wasting their precious resources on maintaining the illusion of defending themselves. It's through the 6th Gift of Diplomacy that the human race will rediscover its true nature as kindly, friendly, trusting and above all, loving.

The 6th Gift is all about alchemy. It's an aspect of the Ring of Alchemy. Alchemy is about the transformation of the gross into the subtle. It's the path of evolution to move through progressive periods of refinement, but true alchemy can only happen inside a human being first. It's part of what it means to live as an embodiment of our higher purpose. When we begin to meet our shadows and transform them into creative service, then we witness alchemy in action, and alchemy is a chain reaction. The more the heart opens, the more heart opening experiences occur. Life changes around us; it draws elements around us that further support more opening. It invites synchronicities and miracles. There's much magic in this 6th Gift.

THE 6TH SIDDHI — PEACE

The 6th Siddhi is funny. It's funny because it's what gives the New Age a bad name! It's what creates idealists, dreamers, wackos, love-and-lighters! It's the ideal of world peace. Nowadays there's a great deal of cynicism around this idea of world peace. There's a projection field from the Shadow that world peace is unattainable, that it's the domain of the dreamer, not the realist. All these people who do ceremonies for world peace, who have conferences around it, who meditate for it, they appear to be getting nowhere. War is still rife everywhere. Atrocities seem more prevalent than ever - thus the cynicism.

We do know something though. Peace has to be found on the inside before it can manifest on the outside. There's no other way. Humanity must discover its true nature. The good news is that our nature is peace, the 6th Siddhi. We live at an amazing crossroads. The world seems more chaotic and unpredictable than ever, and our general level of denial about our way of life seems unstoppable. Yet within all this external chaos, a tiny humble wildflower is growing up through the cracks in the pavement. It's appearing everywhere, all across the human genome, but at first it only takes root in certain people. It's a virus called love. Peace only comes about when love is allowed to expand. Peace is underneath everything. It's there when we all just stop what we're doing and listen. There it is. The birds are singing, the stars are wheeling through space, the ocean comes rolling in, the wind drops. Silence descends - inner silence. Any human being who has discovered the true nature of being has discovered peace, and with it, all seeking comes to an end. Peace, as Christ said, passeth all understanding. It's there when the love has burned through all the karma in our DNA, when all the Shadows have been transformed, when the fire of devotion has burned us clean. It's the final flowering of alchemy. It's the gold, the unio mystica, when all extremes are neutralised, as this Siddhi is described in the gene keys book, which speaks of all the hydrogen ions being neutralised within the body, so that the atomic structure of our body begins to undergo radical changes.

This 6th Siddhi is really, really out there. It's 'woo woo' land. The sceptics love this one. It's about living off light. It's our future. The shift we're going through now at a genetic level is just the very beginning. As our solar plexus opens us up to the new quantum awareness, our bodies will have to mutate. This kind of thing takes time! Unless we have a certain configuration of Siddhis, there're no short-cuts through this one. Evolution moves to greater and greater efficiency. Eventually, we'll need a higher vehicle to house this awareness. Our understanding now about the body is medieval compared to what our understanding will be in the future. Right now, there's no scientific proof, at least in the mainstream, for the subtle bodies, not even for the etheric body, which is the densest after the physical. Even acupuncture is not scientifically proven.

Physics is suggesting that there must be dimensions that we can't see or measure. We call these the subtle bodies, the causal body, the atmic body, etc. They are dimensions beyond our current understanding. Perhaps we'll never develop instruments to measure them. Why would we, when we would have to heighten our consciousness to prove that they exist? Yet they do exist, and always have done. They've been discovered aeons ago. Every person who has passed through the portal of enlightenment is proof that peace is our true original nature. One day, because of this 6th Siddhi, we'll evolve beyond the physical form. Our whole ecosystem will take us with it. Not just us humans, but the whole of Gaia.

The 6th Gene Key is about the colours of culture. It's about cultural and genetic divides. This is why we've created so many beautiful cultures; look at all our flags, costumes, folk music, and customs. We've differentiated consciousness so beautifully, and yet it's also led to conflict and diplomacy. We can also see this differentiation if we look at the big picture, like the kinds of changes that are happening in our nations, the EU, the USA, etc. It's a single culture that's emerging. The music is merging, the gene pools are merging, and yet the old divides still remain. The extremes are being neutralised, and they don't like that! But the news is good; it's always good at the Siddhic frequency. We get to keep the lovely bits of the past and unify everything else. Nature wants all those colours. They're her beauty. Nature loves beauty. Peace is on the way, but it's coming on the inside first. It's coming on an individual level, then gradually through relationships, then into families and communities, and then the world.

It's an internal mutation, is peace. Inner peace requires a physical mutation. It's genetic, and at some level it's impersonal. Not everyone will mutate. The old human is being bred out, but will still stick around while the new one spreads. The new one will be calm and peaceful. This 6th Siddhi is so christlike. It's about our radiance. Our skin and eyes will radiate the higher frequencies. We will radiate peace, and nothing can disturb that peace, not even death. As we saw in the beginning of this Key, this is about dropping defences. It's not possible for another being to take away our life, because we are life. Even if our host body dies, our consciousness is not localised there, so it's not a big deal. That level of trust and knowing generates a kind of peace that passeth all understanding, and that's where we are all heading.

THE 64 WAYS

THE 7TH WAY

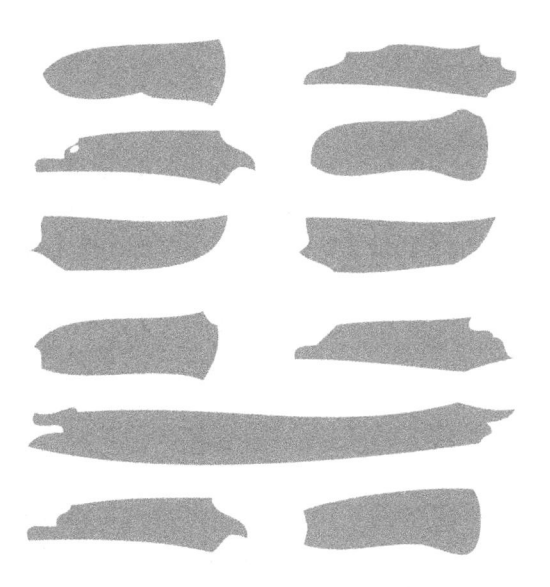

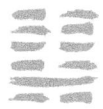

Gene Key 7

THE WAY OF GUIDANCE

The Transformational Way of the 7th Gene Key moves from Division to Virtue. It's the Way of Guidance.

The 7th Gene Key is one of the truly global Gene Keys. It's far-off aim is nothing short of complete Global Realisation, which gives us some idea of its weight in the genome. All those people who have this Gene Key in their Profiles have a profound responsibility resting on their shoulders - to guide humanity into the future, hopefully a new and better future. The 7th Shadow however, also exerts a powerful influence on the direction of our species through this 7th Gene Key. In the Gene Keys book, the title of the Gift is 'The Power Behind the Throne'. These are influential people placed throughout society. Depending on their agenda, their frequency, they collectively pull humanity towards further chaos or towards integration and wholeness.

The 7th Gene Key definitely has potent leadership potential, but they aren't always leaders per se. They are people with influence. In any group, the 7th Gene Key carries this power that when it speaks, others will listen. They may not like what they hear, but the aura of the 7th Gene Key has a frequency that sounds as though it knows what it's talking about. We naturally tend to listen to these people. Think about this though. If someone has an agenda to make as much money as they can, without a care for anyone else, then just through the power of this Gene Key, the chances are they'll find people who will listen, follow, and help them achieve their aim. The 7th Shadow can really take advantage of the Shadow, and remember the Shadow is the victim frequency.

The Dilemma of the 7th Shadow is Boundaries. If we don't have a strong sense of our own core stability, we're at risk of being pulled into the current of someone's 7th Gene Key

Shadow: Division **Gift**: Guidance **Programming Partner**: Gene Key 13
Dilemma: Boundaries **Siddhi**: Virtue **Codon Ring**: The Ring of Union

---

agenda. It can sound exciting and enticing. It can sound captivating and filled with promise. If we aren't discerning, we'll very likely fall victim to this energy in the world. The first aspect of understanding this Shadow is therefore to learn how to have strong boundaries, to have restraint. On the other side, it's also to realise that the Shadow is the Shadow of Division. If we don't have a clear intention that's grounded and rooted in service, then division is what we'll create.

The 7th Gene Key is part of the Ring of Union, a genetic coding family that governs how we relate with others. The 7th Gene Key and a selfish or self-obsessed agenda can create a real mess in the world. This is why boundaries are so important. It's not enough to have good intentions. We have to be able to show Understanding and Commitment, two key Gifts of this codon group, not to mention the 7th Gene Key's Programming Partner, the 13th Gift of Discernment. The 7th Shadow isn't good at boundaries, and often its very eagerness to be of service without the proper maturity, support, and ability to listen is a cocktail for eventual disappointment. Many projects are begun by the 7th Gene Key that end up a divisive situation in which people are hurt, resentful, and plain angry at the lack of clarity, commitment, and humility coming from the 7th Gene Key.

The 7th Gift - Guidance

The Gift of Guidance is often misunderstood at the Shadow frequency. With the Shadow, we can offer and proffer guidance without awareness, and even more importantly, without invitation. There's a deep need for recognition coming from this Shadow. It craves attention and feeds the will to power. If we have this Gene Key, we need to examine our motives for guiding others very carefully. This is the Gift of sages, and we should only guide when we're truly asked, rather than being the initiator. And when we are asked, we need to take our time and consider the person and situation carefully before we decide to help. We need to let them know we are considering their request and then be honest about what we have decided. Sometimes the best guidance is not to guide. This takes a deep strength. Most people actually don't need guidance; they need someone to listen. Sometimes I'm amazed at the role I find myself in. When I go into the world as a teacher, which is actually quite rare, people come to talk with me and they often do most of the talking. I listen, but they're often so desperate they forget about me. I could be anyone. I don't really mind, but if they were able to be a bit more quiet, a bit more more present in their body, we could exchange something deeper than simply their urge to be heard and seen. The other beauty of the Gift of Guidance is that it knows how to be still. Guidance is really about being with someone. It's about presence. It's about resonating with them, taking them in, drawing their energies into our cells, our blood, our heart. This is the deepest form of guidance - guidance through embodiment. This is guidance through non-guidance.

One of my favourite pastimes these days is drinking rare and fine tea. It's become a teaching that accompanies the Gene Keys. It's entered into the bloodstream of our community. Many of us are doing it and it's a wonderful form of guidance. We sit with someone and prepare a fine tea and as we pour and drink the tea together, the ritual of this act brings us closer. We are entering the field of guidance. It isn't even from one person to the other; it's in the field that lies between us and the other. It's a true dialogue - what the Japanese call a haragei - a dance between two bellies, between two haras. The guidance comes from life, the Tao, the simple act of being together without much of an agenda. It's an exquisite thing. It's beauty in action. The Gift arises on its own out of the fertile field of the Shadow. We sit, cultivate the presence, and then the Gift just floats up into the space. Each of the 64 Gifts carries its own form of guidance. We're really just being hosts for each other. This is the magic present in the Ring of Union, that guidance comes from reflecting, pausing and truly being together. When we just sit, relax in each other's aura and talk about ordinary things, the invisible enters.

The 7th Siddhi - Virtue

When we use the word virtue as a Siddhi, we need to realise that we're using a word in its broadest, most multidimensional capacity. English, as a modern language, has the great advantage of being universal in potential, but the great disadvantage of also being somewhat one-dimensional. Other more ancient languages, or languages derived from scripts and pictograms, have at their disposal many dimensions for every word. For example, one Chinese term for virtue might be te or de, but this word also has many other meanings, such as 'telesmic power', or 'moral fortitude' or even simply, 'power'. When we think of virtue, we can think of the source of all that is best in us. We can think of the qualities latent in our souls. We can picture those aspects of our essence that will travel onwards when we die and give up our body. This virtue is the light inside, the illuminated dream of eternity hidden in our bones. How shall we find our hidden virtue? How shall we invite its aroma to be released into the air of our lives? Here are some ways:

~We can cease thinking or speaking of others in a negative light. Virtue is as delicate as a wild orchid. It can't thrive or even breathe when we cast our Shadows on each other. We must protect our virtue from such thoughts, and if others are speaking ill of others, we must protect ourselves from those sick winds.

~We can be forgiving towards others and let them feel the warmth of our care for them.

~We can realise that the way we think of others is like the sunlight or the darkness cast before the flower of our virtue. If we do this over time, the flower of our virtue will return to our heart. It will grow strong and release its sweet perfume far and wide, stirring magical currents and wonderful things.

We've seen that the 7th Gene Key has a quality of leadership and influence. In the original translation, it's known as 'The Army', and there's a lot of commentary on this idea of the army and the general. I'd like to move away from this cultural and historical image. The structure of this hexagram and this Gene Key has more to do with the water that's hidden beneath the earth. Like our inner virtue, it's hidden until it rises to the surface in mysterious places and ways, as springs do. People are naturally drawn to springs. Rivers and lakes flow from springs. Towns and settlements form around them. Springs are healing places for all creatures to come and be together. Virtue is also something we can accumulate, just as water accumulates beneath the ground over the centuries. We accumulate virtue through our positive actions, thoughts and deeds. We don't see the drops of water filling the great lakes below but every drop brings the water closer to the surface. One day, when our virtue is brimming over, suddenly it erupts through the cracks of our lives and begins to flow from our hearts, through our aura as effervescent light and as tangible goodwill and benevolence.

I actually like the idea of an 'army of virtues', arming themselves to combat the negativity of the world. Someone asked me recently what my definition of synarchy was. Synarchy is the 44th Siddhi; it's the highest form of human government. My answer was that synarchy is a hierarchy of virtue. It's a world in which the lowliest and humblest rise naturally to the top. It's exactly the opposite to what we see today where wealth favours the striver. One day wealth will no longer rise but will sink down to the ocean floor. There it will come to rest beside the humble ones, the true sages, who have silently, invisibly over the millennia remained hidden from view, cultivating virtue and love, holding the vision of harmony and a higher world on behalf of us all. This is where all can drink from the same inextinguishable spring - the spring of virtues.

THE 64 WAYS

The 8th Way

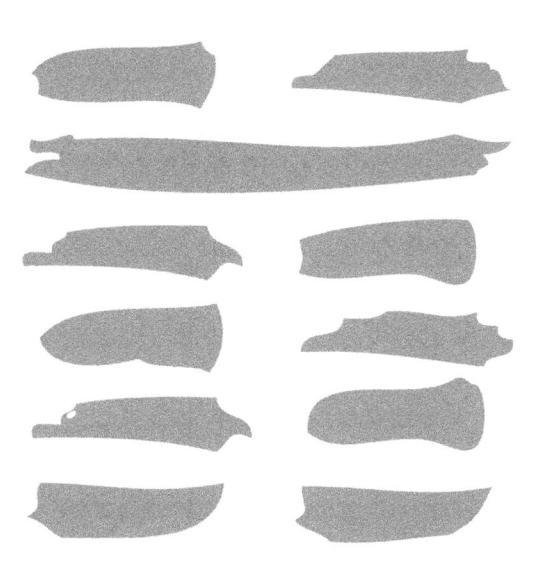

Gene Key 8

THE WAY OF STYLE

The Transformational Way of the 8th Gene Key moves from Mediocrity to Exquisiteness. It's the Way of Style.

Every Shadow state involves being a victim of something or someone. That's the hallmark of all awareness that remains rooted in fear. Here with the 8th Shadow we have a pattern rooted in the deep-seated fear of what others may or may not think of us. It all has to do with image - the image we project to the world, the image we have of ourselves and the image we have of others' image of us. Ahh, it's another tangled web, this Shadow. The Dilemma is imitation, and at the Shadow consciousness we are always a victim of imitation at some level.

In its repressed state, as it moves and drives vast numbers of human beings, this 8th Shadow maintains the status quo. It's that part of us that won't leave the comfort zone of the status quo. It manifests in our willingness to become institutionalised, homogenised, to live an ordinary, mundane, monotonous, and above all, safe life. My image of this Shadow is a kind of genetic suburbia. It's a space inside that's laid down through our conditioning as we develop through our early childhood. I also sometimes refer to this as 'maintenance consciousness'. These are people who exist in the world simply at a maintenance level; they maintain the institutions, the systems, the structures but they don't add anything to the world. They may add something through their goodwill and kindness. Of course at an inner level, everyone evolves in their lives but externally these people just maintain the machine that purports to make us all feel safe.

When we're not aware of the fear that drives us, we live very superficially. We live in a grey world, a world of mediocrity. We may be successful, glamorous, popular or kind.

| **Shadow**: Mediocrity | **Gift**: Style | **Programming Partner:** Gene Key 14 |
| **Dilemma**: Imitation | **Siddhi**: Exquisiteness | **Codon Ring:** The Ring of Water |

We may even appear interesting to others and the media. But underneath we are mediocre. What do we really mean by mediocrity? I'm not talking about externals but the quality of our consciousness. It's not possible to experience the peaks of consciousness when we repress the fear inside us. We can distract ourselves from the fear in a million ways, but then we will never know ecstasy. There are billions of people across our planet, and very few of us remember the ecstasy that was present all around us as a young child. We have forgotten the light that every child emanates, and which gradually over time, through education, upbringing, local and global conditioning, becomes throttled and grows dim. We might be thinking, 'that isn't me, I'm no victim of mediocrity, I've escaped all that humdrum existence, I'm different, I'm following the alternative route, the path less travelled', but we have to be really honest with ourselves. Many people believe the path less travelled is far for the common path. But in the West we now have a whole alternative lifestyle movement. We can allegedly escape the rat-race, drop out of the grey mediocre world of the masses and become more colourful, do yoga, travel to exotic places, study with great teachers, be a gypsy, an artist, live a right brain life. But still we need to look carefully and honestly at our lives. Is this really the path less travelled? Or are we still a victim of mediocrity? By this I mean, are we reacting to mediocrity or is our life a reaction to not wanting to be mediocre? Remember the Dilemma is about imitation. How many people now are living alternative lifestyles? Is it a new kind of surburbia? Is it a new kind of security to be a seeker or an outcast?

The Shadow states can sometimes be so subtle and we can easily become ensnared in their promises of security. I'm not saying these things as a judgment of anyone's lifestyle. This 8th Shadow is really a big one for us all. It's about image, style, wanting to look good in the eyes of society. It's about wanting to do the right thing or it's about reacting to all that and wanting to be seen as the opposite, someone who never does the right thing. 'I'm someone who doesn't care what others think!' Ah, but we do care. We want them to see us that way. We want them to see us as a rebel. We're part of a rebellious counter-movement and even though we may claim to be different in fact we're imitating all the other rebels, outcasts, seekers. We're not a true rebel; we've simply become a victim of mediocrity. We've become a reactionary. Our art doesn't contain true genius. Our dance is still subtly self-conscious. Our music doesn't rise to the ecstatic planes. It's still mediocre. It may be colourful, interesting, exotic even, but it doesn't contain genius. This 8th Shadow is all about image. It's all about investment in our image. If we keep our image intact, whether we're boring or super-hip, we're still not a true rebel. Subtly, we still have an image in mind of who we are. The true rebel, the one who has truly released their inner light, hasn't even a breath of imitation about them. They're constantly transcending all definitions of who they are. They can't ever step in the same river twice. They've truly taken the path less travelled. We all need to be wary of this Shadow. The Shadow states can be slippery as hell; they are after all, the pathways criss-crossing hell, because that's what the Shadow state is. It's hell.

The 8th Gift of Style

We've already seen at the Shadow frequency how the notion of image governs this Gene Key. We can see how deeply we become victims of 'life-style'. However, the Gift of Style is not about that, despite how the word makes it sound. This isn't life-style. It's not about how we look, what we wear, what we do. Again it's about the quality of our consciousness. The Gift frequencies all resonate with genius. It's where and how the Shadow is transformed from potential into kinetic energy. This is why the Gift frequency releases such a tide of creativity. It's the atomic explosion that occurs as all those definitions of who we are begin to melt, and we begin to enter another dimension, a way of living that's far more outrageous than anything we could ever dream up ourselves. The 8th Gift is the Gift of Style, and true style is always rebellious. It's rebellious because it's always recreating itself. It isn't afraid of the mundane material plane, and it isn't in reaction to it either. This is a state that's always exploring new paradigms, that's always expanding out of its boundaries into new areas. The Programming Partner here is the 14th Gift of Competence. These are people who aren't afraid of trying new things; they're not afraid of constantly redefining themselves. Their competence derives from their lack of a fixed self image. They can be a plumber one moment and a pirate the next.

The 8th Gift has no investment in its own image. It's the process in which self-image is being short-circuited. The moment we surrender to life, we surrender to a dance that's so mysterious we can never follow it with our mind. We drop all our ideas of who and what kind of person we are, like - I'm a kind person, I'm a warrior, I'm angry, I'm masculine, I'm feminine, I'm a bad boy, I'm a tomboy, I'm funny, I'm enlightened, I'm not enlightened. All of it has to go into the alchemical cauldron here at the Gift frequency. This is the genius of non-imitation. All genius has this quality. It's always surprising, surpassing, scintillating itself. It's capable of anything and everything. In this sense the 8th Shadow is rebellious. It's rebellious to its own image of itself. It won't allow us to rest anywhere with an image of who we are. It's our unique, always changing, always new style, not a fixed style. It's life sporting with itself.

We can feel perhaps how mad this Gift is, the level of surrender it demands. Yet all these gifts are a fractal aspect of a whole. All awakening has to pass through this phase in which self-image is short-circuited, in which we constantly confuse our mind with the paradox of our own existence. We can ask ourselves how surrendered we are; would we give up our alternative lifestyle if the calling came? How mad are we really? The Gift of Style bridges the paradoxes, unites the extremes, unifies male and female by erasing our ideas of what they are mentally and emotionally, and shows us how to live them internally. As we emanate this rebellious inner spirit, this great inner light, then we begin to radiate our true style. Our style is in our radiance, our aura, the timbre of our voice, as we allow ourself to rest in the uncertainty and vulnerability of life. The Gift of Style invites us to be in the world all the way rather than in reaction to it. These are people who may live deeply rebellious inner lives, but lead utterly ordinary outer lives.

We need not fear mediocrity, as long as our heart is open and singing. We don't need to react to it and find ourselves at odds with the status quo. True style is found in the marketplace, living as an example of a true rebellious human being, unchained by external definitions and unfettered by conditioning, ancestral or cultural. True style is happy to merge with the masses, and yet it can never, ever be missed, so beautiful and so unusual is its creative vigour and open-heartedness. As the Gene Keys say, true style is more than skin deep. It goes all the way to the Source.

The 8th Siddhi — Exquisiteness

This is quite a Way, from mediocrity to style. We can feel how different the word style here is from our modern definitions. We tend to see it as something fixed, yet in this Gene Key it's describing the continual arcing of consciousness as it surprises itself by mutating in every living moment. This constant inner outpouring of the mystery is brought to its peak here in the 8th Siddhi – the Siddhi of Exquisiteness. These words for the Siddhis are funny. How do we use a word for a state that exists beyond words? We're only describing genetic effects of that state. The cause is beyond words, but we can somewhat envisage the effects. It always has to be a bit of a story, a conjuring trick, so it's good not to get too attached at this level to the words. I'll try to enter the field and bring some of its energy into my words.

Certain Gene Keys trigger spontaneous images inside me. This is one of them. I always see a diamond here. A diamond. Why do I see a diamond? Well, it's a metaphor, a symbol, an emblem for Exquisiteness. The diamond is multifaceted, just like the Self, and yet it's also one, indivisibly beautiful. It's also rare, unique and geometrically perfect. The octahedral shape of the diamond is universal to all life forms, from DNA helices to the universal lattice that holds together all creation. The original name of this 8th Hexagram in the I Ching is Holding Together. The universe is held together by this exquisite, invisible unity, and it's also why this 8th Gene Key is allied to the 2nd Gene Key of Unity. This is the Codon Ring of Water, and these 2 Gene Keys are the two great feminine archetypes. Perhaps that's why they say 'diamonds are a girl's best friend'!

Yet on its own the diamond is not enough of a symbol to convey the other part of this 8th Siddhi. We're each exquisite, indivisible, unique alonenesses, standing like jewels in the sparkling flood of spacetime. The 8th Siddhi also conveys the essence of the feminine quality of flow. The diamond is brittle, just like the individual who doesn't know its true nature as one with all that is. This Siddhi is also fluid, ever-changing, curving, unpredictable, yielding and weak. It's weak in the most mystical sense of the word. The diamond may be strong, but water is weak. It has no fixed substance, and therefore it has the kind of weakness that nothing can stick to it. It's magnetically weak. It attracts no karma, no agenda, no attention, no opposition. It's like a monopole, an element resting in infinity. The 8th Siddhi is completely at rest. This is the ultimate rebellion – to do nothing. We become an anti-rebel. We move beyond the game of rebellion and individuality. We enter the paradox, and in finding ourself, we've simultaneously lost ourself.

I can only move into paradoxical wordplay when I enter the spirit of one of these Siddhis. It all becomes so fluid, so voluptuously slippery when words dance along the banks of the wordless. The 8th Siddhi has embraced the wordless world of impermanence. It's found the permanence of consciousness within the impermanence of form, and that's what releases its full atomic beauty.

> *Thus shall you think of this fleeting world:*
> *A star at dawn, a bubble in a stream,*
> *A flash of lightning in a summer cloud,*
> *A flickering lamp, a phantom, and a dream.*

These words, famous words from the oldest of all the great sutras of India, the aptly named Diamond Sutra, capture the essence of this truth of impermanence. When we think about our life, the people and places we love, the books, teachings, films, stories, children, sun, moon, ocean, mountains, trees and stars - they're all fading away. Along with us, the self that we recognise, we'll all soon be gone. In a sniff we could be gone. One asteroid, and puff, it's all gone. To enter the siddhic realm is to let go of all history as though it never even happened. Millions of years of evolution, story, poetry, wisdom, love, humanity's final wonderful flowering, and then puff, it's just all erased, with no traces. A whole story, just forgotten. All of our drama, our evolution, our striving, our seeking, all one day gone and then we rest. Consciousness just rests. The 8th Siddhi is completely at ease. When we fall into this fluid state, where our heart sits floating like a diamond lotus on the ever-changing waters of life, then our essence will be at ease. Our essence is at ease. It was all just a joke. It was all just a game. As all the poets have always known, our beautiful, exquisite world and all of us, our souls, are nothing more than a puff of dust in the wind…

> *Thus shall you think of this fleeting world:*
> *A star at dawn, a bubble in a stream,*
> *A flash of lightning in a summer cloud,*
> *A flickering lamp, a phantom, and a dream.*

THE 64 WAYS

THE 9TH WAY

Gene Key 9

THE WAY OF DETERMINATION

The Transformational Way of the 9th Gene Key moves from Inertia to Invincibility, and it's the Way of Determination.

The Taming Power of the Small - this is the lovely name given to this hexagram in the original translation of the I Ching, perhaps one of the more overlooked Gene Keys, and very worth looking into in more depth. Originally, the symbolism here is of the wind and sky accompanied by the threat of rain, and the wind is only just strong enough to keep the rains at bay. At the time when the I Ching was written, King Wen, one of its originators, was threatened with war from his neighbours, and only managed to keep them calm by a continuous stream of friendliness, hence the meaning of this hexagram. I like this image. It makes me smile - the continuous stream of friendliness that keeps war at bay. This is the Shadow of Inertia. The elemental energy in this Gene Key brings a focus on subtle activities, rather than grand plans and gestures. Life can be overwhelming at times. Even the best laid plans can go awry, as one Scottish poet put it. Life can get us down. This is a truth we have to accept. The I Ching and the Gene Keys are maps of the changing cosmic forces of our lives, and how we respond to challenges dictates the pattern of our destiny. If we succumb to the Shadow frequency or indulge our negativity for too long, it will drain us of our life force. It will suck us dry.

The evolutionary movement towards awareness, towards the light, can be fraught with disappointments. We make a grand leap only to have a grander fall. Sometimes we feel we're back where we started. Sometimes we feel we haven't got anywhere at all. These are the kinds of feelings that plague the 9th Shadow. It's part of the Codon Ring called the Ring of Light. At the Shadow this is the Ring of Darkness. The darkness presses in upon us. It coerces us to yield to it, and causes us inertia. Sometimes when we gaze at the world,

Shadow: Inertia	**Gift**: Determination	**Programming Partner:** Gene Key 16
Dilemma: Perspective	**Siddhi:** Invincibility	**Codon Ring:** The Ring of Light

it's as though we're standing before a vast mountain that stretches far, far above us. How will we ever get up and over that impossible looking peak? The very looking at it makes our knees feel weak. What's the point even trying, we think. These are the thoughts and feelings that drag at us and make us sag. Many of us live exhausting lives, and spend a great deal of our lives labouring under fatigue. We don't live beautifully, simply. We don't spend time with the elements, with the sun, with the trees.

On the way into town this morning I decided to stop the car, and get out and enjoy the sun. It was a beautiful day. My mind wanted to get on with the jobs I had to do. Just do the things on your list, the mind says, and then you'll be able to rest. That's the mind for you. As I started to enjoy the sun, I forgot all about my list and the jobs I had to do. I just entered into concert with the sun and the elements. I had the most wonderful time. I was an hour or so, just adrift. This is exactly what the 9th Shadow doesn't want us to do. It wants us to be a victim. It doesn't want us to cultivate our own essence. It wants us to lie down and give up.

The Dilemma of this Gene Key is perspective. If we're looking up at the whole mountain, we'll feel overwhelmed. If however, we decide just to look down at our feet, we'll be captivated. The Taming Power of the Small teaches us to focus on small changes, rather than attempting great things. This is how we keep the Shadow at bay. It's how people attain great things. They focus on small goals, small successes, and lots of small successes add up to victory. So if we bring our attention to the small, to the details that make up our life, we can make a small change. If we have a negative pattern that's undermining us, it's better not to take the whole thing on all at once. It will floor us. Just make a small change. We might be trying not to react in a charged situation with someone, but we need to not expect miracles. If we don't react, even if it's just once, then we can congratulate ourself inwardly on that success. Hug that victory close. If we do it once, we can do it again. This is the change in perspective that's needed to move beyond the grip of the 9th Shadow. Look at the small things. Stay in the present. We won't even have noticed, but one day we'll find ourself halfway up the mountain. That's how we bring the light of awareness into our lives. Small steps. Small steps.

The 9th Gift - Determination

This is the Gift of Determination. Determination may be a misunderstood term. It sounds like it involves a great deal of power, or force, or discipline, or willpower. Again, this is why we fall victim to the Shadow of Inertia, because we see how much energy it will take to get from A to Z, and we feel that we don't have that kind of energy or commitment. We've just seen that it's really about small steps. We take a first step. Actually, the first step is the hardest. On the other hand it's easy, because it's just one step, but the full weight of inertia is before us. In the beginning, we have to be more brave and determined. Maybe there's something we'd like to do in our lives, but are afraid to begin. So we just take that first step. What a threshold something so simple can be, and it's really just our mind in the way. Our mind is seeing the mountain, but if we look down at our feet, we can take that first step. Once we've made that first step, every single step after becomes easier. There may be big obstacles and breakthroughs on our journey, but that first step is with us every other step. Its power is incalculable. Even if we fall from the path, that first step can bring us back, and then we come to the power of repetition.

The Programming Partner of this Gene Key is the 16th Gift of Versatility and the Siddhi of Mastery. Versatility comes through repetition. We do something over and over until it becomes imprinted, not just inside our cellular being, but also within the cosmos. There are forces and laws that uphold the cosmos, and they're irrefutable. For example, if we pray for something over and over from our heart, one day that prayer must be granted, as long as it's a selfless prayer.

We can only be versatile when we've determined the pathway forwards. This is the beauty of this word determination. It's also the notion of pre-determination - that once we get in the groove, the practise we're doing kind of holds itself up. The cosmos steps in to help us attain it, and it feels like this is something that just wants to happen.

It's like my son, Ambrose, who's eleven and at that stage in his development when he has a body like Adonis, where everything's in proportion. He went to this version of the Olympic Games that the Steiner Waldorf Schools hold. All the boys and girls at his stage come together to reenact the Olympic Games. It mirrors their stage of physical development. Anyway, Ambrose knows that his bigger brother at that same stage won the marathon, not actually a real marathon, but about a mile. It's a big deal at that age. There are about 300 of them, and it's the race that has the most kudos. Ambrose really wants to win this thing, and it's a big ask. There are a lot of others who also want to win it. Ambrose isn't the tallest, or the wiriest, or even the most muscular kid. He's quite average in height and build; there's no clear advantage. It turns out he has one advantage - his will. He won the race. I didn't think I could handle another one. I was almost in tears when my eldest boy won it four years ago. I had all those emotions well up in me again, that fatherly pride and the ecstasy of knowing that he had attained what he wanted so much. He was pitted against faster boys and maybe if he'd raced again he might not have won. But he knew he only had to win it once, so he threw all his will into it. There wasn't an ounce of his being left out of his effort. It was almost as though he knew it was a defining moment in his inner life. If he hadn't won it would also have been fine, but for me it was a lesson in will. If we can make one breakthrough inside ourself, we can make others. We will make others. Ambrose's victory was a big one, but there were many small ones that preceded it, not least his brother's paving the way for him.

The Gift of Determination can also include working together and encouraging and learning from others. We create our karma of tomorrow, today. That's the power of focusing on the present, so whatever our difficulties in life, we can bring our attention and determination into the small, everyday, local details and make our changes there. That's the foundation of magic, the transmutation of the small, the Taming Power of the Small, into light, into truth.

GENE KEY 9

THE 9TH SIDDHI - INVINCIBILITY

I love the playful nature of the I Ching. We have these two Gene Keys, the 9th Gene Key, the Taming Power of the Small and the 26th Gene Key, the Taming Power of the Great, so they're intimately connected. Their Siddhis are Invincibility and Invisibility. Just a letter or two of difference in the word. Again we have a word that sounds like it's so powerful. Invincibility. It sounds like a great Archangel wielding a great power. That's our masculine word bias in English, because if we read the Tao Te Ching, it will tell us that the invincible is in the weak, not the strong. We come back to the origin of this hexagram in the I Ching - it's about weakness leading strength. Remember? The old King controlled his warring neighbours through friendliness, not through any show of strength. Through friendliness, kindness.

The 9th Siddhi can have special powers. Along with the 26th Siddhi, the 9th Siddhi is about eternity in a grain of sand. I'm reminded of Mother Julian, Julian of Norwich, the Medieval mystic - you can find out all about her in my free series, the Ecstatics. She was a mystic who received God's transmission in a series of showings or revelations. In one of her revelations, she's famously shown a tiny object before her, the size of a hazelnut. She marvels at it, and asks God what it is, to which He/She replies, 'it is all that ever was, and all that ever shall be'. In icons of Mother Julian, you'll see her holding this tiny hazelnut - this essence of the world. This is the magic of the 9th Siddhi, that it can reduce everything down to its essence - and the essence is love.

The most powerful force in the universe is the feminine. It's Water. It's the void. It's tenderness. It's the Puer Aeternis. I have to tell you another story here. These are my personal contemplations, after all. I apologise that it's also about my children. If you have children of your own, you will know that they are the greatest teachers of Truth. This morning I went out to see the sunrise with my daughter, who's nine. There we are watching the most exquisite jewel of a sunrise, and there's all this mist hanging over the meadows, and the golden light is streaked through in a beatific haze. It's magical. Otherworldly. Ursula turns to me and says, 'Daddy, can I run into that?' Well, I'm not going to say no, even though it's soaking wet long grass. I mean I had the same feeling.

So off she goes running and leaping into the golden dawn, skipping through the long, damp, misty grass. As I watched her, I realised I was watching something immortal. If I could carry any single memory with me until the end of time, I would choose that moment - the young innocent girl skipping through a field of magical misty light. It was rapturous, enchanting. Afterwards, as I contemplate it, I realise that that is Invincibility. It isn't me, the father, the strong, the protector, the yang. It's the mystery of the childlike, the innocent, the weak. You see it isn't really weak, it's just so delicate. This is the Puer Aeternus, the immortal child, the Golden Child. It's a myth that has crept out into the world.

It's this spirit that makes us invincible - all the yin qualities - softness, surrender, yielding, play, subtlety. That is God, the qualities of the Divine, of the Ring of Light. To be invincible, we must give up our identity, our attachment to the form. We must dive into life, and die to be reborn in eternity. Only that which has already died can be invincible, and then of course, there is no death. There is only our love, cradled in the palm of love, like a tiny hazelnut, eternal and precious and sweet beyond measure.

THE 10TH WAY

Gene Key 10

THE WAY OF NATURALNESS

The Transformational Way of the 10th Gene Key moves from the Self Obsession to Being, and it's the Way of Naturalness.

If we have this Gene Key somewhere in our Profile, or are drawn to or contemplating it, we may be in for a surprise, or even a shock. Whatever we're seeking in life, however hungry or exhausted or frustrated, this Gene Key offers us a way out. The problem is that we may not want to take it. The reason is that it's too easy. We humans often don't do easy. We like to make things as hard as possible for ourselves. It seems to be the habit of the ego. The harder we struggle, the more we feel we exist. The Dilemma here is ease. It cuts very, very deep, does this Gene Key. In this modern, fast-paced world, this Gene Key has become like a forgotten backwater in our genes. It's as though we're all racing past this wonderful treasure. We pass it every day on our way to work. Because of our intensity, expectations, and longing, we miss it within our relationships. Even in the quietness of our inner life, we rarely stop to give it even the smallest moment of our time. The ancients always spoke of this thing - this elusive thing that we all seek - and they also spoke of it being right under our noses. Well, here it is in this Gene Key. The great sage Chuang Tzu spoke it in his immortal words, 'Easy is right'. If we want to really know what this Gene Key is all about, we can make these three words our creed. Contemplate them over and over again. We really have to try and understand what they mean for us.

This is the Shadow of Self Obsession. We all suffer from this disease. We worry about our lives, our future, our clothes, about what others think of us. Even if we don't worry on the outside, we're running from ourselves. We hide in our business, our jobs, our studies, our busyness. We've forgotten what it feels like to do nothing. We've forgotten how dreamy life can be. We've forgotten completely how to relax. We're obsessed with knowing where

Shadow: Self-obsession   **Gift**: Naturalness   **Programming Partner:** Gene Key 15
Dilemma: Ease   **Siddhi:** Being   **Codon Ring:** The Ring of Humanity

---

we're going, who we are, with finding our purpose. If we've been drawn to the Gene Keys, it may be partly because this Shadow is driving us. We needn't worry or rush into self-judgment. We only need to see the pattern in our life. That's all this Gene Key asks. This is how transformation occurs - through doing nothing and simply seeing how manic we've become. If we take this Shadow deeply into ourself, explore it, and get to know it intimately, our life will just change. We won't be able to help it. Our awareness will turn inwards, but without becoming obsessed. We'll slow down. We'll begin to enjoy life, to experience it. So few of us really experience life, we're so obsessed with our problems and challenges. We've become a deeply selfish species.

Think about all the people in the world who are obsessed with finding their perfect partner - their soul mate. That can become a secret obsession that lasts an entire lifetime. Think about all the people striving, striving to make more money, to find more comfort. That can last a lifetime. Our families are lacking in true love, in true safety for our children. Was our adolescence a safe place? Did we feel that loving, joyful holding from our parents? If we did we're one of the rare ones. We don't need intervention. We don't need guidance - not really. We don't need advice. We need to feel love and joyfulness and acceptance around us. We need to feel a sense of play. Our obsession with the 'dream' is the very thing that undermines our ability to relax in life. We don't need a dream. Life takes care of everything for us. We've forgotten this simplest truth - that life takes care of everything. Without this truth we're doomed to be a tight person living in a tight life. We're angry, frustrated. We're bored, dissatisfied, ungrateful. I'm sorry if this seems like a negative ranting monologue but this Gene Key has a certain ruthlessness to it. I said it'll cut to the bone. It's remarkable how something so soft and simple can be so harsh and unforgiving. Why are we self-obsessed?

Are we endlessly chasing our own tail, putting off our relaxation until tomorrow, until Friday, until the holidays? What kind of a life is this where only a few weeks of a year we relax? When we add all that up at the end of our days, we'll see what our life has really amounted to.

Ease is before us but we don't take that path. We take the hard path, the steep path, the path of toil and struggle and distraction. The one who decides to take the easy path swiftly finds ecstasy, playfulness, a purity and simplicity of being. The easy path goes through gardens of delight. It has seats placed in beautiful places for us to rest. It has little tea-houses with kind and wise old hosts waiting to serve us. It's lined with friends and friendships. Friendship is central to this path. It's given central stage, but most of us won't take this path in life. We may want to. We may like the sound of it, but our pattern of self-obsession, our addiction to the drama and the struggle is too great. So we'll likely turn away. Think about that.

THE 10TH GIFT - NATURALNESS

Nowhere is our self-obsession more pronounced than in the spiritual life. The more spiritual we become, the more achingly serious we become, and the more we think we know. But we have to admit at a certain point that we know nothing, absolutely nothing. Do you think I know any of this? Everything to do with the Gene Keys comes out of nothing, out of my not-knowing. Don't ask me what I know. I can't tell you. If I do this same contemplation tomorrow, it'll come out completely differently. I may say the opposite. This isn't science. This isn't dogma. It's nonsense. It doesn't need a sense of continuity. It's wisdom. Truth flows from a sense of naturalness, a place of flow, of playfulness. We have nothing to defend with this Gift. There's no need to defend any position or opinion, because we don't really have one. Spirituality can be the greatest trap. Under its veneer, we may one day see that we've quietly taken on another set of views and opinions - new layers of complexity and thought. I mentioned earlier that this Gene Key gives us a way out. It does. It truly does. This way out is naturalness. How to be natural? It can't be done. There is no 'way' to be natural. Naturalness is actually a process of realisation. We begin to realise that everything is natural.

We can't even say that the Shadow is unnatural and the Gift is natural. Self-obsession is natural at the beginning and then it naturally dissipates as our heart opens. I listen to my children arguing. It's natural. I listen to the birds singing, it's natural. I feel my laziness, I feel my seriousness, I see pain, beauty - any state between the Shadow and the Siddhi and I see only that which is natural. The Gift of Naturalness is a softening of our edges, it's a great allowing, a great place of defencelessness. Easy is right. Where will those words go inside us? The ancient Taoists teach the art of wu wei - the subtle art of inaction - of doing nothing. We don't act and everything gets done. It doesn't mean that literally. This is a subtle thing to understand. Many have misunderstood these words. All the Advaita teachers out there in the world at the moment - you know, these people who say that there's nothing to do, no spiritual path, no enlightened state, no unenlightened state. They're right, but they're still there saying it. Why are they saying it? Many times they're saying it, but they're not living it. If they were living it, they would have disappeared into their own lives with no need to teach.

I don't wish to be harsh or judgmental, but this is such a subtle truth. You can't decide to be natural, and then go and make a career of it. This Gene Key is easier than that. Some of those teachers are utterly authentic. All are behaving naturally, because you cannot but behave naturally, but you can also be naturally mistaken. So be very, very careful when it comes to these subtleties. We can see the truth easily enough. Easy is right. If it's playful, if it doesn't take itself too seriously, if it's fresh, original, then it's something emerging from nothing. If it's repetition, if we've heard it before somewhere, then perhaps it's not so pure.

Wu wei is so subtle. It's something we cultivate inside ourself over time. It can so easily be mistaken. We must be careful of any spiritual path with this Gene Key. If we're naturally drawn to one, it can be our learning, but not our home. We must allow ourselves to become softer, more open, more yielding. That's the pathless path - that's what we mean by naturalness.

The 10th Siddhi - Being

When I wrote this Siddhi in the original Gene Keys book, I had such fun. I spoke of the way of the Bodhisattva and the Arhat - two paths or revelations to truth. The Bodhisattva is of the 15th Gene Key - the Siddhi of Florescence - a path of marvellous and colourful service. The Bodhisattva vows to stay on the path until all beings are enlightened. It's a path of sacrifice and service. Then there's the Arhat - the Arhat sees that all beings are already enlightened, so why the fuss and bother? If they're all enlightened, what am I going to do? There seems to be no point in doing anything. This 10th Siddhi is so normal that it seems radical. It's about meaningless-ness. There's no meaning to life. There's no hidden secret. There's just the beauty of this moment turning into the next. Naturalness arrives at Being. It's always arriving there in fact, but Being is too simple to describe. It isn't even in relation to non being. The Buddhists speak of being and non being. This Siddhi is beyond both. It isn't a polarity.

I don't know if you're understanding me in this Gene Key, or if what I'm saying is of any use to you. If you hear what's really coming through, you may experience a spontaneous sense of deep relaxedness pervading your inner being - an utter acceptance of that which is. There is nothing that is not natural. This gets us out of the game. But again, it's so subtle. We can't stop seeking unless the seeking naturally exhausts itself. Many have made that mistake - they hear this truth, and then they stop seeking, because the attraction of stopping and arriving is so great. It's exhausting to seek. Not seeking must be such a restful thing. So we try it out - our mind buys into this idea. Then we can look at all the seekers in the world and sort of pity them. Have you experienced this? Do you know someone like this? Spiritual people become so entrenched in their viewpoints. If we want to believe in angels, if we just naturally know that there are angels, then that is our naturalness. If we're a scientific materialist, that is our naturalness. Being is the most inclusive, gentle, and non superior state. It very rarely becomes a spiritual teacher. If it does, then it's with great reluctance, or with great playfulness. Being has no need for teachers or teachings. The moment is the teaching. The Arhat may seem like a selfish person - we can see a higher mirror here of the self obsession in the Shadow, but this Siddhi isn't interested in itself at all.

It has nothing to discover, nothing to do. Thus everything gets done through it.

How can I possibly make this practical? There is nothing practical about this Siddhi. Practicality is the Bodhisattva's path - to be helpful, useful - to try and help people move beyond their suffering. It appears very noble and pure, and it is. But the Arhat is just as pure. It's not that they won't be kind and helpful, but they haven't got any agenda. They haven't made any vow to help all beings. They are just content - utterly content. Being is a state beyond extremes. Its sole characteristic is its neutrality. It's so neutral that it shows up all other extremes very, very clearly. If we've ever met one of these people, we would either not even know it, on account of their ordinariness, or we'd be deeply disturbed at the depth of our unrelaxedness.

The 10th Siddhi also knows laughter. Not that laughter is an agenda, but that pure Being alone sees the great human joke. This Gene Key lives within the Codon Ring called the Ring of Humanity, and it connects across to the Ring of Seeking, through its Programming Partner, the 15th Gene Key. Its role is to show up seeking. But it isn't in contradiction to seeking. That's where you must get the subtlety here. One is not better than another. If we do get the big joke in this Gene Key, then we may come to the end of our spiritual path quicker than we thought! But please don't be seduced by it. If it dawns in us, it will dawn in us. Our seeking must exhaust itself naturally. This is a Siddhi we're unlikely to see. It's our natural state, but because of that it's unnoticeable. That is unless we spend some time around it. If we do, we'll see that the ordinary hides the extraordinary. The world was once a place populated by this Siddhi. One day it will be so again. Chuang Tzu says it thus, with his wonderful irreverent humour:

Dull and unwitting, men have no wisdom; thus their virtue does not depart from them.
Dull and unwitting, they have no desire; this is called uncarved simplicity.
In uncarved simplicity, the people attain their true nature.
Then along comes the sage, huffing and puffing after benevolence, reaching on tiptoe for righteousness,
and for the first time the world has doubts.

THE 11TH WAY

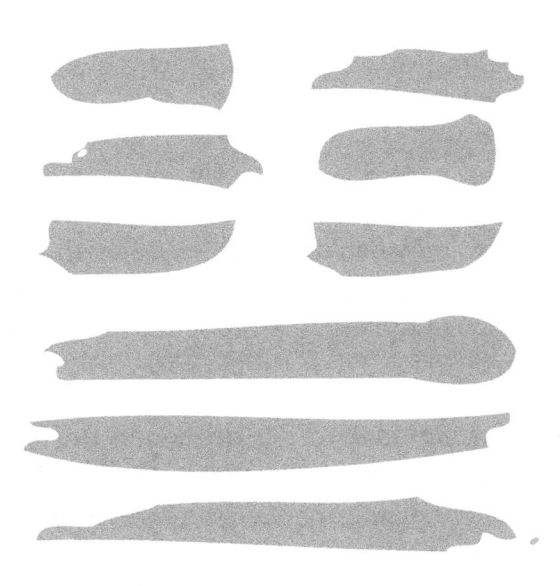

Gene Key 11
THE WAY OF IDEALISM

The Transformational Way of the 11th Gene Key moves from Obscurity to Light, and it's the Way of Idealism.

Ah, I've been looking forward to this one. It's a powerful wake-up call for many in the so-called New Age. Here we have the Shadow of Obscurity and the Gift of Idealism. We can perhaps feel the connection between these two words-obscurity and idealism. When does idealism become obscure and when does it shine out with light? Obscurity is about being lost in the clouds. It's about being lost in the details, the trivia, the miasmas of the mind and its beliefs. Obscurity refers to an obscuration of the inner light, whereas idealism is a dynamic, creative and self-enriching process.

The Dilemma of this Transformational Way is belief and this is a word that we must understand correctly. We sometimes say: 'I believe in myself', which is an affirmation of one's own integrity. There's also the idea of belief as a rigid inner mechanism for coping with life. It was Carl Jung who said it best in a famous interview: 'Mr. Jung' probed the interviewer, 'Does this mean that you believe in God?' to which the great man replied, 'I don't believe. I know.'

So the 11th Shadow is about fluffiness. It's about believing one's own or someone else's propaganda. At the Shadow frequency we're easily led into other people's obscurity, their belief systems, which may have been woven into elaborate systems of methodologies. Institutionalised religion is a net of beliefs designed to lift us out of our fears and give us an ideal to strive for. It's a noble goal, but unfortunately it creates more slaves than rebels. If we have the 11th Gene Key in our Profile, or if we're in a deep contemplation of it, we can have a long hard look at our tendency to be drawn in by systems or ideologies

Shadow: Obscurity **Gift:** Idealism **Programming Partner:** Gene Key 12
Dilemma: Belief **Siddhi:** Light **Codon Ring:** The Ring of Light

---

that promise the Light, the 11th Siddhi. This will also be a good test of the Gene Keys themselves. Are they for real, or just a set of fantasies? Such a divide there is between the Light itself, and the promise of the Light. That's the nub of this whole Gene Key.

Of course, the other side of this word obscurity is about being forgotten. It's about being lost in obscurity; we're referring here to the inner world rather than the outer. We're lost in obscurity whenever we become a victim of our beliefs. I want to make this absolutely clear - there's nothing wrong with having a belief, but we have to be able to see that belief as a construct of our mind. Belief and knowing are two very different things.

How do we tell whether something is false or genuine? Sometimes the only way is to go in. To go down the wormhole into the system or teacher, and then our experience will show us. It's interesting that the 12th Gene Key, the next in the sequence, and the Programming Partner here, is the Shadow of Vanity and the Gift of Discrimination, because that's how obscurity gets us - it feeds our vanity. It promises us riches, or it promises us the Light if we do such and such. We have to learn the art of discriminating between the genuine voices and the less than genuine. That's an essential aspect of taking any spiritual path. Sometimes a mistake is pure gold, so we needn't beat ourselves up. A mistake that shows us our tendency towards the inessential, towards something that hooks our beliefs, can be a massive wake-up call. If we look at the field of health today, we can see this same thing - there's an army of doctors, experts, healers, therapists and they all promise to help us with our health, whether that's through prescribing us medication or holding a purple amethyst over our third eye or whatever. A great deal of it is just obscurity. A great deal of it is simply the placebo effect - we buy into a belief, and it appears to work. There's nothing wrong with any of that, but at a certain point in our path, we realise that everything comes down to us, to what's inside us. What's beneath all this? What's belief? It's something we decide in our mind. That's the key. Our mind becomes convinced of a truth, and then we put that truth into our body, into our DNA, and it manifests. As I said, I'm not saying it's all rubbish. Not at all. But I am saying that at the Shadow frequency we tend to give away our authority to others. We want someone else to do it for us. It's like this Gene Keys business with our Hologenetic Profile. If I started offering readings, can you imagine how popular that would be? I'd be booked solid every day. And because we don't do it that way, it's a much harder sell! We have to do our reading on ourself. It's not just about believing what I say. That's the whole problem with us in the first place. We won't take responsibility for our own life, our health, our purpose, our relationships, our karma.

Think about science. Science is not supposed to be about belief. It's supposed to be absolutely open. But scientists become believers too, and they believe in theories, logic, and their own opinions. A good scientist is never a believer; they remain always open. They're available for their views and perspective to always be changing and adapting. Yes, scientists should be the most open-minded people on the planet. As should religious people. But see how obscurity works, even scientists can obscure the truth. They can prove anything if they believe in it enough. They can become fanatics, and then they believe that only their view is right. A sad situation that is. Obscurity robs us of creativity. We get caught up in a mental net, a net of ideas, and no matter how well intended it is, it keeps us from actually making any progress. It's not quite a dead-end street in fact, it's more an eternal loop. Obscurity traps us, it distances us from the inner Light. Beware the siren song of belief. We don't want to believe. We want to know, and to know, we must take our own journey, not someone else's.

Take the example of these 64 Ways. These are my contemplations on the 64 Gene Keys, and I hope they're inspiring, but ultimately we must do our own journey of contemplation. We must find our unique path through this wisdom. We must see them playing out in our life. That's why I don't create trainings and teachers, because then I've created a system that actually obscures the truth and looks like it has real substance. Then we stifle the magic.

You see obscurity is only about giving away our own inner light. It's fine to find a guide, or follow a system or any of these things, but we must be careful about our own beliefs. The system or the teacher is just a raft to get us to the other side, and sooner or later, we must step off the raft. Obscurity is our addiction to the raft, our addiction to seeking rather than finding, to believing rather than knowing, to dreaming rather than doing.

The 11th Gift of Idealism

The 11th Gift is our way to ensure we're never a victim of belief or obscurity. It will give us the lift and clarity necessary to carry us all the way out of the confusion of the Shadow frequency up into the more refined atmosphere that we call the Light.

Idealism is often seen as the opposite to realism. Again, I'd like to claim back this beautiful word. In the 60th Gene Key I have claimed back the word realism and hopefully imbued it with some long-needed magic to keep it from being so dry. Idealism has also been around a long time. In the Rig Veda, the ancient Hindu holy text, idealism was espoused as the notion that consciousness pervades everything in the universe. Many great philosophers and movements picked up this idea and developed it; Plato, Kant, Hegel, Russell, and Kierkegaard have all helped develop this concept down the centuries, but I don't want to discuss metaphysics. Since we're talking about the Gift frequency here, we're talking about creativity and action, so let's make this practical.

To have an ideal at the core of our life is to live a life of great expansion and purpose. The trick with the 11th Gene Key is to see that the ideal itself is not something literal and personal. What I mean by this is that our ideal is simply the carrot we use that draws our frequency upwards. For example, the highest ideal anyone can have is to be committed to creating heaven on earth, but most people would say, 'well, that's not realistic!' See how these words work! But that's not the point. This is what underpins the Christian Gnosis and the Buddhist Bodhissatva vow-that we must strive for the highest, most outlandish ideal and then all our energies begin to organise themselves around that ideal.

Obscurity is when we get caught in an expectation. I know this personally because when I first had my experience of the higher light, my mind refracted that as a series of images that I then thought I had to manifest in the world. For example, I was shown a castle (I actually went there physically), and I saw the castle as a kind of symbolic Camelot where people could come and study higher consciousness, and people would come from all around the world to this beacon of the new consciousness. I thought that was literal, but the 11th Gene Key operates through the right brain, through symbol and archetype, so we have to be very careful about being a victim of this kind of fantasy. The castle is a symbol for a great ideal - the ideal of Synarchy, a higher organising principle of virtue, service, and fellowship. It may even manifest as a castle one day (one must always remain open), but the point is that the ideal itself carries the Light into our DNA, and ignites the light in our DNA.

That is how the 11th Gift works. Our ideal energises us. It illuminates us. It enlightens us. It gets us out of bed in the morning with enthusiasm. It's the mental, emotional, and physical shell into which we can pour all our highest aspirations. If for example, we carry this ideal of a perfect world and we're in the business world, it will affect every decision we make. It will inform every relationship we enter into. It becomes an impulse at the core of our approach to business, and the same with relationships, health, family, eating, everything. Our ideal animates our life, so the higher and richer we can make it, the more power it will have in our life.

The thing we need to understand about the Light is that it's all-pervasive. It unites all forms and manifestations of phenomena. If for example, we set ourself up as someone who channels the ascended masters, then we had better realise that that is nothing more than a brand. The ascended masters are aspects of our higher consciousness. They're not 'up there,' separate to our own greater being. Otherwise we are caught in obscurity, and we'll capture others in obscurity. It's all about vanity (the Shadow of the programming partner here), because secretly, it makes us feel special that the masters have selected us to be their vessel. I don't wish to be harsh on the New Age, but these Shadows really don't serve us. They only disempower. As long as we get the joke, then it's okay to brand ourselves with these kinds of stories. If we believe the story, then we get lost in it.

Idealism is paired with the 12th Gift of Discrimination, its Programming Partner, and that's the power to use an ideal without being caught in the dilemma of believing it as literal.

For millennia, the great mystical teachings have used the idea of the Divine Ideal as a technique to raise the frequency of our consciousness. And the ideal is real. At the siddhic level, as we'll see, the ideal is already here, but we need to learn to detach our ego from the ideal. That's what spiritual maturity is - to see through the spiritual ego. If we have the 11th Gift, or are contemplating it, then we can use the beautiful richness of our right brain visions and archetypes to launch our life onto a higher level. That's our greatest Gift - to catch others on fire with the Light that burns in our hearts. Our Gift is our heart, our love, our devotion. It's not our ideal. It's our willingness to stay open, to know that anything is possible. That creates such a powerful field in the world. It's not the brand, it's the product, and we're the product. The ideal is simply the delivery mechanism. The true idealist knows this deeply in their being, and it's what makes them so deeply realistic. It's the delicious paradox of the 11th Gene Key.

The 11th Siddhi - Light

Many of you listening to or reading this will be familiar with the Hindu notion of the world being seen as a maya, an illusion or construct created by the mind. To us here in the phenomenal world of object and matter and cause and effect, this seems a distant and dreamlike notion at best. Mostly we might be tempted to see it as a colourful ancient metaphor. The only thing is, it's true. The world that most of us think we see and experience is not the real world. It's a dim reflection of the real world; the real world (a funny concept in itself) is that of pure light. We use the word light as a metaphor here, because it isn't really light, but light is the closest concept to it. I'm talking about the light of consciousness. Let's do a little meditation. Close your eyes, take a deep breath and imagine your life for a moment-your physical body, your home, your friends, your family, your car if you have one, your things. Now just imagine for a moment that none of that is real. It's all just part of a dream you had once. That's the view from the enlightened state. Ok so let's go on. Now imagine that the life that you think is yours is shrouded in darkness. You can't see the truth. It's all been a lie, a fantasy. Everywhere you look, all you can see is darkness. Look up, look down, look all around. All is dark. You're completely asleep. Now somehow, through the spirit of grace, you see a single pinprick of light in the darkness. Just a speck of light. Watch the light. See its tremendous beauty as it hangs there in the darkness-an eye in the void. What is it? What is this light, this first light, this pure light? I'll tell you what it is. It's a single moment of pure awareness. Now imagine yourself going through your daily chores, getting up, putting on your clothes, eating, going to work, coming home, maybe shopping, eating again, going to bed again. All darkness - an unaware life, a sleeping life. But you had one moment in the day - a moment of pure awareness. A moment when everything paused. Maybe you were sitting down. Maybe you were standing up. But for that short moment, you were aware of the inner light shining.

All your thoughts ceased in that pause. It was wonderful. It was like a holiday from Samsara, the endless wheel of life. Now look up again and see another pinprick of light shining in the sky of your life-another moment of light. Now there are two lights. One leads to two. And now three, and another, and another, and another. Let the lights continue to form, like the first shining stars in the night sky, and your view of life is changing. you're becoming more mindful, more heartful, more aware. The moments of presence keep appearing in the gaps, in the pauses, between the breaths. They just keep coming, and the more you become aware of these moments, the more keep coming. Soon there are thousands of lights in that dark sky, even millions. How beautiful they are. Now your daily life is filled with those moments. They well up every time you pause, maybe when you're doing the dishes, when a stranger engages you in casual meaningless conversation, or when you find yourself sitting at a red traffic light in your car, listening to a piece of music... Your life takes on a new meaning. A new higher purpose is shining through. Your ideal is burning strong in your breast. You find ways of stretching out those moments. You pause more and more often. You smile more. The tension is leaving your body. The anxiety is diminishing. The desires that led you out into the distractions of the world, your hunger to end your suffering, to block out the anxiety, the discomfort, it's all funnelled in one direction - to presence more of that light. At a certain point you're just hooked. You find yourself spontaneously meditating, maybe dancing, or you're changing your life around to enable more presence to enter.

Now when you look at that night sky that was your life, you see huge clusters of stars coalescing to form radiant suns, and the background is falling away... At a certain point there's more light than darkness. Now you really bring an intensity of focus to the dark patches. They leap into view. You give them your breath, your attention, your compassion, these shadows. One by one they diminish as the light cracks through from inside them.

Now even your movement becomes a pause, as the awareness saturates your daily chores and activity. Now your life is pristine and the final vestiges of darkness evaporate. There's nothing now but the radiance of light. The pure awareness has extinguished all the Shadow. Now what you thought of as yourself has also fallen away. All that is left is the pure light, the light of consciousness. That's who we really are. That's the 11th Siddhi. The glory of God. The ineffable radiance of the Presence. The rainbow body. And it's within us right now. We are the peace that passeth all understanding. Tat tvam asi. That art Thou. Namaste. I bow to the God inside you.

THE 12TH WAY

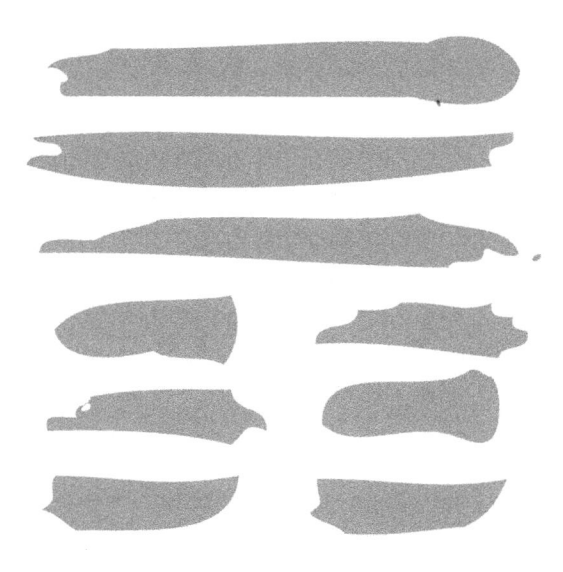

Gene Key 12

THE WAY OF DISCRIMINATION

The Transformational Way of the 12th Gene Key moves from Vanity to Purity. It's the path of Discrimination.

This is quite an exciting Gene Key for me. I'm excited to explore it simply because it's so mysterious. It's fun to enter on this kind of a journey using the art of contemplation. The Gene Keys are a living wisdom, a transmission - which means there are no experts. There is only our listening. The deeper we listen, the deeper the mystery opens up before us. And this 12th Gene Key is unique because it's an anomaly. It's a point of closure. If the human journey ever comes to an end, this Gene Key will close it. There is an aspect of the Gene Keys called the 22 Codon Rings, which groups the Keys together in a mysterious but wonderful pattern according to the structure of the genetic code.

Let's just pause for a moment to consider the miracle of the genetic code. It's a code that dictates how all organic life is built. It's literally an instruction manual, and the body has to follow it exactly. Within this matrix, there are three specific codes that signal when the body has to stop building proteins. These are called the Stop Codons. They are chemical signatures that geneticists sometimes liken to traffic lights, and essentially they control the way in which chemicals are built. The Gene Keys offer us a mirror of this process, and the 12th Gene Key is the third and final of these 3 Stop Codons, which are known as the Ring of Trials.

However, the 12th Gene Key also has another secret - it is part of the Ring of Secrets - which is a code within a code, and it's the only place in the Gene Keys you see this happen. It isn't even reflected in our genetics as far as I know. It's a secret. There must always be secrets. There are codes inside the human body that are dormant, that will

Shadow: Vanity   **Gift:** Discrimination   **Programming Partner:** Gene Key 11
Dilemma: Aloneness   **Siddhi:** Purity   **Codon Ring:** The Ring of Trials

---

only be switched on at a highly specific time in our evolution. Maybe they are waiting for the conditions to be right. Maybe they are awakened through mutations in radiation, or very high frequencies. So this Gene Key conceals something. It is holding something vast back. It is like a dam behind which an ocean is waiting.

So let's have a look at this and see how we can make it practical. At the shadow frequency, the essence of this Shadow of Vanity is really the dilemma of aloneness. It's the dilemma of being alone on one hand and the dilemma of wanting to belong and be part of something and others on the other hand. It's the balance between our relationships and our aloneness. This is our dilemma if we have the 12th Gene Key, the 12th Shadow. So it's all about how we deal with relationships and at a collective level the 12th Shadow is very, very profound because it all hinges on a single deep, unconscious fear. And that fear is the fear that another person can take away our freedom or our independence in some way.

And we can see that this is a deep victim belief structure, that another can do something to us that takes something away from us. And this is actually the foundation of vanity. Vanity is the belief, the false belief that we actually exist as individuals. That may sound funny but actually the truth is that from the view of the heart or from the purity of the Siddhi, there is only One being here. There is only one of anything because we all are a single consciousness. Now, that's a very lofty concept for some people. However, the deep dilemma if we're operating out of the 12th Shadow is this fear that others can take away the spirit of our freedom. At the shadow level it's this same fear that makes us very emotionally cautious. This is a hallmark of this Gene Key - emotional caution. At the same time we can be very volatile beneath the surface. Even so, people with the 12th Gene Key can sometimes appear very collected and calm and yet there are deep seated boundaries within them that probably evolved in early childhood. And these boundaries are designed to keep others away, in order to prevent them from causing us hurt. So through the 12th Shadow we really only allow people to come into our heart occasionally in tiny, controlled bursts. An unconscious childhood fear is dictating all of that. And what this means is that other people can become very frustrated with us because they're always left wanting more, on account of us being so guarded. This represents one extreme, one side of the spectrum. The other side has the opposite effect. The 12th Shadow can appear extremely emotional and maybe even a bit crazy, and this can obviously dominate our life and dog our relationships. We have to remember that this is really about the fear beneath the surface. All the shadow frequencies are about fear. Our fear prevents us from loving fully or from receiving love. To receive another's love can be terrifying for this Shadow. The result of all this is that we can end up being the kind of person who's always looking for more space but ironically, it's never enough for us. It's just never enough. So relationships can really be the 12th Shadow's nemesis.

The other thing to know about this 12th Gene Key is that it is so sharp and clever. It has a laser-like mind, which can make us believe that we alone can see the real reasons for everything. One can so easily use this mind to push others away, or make them wrong. Vanity creates all manner of unconscious belief systems that help keep people away from our heart. In essence, this 12th Shadow is a great fear key, with this deep fear of being emotionally overwhelmed; of not being able to cope with the voltage and the frequency of emotions when they run away inside us. And so the 12th Shadow can be very much a person that really holds it all together on the surface but underneath there's a deeply open, loving being who just doesn't want to admit what's really there underneath.

The 12th Gift of Discrimination

At the Gift level, this is the Transformational Way of Discrimination and the gift level is all about genius. So the essence of discrimination is about being able to discriminate between behaviour that is coming from your heart and behaviour that is coming from your mind. So it's about balancing emotions and mind.

And when I say heart, I don't mean emotions. I mean in a way, soul. I mean something beyond emotions. I am referring to emotions once they've been refined and purified. You see, the real genius of the 12th Gift is about refinement. Our life is a life of gradual and constant refinement. And we have to learn to use our Gift of Discrimination on ourself. At the Shadow level we used this same gift on others, to keep them away, but now we turn this Gift upon ourself. That's quite a turning point. When we look at ourself with utter honesty then it allows us to see where we're holding back from others out of fear. And the fear is there in all human beings - it's the vanity of our separateness. So this Gift is a breakthrough Gift - we use that laser-like honesty to break down our own self-imposed mental boundaries. And then of course we experience an opening. It doesn't have to be all at once - often it is gradual - but it begins to re-imprint us. The emotions we feared would be so overwhelming are actually not at all. They rise up sometimes and then they fall back again, but now we are beginning to remember what love feels like, we no longer need to be afraid.

It is through this Gift of Discrimination that we begin to let others in. And as we let the world in once again, so our heart begins to swell - and not in any co-dependent relationship, but just the feeling of love, of self love, of the love of life. And the process continues - we have to let it all in. We have to let in all the emotions of the world and the wounds of the world and the wounds of others into our being, into our heart. It's our greatest fear but as we learn to discriminate, we realise that other people can't touch us. We slowly realise that nothing exists outside us, and nothing can touch the purity that's in our heart. So we let the world into our heart and finally we taste that freedom that we have sought for so long.

As our search deepens, through this inner discrimination, we also realise that we don't want to be alone. We really don't. We want to live in love with an open heart. That's the 12th Gift. And the aloneness we are seeking is really not aloneness but purity. It's the purity of our own heart and it doesn't depend on any external conditions. That's the beautiful secret we learn through this Gift.

If we have the 12th Gene Key and the 12th Gift, then we need to realise that emotions are not the enemy. We have to let life and let love into our heart. If necessary, we have to also let it wound us. We must hold nothing back. This is such a real powerful thing because we realise that nothing or no one can really wound us. The pain may remind us of a childhood belief system that we're holding but that's not who we are. Thus it is through this Gift that we stop being an observer of love and life and we become an embodiment of love. And our true genius is to help others also make this same leap.

The 12th Gift is a great Gift of love. And by the way, the genius of this Gift is also very acoustic. It's really rooted in sound and in the use of our voice. When we really come from this pure place inside, rather than the shadow and the fear, then our voice has a real power to stir the heart and soul of others.

The 12th Siddhi - Purity

The Siddhi is the divine essence of life, and the 12th Siddhi shows us that we are nothing but purity. And this is what's hiding all along in vanity. The only purity there is, is purity of heart. There's no other purity. And nothing or no one can ever take that away from us. No matter what they try, no matter what they do to us, no matter how horrendous the outer conditions might get, no one can touch the purity of our heart - that is the marvellous realisation of the 12th Siddhi. In other words, we can be locked up in prison but they can never stop our love. They can do anything to us but they can never stop our love. Because when we get in touch with our heart, when we really get in tune with it, then all of our relationships and all of our dilemmas are instantly resolved. Because we cannot be tarnished by anyone or anything external because there is no external. It's all just us. It's all manifestations of one thing.

So, if we have this Siddhi, our purity will always be tested. That's part of the transformational journey through this Gene Key. It's why it's part of what's called the Ring of Trials. And because this is also the Ring of Secrets, there's a secret for us all to learn: It's that everything and everyone is inside us, so we simply have to let it all in. Because there is no other, there is only one. I know that sounds very 'new-agey', but it remains a truth. And the 12th Gene Key and its Siddhi is about letting life's experiences polish our heart. It's a journey of refinement. And then we can let our heart shine out. It's the love that we experienced as a child, that purity, that innocence. That we are each here to remember that again and again and again, until we've embodied it. Ultimately, it's about our purity of heart, particularly through our speech and our voice or our song or our chant, and sometimes also through our silence. Our purity will remind all others that they too are of the same heart, the one heart.

We are here for love. There is no other reason for existence. These 64 words for the Siddhis are nothing but the multitudinous names of love. Purity is the very heart of love, the soul of existence. If you have this Gene Key, or if you are contemplating it in any depth remember this - let love sing through you. And I don't mean emotional love, sentimental love. Look at the 64 Siddhis. Look at the many names of love. In my short program called 'Dare to be Divine', I explore these names, or at least I introduce them. It really doesn't matter what our name is. It doesn't matter what our Profile is or when we were born. The words are not the territory. The territory is the living, breathing expression of Love, and love is pure. Nothing else matters but love. It is waiting to break through inside each of us. It is our essence, it's our heartbeat and it's our home.

THE 13TH WAY

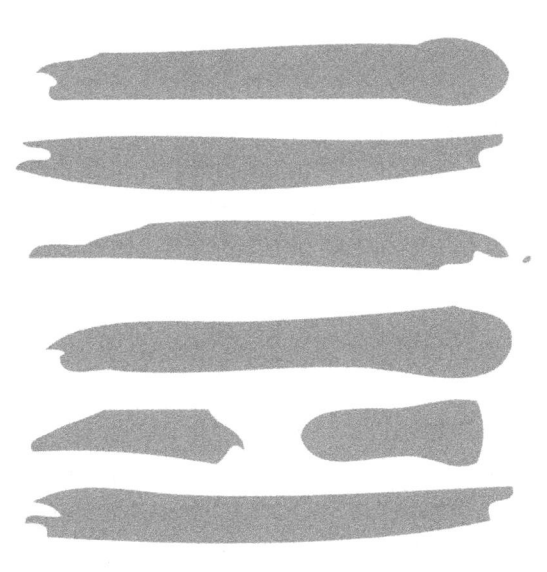

Gene Key 13

THE WAY OF DISCERNMENT

The Transformational Way of the 13th Gene Key moves from Discord to Empathy, and it's the Way of Discernment.

Secrets - the Gene Keys are a reservoir of secrets hiding inside the coils of the human genetic code. This is why the secrets are not really very well hidden, because they're inside us. Anytime anyone really decides to go deep within, they will always, sooner or later, discover the secrets. They're all known already; they're open secrets. The great sages and masters and ecstatics down the ages have discovered and shared them with us. The secrets of love, of wisdom, of surrender. They're all readily available, through the teachings, the embodied teachers, the elders, and the living role models who openly share them because they've discovered them for themselves.

The challenge is to just listen, to open our eyes, minds, and hearts, and read the secrets that are written all around us, inside us. Yet at the Shadow frequency, we don't listen. We can't hear the secrets. We allow our lives to get too busy, and there's simply too much noise inside our heads. There are too many layers of armour around our hearts. The great secret of the 13th Gene Key is listening, but the Dilemma of its Shadow is pessimism. We may hear the good news, but we don't believe it. We can't quite bring ourselves to believe it. How can so many be so wrong, and just me and maybe a few others be right? That's what the Shadow whispers in our ear.

The mass consciousness of humanity is still operating for the most part at the Shadow frequencies. The old reptilian brain still dominates, and that means we only hear the frequency band that it hears; 'survival', it whispers, 'security', it whispers, 'certainty', it whispers.

Shadow: Discord **Gift**: Discernment **Programming Partner:** Gene Key 7
Dilemma: Pessimism **Siddhi:** Empathy **Codon Ring:** The Ring of Purification

---

Pessimism is not the same as cynicism. It's not really a choice. It's a sense of hopelessness. It's a sense that things are out of kilter, that our dreams can never really come true. It's a sense that magic and idealism are things we only have when we're a child. When we become an adult we have to put on a serious hat and work; life isn't really fair, and the world is going down the tubes. It's what people refer to as the 'real world', a concept I find wryly amusing, since reality is so wholly subjective. Everyone in the real world has to worry. We have to worry. We get the distinct impression that things are in decline, that it's getting more and more out of control. No matter which generation we're born in, we always think that the end of the world is just around the corner. 'The world's changed since I was a child', we'll hear ourselves say, or 'in my day, things were simpler, in my day, people cared more, things were better'. This is the unconscious energetic of pessimism at work.

The 13th Shadow is discord, and discord is an acoustic term. It's about hearing only Shadow frequencies, unnerving sounds. It's about only seeing the crises, only reporting the bad news, only being tuned into the vibrations of chaos. It's the programming of the mass consciousness. We believe what we are told to believe, until we break out of that and question the status quo.

This Gene Key cuts very deep into some of the most entrenched human patterns. The original name is The Fellowship of Man. It's about the human emotional connection. It's what has brought us together around the council fires forever. It's about listening to each other. Yet at its Shadow frequency, it's riddled with distrust. One human distrusting another, one tribe distrusting another; it's about us distrusting life. It's about distrusting the story of life. Life is a story and it follows a natural evolutionary curve. That curve does not by design lead to chaos. But even science would have us believe this, that life is entropy, that all life moves from order to disorder. If there's anything that leads to pessimism it's a statement like that. Well, we are screwed then!

This frequency is everywhere. The real world has always involved suffering. That's what we do. It's always been this way. It's all across the news. It's in most communities, families, relationships, in our own body, our chemistry, but only if we're gullible enough to believe in it and deaf enough to hear it. This Gene Key carries a lot of weight. It drags behind it the experiential weight of human history. It's essentially misanthropic, believing that we humans are really pretty weak and not that great. We're just a tiny, abandoned corner of the cosmos and victims of the vagaries of fate. That's discord. It's about only hearing the heaviness, and when I say hearing, I don't mean only aurally acoustic. This is emotional hearing. We hear from our solar plexus. To be at the Shadow frequency is to be weighed down by the human wound. It means we don't see the beauty around us. We don't see the hope, the best in others. We don't see the interconnectedness of things. We don't experience the magical, holographic dimensions or trust in the inherent mysterious purpose of the present moment. We just don't see; we can't hear it. We can't hear love. We've forgotten about love. It's the greatest secret of them all, and here in this 13th Shadow, we've simply forgotten. I tell you, it's depressing as hell when we forget about love, and it keeps us in hell.

The 13th Gift – Discernment

How do we break the pattern? How do we tune ourselves back into love? How do we rebuild the Fellowship of Man? Easy. We listen. We learn to listen again. We listen inwardly. We listen to our responses. We listen to our body, our chemistry. We listen to our heart. Out there in the New Age circuit, there are literally tens of thousands of teachers, all flooding the circuit with one single message. In all their different, funky, sometimes fantastical, sometimes fanatical ways, all they're saying is: listen to your heart. Listen to your heart. This is the secret. It's always been the secret!

This is a collective voice coming alive again in humanity. It's reminding us to listen. Even if some of the teachers aren't living it themselves, it doesn't matter. It's a collective phenomenon. This is a collective Gene Key – the Fellowship of Man. We're a fellowship.

We only realise our fellowship when we begin to listen to one another. This is the dream of the United States, of the United Nations, of the European Union. We've begun to create these circles, these council fires, where we try to listen again to each other's needs and agendas. We're not very good at it. We've fallen out of practise. But it's a start.

The 13th Gift is the Gift of Discernment. It's about discerning the voice of the heart from the voice of the mind. Not that the mind is wrong, but that if it comes before the heart, we'll again have discord. We have to discern the heart first, then bring in the mind. The heart doesn't mean the emotions either. Listening to our heart means to fall into silence, into quietness. The impulse of our heart arises from stillness. As it arises it becomes freedom, and carries great excitement with it, great certainty. There's a great leadership potential in this Gene Key. It's paired with the 7th Gene Key whose Gift is Guidance. We only become a good guide if we know how to listen. To really listen is to discern our own agendas, our own opinions running underneath, even while someone else is talking. You know that one? Someone is talking to us and our mind is busy formulating an answer, so that we don't really hear them. This is emotional listening, and that's different from heart listening. Discernment means to listen through osmosis. We're listening beyond our ears. We're listening for the hidden notes and chords in someone's speech, or actions, or body language, or heart.

This is the gift of hearing another's heart. We can only do that when we can hear our own heart. The heart exists on a higher plane, at a higher frequency than the mind or emotions. This is what the Gift frequency is; it's sometimes known as the causal plane. When we hit this higher frequency, our mind becomes more still, and we begin to hear what's really being said. We begin to listen to the evolutionary impulse moving behind events, behind everything. We begin to feel the hidden higher purpose behind everything. We begin to remember the secret. When we listen from our heart, our soul, then we begin to see hope in everything around us. In listening to a higher frequency, we first of all have to resonate at that frequency. Our whole body has to vibrate at a higher frequency, and then we feel more of the truth. We feel through our body, our organs, particularly through our belly, and we begin to feel the higher purpose within things.

The more we listen in this way, holding someone's higher purpose always foremost, the more we'll emanate that through our listening, and the more others will feel that trust emanating from us.

We may begin to see that the Gift of Discernment is truly transformative. It transforms us, and invites transformation in the other. This is why it's called the Fellowship of Man, because true, deep, heart listening brings human beings into sympathy. It brings us into resonance. This is what creates melodic resonance, this 13th Gene Key. The deeper we listen to our lives, our relationships, our DNA, the more subtle levels and dimensions open up. A human life is a masterpiece of lilting melodies woven in light. This is what contemplation is. It's the art of listening inwardly. There is nothing outside yourself. We become an ear, a receiving dish for the higher frequencies, and the more we receive them, the more we amplify them.

This 13th Gift, the Gift of Discernment, is what will ultimately bring human beings together into a higher harmony, into synarchy. As we learn to listen into each other, through the layers of the aura, we'll realise and open up the quantum field that interconnects us all. Our listening is then no longer passive, but becomes an aspect of our radiance. We listen with love, and we discern only love. Even the Shadow consciousness field, ever rooted in pessimism, becomes charged by the quality of our listening. This is when listening becomes the greatest balm to our human wounds, and then finally, we can make the quantum leap that's needed in order to overcome the patterns of our collective history. Listening is awesome. It's one of the greatest yin powers in the universe, and because it's so giving, trusting, without agenda, it alone has the power to bring permanent change to our world. The deeper we listen, the more optimistic we'll become. The deeper we listen, the higher our spirit can rise; the deeper we listen, the more we'll hear only one thing, love.

The 13th Siddhi – Empathy

The Transformational Way through this Gene Key moves from discord at the Shadow frequency, to Sympathy at the Gift, and Empathy at the Siddhi. We can see how acoustic this phenomenon of listening is. It involves the ears. It involves the inner ear. It involves the belly. It involves the entire aura. It's about digestion. This is why digestion is rooted in the belly, because the intestines are the great discerners. They sift and draw out the nutrients and dispose of the dross. That's digestion. It's an alchemical process that goes on in every quadrant of the universe. Everything is digesting everything else all the time. That's what listening is; that's what contemplation is, it's digestion.

13 is a secret number. It has always been so. It's a master number. The 13th sign of the zodiac is Arachne, and Arachne is the spider with her eight legs representing the eight directions. As she sits at the centre of her cosmic web, she listens. She listens to the vibrations of the cosmos through her legs. This is the symbolism of the number 13. We can see how at the Shadow frequency, the projections on this number are always rooted in pessimism, and so it's come to be known as an unlucky number - the number of discord. Yet it's also the master number. The cosmic geometry is arranged as a 12-fold geometry woven around a single 13th centre. It's the Christ number.

Empathy is such a beautiful word. 'Syn' means with, whereas 'em' means within, or inside. We enter inside another person. We enter into true fellowship, not just with another, but with all beings. This is where the great teachings come from, Buddha spoke of the current of metta - of loving kindness – that state which naturally emanates from all human beings and connects all beings. Likewise Christ's most central message was the same – 'love thy neighbour as thyself'. That has often been misinterpreted, it really means 'know thy neighbour as thyself'. Our neighbour is not separate from us, our neighbour is us. And then we know Love.

Empathy is all embracing. It includes the Shadow and the Gift, and yet it is beyond both. It's a witnessing, it's an acceptance so profound that it brings all beings into the centre of the wheel. Empathy is a pure centripetal force, like a black hole. It draws all beings inwards, inside ourselves. It embraces every aspect of life. It sucks in the past and the future, bending them inwards as they hurtle into the stillpoint at our core. There is a place inside every human being, a place inside us, where we're nothing more than a simple listening presence. That's all we are – we're the universe listening to itself.

GENE KEY 13

As this Siddhi takes us, it sucks us into the beyond. It delivers us into the absolute. It's an arrow leading right through the centre of our heart. To empathise with another is to allow their suffering deeply into our heart. It's to let their pain into every cell of our being so that we can feel it with them. As we allow this level of surrender, the miracle of grace occurs, and we hear the harmony within the discord. We feel the miracle of Empathy flooding our being. As it annihilates all that past memory, all that karma, suffering, and experience, we experience the truth, we witness utter purification, as we disappear into the quantum field of existence, and become one with all that is. This Gene Key is an aspect of the Codon Ring called the Ring of Purification. How purifying just listening can be. Try it some time…it's magical.

It's a funny thing, doing these Gene Keys. As I enter into each, their transmission starts to move inside me like a memory, opening up the universal codes. Right from the beginning of this 13th Gene Key, I've been aware of a sound, a gentle humming sound moving somewhere between my thoughts. Now as I come to the Siddhi I know exactly what it is. I hear it fully. It's the Gayatri Mantra, the most sacred and ancient mantra of the Vedas.

Om Bhur bhuvah svah
Tat savitur varenyam
Bhargo Devasya dheemahi
Dheeyo yonah prachodayaat

Some things are untranslatable in language, but essentially what this mantra represents is the power of the 13th Siddhi. He or she who listens inwardly and relaxedly, will experience the darkness and discord being purified by the inner light, the inner radiance, which progressively breaks through and illuminates our being with the truth of our divine essence. This is what Empathy is – it's our full remembrance of the greatest secret there has ever been – the secret of our union with all that is. Now that's something worth digesting.

THE 64 WAYS

THE 14TH WAY

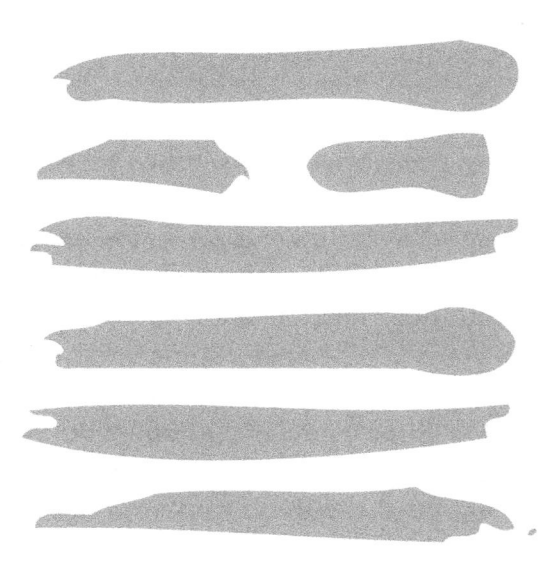

Gene Key 14

THE WAY OF COMPETENCE

The Transformational Way of the 14th Gene Key moves from Compromise to Bounteousness, and it's the Way of Competence.

In life, the compromises begin early. In fact we're even born compromised, because we come into the world carrying the seed of a sacred wound that was passed into us through our ancestral DNA at the point of conception. Everything on the human plane is about making compromises, because we're not quite born whole. We're born with a question mark etched on our soul, and our lives will revolve around that question mark. There are many ways we can interpret this question, for example, 'What is my purpose?', 'Why do I feel uncomfortable?' and of course, 'Who am I?' These questions only arise consciously later in our lives. For many of us, they never become conscious at all but drive us at an unconscious level. This is the first thing to understand about this Shadow - compromise is the norm. To learn how to stop compromising is the journey to awakening. It's the journey out of the darkness into the light. I also want to get the basic definition of compromise really clear, because it's so easily misunderstood.

There are 2 types of compromise - inner and outer. Outer compromise is for example when we decide we want to go out for a meal with our best friend. We're really excited about it but then our wife or husband tells us that they would really prefer that we stayed in because they're feeling unwell. So we make an outer compromise. We may be disappointed but we cancel our engagement and stay in. Another possibility is that we decide to go against our partner's wishes; convince them that they'll be fine and go out anyway. We don't make the outer compromise.

Shadow: Compromise **Gift**: Competence **Programming Partner:** Gene Key 8
Dilemma: Self-Belief **Siddhi:** Bounteousness **Codon Ring:** The Ring of Fire

---

What's interesting about this scenario is what's going on on the inside. If we decide to stay because our love for our partner is greater than our disappointment, then we haven't made an inner compromise. We've honoured the integrity of our love and relationship. If on the other hand, we decide to go out and enjoy ourself while our partner stays at home feeling terrible, perhaps we've made an inner compromise, a compromise of our love, of the integrity of our relationship, and even our own honour.

It's interesting to consider these things in our life. Life is filled with outer compromises. To live without outer compromises would involve a huge selfishness. The inside is where the gold lies hidden, to learn how to overcome our selfish tendencies to compromise our higher self, our integrity. To live without inner compromise is to live a life of deep honour and virtue. Ultimately the question is one of the heart. Have we compromised love? What would love do in this situation?

Sometimes it's a delicate balance in life to stay with what truly feels right inside when faced with an external pressure. There is often a great deal of expectation to behave in a certain way in society. To thread our way through these decisions, we need to really examine our motives in life. One thing that always holds true is the result of inner compromises. When we make an inner compromise, we don't feel good. A part of us shrinks. A part of us contracts. It becomes a habit for most of us - this compromising of our highest dreams. At some point we just begin to let them slide away, and we accept a second best life, a lacklustre life, a fearful life.

Let's think about the decisions we make. We can change the pattern. On the outside, remember there will always be many, many compromises. On the inside, we can stay with what feels true to our hearts. The Dilemma of this Shadow is self belief. People have stopped believing in themselves. People are content to be tiny little ants running about just maintaining the world. Ra, my teacher from my Human Design days, had a terrible expression for such people, but it's true - he called them 'furniture'. That was his dark sense of humour. It's true that if we compromise our hearts in life, we're nothing more than furniture on the great movie set. To live a life of genius, we have to start believing in ourselves again. We have to get in touch with our hearts and our dreams.

We may also feel that we're trapped, if we've been living a very compromised life. But we're never trapped. If we begin right now to make small decisions and actions that don't compromise our sense of inner integrity, then even one uncompromising act a day will make a difference. The more we learn not to compromise, the more we'll begin to believe in ourselves again. Eventually we'll become so attuned to the inner voice that wants to rob us of our vitality, that we'll learn to discern the voice that says 'yes!'

One of the qualities that comes from this Shadow is poverty - poverty consciousness. In this Gene Key, we'll find the secrets of poverty and prosperity. It's part of the Codon Ring called the Ring of Fire, so it's paired with the 1st Gene Key, the most creative capacity in the universe. Prosperity comes from genius, creative uniqueness. If we have the 14th Gene Key or are contemplating it deeply in our lives, it can bring about an enhancement of our physical, emotional, and mental capacity to succeed and excel in life. It's a Gene Key of great fortune, which is why the Shadow creates the opposite - people who just seem to attract bad luck. It's about inner fire, and making inner decisions in life that ignite the fire rather than ones that douse the flames of our love. We'll have to make sacrifices and have many disappointments. We all do, but somewhere inside we'll begin believing in ourselves again. When we light this fire and keep fuelling it, nothing will be able to get us down.

The 14th Shadow pulls our energy down. It makes our spine droop, and causes problems in our posture, internal organs, and glands. The road back is clear; to give ourselves permission to believe in ourselves again. We just need to dream, and take actions that bring us closer to those dreams. In the beginning those actions may be limited in their scope. But just by taking them, we'll re-ignite the fire inside. Often it's not so much about what we're here to do in life as how we do it, the quality we bring to our role, the joyousness, the sense of personal power. An examination of this Shadow in our life often leads to an inner turning and a challenging of our own tendency to take the easy path. This isn't the easy path that leads upwards (that comes later), but the easy path that leads downwards in ever decreasing spirals. We don't want to be making those kinds of inner compromises. So we have to take a stand, summon the inner fire, change ourselves from the inside, and pull ourselves out of the Shadow back up into the light.

The 14th Gift - Competence

In the original I Ching, we can see that every hexagram is made up of six lines - combinations of Yin and Yang lines, broken and unbroken. The unbroken lines represent the Yang, masculine principle, and the broken lines are the Yin, feminine principle. When we look for example at the 1st Gene Key or hexagram (which is related to this one through its Codon Ring), we see it's made up only of Yang lines.

It's only about the masculine principle, which is what makes it all about Fire. When we look at this 14th Gene Key however, we see it has all Yang lines except one, so we might think it's also very Yang, very masculine. In a way it is, but with one big difference; the Yin line is in the most powerful position in the hexagram, the 5th line. The 5th line of the hexagram is traditionally the ruler of the hexagram.

We see here huge creative force with the guidance of deep femininity. Doesn't that sound good? This is the key to material success. If only today's businesspeople knew this secret. Ah well, they will find out soon enough. It's not about women being at the top either, necessarily, although that is a natural tendency of higher consciousness. This is about a wealth generating force that is guided by an ideal of nobility, sensitivity, and service. The ancient Chinese named this Gene Key 'Possession in Great Measure'. They recognised that this combination pointed towards huge success in any endeavour.

This is why the 14th Shadow is about poverty consciousness. It's as though we have this huge inheritance inside us, and yet we're so miserly that we refuse to spend any of it, and we and our family are starving. All our friends are starving, and it's within our power to help everyone, but we don't. This is a powerful thing to think about if we have the 14th Gene Key, or are contemplating it and applying its power to our life. Especially if we're born with it, it's like being born with a silver spoon in our mouth. We have vast good fortune if we have this Gene Key in our birth chart. It's even good fortune to have a friend with it, because as we'll see, it's contagious.

The 14th Gift is Competence. It's an emerging Gift in the genetic matrix, because it has a lot to do with the collective awakening rather than being an individual Gift. If this Gift is applied for selfish ends it will lead to great misfortune. Great wealth without an ideal of service ends in disaster. Competence is about part of something transcendent, something huge. The 14th Gene Key is one of the Gene Keys that will change our world. It has a particular power in business because it's a driving force of abundance. It's mostly fire after all, so it has this deep inner drive to amass great fortune. The image the Chinese used was the wagon piled up with treasures. It's really funny, but all that treasure has to have a purpose. We have to begin with a vision.

If we're contemplating this Gene Key, we have to consider carefully what service we want to offer the world. This is the place to begin. If necessary, you can spend several months getting this question crystal clear. When we know, it's as though that 5th line in the hexagram - that leader - suddenly knows what to do, and we can launch our ship. Once we have a clear vision, it's all downhill from there (I mean in a good way). The forces of the cosmos bend to our will; they have no choice but to serve our vision. But we must be patient. We must have our vision absolutely clear inside us and continually nurture it. The danger of this Gene Key is always greed. The danger is that at any time we may be tempted to compromise our dream and to compromise our integrity for some kind of shortcut.

The wagon rolls at its own sedate pace, and the more patient we are the more it picks up speed. Competence is an electric force, a dynamic Gift - it's not just about being good at things. It contains the spark of enthusiasm that creates a cohesive team, that inspires a group to achieve great things. Oh there's a lot of excitement in this Gene Key. It will change our world through the integration of the power of the unit - a small team, from 3 to 15 people. Beyond that it becomes what's called a network. The small team is the power unit of collective transmutation. All we need is one 14th Gene Key in the team, because its power gets transferred through the group aura by means of the vision of higher service that the group holds. This is the basis of the principle of Syntropy - the mechanics of collective prosperity, whereby the total energy (or money) through a system is exponentially increased through an ideal rooted in a higher level of consciousness.

The 14th Gene Key is an indicator of success within an organism. The more 14's one has, the greater the inheritance. It isn't only about money, though it truly does magnetise money; it's also about love. This is Possession in Great Measure, and that's the definition of love. He or she who loves unconditionally generates, like the sun, huge inner wealth and radiance. This in turn generates friends, opportunities, blessings and above all, more love. Love begets love. Remember this always. It's a Divine formula - the more consistently we love someone, the more our love will over time melt them. Love is a fire. It cannot be resisted. This is why Jesus challenged us to love our enemies. That is the highest formula of all, because when we can do that, they will transform into our friends. It won't happen overnight, but it will happen. But our love must be unconditional. It must be disinterested and without strings.

The 14th Gift is a wonderful power to have inside. The key is not to isolate ourselves. You'd be surprised how many 14th Gene Keys do this. They would rather work alone, but this is only fear. If we dig a little, we'll find the fear. Most of the time it's the fear of success. It's the fear of being powerful. Poverty consciousness, which is what the Shadow field is built upon, does not want us to be great. It wants to keep us small. It hides behind false humility. We have to remember when we were young. When we're young, we all have these dreams of being great - we want to be pilots or astronauts or princesses or gold medallists or kings. It's because we are great, but we learn to compromise that greatness inside. It's up to us to come out from behind that self imposed exile. All those fairy tales about the lost prince or princess living in exile in poverty until all of a sudden one day they rediscover their inheritance, get married, and live happily ever after. Do we think those stories are just stories for children? No. Those are stories for adults. The children don't need them. We do.

So let's start believing in ourselves again. Get ourselves behind the wheels of the wagon, and give it a little shove. In the beginning it'll take some time to build up the momentum, but after awhile, we'll see magic occurring in our lives. People will come from far and wide to help us. We won't believe how much joy our hearts are capable of bearing, and our only wish will be to keep distributing our good fortune, to help others, to bring them up onto the wagon so that they too can share in the treasures that the collective life brings.

The 14th Siddhi - Bounteousness

Contemplating and recording these Gene Keys is an amazing process for me. One of the things you may have been discovering yourself is that when you enter into contemplation of a particular Gene Key, it comes alive in your life. Our life begins to send us the experiences we need to unlock that teaching. Here I am in the midst of this deep contemplation of the unconscious meaning of fire, and the Ring of Fire, through this 14th Gene Key, and then yesterday a friend came over and taught me how to make physical fire.

Let me share with you what an incredible experience it is to make fire with your own two hands - to gather wood, axe out your gear, set up your friction bow, tension it and carve a spindle from the raw materials in your environment, and then to create the friction, and see the first whiffs of smoke. You look down, and there before you is a tiny, tiny ember. What a moment! Out of nothing comes this tiny delicate spark, and you pick it up like it's the most precious jewel in all existence. You drop it into the middle of a pile of tinder, and then you gently blow it in your hands. It's a delicate art, it easily goes out. But you persist, and then presto, you get a flame. For me, it was like my whole heart burst open at the same time. And it's not easy. You go through quite a process, but the result is such a feeling of inner power. Talk about self-belief. There is a new me here now. There was me before I made fire, and now there is me who knows how to make fire. And it's a different me. I recommend it heartily for anyone.

The most memorable part is that tiny ember. I could imagine being alone and out in the cold wilderness with night coming in, and that ember, no bigger than a flea, is my lifeline. It came out of nothing, well, it came from the sun ultimately, because it's the sun's energy stored in that wood. This is the basis of prosperity, and it's the basis of the Siddhi of Bounteousness, symbolically speaking. It's about gratitude. I was so grateful to that little spark. I was so grateful to the elements for giving me that gift. Bounteousness comes from that vast sense of gratitude. It's the gratitude for the spark of life. When we nurture that spark of gratitude inside ourselves, then it becomes a steady flame. When we continue to nurture it, it becomes a fire. When we nurture the fire, it becomes a Sun inside us, and the Sun is bounteousness.

The Sun gives of itself endlessly, tirelessly. Its gratitude is infinite. It's continually refuelled through the power of its own giving. This is bounteousness. It's to give and give and give. There is no whiff of take. Take has all gone when we get to this Siddhi. We've reached unity, and unity is based on love and giving. Of course, with giving comes receiving, but receiving is different from taking. Receiving fuels our gratitude. The more we give, the more we're given, and the more we're given, the more grateful we feel.

The highest formulas of the Gene Keys have yet to be revealed. The transmission holds many high secrets. One of these is the art of white magic. White magic is based on the law of earthly and celestial correspondences. Every Gene Key has a relationship to a star, an element, a geometry, a codon in our DNA, an animal, a plant, etc. This law of correspondences allows us at the higher level to draw into ourselves all the elements of the holographic universe. It allows us to become a creator, a magician, in effect, it allows us to be like God. I know that sounds arrogant, but this is where we're heading as a species - once we've purified our Shadow nature, God works through us, and He/She works through the Siddhis.

The 14th Gene Key represents the element of gold. Its Programming Partner, the 8th Gene Key, represents silver. They form the Ring of Fire and Water, along with the 1st and 2nd Gene Keys. The 14th Siddhi carries within it the power of materialisation. It can create something out of nothing. This is what alchemy is. We can only do this at the very peak of consciousness. We must have turned ourselves into gold first. There can be no vestige of Shadow left inside us, and then we can work miracles. There are a group of Siddhis, which I call the 'Miracle Siddhis', and the 14th is one of these. You can learn the others in my 'Dare to be Divine' course.

The value of knowing such a thing is that we can see the very highest archetype of our consciousness. We'll see this power of materialisation at different levels. It's about magnetising good fortune. As we ascend the ladder of frequency, more will come to us: more joy, more love, more money, more friends, more of everything beautiful. The formula that takes us there? One word-gratitude. We must look at our lives every day and count our blessings. This is the most powerful thing we can do in our lives. Focus on all the beauties in our lives rather than the hardships. In fact, learn to look at even our hardships with gratitude, because then we will turn them into gold as well. This is the Midas touch, it's Possession in Great Measure. It's the spirit of philanthropy, of gold, of the Sun, of all the riches under the Sun. They can all be ours when we learn to give of ourselves unconditionally, just like the Sun. I think Yeats said it best in his alchemical poem:

The Song of Wandering Aengus

I went out to the hazel wood,
Because a fire was in my head,
And cut and peeled a hazel wand,
And hooked a berry to a thread;
And when white moths were on the wing,
And moth-like stars were flickering out,
I dropped the berry in a stream
And caught a little silver trout.
When I had laid it on the floor
I went to blow the fire aflame,
But something rustled on the floor,
And some one called me by my name:

It had become a glimmering girl
With apple blossom in her hair
Who called me by my name and ran
And faded through the brightening air.

Though I am old with wandering
Through hollow lands and hilly lands,
I will find out where she has gone,
And kiss her lips and take her hands;
And walk among long dappled grass,

*And pluck till time and times are done
The silver apples of the moon,
The golden apples of the sun.*

The 15th Way

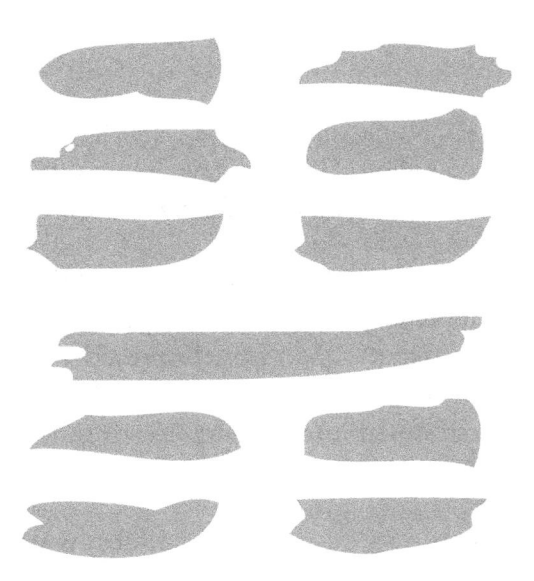

Gene Key 15

THE WAY OF MAGNETISM

The Transformational Way of the 15th Gene Key moves from Dullness to Florescence, and it's the Way of Magnetism.

The 15th Gene Key is vast. It encompasses all other Gene Keys. Its reach is so broad and generous - its heart so open and giving. Here we have humanity at its peak. Here we have nature in its most abundant form, giving birth endlessly to the creative ideas of God.

Then we have the Shadow. There must always be a Shadow, and there will always be those who hide in the Shadow. They tend to hide in numbers, together, where they feel the illusion of safety. This is the Shadow of Dullness, but it isn't the remarkable dullness of the Taoist or the dullness that makes for a smooth surface, the simple and beautiful sheen of the simple. This dullness is death. This is the stifled imagination. This is the comfort of the crowd, the shirking of self responsibility. This is cowardice and comfort and indolence.

Dullness is repetition. Dullness is over-stimulation. Dullness is the terror of being wrong. Dullness is bad behaviour, lack of courtesy and friendliness. We may not think of ourselves as dull, but every aspect of our life that doesn't lend itself to change has the potential to be caught in the Shadow of this great Gene Key. The I Ching is called the Book of Changes for a reason. We must change. We must change or die. The Dilemma here is Comfort and our modern world provides us comfort in spades.

We are so comfortable that we don't need to lift a hand to help others. Our comfort blinds us. Our comfort is like a great quilt filled with goose down. It's like modern houses; they're so warm. We don't feel the cold anymore. A couple of years ago, we had all the windows redone on our house, with wooden window frames. We redesigned their shape to make them more generous, appealing, and elegant to the eye. I asked the architect if he could

Shadow: Dullness			**Gift:** Magnetism			**Programming Partner:** Gene Key 10
Dilemma: Comfort			**Siddhi:** Florescence			**Codon Ring:** The Ring of Seeking

---

design them so that they leave a draught. He smiled and said no one had ever asked that before! The obsession nowadays is to keep out all draughts. They're the demons. We have to live inside non-breathing plastic-lined boxes. But draughts are essential. They keep the air from stagnating. They give rise to the little noises that every house should have. There's nothing worse than a silent house. A house is a living thing. It needs to breathe like us. Anyway, he designed a hidden notch in the end of each window that allows us to lock the windows a tiny bit open. So I was happy - eccentric man that I am.

The point is we get stuck with our comforts. We complain about the most unbelievable things. If our food is late in a restaurant, we complain. If the price of fuel goes up a few pennies, we complain. We've become so spoilt, so used to comfort that we've lost all our edges. Many of us don't even know what it feels like to be hungry anymore. We eat before we're hungry, so we miss out on that feeling of emptiness that gives life its edge. At every turn we dull our senses - we dull them with technology, smart phones, films. We dull ourselves with the inessential trivia of our voyeurism.

I'm also to blame. We're all to blame. The 15th Gene Key is a gauntlet thrown down before each of us on how to turn away from dullness, and take up the baton of thrill, adventure, growth, in a world that drags us from every corner. Once many years ago, when I was living in the Highlands of Scotland in a small cottage, I took some magic mushrooms. They grew just around my door, and one day I picked them, brewed them up, and went on a journey. I told myself that whatever happened I would retain my smile. I would smile at whatever occurred. This turned out to be an error.

At one point, as I sat in silence with my eyes closed, smiling softly, I suddenly felt all these little creatures like demons or goblins. They had fastened grappling hooks and ropes to the ends of my mouth, and they were pulling down on my smile to make me stop smiling.

My mind battled with them for some time, until finally I let go, stopped smiling, and they were gone! Again, the point of the story is that those demons are now built into our society. From all quadrants, comfort is like a siren song to blunt our sharp edges, to make us soft and take life for granted.

Never take life for granted. Only death teaches this. Death and suffering. Be grateful for suffering. See it for the gift that it is. It's the only way that nature reaches us sometimes. She reaches out from inside us and shouts, screams - Awaken! Life is immense. Get outside. Take off your clothes. Let the draughts into your house!

THE 15TH GIFT - MAGNETISM

Magnetism. What is magnetism? Sometimes we speak about people with magnetic personalities, but we're not talking about that here. That's charisma - an overflowing of the life force beneath the surface. True magnetism comes from way below the surface; it arises from the very depths of life. It may not so much as flicker through one's personality. It may remain hidden from view. If we spend some time around a truly magnetic being, we'll soon feel there's something there - something indefinable, something we can't quite put our name on, as though the great mystery swirls around the person like silent, hidden flames…

The 15th Gene Key is a polygamist. Not in the literal sense, but in the sense that they're a lover of all aspects of creation, especially the human. They love the stars, the birds, the rocks, the cities, the garbage dumps, the places where people gather. In today's society, the 15th Gene Key has much to teach the rest of us. This is the Gift of loving the time one is in. This is the appreciator of all expressions of humanity - from the lowest to the highest. I had a girlfriend like that once, many moons ago. She taught me how to see everyone in a new light. She would look at someone for example, and at first glance that person might not offer much in the way of inspiration. They might look rather ordinary, perhaps repressed or angry or uptight even. She would bring that person alive. She would imagine their life. She would dream them into reality. She would describe their struggle, their oddities, their humanity. She'd do all of this in her imagination. By the time she had finished, you'd love that person! That's quite a rare gift.

To be magnetic is to love everyone. It doesn't mean we have to like them, but through our heart we can feel their essence, so we can resonate with them entirely. We can always find something worthy and worthwhile in everyone. There is great positivity in this Gift. It's not forced positivity, like we often find in the New Age. It's a truly humble, noble heart, who genuinely appreciates the whole farce of life. It takes great humour to love that widely, to love the monotonous, the mediocre, the drab. But remember this was the Shadow of Dullness - so the 15th Gift has to have transformed that - the grey of the Shadow becomes the colour of the Gift. Everyone is welcome here. Everyone is accepted.

There's one more very important dimension to this 15th Gene Key, which is its seeking. It's one of the Gene Keys that make up the Ring of Seeking. In this case it seeks betterment. It seeks advancement for all. It's truly the most benevolent of all Gene Keys. Its benevolence is what makes it one of the great Gene Keys of love. This is why mythically it's connected to the figure of the Bodhisattva - the sage who decides to hold back his or her own enlightenment for the sake of others. One who remains behind to teach others, rather than pressing on towards the ultimate goal of becoming one with the Divine.

This is where the Gift begins to bleed into the Siddhi, as all this benevolence is transformed on the lower planes into love as service, into karma yoga - the yoga of Divine service. Such magnanimous hearts ring out like bells in the evolutionary storylines of humanity. These truly are our saints, our saviours, our role models, here to remind us of the profound and endless potential there lies within every human being.

The 15th Siddhi - Florescence

In many ancient traditions and folk stories there are myths of cities within the core of the earth. The Tibetans speak of Shambhala, the mythical kingdom buried in a hidden valley in the Himalayas. In their more esoteric scripts there are detailed descriptions of Shambhala, at whose heart lies a mythical inner mountain, Mount Meru. This is the symbol of this hexagram - the Mountain in the Earth. This should tell us that this is the most grounded and earthy of all the Gene Keys.

This is why in my book in this Gene Key I speak of the Schumann Resonance, the natural energy frequency that's emitted by the earth. It's like the breath pattern of Gaia. To be in harmony with this is to be at peace. As I've contemplated this 15th Gene Key, I've come to see a new dimension opening up in its Siddhi. In the Gift, its benevolence shines through, but when that benevolence ripens fully, something extraordinary happens - the fruit falls back to the earth. We see this sometimes with the greatest sages - they come down off the mountain and become utterly ordinary. They even behave a bit madly.

Deep harmony frees us to behave spontaneously because whatever we do, our behaviour emerges from that mountain of benevolence inside us. The ancients called this hexagram 'Modesty', but I think it's been misunderstood. The traditional version of modesty is the expression of outer humility, but sometimes extreme humility doesn't feel very human. It feels like a Divine expression, and this Siddhi is about staying human. Sometimes a great teacher will behave in a way that appears angry or weak. Such teachers will use human devices, human feelings and emotions to remain close to the people around them, rather than becoming so elevated that they're put on a pedestal.

The ultimate modesty is to allow another to believe we're weak or flawed, just as a means of loving them. This is a deeper meaning of the word Florescence. It means to use any and all behaviour to create illumination. It means to stay close to all beings, especially human beings. Imagine if we were a God and decided to become human - what costume would we choose?

Would we play a Holy man and have lots of people crowd around us and worship us? really? I don't think so. If we were really a God, we would play tricks. We would conceal ourself as all manner of beings, and then we would work behind the scenes, influencing on levels unseen.

The 15th Gene Key concerns the magnetism of the human aura. The 15th Siddhi works primarily through its aura. Whatever behaviour it pretends on the surface, it's just a subterfuge. Beneath the surface, down within the inner mountains, the real work is occurring. The aura is alive. It's a rippling resplendent field of multi-dimensional colour and reality. The 15th Siddhi concerns the subtle colours of the higher dimensions. If we spend some time with the Seven Sacred Seals teachings, a mystical aspect of the Gene Keys, we'll come into touch with these auric signatures, these angelic colours. They're aspects of the intelligence of light, which is why they're common to all forms. They're just hidden from the human eye. We can only perceive them through the eyes of love and the depth of our benevolence.

Perhaps we can sense the mysteries of this 15th Siddhi that lie on other planes beyond our reach. Now I'll bring it back to earth. For us, listening to or reading this Gene Key, the secret is the earth and humanity. We must stay close to the earth. We must stay close to humans, and never allow ourselves to become too holy. Hildegard von Bingen, a well known medieval mystic who lived very close to the earth, spoke of a force she called *viriditas*. Viriditas means the power of greenness, the fecund life force of nature, of earth. This greenness can be imbibed by anyone spending time out in nature. It's a tangible life force that emanates from plants. It's especially powerful when the sun shines through or onto the green leaves and stems of plants. That's when they seem to glow with this incredible health-giving power.

Stay close to this forcefield, this wonderful homely magnetism that connects us all - that's the clarion call of the 15th Siddhi. The holiest of people are always the gardeners, because they're the closest to the earth, to this viriditas. Of all people the gardener knows the meaning of Florescence, the power of greenness. And the gardener knows another thing - they know the magic of rhythm. Everything comes at its proper time. All beings flower in the end, so why not spread some joy while we're here? Why not take our clothes off and dance amidst the gold and the green?

The 16th Way

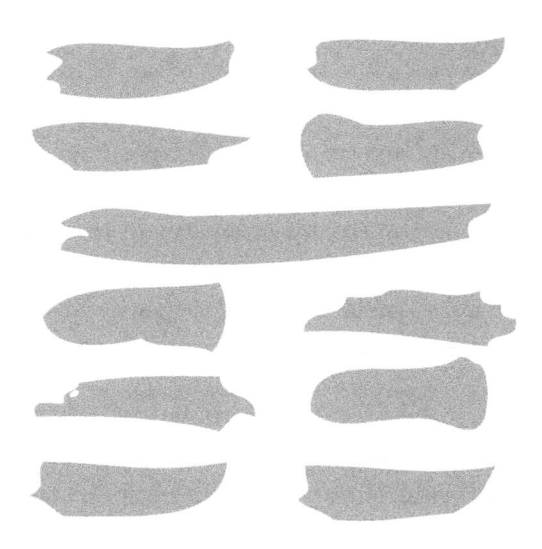

Gene Key 16

THE WAY OF VERSATILITY

The Transformational Way of the 16th Gene Key moves from Indifference to Mastery, and it's the Way of Versatility.

It's really amazing when we look at all the Gene Keys as a whole. We see all these qualities and frequencies. We also see how certain Shadow frequencies underpin so much of our collective behaviour patterns. This 16th Gene Key is one of those interesting Gene Keys that has an exponential affect on the world, especially at the Shadow frequency. It's the Shadow of Indifference. It's what the world is like when love is excluded. Recently I was listening to all these great writers and thinkers talking about what it means to be human. The question was what makes us human? There were some interesting responses.

My response would be this - to be human is to have the ability, even the tendency, to overcome indifference. Indifference makes us inhuman. Humanity is all about caring, for each other, for the world, and it's about caring what happens in the future as well as the present. This is uniquely human, but the Shadow frequency drops us below this definition. To not care is to be dead. If we don't care, we might as well be dead. I know that sounds harsh, but until we can feel the love that we're born with, we're not really here. As we look at the world, so many people aren't really here. They're just bodies going through the motions They have become automatons. The Shadow frequency is like watching one of those zombie movies.

Why are we indifferent? Because we're lazy. Laziness is the Dilemma of the 16th Gene Key. We're too lazy to care. We can't be bothered. We're trapped by our indifference. We don't know how to get out of it. When I speak of laziness here, I mean at a very deep level; we're too lazy to even take a look inside our hearts. We get into our comfort zone, with

Shadow: Indifference   **Gift:** Versatility   **Programming Partner:** Gene Key 9
Dilemma: Laziness   **Siddhi:** Mastery   **Codon Ring:** The Ring of Prosperity

---

our emails and our jobs and our safe little worlds, and we just get lazy. Awakening takes discipline. Anything worthwhile takes discipline. To unlock our genius we have to work hard, at least at an internal level. We have to really look into our own hearts. Very few people are willing to look into their hearts. What happens when we do is a breakthrough, always a breakthrough.

This 16th Shadow governs huge swathes of the human race. There is safety in numbers. If no one else is really bothering, why should I? I'll just tag along, and do my own thing. But the world is really screwed up in certain areas, like money for example. This 16th Gene Key is part of the Ring of Prosperity - a codon group that designs behaviour across whole gene pools. In the name of money we can be as indifferent as we like. This is the norm in our society. We can do anything and get away with it if we have a lot of money.

Look at corporate greed for example. Where does the buck stop? They're polluting our planet, but we don't know who 'they' are. When we actually find these people, they're usually quite normal people with families and the same issues as the rest of us. They don't question their behaviour because no one else does. We're all indifferent together. We're all too goddam lazy to wake up. To wake up we'll have to push against the flow bigtime. At least that's how we might imagine it. Waking up isn't draining though; it's the opposite. It gives us vast energy and makes us feel alive. To open and live from our heart makes us stand out on our planet.

The 16th Shadow is all about wasted talent. If we have this Shadow in our Profile, then we may recognise this theme. We have so much potential but no discipline, so we waste our gifts. We ignore our genius. Our fear makes us lazy, but that's all it is, just fear. We're afraid that if we open our heart up to life and all its suffering, we'll drown and be overwhelmed, but we won't. The heart can't be overwhelmed. It just opens more to encompass the change.

If we have this Gene Key, then it's time for us to wake up. No one's ever going to come to help us. This is something we have to do ourself. Alone. When we do overcome our laziness, our life will never be the same again. We'll be flooded with purpose, our relationships will soar, and our life will move onto a whole new plane of being. Let's do it!

The 16th Gift - Versatility

This is such a great Gift. You won't believe what lies hidden behind laziness and indifference. I want to be clear one more time about this laziness, because there's a laziness that's powerful, but that's a different quality. The powerful version of laziness is about effortlessness. It's about ease and relaxedness. It's a quality associated with flow, but it doesn't come from indifference. Indifference is more about sloth, about being stuck, and it takes something powerful to get us out of such a state. Ironically though, this same quality of ease runs all the way through this Gene Key. The Gift of Versatility emerges in our life as a kind of effortlessness.

To be Versatile means to be multi-faceted. It means we can easily transfer our talent across a number of fields. Once we've cracked through the resistance and our heart begins to warm, then we find self discipline easy. It's not really possible to get to the highest frequencies without huge inner discipline, but the nature of this discipline changes as the frequency rises. It becomes easier. We have to begin with passion and focus, and then we'll find we have the energy necessary to follow through with things. The 16th Gene Key opens humanity up to so many creative possibilities. It's the domain of the polymath.

I love this term 'polymath'. It's fallen out of vogue these days, which I think shows our level of indifference. A polymath is someone whose wisdom spans many different fields of knowledge and endeavour. The term was coined during the Renaissance, when certain spirited individuals and geniuses dedicated themselves to higher knowledge and understanding over a wide range of fields, from physical excellence to intellectual understanding. Through the power of this 16th Gift, I see a new rising up of the polymath in our society. The problem with the modern approach is its specialisation. People at university, for example, become so specialised in their approach that they become kind of myopic. If we had an education system that was set up differently, we might even begin with specialisation. As we see into the holographic truth of a single subject, we can see how that same higher theme or strain runs through all subjects.

The 16th Gift learns holographically, using heart, body, and mind all synthesised. This Gene Key is about excellence. Once indifference is taken out of the equation, all that skill and natural talent can be used to serve the whole, rather than individual fame and fortune. We can only truly prosper when we're helping others, and when we're helping them with integrity. So many people in the world think they're helping the whole, but because they don't see the big picture and aren't listening to the whole, they don't realise that they're not helping at all. To serve life is to respect every level of society. It's to revere the chain of life. It's to understand the interconnectedness of all things. This is where the Gift of Versatility comes from, from this holographic wisdom.

This Gene Key isn't just about being intellectual, though it will probably have a very keen intellect. It's about an expansion of intelligence, that includes our IQ, EQ, and SQ. If you know The Golden Path, you'll know exactly what this means. Higher intelligence is a fusion of heart, mind, and spirit. We need a new type of thinker in the world, who isn't sunk in their mind alone, whose spirit isn't for sale to the highest bidder, and whose emotional life has matured enough, so they can use their feminine qualities in harmony with their masculine. There aren't many of them yet, but the time of the polymath is coming, and one day I envisage them leading us in business, education, science, and all arenas. They've found the versatility of the higher faculties latent in the human heart, and they're dedicated to serving the vision that flows from that heart. Bring it on I say!

The 16th Siddhi - Mastery

What is Mastery? What is a master? This is the question that this Siddhi invites. Is a master some white-bearded Indian yogi with flowers around his neck? Or is a master something less definable? Most people who have tried to answer this question have been men. Even the word 'master' is a male word, so I think it's overdue for an overhaul in understanding. Let's start with a completely fresh slate on this one. A master is the opposite end of the spectrum to indifference. A master must be extremely sensitive, though not in a weak way. This is sensitivity as strength. A master feels everything, and this already sounds a lot more feminine. The master is a receiver, an open book, and the master must also be a paradox. The master combines the focus of the yang with the receptivity of the yin.

The leap from the Gift to the Siddhi is not really so far. Versatility requires viscosity, flexibility, and openness. What happens after the heart has opened? The Gift describes the process of the actual opening of our heart. It opens, it closes, we open it again, it closes again. It's a stretching, a process, a learning. We're carving ourself into being. At a certain point we've just learned the trick. Our heart softens to such an extent that it's no longer necessary to close it off. We've mastered the art, and the art is life. To be a master means to be a master of living. This isn't about skill or talent anymore. It's reached the essential. The greatest art is to live well. We're never taught this. No one even mentions it when we're young. The art of living well. That would be a great open university course. It's exactly what the Gene Keys Golden Path is - it's about Purpose, Partnership, Prosperity - the 3 'P's. When these three have been integrated and become a seamless symphony in our life, we can be said to be a master. This is quite different from the old image of mastery. Perhaps we thought it needed hours of meditation every day or that it was the domain of the ascetic.

But I tell you, it isn't; it's for the ordinary human being. Mastery is for everyone. It isn't exclusive or elite. We needn't go to India in the winter for long silent retreats. The most powerful place we can discover Mastery is in our everyday life. There are people who already exhibit this Siddhi. I'm sure you know one. They glide through life. They give of themselves, but not out of avoidance of some deep issue. They just give because they want to. They're cheerful, and it's not a feigned cheerfulness. It's a bubbling up of life. They're the least indifferent people we'll find. Think of such a person. I bet they're ordinary. I bet they pass almost unnoticed in the world. I'm sure they're appreciated and loved, but I bet others don't see them as a master. I'm sure they themselves don't see that.

Such people are scattered throughout the world in every community. They aren't perfect, but they have somehow mastered the art of living. They may not be rich, but we can tell they're prospering. They may not have a rose-tinted tantric love and light relationship, but we can tell they're devoted to someone. They may not be living a big public life where they're recognised, but they've found something inside. It's their higher purpose and they emanate it as a jewel-like frequency. They live well. Such people are precious, because they remind us of why we're here. We're here to learn how to live well. That's what Mastery is. It doesn't seem so hard, but I assure you it does take inner discipline. That discipline is something we find when we're ready, but we're really born ready.

There's a wonderful softness to this 16th Siddhi. We can see why it's allied to the 9th Siddhi of Invincibility. Only the ordinary person is invincible, and the master is a master of ordinariness. This is why they become extra-ordinary. Don't you love how words work?

Versatility doesn't get as much attention as specialisation. Specialisation makes us seem special. We become an expert in something, and everyone wants our opinion. We become powerful in the world, but that's not inner power. That's not real prosperity. Real prosperity is found in the detail. It's found in the little things, the flower in the pavement, the smile of a child, giving someone our last mouthful of dessert. All those little things add up to Mastery, but in and of themselves they don't seem like much. When they all come together, we have Mastery.

Mastery is all about time. It's about where we focus our awareness. This is prosperity. It's about how we invest our time. If we invest it in the inessential, then the energy flows away from us. I learn so much from my little daughter. Sometimes in the mornings I wake up early to write. I love that time before the children are even awake. She often senses I'm awake and appears and climbs into bed with me. She makes me close my laptop. I've learned to close it when she appears. Those are the most precious times of my life. They'll be gone in just a few years as she grows up. That sweetness between a father and young daughter - no power in this world should come between that. We look at our lives, and find those examples when life calls us to our Mastery. It calls us out of our indifference. That's richness. That's wealth. That's the only thing worth living for.

THE 17TH WAY

Gene Key 17

THE WAY OF FAR-SIGHTEDNESS

The Transformational Way of the 17th Gene Key moves from Opinion to Omniscience, and it's the Way of Far-sightedness.

It's fascinating how certain Gene Keys seem to be connected to certain archetypes in our consciousness. In the Gene Keys book, the chapter heading for this 17th Gene Key is called 'The Eye'. Immediately we know that it's about how we see the world, and more than that, how we think about the world. In the Venus Sequence we learn about the three stages of imprinting in our childhood - the first seven year cycle, which governs our physicality, the second seven years, which govern our emotional life, and the third seven years, from 14 to 21, when our mind develops its primary thought patterns - our psychology. This 17th Transformational Way is about how the architecture of our mind is built during this last teenage cycle.

The Shadow is Opinion, and those with strong opinions may object to that! What's wrong with having an opinion, we may ask? Why is it a Shadow? Well, it's not so much about having an opinion as being trapped and victimised by our opinion. We often think of opinions as our own, as though they define us. We say, 'this is my opinion, or in my opinion…' At the Shadow frequency our opinions define and limit us. They aren't who we are because they can change at any moment. The strongest opinions become meshed into a worldview that forms around wound experiences from earlier childhood cycles. They crystalise in our mental consciousness as we try to cope with the world as teenagers.

The Dilemma brings the other half of the story, and it's the Dilemma of Politics. By Politics, we don't mean the external means of government, but the internal means by which the Shadow mind works, and it works by taking sides. It takes on a single monocular limiting view.

Shadow: Opinion **Gift:** Far-sightedness **Programming Partner:** Gene Key 18
Dilemma: Politics **Siddhi:** Omniscience **Codon Ring:** The Ring of Humanity

---

It does this out of emotional insecurity, and it will even build a whole life around that wound. This leads to division in the world, to left and right, democratic and republican, labour and conservative, liberal and traditional. It leads to politics - emotional, sexual, and intellectual politics. The intellectual mind is all about politics. The political mind is always the defensive mind. It has an investment in feeling safe through its opinion, so when it's challenged, it hardens even further around that wound.

Think about the views we hold about the world. Is our view of the world lopsided or can we look with equanimity? If we're listening to or reading this, then we may be spiritually lopsided. Perhaps we've taken up residence in a spiritual view of the universe? It's an interesting contemplation to do - to look at the opinions we hold, consciously or unconsciously and see how they trap us. Think about something in your life that concerns you. Is there a 'should' attached to it? 'Things shouldn't be like this.' It may not be comfortable to observe, but our opinion is often the first stage of denial of what is, of the way things actually are. Only when we're able to see through the structure of our opinions and worldview, only then is transformation possible.

We think politics is the only way to sort out our differences. We think it's the norm; we even think it's healthy. We think that we have to have one person on one side with an opinion, and another on the other side with the opposite opinion. All we really have then is argumentation. When we look at our leaders, they spend most of their time arguing. Don't they look a bit like teenagers arguing with their parents? The thing is, we get stuck with our worldview and carry it out into the world. It becomes who we think we are, and then we have to defend our worldview, otherwise who are we? Who are we without our opinions? Let's think about that.

It's a good idea to contemplate your life between the ages of 14 and 21, and the opinions you formed during that time about the world. Here's one of mine as an example: 'I can't be happy unless I pretend'. That's an unconscious opinion about the world I carried as a teenager and beyond, until I became aware of it. If we dig in, we'll find these beliefs. Many of us are caught in a net of similar opinions that simply don't serve us anymore. We have to see them to let go of them.

We humans are a dichotomy, a dilemma. We're two contrary views. We have two eyes and two hemispheres of the brain, always we have two.

Because it's so uncomfortable being two, we choose one and let it dominate and we pretend to feel safer. That's how the political mind works - logic or intuition. It's one or the other. The 17th Shadow has a distinct leaning towards the logical, the scientific, towards the left brain view.

I find it hilarious whenever I come across an alleged skeptic. These people often carry the 17th Gene Key somewhere. They claim skepticism, but they're usually masquerading dogmatists who've already made up their minds. Logic is their God, and they can't accept anything for truth unless there's evidence. The true skeptic however, is coming from the 17th Gift; they don't have a bias at all. They remain open. They're even skeptical of their skepticism. That's my definition of a pure skeptic. They don't have a viewpoint to defend, so we'll not find any aggressiveness or defensiveness in them. It's rare to find a person who's transcended the dilemma of the political mind - a person who can see both sides of an argument and embrace both logic and intuition equally. We can use this Shadow to dig into those places in our minds where we feel the need to defend a viewpoint. We can have a view of course, but that view doesn't have to define us. As long as we're aware that any single view is not the whole story, then we've freed ourselves from the clutches of the political mind, the opinionated mind, the victim mind.

The 17th Gift - Far-sightedness

We need to understand something fully before we can transcend it. This is what genius is all about. We learn something, then we unlearn it, then we transcend it, but our transcendence includes it. This is what compassion is - the view from the Siddhi. We know what it's like to be opinionated; we understand it in our bones. When we come across it in another, we needn't fight them or react. We can simply let them have their process. We don't have to try and convert them. In fact we won't be able to, so it's better to forget that path!

We also don't have to kill people with kindness. The opinionated person doesn't know what to do with that genuinely loving intelligence. We speak our truth and let our heart shimmer with our truth, but we aren't trying to convert. That's where the power lies; it's the way of non-attachment. The 17th Gift is awesome; it's the power of far-sightedness. It's the Gift of seeing the matrix, the whole matrix, with all its detail. Once we've seen it we can never go back to the land of opinion and division. This is the domain of the heart-mind, this Gift. We merge the opposites, looking with intuition and intellect, and rise up to a higher level of functioning. The 17th Gift is about seeing with our causal body. Our causal body is the subtle equipment that humans have to look at something beyond the mind.

The causal plane lies beyond the mental plane; it's the realm of archetypal wisdom. It's not about knowledge; it's about the direct seeing of Truth. We perceive Truth through our whole body. It's from here that revelations, insights, epiphanies, satoris, breakthroughs arise. Every genius that's ever lived has seen with this eye. They've lifted themselves up to look at life through wider eyes. Many were not able to live there, but they captured it through their art or science or particular stream of genius. It's why genius is always ahead of its time. It's Farsighted. It sees where we have come from, and it sees where we're going.

The Gift frequency is always a process. It's the process of dismantling the Shadow. As we drop our fixed views and opinions, our cells open us up to this higher mind. The process is like having contractions; a breakthrough occurs, and we have sight of the higher realm, a higher truth that exists beyond the world we see. We see into the interdependent self-originating cosmos. We see into the hologram. At the beginning, we can't sustain this view through the 17th Gift. It can be something of a trial to see that higher view and then return to our normal functioning, but we need gaps and pauses between the contractions. We need them to integrate the truths. It's too much for most of us to see it all at once. We're lowered gently into the ocean and we have to get used to it. After an epiphany, a powerful charge is rushing through our body and we feel so powerful. Yet we have to ground that insight into our daily life, so we're given time.

When I was a student at university, I used to drive my English tutor mad. I was into meditation and we were studying the creative imagination and the nature of identity in literature. You can imagine I loved that. I remember once asking our small study group to imagine what it might feel like to look through an eye with 360 degree vision. What would it be like if our eye was just suspended in space and we could see through that? What would the world look like? I used to blow their minds with my ideas! I'm sure they dreaded when I came to tutorials!

This is what it means to see through the eye of wisdom. As I said, the 17th Gene Key favours the left brain approach, so it can really see into the architecture of life. It sees the fractals and patterns of existence. It sees the synarchies of creative evolution. It sees through the heart. The 17th Gift knows how to overcome politics, and get communities working together. We don't really get anywhere by arguing, disempowering, and jostling for position. We work with each other through empowering, affirming, and listening. This isn't idealistic. This is eminently practical. Efficiency is about working with higher values. We're not children, but we behave like them. In fact, we're much worse than children, because we don't have their capacity to let go.

Left brain genius is all about mastering technique in order to transcend technique. A left brain musical genius, for example, is very different from a right brain musical genius. The left brain works in hierarchies, levels, sequences. The right brain works illogically and makes quantum leaps, but they both lead to the same place-transcendence.

Think about the truly healthy teenage mind. Think about how open it is. Think about how revolutionary it is. Think about how far ahead it sees. Why do you think young adults are so into science fiction? It's the Gift of Far-sightedness. We all have that Gift, regardless of our profiles. The 17th Gift is about reclaiming that mind, that causal view beyond the veil of the world. It's about letting the open heart see through that kind of a mind. It precipitates a creative revolution. Let's open our hearts that wide and then look at life, and we'll see what the 17th Gift sees. We'll see the beauty, the magic, and the miracle of the true nature of the dreamworld in which we live.

The 17th Siddhi - Omniscience

The 17th Siddhi activates the fullest expression of the pituitary gland. Each of the endocrine glands has a different higher purpose in our biology. The pituitary operating at its genetic zenith gives us the experience of the opening of the so-called third eye. It's funny when we think about it, because the third eye isn't really in the forehead between our two eyes. That's just a metaphor. I experienced a third eye opening on a large scale back during my mystical experience when all this first opened in me.

Traditionally we see the third eye between the two eyes, because it does indeed represent the transcendence of the dualistic view through our senses. It's the third transcendent view of the whole. In my experience, the third eye is actually at the heart of every single cell in our body. When it opens, our entire body becomes the eye. We open in a way that defies belief. We become the 360 degree eye floating in space-time, and we bring an end to space-time. Little did I know what I was saying back in that tutorial at university all those years ago. My words have come back to haunt me. The experience of the 17th Siddhi is akin to being seen through, rather than seeing. We cease to be, so we ourselves don't see. The cosmos sees itself through us. I imagine it must be something like that when we die…such a beautiful phenomenon. Nothing whatsoever to fear…the beauty of that cosmic sunset that brings an end to our individuated existence.

The 17th Siddhi is rather unusual. I think it may also be rather rare. It's a Gift of Grace. It's one of the agents of Grace - one of the Seven Sacred Seals spoken of in the 22nd Gene Key and its beautiful transmission. The 17th Siddhi is one of the Siddhis that will bring an end to the sacred wound of denial. It comes to end the second line wound. If you've done Part 2 of the Golden Path Program, you'll know what I'm talking about. The second line wound is our sexual wound. It's the wound of violence, rage and pure denial. The only way humans can do some of the deplorable things we've done is because we have the wound of denial. We couldn't live with ourselves otherwise. We can see that at the Shadow frequency there's also a kind of death, but it's the death of conscience or self-responsibility.

With the 17th Siddhi comes Omniscience. It's a collective phenomenon. Humanity is the eye that we will one day see through. Once that eye opens up in our genome, our racial gene pools, it will change our Shadow nature forever. How can we harm another when we realise that they're part of us? How can we harm another when we're feeling so good? The 17th Siddhi is part of the tradition of sudden awakening. When someone sees through their denial, it shatters them wide open to the core. This is St. Paul on the road to Damascus; this is a thunderbolt.

When we mutate, we'll mutate swiftly. The 17th Gene Key acts fast. It's the master of efficiency remember. One never knows where lightning will strike, so this is one of the most unpredictable places in the human genome. It could transform the human race overnight. My hunch is that this Siddhi comes towards the end of our evolution, and follows fast on the heels of our heart opening. It'll literally bring an instant end to fighting at all levels, even in children. We know how siblings love to fight and provoke each other, and we parents just wonder at the pain of it. Why do they do that, the sweet little cherubs? It's because it's in our DNA. One day it'll be transformed just like that. A new kind of child will come into the world, one with no violence in their system, with no memory even of violence. That's something to contemplate…

I want to finish with an image of the 17th Siddhi. You know I like to do that sometimes. Well in the Gene Keys Synthesis, one of the approaches is called the Dream Arc. It's a shamanic way into the matrix of the 64 Codons. Every Shadow, Gift, and Siddhi has a totem animal, insect or bird connected to it. I brought this transmission through a few years back, and it's really an exciting right brain approach. It's also a kind of Dream Yoga using the Gene Keys. Anyway, the 17th Siddhi is the peregrine falcon. All the Siddhis are birds because they represent the alpha state, the higher consciousness. The falcon is seen by many traditions as a symbol of higher sight. The best known of these is probably the Egyptian tradition, which is where we get the all-seeing omniscient eye of Horus. Horus had the head of a falcon.

If you've ever seen a falcon in the hands of a falconer, you will know that they always keep a hood over the bird's head. This is because the eyes of the falcon are a complete marvel of creation. They can see the 'O' in a packet of Marlboro cigarettes from a mile up in the sky, while moving at speeds of up to 200 miles an hour!

With the hood on, the falcon is docile, almost in a trance. All its primary awareness systems are on standby, but the moment he removes that hood, my God, that system instantly comes online! Those eyes are connected directly into the bird's central nervous system, so what the eye sees is instantly translated into action, without any additional cognition.

When the falcon is released into the air to hunt, it becomes this all-seeing eye connected to a 200 mile an hour killing machine. It's no wonder the falcon became the royal bird; it's an awesome creature. The moment those eyes see the prey, the bird is instantly in action. There's no time delay between seeing and acting. I leave you with this image, because our future awareness is like that, except instead of being predatory, it's revelatory. There's no time delay between seeing and acting. At the lower frequency that's the definition of denial, but at the highest frequency, it leads to a world imbued with a living awareness, an all-pervasive intelligence that bridges all creatures and all things. It's the Omniscience of God spoken of in the Bible. It's our legacy. It's the natural outcome of our evolution.

The 18th Way

Gene Key 18

THE WAY OF INTEGRITY

The Transformational Way of the 18th Gene Key moves from Judgment to Perfection, and it's the Way of Integrity.

This is a lovely Gene Key, this 18th Gene Key. At least I'm very drawn to it, but for no good reason. It's not in my Profile. It's not even in my Integral Human Design matrix. I don't have anything to do with the 18th Gene Key. And yet I do! This is a great clue for anyone who's working with the Gene Keys. We can work with our Profile and our Golden Path, and this is really essential. In addition to this, we can make room for the Gene Keys to come into us in other ways, in mysterious ways. This one has done that with me. For a good six months, my contemplation has been strongly flavoured with the 18th Siddhi of Perfection. I intuitively feel drawn to this word, to this energy field, and my inner being loves to explore what it feels like. Along the way I've also gotten to know its other sides, the Shadow and the Gift, and I see it everywhere in the world and in myself.

I hope you're inspired by it, as I've been. Let's begin with the Shadow of Judgment. It's quite an obvious one. We all make judgments all the time. It's something that comes through our minds. Our minds pick up on our emotional responses, our physical feelings, and then they create detailed judgments out of that. It's really intriguing. Anything out of our comfort zone leads to a judgment of one sort or another, and it's all based on the observation of flaws. That's the Dilemma here. judgment is based on the perceived notion of flaws, mistakes, errors.

Interestingly, we can't really go there without including the Siddhi right from the beginning - this notion of Perfection, because the idea that the universe is not perfect is bred into us. The Shadow believes it, swallows it hook, line, and sinker and then all we see are the flaws in life. This Shadow likes to find flaws. It has a knack for finding flaws. You know when it really takes root? In our teenage years.

Shadow: Judgment **Gift**: Integrity **Programming Partner**: Gene Key 17
Dilemma: Flaws **Siddhi**: Perfection **Codon Ring**: The Ring of Matter

---

Between the ages of 14 and 21, we're so riddled with insecurity that our mind learns to try and escape the flaws. You know, the flaws that our parents make every day, the flaws of our teachers, the flaws of our friends, the flaws of our enemies at school. The mind constructs a way of keeping the emotional insecurity in check. We fix ourselves into a fixed thought-realm. It usually comes from the people we spend the most time with, our friends. It may make us feel like a rebel, or outcast, or conformist, or non-conformist, but the point is it freezes our mind. It fixes us mentally and thus it stops our mind from expanding naturally and freely.

These Gene Keys are really quite amazing; they describe genetic processes of shut-down at every level. Gradually as we grow up into young adults, we fix the idea inside our minds that the world we're coming into is deeply flawed. It's really far from perfect. The 18th Gene Key is part of the Codon Ring of Matter, and this collection of genetic markers determines the ways in which we all close down from experiencing the world as perfect. The 18th Gene Key governs the 3rd seven year cycle of imprinting, which is our mental imprinting, our IQ in the Golden Path.

Before our teens we don't make these judgments, at least not in the same way. In our 2nd seven year cycle from 8 to 14, we're really making emotional judgments, but that's a whole other ball game. In this 18th Gene Key, we're talking about mental judgments. Let's think about what our life would be like without our mind making these judgments, when we're just sunk into the inherent Perfection of it all. Perfection isn't a judgment - it's a cellular knowing. We'll see what that looks like in a minute when we come to the Siddhi. I just want us to know how this judgment game all began.

There are two types of mental judgments here. There are judgments based on fear, that come out of a defensive, closed heart, and then there are judgments that come from an open heart. We don't ordinarily refer to these as judgments - we call them wisdom. Both see flaws, but the first one becomes a victim of those flaws, whereas the second version uses the flaws creatively. If we have this 18th Gene Key in our Profile, or are contemplating it in our life, we can think about the things we consider flaws. We have a Gift for seeing flaws. If that comes out through a Shadow mentality, it's hell. We're forever seeing what's missing, driven by this misery, and we may spend a lifetime chasing the flaws, trying to perfect them, eternally dissatisfied. Of course, we judge ourselves internally all the time for not being good enough.

When it comes to relationships, we'll judge the other for not being good enough. They will never, ever meet our standards. We can never find a fulfilling relationship until we see the pattern and begin to work with it creatively. The Chinese name for this hexagram is 'Work on What has been Spoilt' - a wonderful name that at first glance might sound depressing, but on closer inspection is actually rather magical. Work on what has been spoilt. That means that we can find the flaws and use them as inspiration to serve the whole in some way. That's the Gift. But the Shadow is just 'what has been spoilt'. There's no work. It's just a curse we carry everywhere we go. Let's look deeply into the mirror of our judgments, especially what happened to our minds through our teenage years. What mental compromises did we make that led to this acute habit of judging the world around us as flawed? More importantly, what can we do about it now, to open up that wonderful mind of ours again to the incredible possibilities latent in this Gene Key?

The 18th Gift - Integrity

The problem with the Shadow and its Dilemma is that unless we can train the lens of this Gene Key on our own behaviour in a compassionate way, we're caught in the inevitable hypocrisy of the judging game. You may remember Jesus calling out at the trial of a young woman who was threatened with death by stoning: 'he that is without sin among you, let him cast the first stone!' A beautiful moment in the gospels. A moment of integrity. It's not so much that we as individuals have integrity, but that life has it. It's built into life. Look at the animal kingdom. We see no judgment. Every creature has its own integrity in the great web of life. Everything has its purpose, its role. Nature as a whole has a certain Perfection to it. But humans don't yet see that way. We're still evolving.

Integrity also has a lot to do with morality, not manmade morals, but moral fibre, the natural morality of a self-conscious human being. Most of us are pretty unselfconscious, especially in our relationships where we revert to our Shadow patterns. Integrity presupposes that we're developing an inner view. Without an inner view, we're lost in the Shadows. As we evolve and begin to awaken, we begin to learn how to take responsibility for our own flaws. We may see the flaws of others, but instead of making them the focus, we train our laser sight on ourselves. We enter a great paradoxical realm - the realm of self-improvement. It's a paradox because our greater Self can't be improved. It's already perfect, remember, but our lesser self definitely has some room for improvement! So our inner journey through the Gift begins.

We learn to use the flaws, our flaws and the flaws of others, even the flaws of humanity, to inspire us. To begin with, most of us give this an outer focus. We try and improve some part of the world in some way. We feel the drive to try and help. This is a noble cause, but it's also flawed. It's flawed, because we can't help the world until we've helped ourself first. This is often the advice given to disciples (especially Western ones) of great realised teachers. The question is how can we help the planet if we don't do something…it's no good just sitting here. The Master will respond, 'you don't know how to help until you are 'you'…. and right now you're still just a victim of your perception of the world's flaws.'

We only really help and enter into the field of integrity when we're no longer in reaction. Our service can't come from anger. It must come from love, from wisdom, from realisation. Integrity has great calm inside it. It isn't showy or provocative. Integrity leads by example. That is its primary method, and because it's in the middle between the Shadow and the Siddhi, it has roots in both. Integrity knows that underneath there's Perfection, but it also acknowledges on the surface that there's work to be done. There are many improvements to be made that will greatly help others and the world as a whole. It's why the Programming Partner is the 17th Gift of Far-sightedness, because integrity sees where things are eventually going. Life does evolve, although it does so sometimes by going back a few steps. Nonetheless, it still evolves. Knowing this, the being of integrity is relaxed deep within and that's where their power derives from. It comes because they're both in the game, but a part of their awareness is also resting outside the game.

This is a Gift that likes a challenge, one that comes to challenge all falsehood. It does that not through pointing out what's wrong, but rather through adopting creative solutions that it's ready to back up. Think about the teenage mind. Think about how elastic and expansive it is. That's your mind. It was never intended to become stale or frozen or opinionated (well at a certain level it was, but you know what I mean). The point is that we can return to that openness once again, to that place of non-judgment. Then our inherent knack of finding flaws turns itself upon our own thinking; it's we who cause the problems. It's our very thinking. We begin to clean out our thinking, and this is an amazing process - it's the return of our true IQ.

A cleaned-out mind is a rare thing. A mind with integrity has terrific power to serve the world. This is what we really mean by genius. Our IQ expands as we reclaim our higher purpose in life. This is another meaning of integrity - to have a deep core stability, to be anchored firmly in a sense of inner purpose, and to have that feeling radiate through our posture, our movement, and our presence. In the East, they call this mind the Yi, the Wisdom Mind, and it's a mind like water. It flows in harmony with the universe. It sees the Perfection and the flaws, and it knows its role in bringing those flaws back into alignment with the greater Perfection. This is after all the Ring of Matter, so this Gene Key has a deep mission to fulfil in the physical world. Integrity is about embodiment and it's also about having grit. That's hidden in the word 'Inte-grity'. It's gritty.

It has real power to serve and improve the whole, and that role requires grit because we'll have to go against the grain, the Shadow, the nay-sayers, the pessimists, the hypocrites, the mass consciousness. Yes, it's really a powerful Gift, is this one, because we'll have to stand out from the crowd, which is the role of integrity. We'll have to be a model of harmony and beauty and inner strength even when everything seems set against us. Especially when everything seems set against us.

The 18th Siddhi - Perfection

Perfection. What on earth is it? Most people would say there's no such thing, or it's unattainable. Not true. Every Siddhi is the realisation of Perfection. It's the embodiment of

Perfection and it's absolutely attainable. It may be very rare, but it's been realised and will continue to be realised. So what is it? Well, there's outer Perfection and inner Perfection. This contemplation is going to be unusual, I can tell already. Let's do inner Perfection first, because it's actually going to be easier to embrace for most people. Inner Perfection is the realisation that the world as it is right now in this very moment is utterly perfect. This is not just an intellectual understanding. It's pervasive across the whole great span of our inner being. It's the culmination of the process of meditation or contemplation - the utter acceptance of what is in each moment.

At a mental level, it's the acceptance of our thinking process, but it also includes detachment. We become a witness to our mind, and then our mind lets go and sinks back into the primordial source of being. We experience Perfection, and every thought arises spontaneously out of that Perfection. Emotionally it's similar in that emotion as we know it ceases, because detachment has saturated our inner life. Eventually all emotional patterns rooted in the past, or the mind, or desire, also fall back into the root of emotion - the still lake of being. The emotions that do arise tend to be higher emotions - ecstatic feelings, which are not really feelings at all. They're waves of bliss imbued with wisdom. Emotion and desire are purified, and then the Perfection of love is experienced continually. This love is unconditional, so it includes what once we considered as ugly or flawed, but now is perceived as perfect. Even the Shadow and its behaviour is experienced as perfect.

There's the Perfection of the physical form, the way it breathes, moves, its rhythms and tempos, and its connection to everything that exists. The Perfection of physicality is experienced as stillness without bounds. One form flows into the next, even though the awareness in each seems to make it feel separate. We tend to think of others as perfect - maybe Christ or Buddha are perfect, whereas we're not. Actually we're perfect right down to the core. I know lots of people say this in the New Age - 'we're all perfect' - 'it's all perfect'. They're right, but it can also be a mental thing. Usually if we need to say it, then it is. To embody it at all times is Perfection, and not to embody it is also Perfection. The Siddhi is always paradoxical like that.

Perfection exists at a higher level of consciousness than humans currently generally access. Perfection is in the higher trinity. It's found in our causal body, our buddhic body, our atmic body. These are the higher dimensions of our inner being. Our consciousness has to rise up into these levels, and these levels have to descend into our form, into our emotional life and into our mental life. This is the process of enlightenment. The Gift level isn't yet capable of Perfection. It's into perfecting. It's expressing the yearning for Perfection as creativity or service, but it hasn't realised it yet. There's a big difference between perfecting and Perfection. In Perfection there's no more perfecting. Have you ever considered that? Striving has ceased. Seeking has come to an end. We've arrived. Life continues to evolve, but it evolves towards greater layers of Perfection. How can this be, we may ask? If Perfection is attained, how can evolution continue? Because Perfection is infinite. It's effervescent. It's life. It's a paradox.

What then about outer Perfection? How can there be inner and outer? Well, there aren't, but we're inside a Siddhi here, so anything goes. Whatever language we need, we'll use. When I talk about outer Perfection, I mean our world. Can it ever be perfect? We know that from the enlightened consciousness it already is, but it also isn't on the outside, right?

There are legends of Eden, Shambhala, Tir na nOg - the heavenly realms. Almost every global culture and mythology has references to heaven, to a perfect world beyond ours. In St. John's Revelation he goes one further and talks of the coming of heaven to earth, the coming down of the New Jerusalem. Other cultures also speak of this idea of the future Eden that we will one day inherit. Is it just mad idealism? Well, from our current scientific materialism perspective it might seem so. The world we live in today is in a hell of a state. But is it really? I want us to let this Siddhi really blow our minds. It should do. You know, a couple of inventions and our world will look very different. An energy invention and a food invention. You know, free energy from nuclear fission or something, and pure nutrition inside a pill, and we're almost there. Most of the battles here are about food and energy. With energy solved, we can even move to places like Mars or the moon and then territory gets solved as well. On the outside, these things are possible, even probable in the future. Maybe heaven on earth isn't as far away as we all think? Of course the inner and the outer are intimately linked. They aren't separate at all. The outer follows the inner.

There's still one more dimension missing from this contemplation, and that's the coming together of the spiritual and the physical, of heaven and earth, of the mystical and the scientific, of technology and consciousness. It's not the way some people think. It's not about cybernetic humans. It's about us realising that we are the technology. Our vehicles are capable of a lot more than we realise, and that's where this inner revolution is going to take us - to the realm of the magical.

I was reading this book recently about a Himalayan renunciate, Swami Rama, and he goes to see all these incredible masters over the course of his life. One of them is called Aghori Baba, this weird wise man who everyone is afraid of, and he lives in a remote cave by the upper Ganges. Any time anyone comes near he shouts at them and throws stones, but our guy goes to see him, and spends some days in his company. They are two renunciates, so they kind of have an understanding. Baba has the extraordinary gift of transforming matter into energy and vice versa, and he's living on his own to perfect his art. That's why he pretends to scare people away. He turns these pebbles into almonds, and manifests all kinds of food out of nothing. By this point in the book you know that you're listening to an authentic voice, and that this is all true.

The point is that we are the next technology to be developed. All we need is the inspiration and this will happen. We all have these latent higher capacities. We have these Siddhis. There's a big incarnation coming, and it's going to open up these pathways of magic, of alchemy, and not just individually, but through the collective. That's more powerful than we can possibly imagine.

There's a higher ideal at the core of our DNA. We call it Synarchy. We'll be its vehicles. As it comes into the world, into form, it will implement the principle of Syntropy - generosity and service throughout humanity. The most efficient means of organisation comes from being awake, because when we're awake, we move in harmony with all that is and then we embrace the miraculous. When this same impulse becomes wisdom, it manifests through Synthesis - the ability to see where everything and everyone are interconnected. Not just to see it, but to know it, remember it, and embody it. That's powerful.

I'm in the strange position of being a prophet and a realist. I see what the world is today. I see the problems, the horrors, the hypocrisy, but I've also seen the future. I've remembered it. And it's Perfection. One day we'll perfect our world. It may well take a period of deep chaos before we get there, because the Shadow must be rooted out and utterly transformed. The future is a seed that lives in the present. That's the paradox. When Jesus said the kingdom of heaven is here now, he was right. He was absolutely right. It is here. But it's also coming.

So see the Perfection that's here now, and see the Perfection that's coming. One is imperfectly perfect and the other is completely perfect, but they're both Truth, because they both resonate now. I know I'm going out on a limb with this Siddhi, but I really, really want us to get it. To hold both sides of the same coin inside ourself and live from that, that's truly to know what Perfection is - it's flawless. What a contemplation!

THE 64 WAYS

THE 19TH WAY

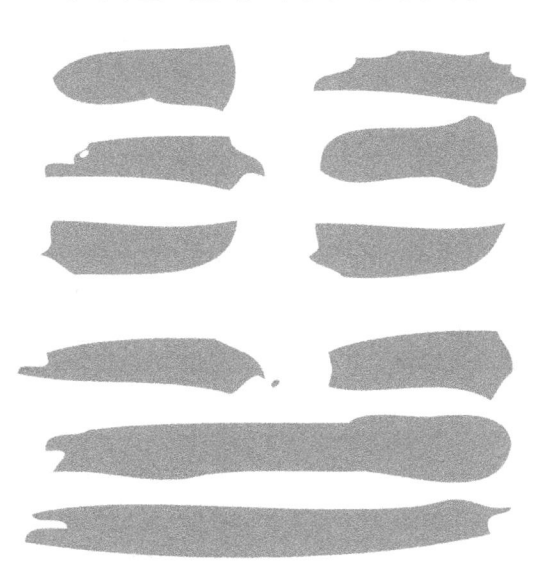

Gene Key 19

THE WAY OF SENSITIVITY

The Transformational Way of the 19th Gene Key moves from Co-dependence to Sacrifice, and it's the Way of Sensitivity.

If we go to the theatre or watch a film, most times the show we watch will utterly possess us. We become one with it as we're watching. We become absorbed in the drama, the characters and the story. We go through many feelings - anticipation, worry, fear, joy, and yet all is an illusion. It's fabricated. If we go behind the curtain, there we'll find the director, actors, stage hands. On a movie set we'll see cameras, microphones and all manner of people and equipment. We'll see many of them holding scripts, and perhaps we'll see the actors in their ordinary clothes practising their lines. So many people - so much effort is being made to trick us!

Our lives are the same as this. We don't see behind the scenes. We don't realise that events are choreographed in other realms. We don't realise that we, and all those around us, are wearing costumes. We don't realise there are directors, stage-hands, and a script. Sometimes the director and the scriptwriter make a spontaneous decision to change the script, and the whole thing is changed, just like that. It's an extraordinary trick we're living in; we're woven into a fabric made of dreams.

The reason we're so easily hoodwinked is because of our attachments, our co-dependence. We agree unconsciously to support each other's illusion. On this earth we're here to learn. This is a schoolroom. Eventually we'll have to learn to stand alone, which means we'll have to break our co-dependence with everything around us. This is what happens when we die. When we die, we suddenly awaken and remember that this was all just a script. We can look back and see how we did.

Shadow: Co-dependence **Gift:** Sensitivity **Programming Partner:** Gene Key 33
Dilemma: Heresy **Siddhi:** Sacrifice **Codon Ring:** The Ring of Gaia

---

In the movies or theatre we see what other characters don't see. For example in Shakespeare's Othello, we see the arch-villain Iago plotting behind Othello's back, weaving the diabolical web of his downfall. But Othello doesn't see any of this or how easily he's manipulated into his dark side. So it is with us - there are forces pitted against us. I don't say this to alarm, but to open our minds and hearts up to other dimensions. These forces are the forces that inhabit the Shadow consciousness field - they would like us to exhaust all our precious life forces. Like vampires, they feed on our desires. On the other side there are angels and beings of light, but they're more respectful, only intervening when utterly necessary or when called out for from the depth of one's being. The universe is teeming with life forms and they're all here alongside us. They aren't far away. We're caught up in the web, in the drama.

This may sound like a naive tale to some, and I am anthropomorphising. If you were a psychologist, you could say the same thing with a different language. I'm using the language of the shaman, because it's more colourful, and also because I think it has more truth. Co-dependence is not just a psychological word referring to our relationships. It has subtle layers and levels to it. We feed other life forms, and they feed on us. The human aura emits a wide array of emanations on different frequency bands. For example, when we take a hallucinogen or get drunk, we experience some of the other wavelengths. When we become embroiled in an argument, we taste another dimension. When we sit quietly by the side of the river, again we enter yet another realm.

There are as many realms as there are humans and creatures. This is the theatre of Gaia. So what does any of this teach us? Well for one thing we're here to learn to loosen our co-dependence with the energetic environment in which we live. Our co-dependence is with our thought forms, our belief structures, our opinions. It's also with our emotional patterns, our unconscious belief that we're a victim, or that we can behave badly and get away with it. We can never do so. The bad one always pays.

The good one is always rewarded. Justice is built into the script, but we don't always see the full story.

The Dilemma of this Shadow is an odd one - it's heresy. The heretic is one who breaks patterns, who speaks out against the status quo. The heretic is one who goes it alone, who's willing to shatter the fabric of his or her world in order to see more. It's a Dilemma because it takes heresy to break out of this world of co-dependence - to see behind the scenes. Often people think of themselves as heretical - we like to think we're open-minded, but usually we're not. Usually we're very fixated with our worldview without realising it. There's a terrific self awareness needed to escape the web of patterns woven around us by our karma and incarnation. Some of the subtlest webs are the spiritual ones, carefully woven from the subtlest material, but a web is a web. We remain co-dependent.

Heresy must throw everything out. It can hold a worldview, but that worldview must be seen as limiting and ultimately false. This Gene Key is about initiation - it's about opening our mind and heart up to other realms, other behaviours, and other possibilities. Our lives can be going in a certain direction, but the script can always change at any moment. My role with this contemplation, this 19th Transformational Way, is simply to show us the extent of the illusion we're living in. My hope is that just from us contemplating this deeply enough, perhaps a heresy will begin to grow inside us.

The 19th Gift - Sensitivity

I realise that the contemplation on the Shadow may not have seemed so practical. It's one thing to say 'yes, well the world we see is not the whole story' - but what do we do with that? I wanted us to really take that in deeply first. The purpose of this wisdom is to bring us into the world, not take us up and away into other dimensions. Please don't get caught in that trap. What the shaman learns is that everyday life is the full life. All the dimensions can be accessed and affected by our behaviour right now.

Think about our dream life. Every night we enter the other world. We take off our clothes and enter into the hinterland of consciousness. The borders of time and space soften. Yet we carry our day with us in there. Our day imprints our dream life, and our dream life imprints our next day. There's a continuity there that's magical. The Gift of Sensitivity is not to be confused with oversensitivity, or hypersensitivity, or sentimentality. Sensitivity is strength. Oversensitivity is an affliction that's imprinted by the Shadow frequency band.

We can re-imprint any of these patterns, given enough time and a deep enough sense of self-love and patience.

The 19th Gift is a gift of healing. It knows how to heal itself because it knows what it needs. The 19th Gift doesn't allow us to burn ourself out. It knows the secret of balance - how to feed one's own needs and balance them with the needs of others. Sensitivity also grows. It grows as we grow. As we allow the heresy of a clear mind and heart to penetrate our lives, it will begin to loosen our attachments to the drama around us. We begin to move closer into life. We come closer to others. We lean into situations instead of trying to shun them or hide from them. Sensitivity makes us more human, more rounded, more wholesome.

We learn to parent ourselves. We learn to ask for support when we need it, and let go of resentments. Our sensitivity is our coming alive. It's our re-joining the human race, settling into the family of creatures and all beings. Sensitivity feels like coming home. Many times we think of sensitivity as a problem that's more likely to harm us than be healing. To say that someone is a sensitive person even means that they may be quite emotionally explosive or reactive. This isn't anything to do with the Gift of Sensitivity. This is a Gift of opening, yes to other realms, but not in a way that's showy. The true sensitive doesn't become a channel. The true sensitive doesn't make any such claims. The true sensitive leans into us as a fellow human, waits for us to open, and if we're very lucky, they may share with us some of the things they see and feel.

The original name for this 19th Hexagram in the I Ching is 'Approach'. It's a beautiful simple word. The sensitive has learned the art of approach. They know how to approach things in the right way. They don't rush headlong into a sacred place. They may linger at the portal. They don't rush to greet a stranger, but they'll allow that person to approach them at the speed they're comfortable. The sensitive doesn't talk so much. They're a listener. With animals they know that the whole secret is the approach. We don't instigate touch - we wait for the animal to feel its own trust, and then allow it to touch us.

If we have this treasured gift, we need to first heal ourself and learn to approach our life in a new way, one that's gentle and meets our primary needs. We need to make sure that we're fed by life, and this is our responsibility, not someone else's. Co-dependence is when the relationship doesn't feel balanced. Our sensitivity knows instantly where the imbalance is, so we can address it openly, sensitively. Sensitivity also learns fast. It learns through insensitivity. We all do and say things that hurt others, sometimes intentionally, sometimes not. Sensitivity is an art we must learn, and when we've learned it, we feel so strong, so connected to life, but we also feel permeable and soft. This is where the heresy of openness one day leads.

The 19th Siddhi - Sacrifice

Heresy always leads to Sacrifice. It always has done and always will do, until the day when the human mind has lost its power over our lives. There are different kinds of Sacrifice. There is the lower Sacrifice - the self-sacrifice, where one gives away one's power for the sake of others. This kind of Sacrifice isn't healthy. If we damage ourself deliberately by serving another, there's no honour in that. The higher Sacrifice takes place internally. We sacrifice our lower impulses for a higher purpose. We fuel that which is highest in our nature rather than those impulses (natural though they are) that lower our frequency.

Speaking ill of others is a good example. Most of us indulge in this behaviour, but it doesn't bring us anything. At least that's how it appears. Through the lens of sensitivity, speaking ill of another person does indeed bring a harsh energy into our aura. It comes back on us at a deep subtle level.

The path to the Siddhis is a path of Sacrifice. We have to sacrifice our negativity. We have to sacrifice our negative projections of others and even of the world. In fact, to reach the highest frequency, we even have to sacrifice our positive projections. To move beyond good and evil, we have to step out of the drama altogether. This is to sacrifice our position as a player in the game. We observe our role in such depth that our role is loosened. We become the consummate actor or actress now that we know the nature of the game. The great Sacrifice for the Siddhi is often not to speak. The Siddhi knows it's misunderstood. It's willing to be misunderstood. If we can see with absolute clarity and another cannot, how will we convey what we see to them?

We know that the 19th Gene Key is about initiation. To be initiated means to undergo some form of Sacrifice in which the being that we were is transmuted and becomes something new. The great initiations spoken of in the 22nd Gene Key occur rarely, because human beings rarely reach a place of surrender at that level. After each initiation we go through a process of stabilisation, which can last many years or incarnations. As our awareness evolves further, it does so gradually. We have to be so very patient. Lifetimes pass with little change. We sit staring out the window at the seasons rushing by, at birth and death. We dress and undress our bodies time after time. We love, leave, lose, and yearn.

Most of us have just a few lines in the great play.

The great lives are so often unseen. Think about all the people who gave their lives for others without those others ever knowing. Think about those people whose virtue has shaped and improved the lives of others without anyone knowing their name. The greatest sacrifices are unseen. Think about our life and what we might be able to sacrifice for others. This planet is a planet of Sacrifice. Everything is connected to everything else through Sacrifice, through the chain of death and rebirth. The Ring of Gaia contains these 3 Siddhis, the 19, the 60, and the 61 - Sacrifice, Justice, and Sanctity. Sacrifice discovers Sanctity through Justice. Whatever we give up, if it truly is selfless, justice will reward us and we'll discover the inner Truth.

The thing is we humans don't see the full spectrum of Justice. We don't remember our past incarnations, so we don't always see why things are the way they are. We have to find out for ourselves, and Sacrifice is our greatest teacher and ally. It will be difficult for many to understand this Siddhi. It can only be truly understood by the one who has lived it, but when we've done so, when we've given ourself selflessly for the sake of the whole, for the sake of Gaia, then we'll know. We'll pass through the great portal of initiation and be forever transformed.

Finally, the 19th Siddhi also says something about our collective future. Our planetary consciousness periodically moves through great epochs, and to move from one epoch to another always involves a great Sacrifice for us all. One day another such transition will occur. To move into a new dimension we'll have to die to what we've been. This is the coming of the so-called Sixth Race, our next epoch, in which the Siddhis, which now seem so extraordinary to us, will become ordinary. They become our waking everyday consciousness. I've spoken and written about this many times, as in the 55th Gene Key. It will come, we're approaching that planetary portal. I can't say when, because it hasn't been given to me to know, and if I did, I wouldn't say anyway. The time isn't important. What is important is that we live our lives with honesty and openness and challenge our own perceptions of the world constantly. The future takes care of itself. The now is our home, so let's live in it to the very best of our ability.

The 20th Way

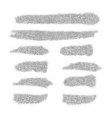

Gene Key 20

THE WAY OF SELF ASSURANCE

The Transformational Way of the 20th Gene Key moves from Superficiality to Presence, and it's the Way of Self-assurance.

The 20th Gene Key is pivotal if you wish to understand the Gene Keys. Its original name in Chinese can be interpreted as Contemplation. It means viewing, in the sense of viewing inwardly and of being viewed. At the Shadow level of being it is about Superficiality and absence, about not being aware of things, or of oneself or others. Contemplation is an art. The whole secret purpose of the Gene Keys is really to foster in us this forgotten art. You notice I don't say 'to teach us'. Contemplation cannot be taught. It can only be cultivated. It is the most subtle of all the arts.

The art of contemplation has 3 levels - the first is simply viewing. You simply begin to look. This is a difficult thing to begin. You must realise that you have been absent, you have been simply living on the surface of life, superficially. You have been living your life without any real self awareness - the dilemma of this Shadow. It can be a painful revelation to look back on one's life and see the debris field of one's relationships, the litter of our dreams and the hurt we have caused others. But this is where we must begin. And then we have to learn to train this lens on the present - on our current life situation and how we are behaving, both behind closed doors in our inner world, and in the outer world. Over time we begin to thread an important connection - that our outer life is built upon the foundation of our inner life. This is the first phase of contemplation.

We also enter into a phase of intense learning that switches spontaneously on and off as we work our way into this Shadow. We begin to see the affects of our presence or absence in the world. We see our mistakes when we were not considering the whole situation, or when we were aware enough to think about the feelings of others. Self awareness comes and goes. Sometimes we are absent, sometimes we are present. For long periods we

Shadow: Superficiality	**Gift:** Self Assurance	**Programming Partner:** Gene Key 34
Dilemma: Self-Awareness	**Siddhi:** Presence	**Codon Ring:** The Ring of Life and Death

are simply absent. Days are consumed by our living in reaction, in stress, without even knowing it. Every now and again we come up for air - an oasis of contemplation reminds us - we pause and remember ourselves. It may be a yoga class. It may be a moment of inspiration or a creative burst of energy. We are reminded of how wonderful a moment of presence is.

We spend a great deal of our time living in the Shadow. Only at times do we pause to enjoy the sun. But this is normal. It is natural. It is the way of things. Evolution comes in its own time. The chop of this hexagram - its shape - is like a tower or an arch. In ancient China these towers were all across the landscape and they are a symbol for gaining a higher view of the realm. The arch also suggests an opening, an invitation to move from one space into another - and that is what this Gene Key does - it calls us from within, to enter on a higher path, a path of awareness.

Contemplation is not just thinking. It is a whole way of being. It is about viewing yourself from a higher level, an objective level. The whole purpose of gaining this view is so that we can learn to see how we create our own suffering. And gentleness is required. This too we have to learn. The two trigrams that make up this hexagram are the gentle wind and the earth, so we have to listen to the whispering wind of awareness and let it blow into all the corners of our life. We are here to learn to be more considerate, to take things more smoothly, to see into the truth of who we are. And to see the depth of our superficiality. It's a good thing to reflect at the end of the day and see how present you were in total during that day. How many moments of presence did you have in comparison to the moments of absence? It's not a competition. There is no judgement. This is simply about seeing what is. It's a hugely valuable thing to see the superficial nature of your life in this way.

GENE KEY 20

THE 20TH GIFT - SELF ASSURANCE

The second layer of contemplation is about viewing oneself in relation to the world. The self awareness really deepens now. A moral view comes into play. It's not imposed at all. It is simply there in every human being, but it requires a certain level of awareness before it can come to the surface. In this deeper level of contemplation we don't only see ourselves and our behaviour, we begin to feel the affect our absence or presence has in the world. We see ourselves through the eyes of others. We become more sympathetic to our environment.

Once we begin to consider the affects of our actions, our thoughts, our words and speech, once we see them deeply, it has a preventative effect in us. Certain addictive patterns fall away and we learn how to be more altruistic and less harmful and toxic in our environment. Of course this is still all a trial and error process. At times we fall back into our old habits and ways, but gradually the awareness begins to show us that those old ways only lead to more pain, so slowly, achingly slowly, we learn. When our natural inner morality rises to the surface we feel more self assured. We manifest the Gift of this Gene Key. It is a Gift that makes us feel more human and gives us a deep sense of purpose in the world.

To have awareness means to be open, like that arch - to receive feedback, even criticism with a certain equanimity. It is not that we are becoming a Zen master, but we are becoming more human, and in doing so, we are more integrated in the world around us. Awareness does that - it brings a sense of calm. Calmness in our modern world really stands out. In fact calmness, genuine calmness - has always stood out. A self assured person is a calm person. And this isn't about confidence or charisma. Those are character traits. I am talking about presence, the Siddhi in this Gene Key. Presence is like the light, and Absence is the lack of light. Presence is moving through this Gene Key in varying degrees - in the Shadow, it is only an occasional visitor, at the Gift it is a regular friend who comes to visit, and whenever she comes, she brings a sense of calm and clarity.

If this is one of your Gene Keys, or you are drawn to it through contemplation, try and recognise how often you are truly calm. See how this Gift of calm can bring increased awareness and comfort to the many daily challenges you face. Allow this calm to settle deeply into your soul. When you are alone and quiet, feel it swirling around you, and cultivate it. How do you cultivate it? Make space for it to grow. Simplify your life as much as you can so that the new awareness finds it easier to take root. Keep your space tidy. Know where things go in your house. Let the daily rituals of your life sing out with this simplicity and beauty, rather than simply being meaningless tasks that you are trying to get done so that you can then enjoy some rare moments of presence.

Most of us listening to this or reading this are what the ancients called vaisyas, householder yogis. We aren't renunciates or monks but people living in the world. The Householder path can still be deeply contemplative if you are able to establish the right rhythms for yourself. So you needn't only get to a deep state of presence during the rare retreats or satsangs or whichever ways you use to connect to your source. Presence does not require a specific environment, but it does thrive in certain soil types, so it is advisable to create those spaces in your everyday life, and to create those pauses where you can enjoy the seasons and the silence and come into a space of inner communion.

The 20th Siddhi - Presence

Contemplation gives you true power. There is a one-liner for you. When you learn the art of contemplation you have more influence on the direction of humanity that the President of the United States. You may not see this on the surface, but it's true. A person living in presence affects the very air around them. They send off radiations of harmony that touch all quadrants of the universe. They are like the gentle wind blowing across the earth.

The third aspect of contemplation is when the contemplation ceases of its own accord. You are no longer seen or the seer. You are simply presence, whether moving or still. Have you ever watched a single leaf falling to the ground with full awareness? Next autumn I encourage you to do so. The leaf is utterly surrendered. The tree has let it go. That is what presence is. It is that let-go. In contemplation you go on firing thoughts, deep thoughts at your core. You fire them from all angles. Then you fire feelings and urges and longings at your core, also from all angles. Everything you do or feel becomes an aspect of your contemplation. You use everything that happens in your life. This is the subtle art of contemplation.

And one day, the tree lets you go. You don't let go. It is a happening. And it goes on happening. Every day the tree lets you go. Every moment the tree lets you go. It goes on doing it over and over, until that's all you are. The Chinese have this beautiful saying - it's from the Taoists - Tzu-jan. It is really untranslatable - it means spontaneously arising, or the of-itself, or the one I like best - self-ablaze. It refers to the dropping of the leaf, to that moment, the mystery of that single never-ending moment. To be in resonance with Tzu-jan is the whole thing. It is the letting go of life and death that gives us our immortality. This Gene Key is part of the Codon Ring of Life and Death. Presence is the only thing that survives death - simply the Presence. I call it 'The Presence' because it alone of the 64 Siddhis requires the definite article. It is the definite article.

The 20th Siddhi also represents the logos - the divine word. This notion of the Word of God is a great mystery. It is the sacred Om, the tone of the divine - the mysterious octave. It is the breath of the Divine, the contemplation of God on you. That's what we are - we are God's contemplations - his or her breaths. We don't really have a say. God is either present or absent in our lives. That is how it appears. That is the game - the in-breath and the out-breath. Now you see me, now you don't. But really the Divine is there all along. It is simply in a process of revelation, and it is all revealed through presence. You can't fake presence. You can try and force it, but it will simply make you tight and uncomfortable. It isn't about will. It's about no will. It's about perfection. Every moment is arising through Tzu-jan. Whether you know it or not. Whether you see it or not. The Siddhi is there all along. How do you cultivate presence then? That is the great question of this Gene Key.

I like to drink tea. I love fine and rare teas. You chose your brew, you adapt it intuitively for the moment, you boil the water, you steep it, you pour it and then before you drink it, you pause. You watch the cup and the steam and you sense the aroma and the deep coloured liquid. These are moments of presence. The presence enters. It doesn't require an elaborate ceremony. It just requires a love of the subtle. And then you drink. So this is how we cultivate presence - through a growing love of the subtle. Presence is everywhere in everything. The weather needn't be calm. You could be in the midst of a hurricane, but the presence is there in its subtlety. You have only to look, not with your eyes but with your being.

This is the beauty of the end of contemplation - that it fires back at you. It keeps breaking over you like a wave. It is endlessly coming to us. Find your tea, whatever it may be and begin there. And one day you will no longer need the vessels, the cups - you won't even need the tea - because it is there in everything, ringing out like a bell, pouring itself all over you, inside your every cell, humming *I come, I come, I come.*

> *Have you not heard his silent steps?*
> *He comes, comes, ever comes.*
> *Every moment and every age, every day and every*
> *night he comes, comes, ever comes.*
> *Many a song have I sung in many a mood of mind,*
> *but all their notes have always proclaimed,*
> *"He comes, comes, ever comes."*
> *In the fragrant days of sunny April through the forest*
> *path he comes, comes, ever comes.*
> *In the rainy gloom of July nights on the thundering*
> *chariot of clouds he comes, comes, ever comes.*
> *In sorrow after sorrow it is his steps that press upon my heart,*
> *and it is the golden touch of his feet that makes my joy to shine.*

Rabindranath Tagore

The 21st Way

Gene Key 21

THE WAY OF AUTHORITY

The Transformational Way of the 21st Gene Key moves from Control to Valour, and it's the way of Authority.

The 21st Gene Key has a bit of a reputation that comes with it. The original name given in the I Ching is 'Biting Through' - it was likened to the jaws that gnaw and chew a difficult obstacle. Traditionally there's quite a bit of heaviness around this hexagram, so I'd like to breathe a new lease of life into it. I find it beautiful because of its trigrams, which are thunder and lightning. Thunder is below and lightning is above. Lightning can also be seen as shining light or illumination. Thunder below and lightning above seems like a pretty good match to me - a harmonic pairing, one that has a far-reaching impact.

The Shadow here is Control. This is both about losing control and trying to maintain control. Life challenges us constantly to strike a balance between maintaining control, and being flexible enough to change to accommodate a new situation. All Shadow states are rooted in fear, and the greatest fear, which is that we may one day cease to be, is what drives this need to keep control. The plot thickens more when we take into consideration the Dilemma of this Shadow, which is discipline. Can we stay in control of our Self? What happens if we give in to our weaknesses? We need enough discipline to keep us from becoming a victim of something or someone outside ourself. On the other hand, too much discipline will create a rebellion or resistance in our environment.

Let's be a bit more specific. As a parent I have had to learn that if we try and control our children too much, we'll fail. If we over-discipline them, they'll eventually become set against us. Too few boundaries also leads to them being out of control. The Shadow exerts control in the old style. It's old school; it uses consequences and punishment to maintain

Shadow: Control	**Gift:** Authority	**Programming Partner:** Gene Key 48
Dilemma: Discipline	**Siddhi:** Valour	**Codon Ring:** The Ring of Humanity

control. The problem with that is that it only works for a while. We should remember that the I Ching was originally used to help people govern their culture; the whole nation in fact. Rulers who are forceful may get what they want for a while but eventually their empires will crumble. It's a universally proven fact. We never seem to learn from history. This Codon Ring is called the Ring of Humanity, and at the Shadow frequency it shows very well the themes that keep humans victims - struggle, self obsession, constriction, opinion, agitation, and control. These are the primary Shadows of humanity.

So discipline is good, but it's a delicate balancing act that the Shadow teaches us. All behaviour creates its own karma. Humanity doesn't really understand or trust in that. Thus we have felt the need to create our own systems of punishment and reward, and those systems are often unjust and easily manipulated by those in positions of power. The secret to parenting that I've learned, and it applies to all life - is to build bonds rather than destroy them. The stronger our bond is with those around us, the more we can trust that life will do the teaching for us. A moral conscience can only grow in a healthy soil. If we take away that health by taking away someone's freedom, that natural morality that comes from learning can't develop fully.

This Gene Key has a lot to do with leadership. It also has to do with taking action and being decisive. One of the Shadow tendencies is to be indecisive, to be a follower. Wherever we have a 21st Gene Key, we have thunder and lightning. We're here to be a force for good, a leader in our arena. It takes great strength to stand in our own dignity as a leader. It requires a certain willingness to don the cloak of ego, even though we realise that we're not that ego. Others may well feel uncomfortable when that decisive power starts coming out of us. The reality is that when thunder booms, people tend to be respectful, not out of fear but out of recognition of authenticity.

There is however a great amount of pain in this Shadow. We either push too hard, not enough, or not at all. It's a steep learning curve. The Programming Partner of this Gene Key is one of the great feminine Gene Keys, the 48th Gene Key - the Well. The Shadow of the 48 is inadequacy. All tyrants feel inadequate deep down inside. As do all sheep. I don't mean to be rude about sheep - it's just an expression. The Chinese character for the 21st hexagram originally contained the figure for a shaman - a wise one who could see beyond the veil, and who could therefore handle difficult situations. Certainly there's a gauntlet thrown down with this Gene Key. If we have it or are contemplating it, then we're challenged to rise above the lower conditions of humanity. We'll probably have to do it alone. Life will test us in this way. Life is grand like that, because it's the Shadow that makes us whole. It makes us into the shaman or warrior or leader. That's the hidden compassion inside every Shadow.

The 21st Gift - Authority

The challenge for every human being is to find their true inner authority. I like that the word authority contains the word 'author'. What is the story we're here to tell? What voice wants to emerge from our depths and lead others out of the darkness toward the light? Out of the morass of the Shadow with its issues of control and being controlled, one day will begin to emerge this inner light of our true authority. Authority comes from openness - from an open mind and an open heart, because only this openness is willing to relinquish control.

The paradox of this Gift is that when one finds the strength to overcome the Shadow, it comes from giving up control, rather than asserting control. We allow the greater power inside us to shine forth, and this power is our natural nobility. Every human has an in-built nobility of spirit. Life calls it out of us. Our destiny, our dharma is permanently calling it out. Whatever we're facing right now in our life, I guarantee it's calling upon our nobility - to face it with candour, with honesty, with craft. This Gene Key is all about the human spirit shining bright in the wilderness. Life supplies each of us with exactly the test we're equipped to handle. If we take up the gauntlet and face the test, then whatever happens, our spirit will have its day.

At the Shadow we can feel how we never rise above the weight of it. We're all stuck down in the fray, competing with each other for scraps around the table, trying to gain our little moments of control - always trying to stay on top of things. The energy involved in that game is tremendous. It leeches us of our life force and we end our days exhausted and dejected. When we rise with authority, we leave those old games and take a stand. We decide to take a stand for something nobler in life. We throw all our energy into something higher. Not that we become arrogant or beyond others, but deep inside we re-imprint our energies. We starve the Shadow into submission and feed those higher aspirations of our soul.

I often make the joke at courses or retreats that if we're given a certain Gene Key by destiny, then we can be sure we're going to need it. If we have the 21st Gene Key, we'll face odds that are stacked against us. But we need to see how wonderful this is rather than let it wear us down. This is all about moving beyond the victim stance. We are not a victim! We are a God! We've been given this rusty old sword, an old nag and sent out to do battle.

There's this wonderful old story from Hungarian folk tales - it's about a magical horse called the Taltos horse. Taltos means shaman here. The youngest son of the King is given exactly this - an old decrepit horse and sent off on a journey to heal his father the King. Basically he discovers that this old horse can speak, and because he alone sees its inner value, it transforms into a powerful and beautiful diamond horse who can fly like the wind, and it helps him to overcome insurmountable obstacles.

The 21st Gene Key has this inner authority. This is part of what I'd like to reclaim for this archetype. The 21st Gift is the shaman warrior. He or she is given these trials in order to polish the sword and learn from the horse. Many times in these old tales the shaman has to give up control - in the Taltos horse myth, he has to let that horse die countless times, but each time the horse comes back stronger and more powerful and resplendent. This is our destiny. We each have this inner nobility to rise above life's challenges.

The Gift of the 21st Gene Key is one of steady and strident refinement. We're here to polish that sword until it shines resplendent. We've been given the sword of authority, and we must learn from it. As we do so, our life will become more polished. It will reflect the hidden qualities of

GENE KEY 21

our soul. With the 21st Gene Key we're called upon to stand tall and meet all obstacles with dignity and courage. In time, others will gravitate towards us, drawn by the very light that they also wish to cultivate inside themselves - the light of our nobility, our only true authority.

THE 21ST SIDDHI - VALOUR

The Siddhi of Valour may sound externally impressive. We need to remember what these Siddhis really are - a mystery revealed from the inner planes only when we're ready, when we've earned it. I've previously defined Valour as courage combined with love. That was a good introduction. Here we must go deeper. We must return to the inner meaning of this hexagram. Remember it's called 'Biting Through'. Only at the Siddhi does this name become clear, because here it's about chewing. We chew something in order to extract nutrient from it, so this is a contemplative practise.

The 21st Siddhi is a shaman, and the true shaman is a deep contemplative. Like the earthworm, we have to take all that soil into us and it must pass through our whole body and come out the other end richer. That's how the earthworm moves. Our life experiences are that soil. Our inner spirit transforms them, and we're the movement itself. The shaman must face death. That's his or her ultimate role - to chew up death, to bite through the veil to the other side and bring back the fruits from the journey. Of course the shaman realises that there is no other side, and that the veil between life and death is false. This is where the Valour comes from - from all those journeys across the river of death.

The things that are hidden from us! The hidden reasons behind people's sufferings, behind the timing of our death. The shaman learns to see through the veil into the hidden meanings. The 21st Siddhi is rewarded with these gifts. They come from learning how to wield the sword of authority. In the beginning, the apprentice uses the sword to hack - to try and control life, and he only experiences punishment. This is his karma. But after some time, we realise that the sword can be used to heal, and then life comes to fruition. Great responsibility comes with the 21st Siddhi. It's what the medievalists called 'noblesse oblige', meaning that rank obliges one to serve.

Thus the 21st Siddhi is here to help others become friends with the material realm, with the karma they've been given. Valour comes together with Wisdom, its Programming Partner, the 48th Gene Key. Wisdom can only be earned through Valour. Ultimately this Siddhi will be needed by all travellers into the beyond, because it takes Valour to die with an open heart. To give up our identity, our attachments, our body, and merge into the limitless light requires the exquisite cocktail of courage and love.

The 21st Siddhi also describes the field that follows a surrendered human being. In other words, once we've given up our 'me-ness', then Valour is all that's left. The Divine operates through valorous acts. We can't own such acts, they're simply the operational mode of consciousness when freed from personal control. Valorous acts are also often paradoxical acts - they often involve great reversals. An example that's just come to me is from the myth of Excalibur. The young Arthur is fighting the great warrior Uriens, who is of the Pendragon line, and therefore believes he should be the next and rightful King. Thus Uriens craves Excalibur, the sword of Kings.

This story is wonderfully caught in John Boorman's classic film, Excalibur. Arthur somehow defeats Uriens in single combat, through his courage and the power of the sword. Instead of killing Uriens, he asks for his life in service, and Uriens replies that he will not pay homage to a mere boy. Then comes the magic moment that even Merlin had not foreseen. Arthur agrees with Uriens and offers him Excalibur. He asks him to knight him. This is a wonderful example of the mystical reversal of the 21st Siddhi. Once Uriens has the sword of power in his hands and the young Arthur kneeling before him, many of Uriens' followers cry out - 'kill him, take the sword, claim your rightful throne'. Uriens undergoes an inner struggle, and finally is overcome by the healing power of Arthur's valorous and selfless act. He knights Arthur and offers his life in service. Only at this moment does he realise that this boy must be the rightful heir, on account of his great trust, bravery, and self-sacrifice.

These are the kinds of acts that can emerge through the 21st Siddhi, but I don't want us to have the idea that it's all about the limelight. This is inner leadership. We might find this Siddhi in a beggar or an ordinary person. The true shaman doesn't usually let us know he or she is a shaman, preferring to operate invisibly until the moment of revelation occurs.

GENE KEY 21

That's what the true meaning of this Gene Key is about - the lightning breaks through only when Grace dictates, and the thunder always precedes it. Be aware therefore that whenever the thunder of intense change comes into our life, the lightning is never far behind.

THE 64 WAYS

THE 22ND WAY

Gene Key 22

THE WAY OF GRACIOUSNESS

The 22nd Transformational Way moves from Dishonour to Grace, and it's the Way of Graciousness.

Whenever I approach this 22nd Gene Key now I always feel a little in awe, and perhaps a little daunted. Like the 55th Gene Key, it completely surprised me when I wrote it. All this amazing and frankly really mysterious, 'out there' knowledge just came pouring out. I never intended the Gene Keys to be very esoteric, but this 22nd Gene Key definitely took them in a new direction. That's what I love about the art of contemplation - you never know what insights will come or when. You just have to begin.

Having said all that, I have a feeling that this Transformational Way is going to be all practicality, because that's what the Divine Feminine is about, and this 22nd Gene Key is the real Divine Feminine. I say 'the real', because I think the Divine Feminine has been misrepresented by the New Age movement. It's not about ladies in flowing robes wafting around campfires. It's also not about some kind of pro-women social revolution either. I don't have a problem with either of these things, but they're not what I understand to be the Divine Feminine. Let's unpack this Gene Key and maybe see what it's really about, at least from the point of view of this knowledge.

Let's begin with the Shadow of Dishonour. What does it mean to dishonour someone? What does it mean to dishonour ourself? Those two questions are ever-connected. When we look at the Dilemma of this Gene Key, we get the answer - it's all about accountability. Life is about learning to be accountable for one's own state. Now that sounds easy, but it really is a huge challenge for humans. It's a challenge because at the Shadow frequency we always revert to a victim stance. If we don't feel comfortable, we immediately look

Shadow: Dishonour
Dilemma: Accountability
Gift: Graciousness
Siddhi: Grace
Programming Partner: Gene Key 47
Codon Ring: The Ring of Divinity

---

for a reason. Maybe we blame the weather (I'm English, remember we always blame the weather), but more often we blame another person. We don't take responsibility for our state. We look for a reason.

The point is that we aren't comfortable being uncomfortable. We deflect our awareness in some way out of the present moment. Why is it so damn hard to remain in the present? Why do all these teachers and mystics keep banging on about being in the now? Why can't they just leave us alone? Well they're right. Although I sometimes wonder how helpful it is to talk about being in the now or not being in the now. The problem can be that we then try and be in the now, which can end up interfering with our naturally occurring Shadow patterns! I know this might sound weird, but it's better to be screwed up and aware, than perfect and pretending to be aware. Dishonour runs deep. We dishonour ourselves every time we don't accept the way we feel or behave. When I say accept, I don't mean morally accept. There are things we do sometimes that really are not morally acceptable, but at a deeper level we can still accept them. It doesn't make them ok, but at least it's honest. In the beginning, we just have to see who we are. All transformation begins with Accountability. We have to accept our Shadows.

When we think about dishonour, we usually think about it in terms of how we might behave towards others, or how others behave towards us. Dishonour is always about us first. We dishonour ourself whenever we blame anything for anything, because there's no fault. We're not perfect. We make mistakes. We just have to be honest about it. The 22nd Gene Key is all about human suffering. It explores the very roots of human suffering. In the Venus Sequence, which is a kind of practical extension of this 22nd Gene Key, there are six essential human wound patterns - repression, denial, shame, rejection, guilt, and separation. None of them are wrong. We manifest them a great deal in our lives. Some of us lean more strongly towards certain ones than others. That's the cosmic deal.

But they aren't wrong. They're the raw material for our transformation.

Let's take guilt for example - is it wrong to feel guilty? We're often told it is. But what if we've done something terrible? Perhaps that guilt is a natural part of our process. Perhaps it is right. The same is true of shame. We're told we need never be ashamed. Well perhaps we ought to be ashamed sometimes. Perhaps if we've harmed another person, then we ought to feel some shame. Perhaps we dishonour our nature if we don't allow ourselves to feel that shame.

Again, the point is that all feelings are journeys. Our suffering is a journey. We have to begin with the knowing that we must honour it. We must even honour dishonour at some level. The word Accountability is a funny one, because it always makes me think of little men in suits and glasses working out numbers! It's like that in a way; we have to see the numbers for what they are - just numbers. Our suffering is like that, our issues are like that; they're just what they are. Imagine if every tax year we had to do a tax return for all our transgressions. That's really taxing! We just have to be honest with our own nature. This honouring of the pattern itself is what begins the process of transformation.

The Programming Partner of the 22 is the 47 - the Shadow of Oppression, and it's all about the junk DNA and karma and stuff we bring with us when we're born - our issues, our sacred wound, our path to awakening. It either oppresses us or it frees us. It's one or the other. Are we going to do our accounts or try and duck the taxman? Will we honour the process or dishonour the wound we carry by avoiding it? It cries out over and over for our attention and our awareness. We have to learn to let it in. Just honesty - self-honesty. That's all that's needed, to not hide from the true numbers inside us, or run or shirk our own program, but face it, deal with it, be accountable for our behaviour, our feelings, our thoughts, our self-judgments. Then we have a chance of letting go of these self-judgments. It's a process of awareness, that's all. It's simple. Contemplation really helps us see these things, because it gives us the space - the pause necessary to see the issue at hand. If we don't stop and look, how will we ever see the pattern?

Let's think about this: we're in a relationship, our partner is really feeling down, and they're projecting some of their state onto us, the way we often do. We get defensive and reactive because it's an injustice. It's nothing to do with us and we know it, but still we aren't being accountable. If we knew it wasn't our stuff then we wouldn't be defensive or reactive. We would be compassionate, or at the very least we might feel a bit sad for them, but we wouldn't get tangled up in their state. It's not so easy to account for oneself, because our own issues get tangled up with the issues of others. This is the Dilemma, and this is what the Venus Sequence is about; it teaches us the practical art of emotional accountancy. Isn't that hilarious? These are my expenses, those are yours. Then we get to work out if we're making any profit, and profit is what happens when the 22nd Gift comes into play…

The 22nd Gift - Graciousness

The 22nd Gift is just fantastic. It'll save our life. It'll save anyone in any situation, anywhere. It's so beautiful and practical and simple. It's graciousness. It's something of a lost quality. For example, here in England I love watching what happens whenever I get to play the gentleman to a stranger, like opening the door for a lady or offering an elderly person my seat on the train. People often say things like 'oh I thought the age of chivalry was over', or 'how nice to meet a gentleman'! It's fun. It also happens to be the way I was brought up, but it's more than that. It's an element of graciousness, which is all about how we treat ourselves and others.

Graciousness isn't just politeness or courtesy, although it may contain both of those qualities. It's a whole cocktail of noble qualities. It's also very refined and often very subtle. It's an attitude carried in our aura and it's rooted in a deep reverence for all life. Graciousness doesn't really have anything to do with upbringing, although it can certainly be imbued from a parent or peer when we're young. Gracious people are really quite rare in the world. Have a think about it, and see if you can bring someone to mind who's truly gracious. That's someone worthy of contemplation. Graciousness stems from our ability to be accountable. When we're accountable for our own aura, our own chemistry, our own emotions, then we move in such a clean way through the world. All our accounts are settled. Our money is laundered. Ok enough, I'll stop with the money metaphors…

It takes time to get clean in that way. We have to know the patterns of our own wounding. We have to disentangle our reactions from those of others. This is what contemplation does - it gives us the space to see what's really going on around us on the emotional level.

GENE KEY 22

I want to be clear here; this is all about the emotions. The 22nd Gene Key is the great emotional valve. The great word for this gift is soul. It's the Gift of Graciousness, and it's the gift of soul. Soul is when we begin to emanate the quality of our essence. It's a refining of our emotions. At the Shadow frequency, emotions are nothing but turbulence. They buffet us around, and disturb us deeply so much of the time. We're caught in the battle between pleasure and pain.

When our Soul shines out, we even begin to let go of the need for pleasure. We become grateful for whatever life brings. That's another quality inherent in graciousness - gratitude. When we feel grateful to life, it's because we're so aware of death, and so our priorities are transformed. As we let go of pleasure, we also let go of pain. The two are inextricably linked. It's not as though they go away. They don't - their delightful musical fugue continues, but we don't shuttle desperately from one to the other. We become accepting of life and its rhythms. We are no longer a victim of the pleasure/pain cycle, so we rise up and our frequency lifts us. We feel equanimous - another lovely word. You see how many wonderful words there are hiding in this Gift. To live with equanimity is to live life lightly but at the same time deeply. It means we pay attention, and it involves having an unquenchable inner calm.

This Gene Key is special as it becomes purified. It is after all the master key in the highest teaching in all the Gene Keys - a transmission known as the Seven Seals. The 22nd Gene Key is the Seventh Seal - it contains the codes for the healing of all humanity's wounds. We can read about it in the 22nd Gene Key. Graciousness is the process of bringing grace into form. It invites grace. Graciousness doesn't exist without challenges. It thrives on challenges. Life will go on testing our graciousness. It needs to be tested so that we can refine it. How graciously do we treat ourselves? How graciously do we treat others? It doesn't mean we have to like everyone, but it does mean that we allow them to be who they are. Graciousness carries a kind of cosmic kindness inside it. When we're gracious, we often hold back from saying something that might stir others up.

Again, it's not that we become holy when we manifest graciousness. We're still as human as anyone else, but we know how to treat people. We treat them with kindness.

We don't allow our own issues to get tangled up with them. When we stop judging ourself then we'll no longer judge others. As we enter deeper into contemplation of our own issues, our agendas and our wounds, so we learn how to be gracious. We learn to be careful without being fearful, how to be warm without being overbearing, and how to be candid without being cruel. It's a balancing act is the Gift frequency. It's a transformational field in which we're steadily refined, and it's all because we learn to stop dishonouring ourselves at the very deepest level.

The 22nd Siddhi - Grace

Thus flows the font of the Divine Feminine. It's really about owning our own stuff. It's about treating oneself and others with dignity, no matter how they behave. I hope this is practical for all who're listening. I'm describing a process that we enter into when we contemplate our lives at this deep level. Whether we use the Gene Keys or not doesn't matter; we can forget all of this and just remember graciousness. It's the greatest teaching I know.

We may well be wondering 'what has all this got to do with the Divine Feminine?' The answer is that it's all about how we treat each other. There are relationship teachers out there who advocate that we express all our emotions all the time. Because we came out of an emotionally repressed generation who experienced a terrible world war, we've reacted and gone too far in the other direction. That's normal and the way of things, but the next generation will need to find the balance between clear and appropriate emotional expression and basic human decency. We don't want to be putting our emotions onto someone else all the time. It's messy. It turns into a real soup.

Graciousness leads to Grace. One more thing before we dive into Grace is that I don't want us to get the notion that graciousness is this kind of 'Breakfast at Tiffany's' thing, where we're all squeaky clean and our behaviour and elocution is all airbrushed. True graciousness can be really gritty. It can be rough around the edges. It's like this old elm floor I've just put into my house. We've been renovating, and I found this beautiful old English elm, all weathered and rough with the elements. Most people would just plane it right down and have it all perfect.

It does look beautiful like that, but we just gave it a light sanding and then put it down. You can see all the weather marks and saw marks, but it's still soft to the touch. Graciousness is like that floor - it's honest, it has a soft touch, it carries a story, with depth and humour, but it isn't perfect. It's just human.

So to Grace, what is grace? Well that can be answered in as many ways as there are stars in the night sky. Here's my spontaneous answer. I'm thinking of the poems of William Wordsworth, a famous English 18th century poet. He was essentially a nature poet and his words, like his name, carry with them the beauty of man's interaction with nature at its highest level. In many of his poems he describes moments of a kind of celestial transport where he's just swept away by some natural phenomenon - maybe it's a storm in the hills, or rowing across a lake in the dead of night and listening to the owls hooting. He calls these moments in our life 'spots of time' - moments that lift us up when we've fallen. These are moments of grace.

We all experience such spots of time. We've all felt the soft touch of grace in our lives. It's worth spending some time in our contemplation calling back those moments and luxuriating in them. They're our markers of grace. Just this morning, while running around the hills here in Devon shortly after dawn, I encountered a little bird, a goldcrest. It was just sitting on the hedgerow before me. It stopped me dead in my tracks. It's a rare little bird, a tiny thing, but with this incredible gold sash on its head. It gave me one of those magical pauses. Once it had flitted away I was off again, but I carried it with me - that little moment of grace, and now here it is embedded forever in this story, in this Gene Key.

Sometimes grace falls on us, and we can't predict when it'll occur. We can't make it happen, but we can prepare the ground through the way we deal with difficulties with graciousness. We have this term: a fall from grace. It's poignant because grace is often about how we deal with the Shadow, about how we deal with our mistakes. It all comes back to accountability. We have to deal with our falls as cleanly and openly as possible. Grace is buried in every Shadow. It almost teases us to take the leap and behave in a new way, instead of being sucked back into the old behaviours.

Sometimes grace hits a whole Gene pool, like here in the UK in 2012 when we hosted the Olympics. It was an incredible atmosphere, in which so many of our athletes did so well, winning so many gold medals. It lifted the whole country onto another plane, especially since we've never been a great sporting realm like Russia or America or China. It gave us a taste of the higher frequencies as a collective. It was a grace that occurred. You could walk through London and everyone would smile and talk openly. That might be normal where you live, but in London it's extraordinary. It was a high. Of course that's just a symbol. Grace comes as a tribute. It's a gift given to us to open us to another possibility. These moments aren't to be missed. They're to be savoured and allowed to mature inside us. They're the stepping stones for a higher life.

Grace can mean many things to many people, but it's also the same for all people. There are states of being that transcend suffering. That's the ultimate meaning of grace. Those states may one day become more readily available to us, and if and when they do, it'll likely be because something inside us mutates to allow us to receive the higher frequencies on a permanent basis. We have to change, but how and when is not in our hands. We can't even say it's for certain. But given that grace exists in the first place, it seems inevitable.

So in our lives, let our contemplation touch upon grace, on those spots of time that come every now and then. The more we pause and listen, the more grateful and gracious our spirit becomes, the more of those experiences we'll have. One day we'll just vanish, evanesce into those higher initiations spoken of in the 22nd Siddhi. I hope this Gene Key strikes a chord with you somewhere deep within. I hope you can grasp a little of what is meant by the Divine Feminine - the spirit of grace - it's practical, unpalpable, numinous, but always available to the one who loves deeply enough.

The 23rd Way

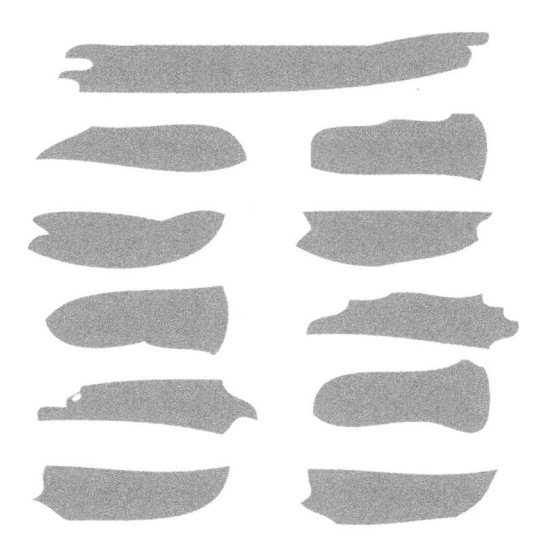

Gene Key 23

THE WAY OF SIMPLICITY

AUTHOR'S NOTE ABOUT THE 23RD GENE KEY

Because of a wonderful mistake, I have made two different versions of the 23rd Gene Key, each with a different Dilemma. The lesson from this is that the Art of Contemplation never yields a fixed formula, but is an exploration of a living transmission of wisdom. Both versions are rooted in their own Truth and compliment each other well. I have thus included both versions. I hope you enjoy this joke as much as I do.

THE 23RD GENE KEY (FIRST VERSION)

The Transformational Way of the 23rd Gene Key moves from Complexity to Quintessence, and it's the Way of Simplicity.

People talk about intelligent design - the idea that life is imbued with a consciousness, and that it can't be the result of a random set of events. Some believe that life is just too complex to have evolved naturally. Others believe only in randomness, and that there's no inherent consciousness beneath the cosmos, but I don't see the universe through any set of beliefs. I'm not a specialist. Religious people can be as specialised as scientists, and the problem with specialisation is that we only see the complexity. Until we can look at the universe with wider eyes, we just can't see the inherent simplicity of creation. To me the universe is so obviously holographic. It repeats the same universal fractal patterns over and over again, but in different iterations.

Here's a thing - most human beings don't design their lives intelligently. We don't design our lives at all. The 23rd Shadow is the Shadow of Complexity. You know what complexity is? It's someone who blunders through life reacting to event after event. We move too fast. We think

Shadow: Complexity   **Gift**: Simplicity   **Programming Partner:** Gene Key 43
Dilemma: Timing / Accumulation   **Siddhi:** Quintessense   **Codon Ring:** The Ring of Life and Death

---

so fast that we miss the obvious. By the time most people are forty, they've already made their lives so complicated that it takes the rest of their lives to get back to some kind of simplicity.

The Gene Keys are a great wisdom for the young. They encourage us to take a few breaths before we decide what we think it is we want to do in life. They encourage a contemplative outlook. With a contemplative outlook, you can consider what kind of life you'd like to live. Once you have a sense of that, you can design it for ourself. What a different kind of life that is from the life that most people lead. Most people blunder along. They meet someone, fall in love, get married, have kids, get a mortgage, get a job to pay off the mortgage, and then they're forty or fifty. And it's mostly over.

I'm not saying that any of that's wrong. I myself fall into that category, but when I was young I didn't have the Gene Keys, and I didn't know what I know now. The Shadow has a tendency to make our lives complicated. If you've studied the Venus Sequence in the Golden Path program, you'll see how I advise people to find a relationship and stay in it, to ride out the hard times, and to use them as transformative opportunities. But most of us blunder in and blunder out again, and the debris we leave behind is extraordinary - legal cases, divorce proceedings, debts, children divided and resentful for life; complexity upon complexity.

The 23rd Gene Key is one of the most topical and important Gene Keys of our modern age. If we ever wanted to make our fortune in today's world, we wouldn't have to go much further than this teaching. So this Transformational Way is going to be nothing but practical.

We have to design our life, and that takes self discipline. It takes care and thought.

We don't want to be a blunderer, or a victim of the status quo and get caught up in this Shadow. There's a fear in this Shadow of the Shadow itself.

People with the 23rd Gene Key can be haunted by their own fears. For example, the fear of a life where they're left out, locked out, abandoned, overwhelmed by chaotic forces. It's a deep irony of course, because this Shadow runs from itself and then creates those very conditions. The 23rd Gene Key wants a clean life, a simple life, and it so rarely creates that, because it never slows down enough to simply design its own life.

Think of all the so-called geniuses out there in the world - great scientists, writers, and thinkers. Look at the mess they make of their lives. That isn't genius. Not to me. Genius is simplicity. Genius is someone who thinks about the quality of their life and the lives of those around them. Have you ever noticed that the cleverest people are often the most deaf.

Think about money. Too little creates complexity, too much creates complexity, but there's a place in the middle that's just perfect. Think about water. Too little and the body is parched, too much and the body is bloated. There's a perfect balance of water in the body. If we're awake and listening, our body tells us what we need. But then someone writes an article somewhere and tells us that it's scientifically proven that we need 4 litres of water a day, and do we believe them? They're complicating our life if we listen to them. There's a simple mechanism inside us that tells us exactly how much water we need so that we don't drink too much and cause all kinds of other problems. It's the same with diet. There's a massive billion dollar industry that tells us what to eat.

Have we gone insane? Is no one listening? Drink when you're thirsty. Eat when you're hungry. Basta! as the Italians say. That's enough. And what shall I eat, you may ask? Well, how about experimenting? If we feel good eating one thing, it's good for us. If we feel bad, it isn't. Do we need any further advice?

The problem is that the 23rd Shadow takes us so far down the road of complexity, because we don't trust the simple, that we end up far, far away from who we really are. That's why people have midlife crises. Because the biological clock kicks in and says: why aren't we fulfilled? We've got to the middle, and what have we got to show for it? The thing is there's no need for big external change. What's needed is many small internal changes to get us back to the simple, the essential. This is why I say we need pauses all the time, to listen inwardly, to be present enough to hear the body.

If we eat when we're not hungry, we create complexity. The body has too much, and we have to shed that somehow to come back to balance. So live simply in the first place. The thing is that we have to design a simple life. We have to be wary of too much success. Too much of anything upsets the balance. Too much of anything creates anxiety. Lucidity of mind requires all the elements within our life must be brought into balance.

Remember this always. Complexity equals anxiety. Simplicity equals serenity. So who's better off, the billionaire or the contemplative? The 23rd Shadow brings us a powerful focus in life. Will this decision make our life more complex, or will it keep it easy? That's an art to master. The Dilemma of the 23rd Shadow is Timing. I'm going to break with tradition and talk about the Dilemma through the lens of the Gift.

The 23rd Gift - Simplicity

Timing. Life runs on rhythms. Life needs different things at different times. When we're young we need adventure. When we're middle aged we need stability and when we're old we need rest. These are generalisations - cliches even. But when we stay with the simple rhythms, generally we'll be happy. It's such a simple recipe.

It doesn't mean by the way that we can't be a billionaire. There are rare exceptions, but to be a billionaire and retain a simple life is a great challenge. Even if we buy a desert island and hide away, we'll still be haunted by what people are doing with all that money of ours. Why hide on our island? Because every one of us knows deep inside that we can only be at peace when our life is simple. Knowing that changes everything. One of the great gifts it brings is knowing how to say no with grace.

When we say no with grace, then our no always has a yes inside it. Simplicity is spaciousness, to retain spaciousness is an art. In a relationship, how do we retain spaciousness? It's not about living in different houses. It's about simplicity. It's about simple communications.

There's no need to lay our issues on the other person. Noticed how that never gets us anywhere? The simplest is to be with them in presence. Words are nice, but when emotions are high they usually lead to complexity. Emotional processing creates complexity. It is complexity. We can't fathom that chemistry. The simplest thing is presence, touch, breath, silence. Maybe music, movement, a walk. Patience. Timing. Simplicity is all about waiting. It's about timing. If we're anxious, everything we do will be off-rhythm. Everything we say will be at the wrong time, even if it's true. Everything we even think will lead towards complexity and confusion.

Here's a tip from me to get back into rhythm. It's right out of the 23rd Gift. It's the heart of simplicity and it's been used, consciously or unconsciously, by all cultures since the dawn of time. Use your hands. I know it sounds unusual but it's a deep wisdom. The hands have a transformational intelligence, and the movement of your hands must be analogue rather than digital.

Digital is a computer keyboard. The hands need to find an analogue rhythm, maybe through a tool or musical instrument or performing a simple menial task; cleaning, cooking, gardening, painting, knitting. It really doesn't matter. This is why the great sages have always gravitated towards both the arts and towards the ordinary. Because the ordinary tasks of life are performed by the hands, and when we're one with the intelligence of our hands, then we return to the vision of simplicity. Try it next time you're feeling anxious. Allow your hands to express the 23rd Gift.

The 23rd Gift is also a Gift of Synchronicity. Speaking at the right time, moving at the right time, moving in rhythm with the cosmos. It takes great intelligence to design a simple life, a handmade life. Have you ever been in someone's home and felt the quality of that life expressed through the hands of the household? You know, pictures on the walls done by the person who lives there, furniture or objects made by the person who lives there? A handmade life is a simple life, a deeply fulfilling life. The contemplative person gives themselves time for their hands to find avenues of mastery, whatever they may be.

Think of a person or people you know, or dream of one, who has a simple life. Consider the elements of that life that appeal to you, that you're secretly yearning. Redesign your life over time to fit that kind of image, and be careful of the siren call of modern culture. Play with it yes. Enjoy its technology and breakthroughs, but be careful not to become a victim of marketing. It wants you to have a complex life. It wants you to spend, spend, spend. And then you end up throwing, throwing, throwing. Be rebellious. Be simple. Be powerful. The 23rd Gift will put you through a transformational process in which you'll gradually simplify every aspect of your life, inner and outer. Your thoughts will become simple, even though they can embrace the complex; your heart will be open and simple, even though it will be compassionate towards the difficulties of others.

And in time, everyone will come to you because you have the one thing they seek the most....simplicity, the greatest of the lost arts...

THE 23RD SIDDHI - QUINTESSENCE

We've seen the practical side of this Gene Key, now let's have a look deeper into its mystical heart. The Gift is the creative field and the Siddhi is where that field emerges from, as well as where it's pointed.

I love words. Here's a beautiful one - Quintessence. It means the essence within the essence. It's a fractal word - it actually means the essence within the essence within the essence and on into infinity. Everything has an essence. Everything is a doorway to the same universal essence. We all have a Quintessence. It's the very soul of who we are, the holographic heart of who we are. For millennia, mankind has sought the Quintessence. We've sought it through science, religion, music, the arts, nature, and each other. We seek it in the eyes of our lover, we sense it in the quiet heartbeat of a sleeping child, sometimes out in the wilderness, we may shout it out from the rooftops of the world.

The Quintessence is everywhere. It's in everything. It's the heartbeat of consciousness. In all our legends and myths, we see the symbol of the Quintessence. It's the hidden treasure, the gold, the pearl, the elixir vitae. One of my favourites is the Chintamani, from Hindu and Buddhist mythology. The Chintamani is the wish-fulfilling jewel, a sacred object that grants anything to the one who finds it. In the western traditions, it's the Holy Grail. The word Chintamani carries over this idea of the preciousness of the hands. The root word 'mani' means jewel, but it also means transformation and is the same root for the modern word for hands. We even see it in the word 'manipulate'. The Chintamani is a symbol meaning that the jewel of life is in our hands. We can take that literally and metaphorically.

When you watch a Japanese tea master preparing tea, you'll feel the jewels that lie in your hands. Our hands are what allowed us to evolve further...as we came down from the trees our hands became free to discover their deepest potential. As we unlocked our true intelligence, so our brain development echoed our hands. So the hands point the way to our Quintessence, but they also are our Quintessence.

Always seek the Quintessence. In our body the Quintessence is the navel. The sparkling pearl, the fractal seed out of which our life grows. And think about time...the universe contains the Quintessence in every moment, so the Quintessence of time is the pause, the moment where we come fully into the present, the eternal now. And think about language. The Quintessence of language is silence. The pauses between the letters and words, the gaps between the atoms. And think about relationships. The Quintessence of our relationships is love. The space into which we merge. The more we dwell in the Quintessence, the more simple life becomes, and the more we stay with the essential.

The 23rd Siddhi is a reminder. Stay with the simple. To express the simple, come into tune with the universal rhythm of life. Before acting, always contemplate the Quintessence. What is the Quintessence of this choice? Where does it come from inside? Is it from the heart of my being, my belly? And let your hands show you the way in life. Your hands are wiser than your head. Your hands dance with your Quintessence. What will your hands leave behind when you're gone? What will you have made from the living clay of this earth? What kind of life will you lead?

When you move from your Quintessence, soon you'll feel it instantly in your belly, and in everything, you'll choose from that place. You'll choose your life from the pause. So fall in love with the pauses in your life. Learn to drift. Learn to love life through your hands. Give time for your hands to shape and express the beauty of your essence. Caress life. Release life. Let it slip through your fingers with a smile. Reach out and touch the world around you. Touch the hearts of those around you. Touch the trees. Touch the creatures of our world. Touch your own body. Stroke your wounded heart back to life.

Hold your palms together in gratitude for this Quintessence. This Ring of Life and Death, for the Quintessence of life is death. And the Quintessence of death? It is Life. What kind of life will you lead?

The 23rd Gene Key (2nd version)

The Shadow: Complexity

The Dilemma: Accumulation

The Transformational Way of the 23rd Gene Key moves from Complexity to Quintessence and it's the path of Simplicity.

If there is any Gene Key that is more practically useful to us in the time we are living through in history right now, it has to be this 23rd Gene Key. It contains some very practical insights for us all. It's fascinating to me how certain Gene Keys have such a contemporary ring to them and this Shadow of Complexity is certainly one of them. Our world has become so complex. It has certainly improved from where it was, but it's also got so complex. The systems we have created, the structures, the way we govern, our economic models, it has all got away from us. What we have lost is the simple and the sustainable.

The Dilemma of this Shadow is Accumulation. It's a word that can be used in many dimensions - we accumulate stuff, we accumulate opinions and beliefs and we accumulate worries. Above all, we accumulate the inessential to the loss of the essential. This is why so many people have lost their way inwardly. It's why a whole generation is coming into the world without a real sense of deep purpose. Technology stimulates, but it doesn't supply purpose, and sooner or later you will have a lot of people getting to their midlife and just crashing. It's not possible to be fulfilled in life without a sense of higher purpose. That's what these Gene Keys are all about. That's why they are here now - because this wisdom will be needed more and more as we move into this new Information Age.

Our education is all about accumulation - of facts, figures, theories, memories. There is rarely anything of deep practical use - like learning how to cultivate vegetables and cook good, clean food. All these children are pouring into the world without knowing the names of the trees around them or their various uses. The simple things have been passed over. You might know how to write a string of html code, but what about how to make rope or darn cloth? And what about even more essential things, like how to treat each other with respect? In the complex world, relationships have become a joke. We all seek the perfect partner, but when we find them we can't hold onto the relationship. We don't know how to. We have lost touch with the essential values of life - deep intimacy, family, community, fellowship.

The 23rd Shadow is driving us like lemmings over the edge of a precipice. And what about us on an individual level? What does this Shadow teach each of us? Well for one thing, to watch out for our tendency towards the complex. I am not saying that we can't enjoy the benefits of the modern world. I'm not an anti-shopper! I love shopping. It can be great fun. But accumulation has become the norm, and so much so that we now see words like 'frugal' as a negative trait. The lesson of the 23rd Gene Key is therefore simple, as it should be - we must accumulate the essential, the higher, the beautiful and the practical. If you are entering into a deep contemplation of this Gene Key, then you should make an inventory of your whole inner and outer life - your beliefs about yourself, about what you are capable of, the places where you have compromised, the opinions you have taken on from your parents, or that you have adopted in reaction to your parents. And we must look at the stuff around us. Do we use it? Does it inspire us? Those are the only 2 questions we need ask.

Think about decisions. Every decision we make in life either makes our life simpler or more complex. Every string of words we speak either makes our life easier or harder. When we treat someone with disrespect, we instantly make our life more complex. If we complain or moan about something, we put out an energy that returns to us. We reinforce our own self belief that we are a victim of something and we accumulate karma. We get hooked into these self-repeating, self-defeating patterns and we simply accrue more karma. This is what karma means - it's the term the Ancients used for accumulation. So we must ask ourself: is our life sticky?, or do we move through our days like a knife slicing through butter? How much stuff - emotions, fears and sickness from other people do we take on? How much sticks to us?

You see how easily we make our lives more complex? It's a disease that runs riot into every corner of our being. In the original I Ching, the old translation of this 23rd hexagram was 'slicing off'. Isn't that beautiful? Slicing off. And its symbol was a knife.

It doesn't take a lot to figure out what this Gene Key is all about. We must cut the ties that bind us. The ties do not come from others. They come from inside us, and it is we who must cut them. If our relationship seems to be failing us, it is our mind that is probably wrong. It is our thinking. We have to simplify the whole of our life to begin to see clearly again who we truly are. Complexity comes from the mind. Thus we have to go to the root cause to deal with this Shadow, and that is where the Gift comes in.

The 23rd Gift - Simplicity

Now let's allow our contemplation of this Gene Key to be transformed into action. There are Gene Keys that are about seeing, and there are Gene Keys that are about doing. This one is both. So here is a challenge: look around your house and find something inessential. Find something that is neither beautiful nor of any real use to you. Then either give it away or throw it away. You have made a good start. Now do the same thing internally. Look at an aspect of your current life situation that is causing you discomfort. Is the way you are approaching that doing you any good? Is it inspiring you to a creative solution, or is it getting you down? So throw out the old mindset and put your mind to finding a creative way into it. Let the very thing that is upsetting you or worrying you be the thing that empowers you.

It takes more energy to turn an issue around than to let it go. We have to upcycle it. We raise our frequency in relation to it. But we will get a lot more energy back from it once we've thrown out our old way of seeing. And in doing this, we are harnessing the secret of free energy. Out of the Shadow that looked so lifeless and depressing, we have found and unleashed a torrent of creative energy. That is simplicity in action. Simplicity is more than just an external way - it is a an all-encompassing mindset, it is an alchemical habit. Everything simplicity touches turns to gold.

This is the beauty and the joy of slicing off - of the 23rd Gift. We slice away the Shadow patterns and we prune the deadwood off, and beneath them we discover the young green shoots of the essential. And the essential is love. It is creativity for a higher purpose. It's all about being aligned with our higher purpose. The moment we begin to tread the path of higher purpose, everything becomes simpler. Life works in harmony with us. And we can apply this to anything. In business, we prune away the inessential and the inefficient. We remove the complex. We stop over-accumulating. It's one of those funny things we do. Sometimes things are growing really well, and then we try and make them expand even more, even though they are big enough. And then we make our lives more complicated again.

It's like in business - a business doesn't need to go on expanding. Some businesses just work best staying at a certain level and they provide a valuable service and enough funds to feed a certain amount of people. If it's working, why interfere? We have become obsessed with expansion, with needing more and more. It is assumed that the purpose of every business is to go on expanding. But that is mad! It's not sustainable. We've lost touch with knowing when we have enough. A small successful business is just that, a small successful business. The headache of that becoming a big business is usually not worth going through. Our life will become so complex. Our relationships may pay the price, our family life will suffer, our time with our children will diminish. We will worry more. Why then do we do it?

Because we have lost touch with the beauty of simplicity. If we have the Gift of Simplicity in our life then we are blessed. We will be fulfilled. We will be much happier more often because we have our priorities right. Simplicity cuts out worry. It enables us to breathe. It enables us to see life clearly. We don't need all this stuff. We don't need it. So let's cultivate a love of simplicity in our life and we will find our joyousness increasing, our sense of freedom growing, our relationships thriving and our bank balance right where it needs to be. No more, no less. And because life is life, it always has its cycles. There will be spontaneous windfalls, and there will be more spartan years, but that is all just the ebb and flow of fate. Simplicity thrives anywhere, regardless of external conditions. It thrives because it is rooted in the essential, in love, in freedom and in the creative human spirit that can turn any situation to its advantage through seeing it simply and behaving accordingly.

The 23rd Siddhi - Quintessence

Now we come to the nub of the matter. Quintessence. A wonderful, wonderful word. It is about the fifth element, the alchemical, mystical substance that turns everything to gold; the elixir of immortality, the panacea of divine wisdom. Whatever culture we come from there are these legends of this mysterious substance; chi, prana, vibuthi, ether… and it is always said to have the magical property of something or other… I love these old legends. And of course they are allegorical - I am not wanting to dismiss magic - because anything is possible - but for my purposes, these legends are allegorical. The fifth element is your true perception. It is clear seeing. The 23rd Gene Key is allied to the 43rd Gene Key, which is the Siddhi of Epiphany. Epiphany and Quintessence - what an exquisite pairing of words! Alchemy, like homoeopathy, goes on distilling and distilling down truth. The 23rd Gene Key is a chef's Gene Key - it's about reduction. It's about sauce.

You make a really good sauce by adding the perfect amount and variety of ingredients and then you reduce it and reduce it. It's the same with whisky. You crush the barley into flour and add water, then you let it ferment and then you put it in a still and distill it. At the end you get an essence, a Quintessence. It's even called the spirit. Everything has a spirit - an unnamed and unnameable Quintessence. Every human being you meet has this inner quality that they radiate. It depends upon your frequency how potently your Quintessence can be felt. Around an awakened being, it is so tangible you can reach out and touch it. You can almost smell it.

So we come from complexity to Quintessence. Life is the distillery. We are the grain. We have to be bashed until we open and release our hearts and our Gifts, and then those Gifts are further refined until they become so pure that they reflect the eternal principle at their core. The motto of this Siddhi is Solve et Coagula, a Latin term from alchemy that refers to the breaking down of elements in order that they can be synthesised at a higher level. This is of course what the Gene Keys are all about. It is what life is all about. My little daughter asked me this morning: 'Daddy, why does life exist?' I didn't answer her directly because we all have to live that question our whole lives, but if I had answered her, I might have said 'Solve et Coagula'.

The amino acids in our bodies are the elements that make us who we are. They are the building blocks. And as we evolve, so we rebuild our chemistry. We have to pull apart the old version first - this hexagram is also known as 'splitting apart' - and then those amino acids can be recombined at higher frequencies. They are the same patterns, the same codons, but activated at a higher frequency, so new hormone combinations are synthesised in the brain. And these chemicals, occurring naturally inside us, allow us to see life as it is, without the lens of our past, as eternally fresh and eternally new.

So I'll tell you what I think this Siddhi is about. It's about smashing things down and rebuilding them so that their true inner beauty can shine forth. It's about exposing the Shadow but not in a negative light - it's about showing people that behind the Shadow lies the light. It's about finding the beauty in ugliness. It's about seeing life in a new and creative way. When we look at the world and all its complexity, if we look only through our mind, we will probably think: how can we ever fix this? We've made such a mess. We'd have to smash it all down in some horrendous apocalyptic event and then begin again. But the 23rd Siddhi sees further than that - it knows that the Quintessence actually lies hidden in the problem, and that just by showing it to people, just by showing them their higher purpose, their Quintessence, the world can be once again made simple and beautiful.

If we take our biggest Shadow that we are currently struggling with and we look deeply into it, we will see that it isn't really a Shadow at all. It's just the way we were seeing it. When we look into the heart of the issue, we will always find something numinous. We will discover an opportunity for radiance in there. This is how we can make art out of ugliness and how we can transform squalor into a garden. We can make the wasted and broken aware of its own spirit and beauty once again. We humans can do absolutely anything. But first we have to find this Quintessence inside - this effulgent, otherworldly beauty, this perfume, this sauce, this celestial aroma emanating from the cooking pot of our being. That is what a Siddhi is - it's an emanation, a distillation of all that is pure and good and worthy and noble. It's the Quintessence, a sizzling, mercurial, scintillating sarabande of consciousness, a steamy dance that brings all the separate parts into a unified, humming whole.

The 24th Way

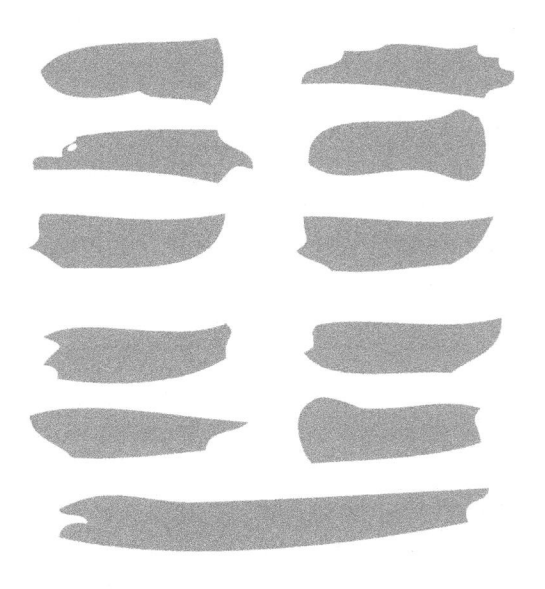

Gene Key 24

THE WAY OF INVENTION

The Transformational Way of the 24th Gene Key moves from Addiction to Silence, and it's the Way of Invention.

The 24th Shadow has great weight inside us. It affects every human being alive. No one escapes the Shadow of Addiction. There are many expressions of addiction, the most commonly acknowledged being drugs, alcohol and substances. Also we know that addictive patterns can include eating, gambling, working, even sex. We don't often look right into the eye of our addictive patterns. It's also not so often that we really see where they spring from, but we're all addicted to something.

Addiction is really misidentification. We identify with the form of the world. Because of the suffering inside, whether we feel it as grief, numbness, boredom, angst, frustration, loneliness, or any other deeply uncomfortable state, we'd like to avoid feeling that state. So we find a pattern of behaviour that temporarily suspends the discomfort. We begin to rely on that pattern so that when we feel the pain come back, and it's usually unconscious, we drop right back into the pattern. Of course it doesn't really take away the pain. It just delays it. It conceals it, distracts us from it, and only ever for a while. Can we see the Dilemma of this Shadow? It's Gravity. That may sound odd, but it actually is the weight of the world. It's the weight of being in a body.

There are two forces in life - the force of gravity, which holds us down, and the force of levity, which lifts us up. We're caught in the middle of this dance between these forces. Gravitational patterns trap us, they cause us to breathe less deeply and contract, and our mind gets fixated and depressed, our systems become rigid and overstressed. They make us feel bad about ourselves, because deep down we know we're avoiding something. They create more heaviness. Levitational patterns (if I may invent a new word) lift us, elevate

Shadow: Addiction **Gift:** Invention **Programming Partner:** Gene Key 44
Dilemma: Gravity **Siddhi:** Silence **Codon Ring:** The Ring of Life and Death

---

us, clarify our thinking and give us hope. Levity gives us a sense of freedom, of vitality, of life. It lifts us beyond what we can see and opens our hearts and souls to a greater vision of what's possible in life. It gives us a sense of purpose.

Our lives are played out in the field of these two patterns. One pulling us down, the other raising us up. It's like a Shakespeare play watching our lives sometimes, as we soar high one moment only to plummet the next. We all know the huge effort it takes to pull ourselves back up once we've fallen. There are so many stories we tell ourselves when we succumb to the force of gravity and fall victim to an addictive pattern. We lie to ourselves in so many ways, and then of course we have guilt, shame, depression, regret, rage and all the feelings that come along for the ride. It's really something being a human.

I think the secret of working with this Shadow, and indeed of being human is just to be honest with ourself. In the well known Twelve Step Program, this is always Step 1 - admitting where we are. Interestingly, Step 2 is about invoking a higher power to bring assistance. Perhaps the best advice here is to really see the deep nature of the Shadow of Addiction in our life. We must look into our everyday patterns. We must put on a pair of glasses that only sees addictive tendencies and train them on ourself. We'll soon find the addictive patterns. What do we do to prevent ourselves from enjoying pauses? What do we do that causes us to miss out on the finer things of life?

When we've seen such things in our life, when we've seen where we cave in to the weight of gravity, then we can go to the Siddhi. The Siddhi reminds us of the true purpose of life. The Siddhi, (and it can be any of the 64 Siddhis in the Gene Keys), is the levity, as the Shadow is the gravity. The beauty of the Siddhi is that it's out of our hands. We can only call upon its power. We can only pray for it, meditate on it or dream about it, but this is enough. We have to remind ourself of the other extreme and put our trust and faith in it. Then we watch and wait and listen and maybe pray. This is all contemplation.

We contemplate the gravity of the Shadow, the beauty and freedom of the Siddhi, and let the Gift come into play. And it will. It will emerge all on its own. Let's take a look at how that works.

The 24th Gift - Invention

Invention is wonderful. Invention is nothing but creativity. The Gift is all about creativity. It's our contemplation sprinting into action. It's effervescent. It's surprising. It's exciting. It's the only thing that has enough oomph, that has enough gravitas, enough chi, to suck us out of the gravity and draw us into the light. It's elegant this whole notion of the trinity. The Shadow, Gift, Siddhi. The elegance is that we have to take a leap of faith and reach out, and then the greater being at the other end of the tunnel reaches out in turn, and we pass through the tunnel into the light.

It's interesting when we consider the Twelve Step Program that's used by AA, because that program does exactly what I'm describing here. Anyone who's ever worked with the Program will recognise what I'm talking about. It's an archetypal, universal process, this transformation. That's why these are called the 64 Transformational Ways. Each Way has a different angle and language, but they're essentially the same. The 24th Gene Key was originally called 'The Return' or 'Returning'. It's about going back to the roots in order to change the pattern. We return to the essential. We examine both where we've begun and where we've reached.

This Gift can be a huge turning point for us if we allow it to be. There's an old Chinese proverb, and it goes:

> *Sow a thought, reap an action; sow an action, reap a habit.*
> *Sow a habit, reap a character; sow a character, reap a destiny.*

Once we've done our Shadow examination and identified an addictive pattern in our nature that drags us down, rather than pulls us up, I want to invite us to sow a thought. Think about this pattern and how we might reinvent it. This is the Gift of Invention. Let something completely new bubble up. What else might we do with this energy? How can we use it to lift us up? We needn't rush to find the answer. Let the answer emerge out of the Siddhi of Silence. Give it time to emerge. This is the art of contemplation we're learning here in the Gene Keys. The soil of contemplation is time. Invention isn't something we do. It's something that happens, that wells up from the unknown.

When that thought does come through, let it reap an action. Let that action be something new, something fresh, something that we might not have done before in that stuck or frustrated state. Then sow that action, and let its roots go deep. If the action has come from the Siddhi, then the action has deep roots, and the next time we're facing the same moment of challenge, the action will happen again. It will reap a habit. This new habit will lift us rather than sink us. We're now transferring the addictive pattern from gravity to levity. In time, the habit will become part of who we are. In fact it won't so much be a habit as a custom. Habits are enforced, whereas customs are followed, so I prefer the word custom here. It's more gentle. This healthy, beautiful custom will become a part of our character. Of course, the finale is that such a custom, rooted as it is in deep selfless love and surrender, rooted in Grace, will reap a brand new destiny.

This is how invention works. This is what invention means. It's not inventiveness. That's different. Inventiveness is a knack, a trait, a skill even. Invention is a mystery. It comes from the Siddhi, and it will reshape our life from the inside out. But first we must be listening. We must be willing to see the Shadow simply for what it is, not something to be avoided, but compost, the most beautiful rich compost for a higher destiny and a higher purpose - our higher purpose.

The 24th Siddhi - Silence

When we arrive at the Siddhi I often have mixed feelings. Sometimes I feel excited because I'm going to venture into the unknown, the unknowable, so I feel anticipation about that. At other times I feel, well, a bit nervous if I'm honest. The question I ask myself sometimes is, 'what right do I have to talk about such a thing? Have I known it in its entirety?' The answer is no but another answer is that I know it if I let myself know it.

What is Silence? How can I speak about Silence? What an absurd predicament. What do I know about Silence? I know that it is a treasure beyond all others. I know that it sparkles with life, like the stars. I know that it's not empty as we might imagine, but pregnant like the cosmos. I know that Silence is not golden but silver, like the jewels of the deep feminine sea. Often we think of Silence as empty. There is such a thing as an empty silence, invented by man, and it's digital silence. Think about that. We've invented an entropic silence, a numb silence. Digital silence is soundless, lifeless, vacuous, but true Silence isn't like that. The Silence of space is alive with light, pulsing light, frequency, wave upon wave of hidden lustre.

Yes true Silence is alive. Let's consider the void. When we think about the Buddhist concept of the void, of emptiness, it feels terrifying to the mind. But that's only the mind's deep fear of annihilation, and that fear is an illusion. There's no such thing. There's only eternity. There can be only eternity. Therefore the fear of annihilation is illogical. Eternity ensures that one thing merely transforms into another. It can never be lost. This is our fear of death. It's hard to find a person who admits that they're afraid of death, but it's only because we won't admit it to ourself. If we had no trace of this fear, we would be a Christ, a Buddha, we'd be a fully embodied Divinity. It's because we harbour this fear beneath all others that we're not that pure awakened one. Any fear we have is really this core fear of annihilation masquerading as something else. It's ok. Fear is safe. Fear is a part of our journey.

It's just that not all our cells have remembered eternity yet. So we harbour fear. But when we let it out, and in, and through, then it transmutes. We transmute some more of those cells. It's just that eternity is such a huge concept for our minds to embrace, and we live in a pretty godless world. We're constantly imprinted by the materialistic worldview. Most of our respected leaders and influential thinkers are materialists, scientists, thinkers, rather than lovers and ecstatics of the great mystery. All this propaganda surrounds us with the feeling that the world is unsafe.

Even the way we behave around death is not really open. We try and fight it off as long as possible. We don't embrace it. We don't celebrate it. It's something we fear. The 24th Gene Key is paired with the 44th Gene Key, which is a magical one. It's about a great Divine Plan where all human lives are part of a great beautiful tapestry, like the Bayeux Tapestry, and collectively all our lives unfold this wonderfully rich story of evolution. In that story we're all approaching the Godhead in our different ways and guises. The Silence is what we keep dipping in and out of. We incarnate from the Silence and, then we excarnate back into the same silent pool. Each time we're refreshed, renewed, and we come back to play another role, and there's a continuity to our roles. The more sensitive and surrendered we become, the more we feel this continuity in our lives and in those around us.

The 24th Gene Key is part of the Ring of Life and Death. Each Gene Key in this Codon Ring answers all the great questions about the universe. The 24th Gene Key, especially with its Siddhi of Silence, is called 'Returning' for a very good reason! We keep returning into form, until we've polished our souls so they shine resplendent. The greater we shine, the closer we come to the end of our particular storyline. At the end of our part, we hand in all our costumes and return to the great source - the Silence from whence we came, and have our time of rest. We also graduate from this plane, this earth plane with its field of gravity. Levity makes it impossible for us to return. Our evolution, such as it is, continues in another form, a form that now knows the timeless truth.

Something has emerged from the Silence, you never know what will come. I hope you've enjoyed the story, and found this particular Gene Key practical as well. Blessings.

The 25th Way

Gene Key 25

THE WAY OF ACCEPTANCE

The 25th Transformational Way goes from Constriction to Universal Love, and it's the Way of Acceptance.

There are certain Gene Keys which occupy a central seat in the genetic code and story of evolution. This 25th Gene Key is one of those. It's a hub Gene Key. We might even say it's the hub Gene Key. Its theme is love. It's the very breath of love. It's also about lack of love and the journey to rediscover and remember love.

It's interesting when we look at a young child, particularly one in their first 3 years, that we don't really get a sense of the Sacred Wound at all. By the Sacred Wound, I mean the germ of suffering that every human being brings into the world. The 25th Shadow is the Shadow of Constriction and the Dilemma of Anxiety. But the young child seems so unconstricted and they appear to have no anxiety. Do we learn it then? How do we become anxious?

We each carry anxiety. We might be aware of it or we might not. But it's there. It's behind the facade. If we close our eyes and are still for a couple of hours, we'll soon touch the anxiety. It doesn't have to manifest as worry, although it often does. Anxiety is a vibration in the cells. It's the vibration of fear. It comes with our sense of mortality. The young child doesn't really know what death is for themselves. They may witness loss through death but they don't yet realise that they will die because they don't have enough sense of 'I'. The anxiety seems to be connected to a sense of 'I', what some call the ego, which I find a confusing term. As we develop a sense of separateness, anxiety begins to tremble inside us, but it isn't learned. It's innate, and it was there all along. It's even there in the young child. It's simply dormant as a code, biding its time. This is the Dilemma of Anxiety - we can't prevent it. We can't relax enough to make it go away. It's a part of our constriction.

Shadow: Constriction **Gift**: Acceptance **Programming Partner**: Gene Key 46
Dilemma: Anxiety **Siddhi**: Universal Love **Codon Ring**: The Ring of Humanity

Angstzustand

The Shadow of Constriction is connected to two primary things - our breath and our thinking. This is why the great meditation traditions train us to follow the breath. If we do that for twenty years and we're lucky, then one day we'll have a breakthrough, and realise that we can exist without thought. Only a certain kind of person will enter a path like that, and what about the rest of us? Is there no hope?

Well, the first step of all transformation is always the same - as Gurdjieff put it, 'realise that you are in prison', or as Buddha said, 'all life is suffering', or some such thing. We're constricted by our mortality, our biological equipment. We've evolved differently from animals. They have fear but they don't have anxiety because they don't have enough self-awareness. Yet anxiety is also the very vibration that inspires the quest for higher knowledge, so we need to get to know it. The biggest Dilemma with anxiety is that we can't think our way out of it. Mental knowledge isn't enough. No amount of psychoanalysis is going to be enough. We have to contact the vibration directly.

In the Golden Path, we talk a great deal about the path of contemplation. At a certain level in the Path, like in the heart of our Venus Sequence, we get to contemplate our anxiety! We carry this sacred wound as a constriction deep in our being. Once we stop trying to run from it (which may take lifetimes), then we have to turn in towards it. It won't kill us. It's there anyway. The moment we bring our awareness into the body, then strangely enough it seems to dissipate, and our breath is the key. How many breaths do we take each day? You might be surprised, about 17,000! How many of those are we aware of? This is the power of contemplation. It brings pauses into our day and slows us down, not necessarily in our outer life, but in our deep rhythms. It brings us into a stately rhythm. It allows more awareness into the day, and that's how we meet anxiety, with awareness.

There's nothing wrong with constriction. It's the starting point of our grand journey. The body is a constriction for awareness. One day our awareness breaks free from the body, connects us into the fundamental patterns of the universe, and that's the Way of Acceptance.

The 25th Gift - Acceptance

A central aspect of Contemplation is coming to terms with our life as it is. This is simple, but paradoxically, not always as easy as it sounds. I break it down into 3 phases - Allow, Accept, and Embrace. The 25th Gift is all about this process.

First we have to allow. Allowing is very spacious. We allow ourself to be a certain way, to feel a certain way. We don't have to accept it or like it. Allowing is the very first breath of awareness. It's the very act of turning within, which is why it's the first stage in contemplation. Allowing also has an additional component; openness. We're saying, 'I'm open for the possibility of breakthrough. I have no idea what that means or looks like, but I'm suffering, and it may not be ok, but at least I'm acknowledging it'.

Allowing is very powerful because it begins with the physical. Whatever we're experiencing in life, however hard, we bring our awareness to our physicality, to the sensations and discomfort in our body. Never mind about our feelings or our thoughts. They'll come later. We begin with the physical. We just allow our body to feel what it feels. There's a kind of odd comfort in the simplicity of that. The body is uncomplicated in that way. After a while we'll feel ourself slowing down and our breath will deepen. Allowing is just staying with the body. Another powerful way of allowing is to do something physical with the body, like running, or exercise, or something with our hands. All these kinds of things can bring our awareness away from the mind and back into the physical cells.

The next layer is acceptance, and it's also this 25th Gift. Acceptance is when we make full contact with our feelings. Once our breath has settled a bit, and we've regained some Core Stability, then we can feel our feelings without being overwhelmed. Emotions are chemical. Once the chemistry is bearable, then we'll feel some space opening around our feelings.

We may weep, or feel numb or angry or afraid, but now at least we're in touch with how we feel. Our awareness can wrap around those feelings. Acceptance happens as we remember our heart. Our heart reminds us that everything is ok. Even in the midst of pain, everything is still ok, at a deeper level. This is when we begin to trust again. With acceptance there's always hope, not blind emotional hope, just the hope of life. Life is hope, life is optimism. Acceptance allows the possibility that transformation may occur.

Allow, accept, and embrace. It's all the process of acceptance. I'm just breaking down the process behind the word. Embrace is when the third component comes in the mind. Allow is of the physical body, accept is of the emotional realm, and embrace is of the mental level. As the heart opens to our experience, so the mind finally lets go. The mind is the chief problem. When the body is filled with anxiety, then the mind runs amok. It's like a mad factory manager trying to keep all the machines from overheating, and in the end he just gives up. The embrace is where the magic happens, embracing pain requires a full and deep capacity to breathe. Now the breath is falling deeply into our belly; we can handle life. No matter how intense our feelings, with an open heart, we can ignite our own transformation.

It's important to discriminate here between embracing something and resignation. When we're resigned, it's a dropping of our head, a yielding to the Shadow without the awareness of the Siddhi. The Gift always straddles both ends of the spectrum. Acceptance is between constriction and love. Resignation is surrendering to the constriction. Many people make this mistake in their Shadow work, and cave in on themselves. They forget there's something higher in their nature. We see people like this everywhere. They've lost hope. They believe that things can never change, never get better. This is a false kind of acceptance. True acceptance is done with our head held high, with a deep breath of courage, almost with a kind of defiance. We turn to the Shadow and say, 'yes I see you, but I don't have to believe in you. You're just the beginning.' Without turning from the Shadow, we open our heart to more.

One of the hardest things for humans to accept is the beauty of life. We rush headlong past it everyday. Without time for pauses and the right attitude, we never break out of the constricted, addictive mindset. The contemplative life allows us time for beauty.

It allows some of the wildness back into our soul. The world has become so tame. Our technology, for all its gifts, is so tame. It's making us docile.

Some years ago, I lived for a year in Maui, Hawaii. It's a place of paradise, heaven on earth. There aren't even any nasty creatures there. The whole place is just so soft, so yielding. You can step naked into the forest and walk on ripe mangoes! I went to a few parties, and found all these people taking drugs like marijuana and ecstasy. I have nothing against those things, but if there's one place we don't need them, it's Hawaii! My point is that it's hard for us to let the beauty of the world in unless we can also accept the suffering inside us. We have to be bold. We have to be inner warriors. We have to breathe, and let the beauty in. And yes, as Kahlil Gibran says, 'love will shatter your dreams and lay you waste, like the North wind', but what a way to go! Love opens us up to higher and higher vistas. It smashes our preconceptions. It shakes the mind to its foundations.

I want to give you something practical. Look at your day through the lens of acceptance. It's an amazing spiritual practise. Look at the things you don't allow to be the way they are. You know, a slow car in front of you when you're in a hurry, a person that irritates you, a rain shower just at the wrong moment, whatever it is, just try allowing it. Surround your day in allowing. You'll have to slow down, because you can't do it otherwise. It means your day will taste very different. It'll be imbued with a new awareness.

The 25th Siddhi - Universal Love

It's funny what happens when we turn our awareness inwards and enter into a period of deep contemplation. With the Gene Keys we contemplate the codes of life inside our cells. When we go deep enough, we get to see that our DNA really contains revelations. It connects us to these Siddhis. Deep within us, within the infinitesimal folds of our physicality lies the possibility for our transcendence. We can never be alone. Our DNA prohibits that. It contains the history of our species as a holographic memory and also, like a seed, contains the holographic imprint of what we could one day become. We can access that seed, that memory imprint. It's readily available for those who turn within. All my insights have come from that place.

Our spiritual evolution drives us to either deny or accept the wounds we carry. There are no other options. It's all a matter of time. We can tread water, we can distract ourself, but eventually it needs to be addressed. The human heart is the most obvious way in. Can we accept life through our heart? Can we learn to contemplate with our heart?

This Siddhi describes the shift from the personal to the universal. Most of us think of love as a personal connection between people or between us and something outside us. The feeling of love bridges that distance bringing us closer into unison. Universal Love lies in another dimensional field. It's the connective tissue that holds together everything. This is why we call it God. It's love. This isn't just anthropomorphising either. It really does have a quality of unifying. When we're on the path towards Realisation, we have to let go of the personal dimension. The personal dimension still retains a certain quality, but we can no longer say that we love someone or something more than anything else.

It's a big mystery this leap from the Gift to the Siddhi. I'm not sure what it takes. It seems to just happen on its own accord as we go on opening and softening our hearts. It's beautiful really, because here we can only achieve through the feminine approach. We can't will our heart to open that much. Our acceptance and our embracing becomes pure surrender. We just bow to life. A friend of mine once showed me how the classic position of prayer, on our knees with our hands clasped together, is actually the only position in which we can remain upright when we're unconscious! It's the same in the Muslim version, except there we collapse completely. These postures were probably discovered by ecstatics as they surrendered all trace of their ego and were then copied by others.

All that love locked away in our DNA. The DNA is just filtering it through the memory - the ancestral memory. This is the embracing of the collective wound. It's the passage to Christhood or Buddhahood. We can't 'get' there. We just have to go on opening, accepting and the path leads us there of its own accord. Even so it's important to always bear the Siddhi in mind.

It's our natural state. It has a certain flavour, a certain peacefulness, universal love, unconditional love. It's not the fiery love of the ecstatic. It's not the Divine Passion. It's after all that has burned away. It's what's left over. It's a deep knowing that emanates from our cells, the knowing that we are one. It transcends and includes personal love. It's the background radiation for all our experiences. Life emerges out of and falls into this love.

It's intriguing that this 25th Gene Key is part of the Codon Ring called the Ring of Humanity, because at its highest level, the 25th Gene Key feels rather inhuman, at least as we know it. This Siddhi concerns the future of humanity, a new kind of human being, a human that knows it's universal, that's moved away from the personal dimension. That would be/will be a very different kind of planet. I don't think it's easy for us to imagine that.

GENE KEY 25

The 25th Siddhi is also one of the Seven Sacred Seals, a mystical group of Gene Keys whose collective role is to heal the Sacred Wound within humanity. The 25th Gene Siddhi is the 3rd Seal, and it heals the human wound of shame. You know, Adam and Eve in the garden covering themselves up. We believe ourselves unworthy at such a deep level, and we've built a civilisation based around that. The manifestation of our unworthiness is greed and selfishness. We're always trying to fill this void we feel inside. One day, when we no longer feel it, we'll no longer be selfish. We'll follow our higher purpose to serve the whole in some way. Our reward will come from service, from philanthropy. This is why the 25th Gene Key always has a strong connection to money. You know how constricting money, or the lack of it can be? Well, the 25th Siddhi has plans. It sees a world without money. It sees a world where giving is the only currency. It knows that's what's coming one day. One fine day.

THE 64 WAYS

The 26th Way

Gene Key 26

THE WAY OF ARTFULNESS

The Transformational Way of the 26th Gene Key moves from Pride to Invisibility, and it's the Way of Artfulness.

The Dilemma of the 26th Shadow is Lack. This is its worldview. It doesn't believe in abundance at a fundamental level. Remember that these Shadows govern huge swathes of the population. So at least a billion people around the world subscribe to this viewpoint. Ironically many of them will be in affluent countries. Almost all of the extremely wealthy are on this list. When we believe that there are never enough resources to go around, we're always in survival mode at a deep unconscious level.

To go with this worldview, the 26th Gene Key is clever. Notice I'm not using the word 'intelligent' here, but clever. Intelligence denotes awareness and realises that a certain degree of altruism is essential for evolution. The 26 however is one of the great 'takers' - a perfect consumer. The cleverness of the 26 is what gives it its pride, its sense of inner self satisfaction. It draws this satisfaction from always finding a bargain. If there's a way to get something cheaper, the 26 will find it. If there's a way to pass the buck, the 26 will do it. If there's a way to shirk blame or responsibility, the 26 is there.

Now there's nothing wrong with saving energy. Saving energy or money is an essential component of an abundant worldview - it's the basis of sustainability. But the 26th Shadow takes shortcuts where there are no shortcuts; it sweeps things under the carpet rather than deal with them. It can edit its own conscience with surprising alacrity. Often the 26th Shadow does these things unconsciously. It doesn't even see that by taking from one place, we're taking from the whole. We can't out-swindle life. Karma will get us in the end.

Shadow: Pride **Gift**: Artfulness **Programming Partner**: Gene Key 45
Dilemma: Lack **Siddhi**: Invisibility **Codon Ring**: The Ring of Light

---

As I said, there's nothing wrong with a bargain, but we need to understand that in life we get what we pay for. This is a universal law. If we underpay someone for a product for example, then somewhere someone has paid the price for that. We may say, well what can I do about that? Right there we have the 26. The 26's all around this globe, and the field created by this fear of Lack, is what creates the attitude that it's someone else's problem. However, when the 26th Gene Key decides to use its cleverness in the service of the whole instead of for depleting the whole, then its whole life and worldview will change. This is what happens at the Gift level.

In relationships the 26th Shadow is the same. It can outsmart us. It can turn a situation around inside its head and make it feel as though it's our fault. It'll do anything to retain its sense of pride and being right. For a 26th Gene Key to admit it's wrong is a big deal. If we have this Gene Key, we can be obsessively defensive in our relationships. When we prove (at least to ourself) that we're right, we're always making someone else wrong. Again, it's the culture of lack we're propagating. There's a certain ruthlessness to this Shadow. In fact, all Shadows have this same ruthlessness in different degrees. At least the 26th Gene Key is openly ruthless! The problem, the Dilemma with this Shadow, is that it can never feel inwardly prosperous. Wherever it goes, whatever it does, however successful it is materially, it will always feel the lack on the inside. Life has this hollowness, this deep-seated fear.

The fear that drives the 26th Shadow is an ancient one that comes from our survivalist roots. It's a deep ancestral fear of not having enough, and that's why it's developed strategies for taking rather than giving. But it's based on a false economy, because if we take from others (directly or indirectly), then those others can no longer support the whole.

The whole continues to founder and can't thrive, thus continuing the cycle of lack. The pride of the 26th that it can survive is a false, self-serving pride. I know this all sounds very dark and depressing. If we look at the world, this is what we see in different degrees. What we need is an entirely new worldview based on giving, philanthropy, and mutual service. Products need to be valued properly according to the time and resources that go into creating them. Professions need to be valued in the same way. In Japan for example, the highest paid person in a traditional community is the teacher. Nowadays, the teachers are one of the lowest paid sectors. The whole world has gone topsy-turvy because of this bargain-culture that we've created. And let's be honest, it's not really about giving the consumers a bargain. It's about making more for ourselves.

The 26 will blame the system, or those at the top of the hierarchy, but they will then use that same hierarchy to get ahead of others. The 26 is thus riddled with hypocrisy. If we have the 26th Gene Key, we need to really do some soul-searching to see where we're living from this sense of lack. We must look into our relationships, finances, diet, everything. Where are we deceiving ourself? People buy cheap food, but then they spend their money on a new tv and say they haven't got enough for high quality food. People will pay more for a bottle of hair conditioner than a Gene Keys course, and still they complain! Our principles have become completely bent and twisted by the 26th Gene Key and its ability to con itself and others. Whoever we are, reading or listening to this, and whether we have this Gene Key in our Profile or not, we can look honestly at our life through the lens of this Shadow. A new level of honesty in our life can utterly change everything and open up a whole new level of possibility for us in health, love, wealth, and all aspects of our life.

The 26th Gift - Artfulness

We can see how this Gene Key is adept at a certain kind of sneakiness. As I said, it's all about what and who that sneakiness is serving. It can after all be put to good use. I love watching the sneakiness in my kids. One of them will come and ask me if they can watch tv early in the morning and I'll say no (sometimes). They'll go and ask their mother, and she doesn't know I've said no, and maybe she says yes. These are the common tricks we learn as kids to get the things we want.

We may think that's harmless, and I'm with you, but there's also a level of dishonesty that's seeded in that. As a parent I do my best to model honesty wherever I can, because I know a small seed can grow in time into something bigger.

That cunning, that shrewdness can be wonderful when put to good use. This is what the 26th Gift is about - the Gift of Artfulness. It's the ability to turn lack into an advantage, not just for oneself, but for all. The 26th Gift is a fast-thinker. It's a 'can-do' Gift. It's likely to exaggerate, so if we have this Gift we need to be careful. The Programming Partner of the 26 is the 45th Gift of Synergy, which is all about working cooperatively. The 26 has to weigh something carefully before it makes a promise, otherwise all those elements that create synergy will collapse into chaos.

I had a wonderful experience of the Gift of Artfulness when I was in Greece in the refugee camp at Idomeni. I went there to bring what help I could in the time of crisis when 12,000 people were all crammed into this makeshift camp on the border of Macedonia. The situation was terrible - you can't imagine - whole families with old women and kids and pregnant women crammed into tiny torn tents, with precious little food, sanitation, with storms and mud and wind. Many of them were also exhausted and in shock from having come right out of the jaws of war.

Anyway, there were so many cultures there - Afghans, Palestinians, Syrians, Africans… they all naturally tended to gather together in their ethnic groups. We were a small team trying to improve the conditions of their shelter, repairing tents, taking around polythene to help cover people from the rain. We got to see how these different cultures were, and one group really stood out - the Kurds. Most people were huddling in their tents waiting for help, doing their best to keep alive, but the Kurds were resourceful and artful. They had sent out groups scouring the local area, and built themselves little spaces from the materials they'd scavenged, encircling their tents with a fire at the centre and shelters around. They had a few musical instruments with them, and were cooking big stews and sharing them. They were playing music to keep up their spirits.

It was a lesson in Artfulness - in how to make the best of a bad situation. Through years of persecution, this was a craft they'd learned - how to use the power of synergy to serve the wider community. I also learned at Idomeni that cultures where there's obvious lack are more generous than cultures where there's an overabundance of resources. These people were happy to share their meagre food with us. They would always invite us to join them around their fires and talk and share food.

The skills that make up the Gift of Artfulness can be put into service to help people, to bring more abundance wherever there's a lack. This is the entire purpose of this Gene Key - to redistribute resources - to give as opposed to take. If we have this Gift, we might like to consider this in light of our whole life. Will we be remembered as a giver or a taker? I don't mean be remembered by other people, I mean by cosmic intelligence, by the Lords of Karma. That's the most worthy contemplation we can do, along with what's our highest potential. The 26 can do anything they put their mind and heart and will to - that's what makes them so impossible at the Shadow frequency. So let's ask ourselves - what's the most we could do to really create positive and lasting change on this planet during this lifetime?

THE 26TH SIDDHI - INVISIBILITY

The 26th Siddhi takes this Gift of Artfulness the whole way. The pride of the ego of the Shadow is perfected in the Siddhi. It's the same energy, but polished to become a shining gem - a jewel put into the service of all that is. Isn't that a beautiful symmetry? This Gene Key is the most magical of all Gene Keys. It's part of the Codon family called the Ring of Light. You know how illusionists use light to trick us into thinking we've seen one thing, and then we see another?

This is the Siddhi of Invisibility. To create vast ripples of awakening, to influence all life to thrive, without anyone even seeing us while we do it. That is Divine Pride. Only us and the gods know what we've done. That's the kind of pride we're allowed to feel towards ourself. Don't be thinking this is for the future. This we can begin right now, whoever we are. The smallest, most insignificant act of selflessness reaches out into the cosmos with tendrils of light that touch the far corners of reality. This is the power of invisible change. We can change the entire cosmos, but only through the selfless act, the selfless thought, the selfless word. It takes time, one of the other partners in the Ring of Light is the 5th Gene Key, which is Patience and Timelessness. In this, time is unimportant; hundreds of years are nothing to this Siddhi.

The hexagram representing this Gene Key is called 'The Taming Power of the Great'. It's about changing the whole universe, and we all have the power to do that. We have all the powers of the cosmos at our fingertips. Think about this 26th Gene Key - we know its great gift is to find the most efficient way of having the greatest impact. That's quite a Siddhi, but it comes from a higher place beyond space and time. The Siddhis emerge from the eternal, boundless Truth. They know that the most efficient way to change the cosmos is to change that which is right in front of us now. That's how we tame the cosmic forces.

There are forces in the universe that are literally waiting for us to engage them. There are vast forces for good, forces of Grace. Great changes are made up of many, many tiny changes, invisible changes. The 26th Siddhi begins with the invisible. The invisible is indivisible. The invisible is infinite. God is invisible. We can't see the whole without becoming the whole. How can the part know the whole unless it surrenders its tiny identity into the ocean? The Siddhi of Invisibility operates in the world without others realising. It has gone far beyond the notion of reward. Its reward is its utter surrender into the benevolence of the One. We all should think about this Siddhi. We all should contemplate it. I hardly ever use the word 'should', but here I am. There are things that need to be said.

Consider how to be an invisible force for good. Contemplate that. How to avoid the limelight? How to use our magician's tricks to have the light fall on someone else, someone that needs it. Then smile secretly to yourself. You did this. No one will ever know it but you and the Lords of Karma. This is the most beautiful of Siddhis. It often plays out through the masters - we don't understand their behaviour. We don't see past the tricks they use, but the true master has his or her own reasons for doing or saying things.

GENE KEY 26

Contemplate Divine Pride. Breathe the breath of the Buddhas into your heart. See yourself as immense. See yourself as a God, moving behind the scenes, orchestrating goodness, love. Make yourself invisible. Don the cloak of Invisibility. Even the smallest selfless acts are magical acts. Go out into the world and make a difference. Make this lifetime really matter. Let it shine our light out into the aeons, influencing the past and the future. Become the Magus. The Magus is a figure who spans the past and the future. He or she is beyond time and space, beyond past and future. The Magus is eternal, omnipresent. The Magus is within each of us, invisible, waiting, waiting, just waiting…

THE 64 WAYS

The 27th Way

Gene Key 27

THE WAY OF ALTRUISM

The Transformational Way of the 27th Gene Key moves from Selfishness to Selflessness, and it's the Way of Altruism.

What is the nature of selfishness? What does it mean to be selfish, and how do we strike the balance between what's right and good for ourselves, and what's right and good for others? This is the Dilemma of this Shadow - the Dilemma of consideration. The difference between the Shadow and Gift in this Gene Key - selfishness and altruism, lies in this single word - consideration. When we're in survival mode, it's not so easy to consider others. The pain and restlessness inside doesn't leave much room for others. This Shadow is about being stuck in a tight room, in a tight little life, with a tight frame of mind.

Many of us would like to give more. We'd like to consider others but we don't have enough for ourselves yet. That's how the thinking goes. When I have enough then I'll be able to help others. That's how people see philanthropy, as a luxury only for the very wealthy, but there are many forms of giving and this Gene Key is all about giving. Selfishness in and of itself is not bad. To look after ourself first is vital. How can we give to others if we don't nurture ourself first? It's more about how and why we give. The question we have to ask ourself is, 'how can I best serve my higher purpose in this situation?' That's the golden question. It's not 'how can I best serve myself?' Those two questions often yield very different answers.

Selfishness derives from ignorance. That's the truth. Ignorance is circumstantial, environmental. It's nurture, not nature. This isn't to say that the moment we have an education we stop being selfish. But when we're brought up in a sensitive way, in an environment of care where love is in abundance, then we tend to grow up with a sense of higher purpose, and that's when selfishness is transcended.

Shadow: Selfishness　　　　**Gift:** Altruism　　　　**Programming Partner:** Gene Key 28
Dilemma: Consideration　　**Siddhi:** Selflessness　　**Codon Ring:** The Ring of Life and Death

---

This whole notion of higher purpose is deeply connected to the theme of selfishness. The Programming Partner of the 27th Gene Key is the 28th Gene Key with its Shadow of Purposelessness. If we grow up without a real sense of a deeper purpose to life, then we'll tend towards selfishness. We can see this manifested in the modern Western culture. Because our religious structures are in decline, we've become more self-centred. Religions always gave us some sense of higher purpose, albeit in a pretty unhealthy way. Religions tell us what higher purpose is instead of letting us find out for ourselves. Some of the most selfish people have profited from religion through the ages, and are still profiting.

The great social disease of today is the lack of a higher purpose. When people feel that lack, they'll do anything to distract themselves. Traditionally, we always went to war, but now we tend to go shopping. The 27th Shadow can be allayed through epigenetic means, in other words, we can stop society being selfish when we bring up our children in an atmosphere of love. By love I don't mean coddling love, I mean that every young child has a sweet, open heart which needs to be continuously nurtured through the values of philanthropy. This is not imposed by the parent, but nurtured. One of the great themes of the 27th Gene Key is the raising of children, and creating a healthy emotional, social, and spiritual atmosphere for them to evolve. Unfortunately, young children are now put under such pressure. Many are in school from the age of four, and this pressure is also there in the social fabric of the home. The modern child is groomed as a consumer, who learns more about taking than giving. As a father myself, I know the detrimental effects of this model. I fight against it every day!

We come into the world unselfish, but we're schooled in selfishness because of the way we've built our society. We need to learn consideration - to consider the feelings of others.

We need to realise that we're connected to everything and everyone on this wonderful planet. A selfish act harms the whole, which therefore harms ourselves. This is the moral message coming from the heart of this Gene Key, but it doesn't come as an imposition. As we shall see, it wells up from inside the human heart, from the very fabric of our DNA.

The 27th Gift - Altruism

Altruism is human nature. If there's any quality that defines the true human being, it's altruism. The Gift of Altruism is equivalent to how deeply we can feel our higher purpose in life. This is of course the central theme of the Gene Keys - how to unlock our higher purpose. When we do unlock it, and it rises up naturally within us, then it always, always has an altruistic ring to it. Since we don't really have a society that encourages it, how do we know and discover what our higher purpose is? The answer is that we must look at the reasons we're unhappy. We must go into the Shadow. This is why so many modern people are searching for something, because it's so lacking in our civilisation. It's such an interesting turning point for humanity. Our external religious structures are falling away, and for the first time we have a very real opportunity to learn to walk without being told how to.

The modern search for truth is a very good thing. It's uncomfortable to admit that one is selfish, but it's also freeing. Selfishness leads to lack of purpose and vice versa, so that when we do finally wake up, a whole new world opens up to us. A life dedicated to something higher? Wow, actually that sounds good, doesn't it? That sounds fulfilling. For the first time we start to consider the feelings of others and the impact of our actions on the world, the environment, and the creatures we share the planet with. Once we begin to feel our higher purpose and unlock that deep wisdom, that open heart, that cellular certainty that there's more to life, then our radiance emerges, our health improves. We begin to glow with the aura of our altruism.

There's no tonic in the world like unconditional giving. There's no power in heaven and earth greater than generosity. Most people think that we need to have a lot in order to give it away, but externally we can have nothing and be the most generous person alive.

Generosity is about how we spend our most precious commodity of all - our time. How do we spend our time? When we give of our heart freely to others, then strangely enough we create more time. Joyousness actually makes time expand. Selfishness makes time contract. A selfish day will pass so quickly because we're not breathing. An altruistic, open-hearted day will move rhythmically, like a great river flowing through the open plains, bringing nourishment to all beings.

The 27th Gift has many insights for us. It's a profound and magical Gene Key. The most important Gift it brings is this unselfish attitude that comes from knowing the connectedness of all life. If we have the 27th Gene Key, or feel mysteriously drawn to it, then we're fortunate. We're a carer, a planetary healer. Healing is the core of this Gene Key.

We heal through our higher purpose, and we heal the planet through our collective higher purpose. Humanity is unique because we alone can destroy our planet, and we alone can heal it. There's a huge global movement towards sustainability, towards a way of life that's rooted in higher values and ethics. Even in the cut-throat world of business, the ultimate domain of selfishness, the idea of social responsibility is flowing everywhere. A new dawn is approaching for humanity, and the 27th Gift is at the heart of the matter.

We all need to get on this wave and ride it. We all need to find our higher purpose. We need to locate its vibration inside us and let it radiate within the cells of our being. we need to let it flow into all our relationships, and then into our work and our actions. We'll instantly begin to prosper. Giving releases the currents of healing. It heals us, and it heals the whole. Giving of ourself out of the joy of our own heart, out of the generosity of our inner being - that's true power. That's what will move mountains. Make no mistake about the power of this Gene Key - it will transform our world.

Out of the 27th Gift we need to create a new global structure. Every Gift has vast creative power. The Siddhi is the being and the Gift is the becoming. They're intimately connected. We shouldn't think of them as separate. Neither should we think of the Siddhi as coming after the Gift. It's the essence of the Gift. The Gift is the Siddhi in action. Through our altruism we'll create a different world for our children. We need a new monetary system based on philanthropy rather than profit. We need a new educational system that considers the whole child rather than being mind-centric. We need new systems of governance that are based on virtue rather than accomplishment. We need to put our energy into finding new technology that can help us create a far more sustainable culture with clean energy that doesn't desecrate our beautiful planet.

The 27th Gift of Altruism is gradually awakening in humanity. It's one of our greatest Gifts. One day we'll see the logic of this altruistic approach and the madness of the selfish approach. In the meantime, it's up to us individuals and groups of like-minded, open hearted souls to help as many people as we can to find their higher purpose in life, because that's what will finally make the difference.

The 27th Siddhi - Selflessness

The 27th Siddhi has two sides to it - one utterly ordinary and one that comes right out of a science fiction book. There have always been stories of great healers among us. The most widely known is of course Jesus, whose many gifts of miraculous healing are well known. The 27th Siddhi is the domain of so-called miraculous healing. When we understand the true nature of life, some of these things don't seem so unusual or unlikely. Our current biological awareness is really quite rudimentary.

Sometimes when I come to these Siddhis, I imagine more advanced races on other planets, or even our own race far in the future. I also track backwards into our past. It wasn't so long ago that we were still in the trees. So armed with that, what might we look like in the next stage of our evolution?

DNA had to mutate in order for the ape to become human. Given the chance and enough time, DNA will mutate again. When it does, one of the first things it will do I imagine, is create a new awareness operating system. The current system experiences itself as separate, so it's no wonder we've been a selfish species. That's how we feel. What if our next awareness is to continuously feel our interconnectivity with all other creatures, even with the inanimate? We can barely imagine that. It means that the life force would flow through us in a totally new way. We would be like the Jedi knights in Star Wars, who feel the force flowing through us. It's a sharp intuition that one.

That kind of awareness would eliminate a sense of self, a sense of separateness. A selfless awareness is beyond our current comprehension but we can feel its truth within our hearts. We feel it when we love and experience rushes of inspiration or ecstasy. It's an orgasmic sensation - to let go of one's self. We all do that as we come closer to death, which is the greatest reminder of our true heritage. We come with no self, and we leave with no self. This 'self' in the middle is an illusion.

Let's get back to Jesus. Is it possible for instantaneous healing to occur? Can a blind man suddenly see? Can a mental illness suddenly be made whole? When we read the 22nd Gene Key and look into the mystical structure of the subtle dimensions that make up the true human being, we might see that anything is possible. The selfless human being is a cosmic being. He or she has access to dimensions that we have little or no awareness of. The very existence of the universe is proof of the existence of infinity, which means that anything is possible. Even today, anything is possible. We needn't assume that science fiction is for the future. Possibility always lies in the domain of the now. So, yes, spontaneous DNA replication is more than certain to exist. As our species mutates, it's likely that the speed and efficiency of the healing mechanisms inside us will expand exponentially.

The 27th Siddhi represents the possibilities of spontaneous healing not just within the human life form, but in all life forms. A mutation in human DNA presupposes a whole string of interconnected mutations throughout the chain of life. If we change, the whole of Gaia changes with us. Perhaps we can see now why the Gift of Altruism precipitates the beginning of such a change. It's not something we can impose from the outside, but a quality that must emerge organically from the inside, and as it does, it'll begin to allow our DNA to mutate and uncover its higher functioning.

This brings us to the ordinary side of the 27th Siddhi. If we want to experience the science fiction version of ourselves, we have to be nicer to each other. That's the simple truth. It's what Jesus said after all. It's what all the sages and saints have said all along.

We have the capacity to be a race of saints - not the puritanical, squeaky clean version, but the rich, orgasmic, selfless kind of saints. We haven't seen so many of those recently. Perhaps that's because they're so ordinary they may pass unnoticed. Selflessness isn't interested in itself! Isn't that funny. It only wishes to serve the whole, and to follow its natural orgasmic impulse to give, to love, and to live in communion with others. When we find ourself contemplating this Gene Key, remember this amazing journey we're all on - selfishness, to altruism, to Selflessness. We come with everything, we leave with everything, we live for everything.

THE 64 WAYS

The 28th Way

Gene Key 28

THE WAY OF TOTALITY

The Transformational Way of the 28th Gene Key moves from Purposelessness to Immortality, and it's the Way of Totality.

Purposelessness has many dimensions to it. It's a manifestation of the great Dilemma of the 28th Gene Key, and therefore it's embedded in all human beings, the Dilemma of Avoidance. We've been avoiding the deepest fear, the fear of death, the meeting with our mortality. The first dimension within this Shadow is the fear of living – this is the repressed side. When we look around the world today, we see great swathes of the population caught in avoidance of the Shadow. We can't live fully without embracing the Shadow.

The great religions have had a lot to do with the suppression of the Shadow consciousness, and they've had a great deal to do with our avoidance of it. This leads to the notion of a hollow life. This may seem cruel and yet it's true. Most people on this planet are either a victim of circumstance (i.e. poverty, disease, war), or in more developed countries they're a victim of the system, and the system includes all institutions that create homogenisation. On a collective level the notion of life purpose only really comes alive when our life is no longer concerned with survival. As the 28th Gene Key reads, 'Survival gives you a powerful purpose'. This Shadow operates in different dimensions depending on our culture, geography, and social status.

The next layer of this Shadow inside us is the fear of dying, which is when it hits us that our life is unfulfilled. This classically comes at around midlife, when men realise their libido is subtly declining, and women, as or before they enter menopause. Sometime after 40, death begins to creep into our consciousness. The fear of dying can create a sudden reaction inside us, a depression, an affair, a divorce, a typical midlife crisis. It usually comes as a kind of unconscious panic that wells up inside. It leads to all kinds of colourful

Shadow: Purposelessness   **Gift:** Totality   **Programming Partner:** Gene Key 27
Dilemma: Avoidance   **Siddhi:** Immortality   **Codon Ring:** The Ring of Illusion

---

crises! This is the risk-taking element of purposelessness. It doesn't just happen to us when we're 40 either, some of us embody the reactive side of this Shadow our whole lives, and many end up dead, in some kind of institution, or at the very least spread across the tabloids! This reactive pattern is also rooted in a deep unconscious fear of mortality, so at this frequency we still remain a victim of the fear. Whether we internalise a fear in our body or externalise a fear through our actions, we're still a victim of it until we see it face to face.

I love the word Avoidance. It's a void dance. We are simply dancing around in a void until we confront our deepest fear of death. I've always been amazed when I hear someone tell me they have no fear of death or dying. It only takes a second to verify if this is true! If it is, I'll be standing before someone so incredibly radiant and surrendered, they're setting the world on fire with their presence. We have to realise that this fear of the void is unconscious. It's buried in the low frequency bands of our DNA. It's a memory code rooted in an older part of our brains. Yet when we raise the frequency field of our aura, suddenly it's no longer there. The body is not afraid to die. Only fear is afraid to die. For most of us, this is a state that we cycle back and forth, in and out of. It's an infuriating business is awakening! However, over time as awareness of our own avoidance becomes more and more acute and refined, we begin to stabilise at a higher frequency, and that's when we begin for the first time to live a higher frequency life.

So if we have this Gene Key in our Profile, or if we are contemplating it, then we should know that this Shadow will set us a tough curriculum - to root out and explore fear. Our life will invite us to explore some deep fears, but we needn't let this make us anxious. Fear is simply a vibration, a frequency that emerges from the chemistry of the body. When we change the chemistry, we change the fear. One of the simplest ways of overcoming deep-seated fear is through loving touch. We simply hold ourself, or we have someone we trust stroke our belly softly. The body recognises love as the antidote to fear, and the beauty of touch is that it bypasses the mind. The other antidote to fear is breath. As we breathe more deeply, over time the fear will subside. Breath brings awareness, and awareness is the great softener - it melts the fear. So let's give ourself these two gifts - regular loving touch and deep breath with awareness.

The 28th Gift - Totality

Joseph Campbell, the great mythologist once said: 'I don't believe people are looking for the meaning of life as much as they're looking for the experience of being alive'. What a beautiful way to capture the essence of the 28th Gift of Totality. We know that every Gene Key represents a kind of human genius, and this 28th Gift displays a genius for being alive, and I mean really being alive. Here's another quote by another genius, Henry Thoreau: 'I went into the woods because I wanted to live deliberately. I wanted to live deep and suck out all the marrow of life... to put to rout all that was not life; and not, when I came to die, discover that I had not lived.'

This is an expression of the kind of genius that emerges through this 28th Gene Key – the path of living life to the hilt, of living totally, holding nothing back. It's here at the Gift level that we finally begin to realise the power of Avoidance. The third phase of this fear is the fear of not living, which is subtly different from the fear of dying. These are the three layers of fear in this Shadow - the fear of living, then the fear of dying and now the fear of not living. The fear of not living is the healthier fear that only comes in when we move through the first two fears! It arises as a pressure inside us and activates a higher evolutionary current that begins the process of awakening. Now we begin to really consider our purpose in life, and we begin to convert the potential energy of the Shadow into the kinetic energy of the Gift, and we become a creative being. There's nothing like purposelessness to give an edge to life. We begin to use purposelessness, turn it to our advantage and transform it into creativity.

It's a great mystical chestnut; this question of the purpose of one's life. We all, sooner or later, want to know what our purpose is. There are so many people out there selling us our life purpose. It may appear to an outsider that the Gene Keys and the Prime Gifts are all about Purpose, since it uses that language. Yet anyone who's moving deeper inside these teachings will tell you that wanting to know the purpose of our life is simply a phase. It actually gets in the way of living, as Joseph Campbell says. What we really want is to experience being alive. There must therefore come a point in our evolution when we let go of mentally needing to know our purpose, and begin to move into the actual living of it.

What the higher reaches of this 28th Gift show us is that true purpose or fulfilment always contains an aspect of service. This is why the Programming Partner of this Gift is the 27th Gift of Altruism. We only really feel fulfilled when we're truly being of service, and that means we become a role model of what it means to be authentic, of what it means to be truly human. It's not about being in a service profession, or even a service role, it's about serving our higher purpose, which is the purpose of the whole. This is when the magic of the 28th Gift kicks in. We begin to live a great life, a life that embraces all seasons, all moods, the whole spectrum.

This 28th Shadow can be deliciously dark. It's a realm populated by all the demons and the dark archetypes that stalk the collective unconscious. This is why many people with this 28th Gene Key in their Profile will find their destiny is drawn into the darker side of human nature. It is here that we have to really meet the dark archetypes and ultimately learn to know them as aspects of our own psyche. Our life becomes romantic, either in a dark or light sense, but we realise ourself at some level as an actor or actress with a rich script before us, and our Totality calls us to play our part to the hilt. Whatever our role; lover, villain, emperor, janitor, it's our plotline, and when we give ourself to it totally, we'll see that it's mythic in origin. This means that we will feel life calling out the hero or heroine inside us. The mythic is even played out on a mundane level, but only when we give ourself totally to the drama. This is the beautiful metaphor of drama, and it's why we are so drawn to it, because it contains the codes of transformation. All drama has transformation woven into it, and that transformation always moves into higher and higher frequencies as the dark nature reveals its hidden light.

Yes, I feel I could talk for a long time about this 28th Gene Key – so rich it is, and so pivotal in our unconscious. It shows us the truth about life, that it can only be understood when it's lived totally, without judgment, without flinching, without hesitation, just trusting in the rush of knowing that our destiny is perfect, exactly as it is right now.

The 28th Siddhi — Immortality

Now here's a word right out of mythology – Immortality. In all mythology, we have stories of immortal beings, of gods and goddesses. For millennia we humans have worshipped them. Even the one God, whether it's the Christian or Moslem or any other version, is known as immortal. Here's the duality - because our bodies die and are mortal, we can only conceive of their opposite, an immortal life beyond our own. Yet what a trick nature has played on us poor humans! This 28th Gene Key is part of the Ring of Illusion, a pair of codings which veil our perception of the whole. Our awakening is an encounter with the nature of these veils.

We humans see from within the confines of our time processing brains. We have no idea whatsoever of what Immortality looks like. Here's the truth - it is in front of us and we just can't see it until we see it. Immortality is to be found only in the present moment. That's the great mystery. Deep inside each of us is a presence that transcends our physical, emotional, and mental form. That presence cannot die. You cannot die. I cannot die. Doesn't that give you goosebumps? Yet the human journey is a metaphor that has grown up around this presence. Have you ever been to a great play? Like a Shakespeare play? One of those incredible tragedies? Romeo and Juliet, or Othello, the kind where this scintillating drama is played out and in the end everyone dies, well, all the really interesting characters? At the end, there's this moment of silence before the curtain falls, and in that moment you're still there, just absorbing it all? And then, imagine everyone leaving, all the actors, players, audience, stage hands, and you remain in your seat. Gradually silence descends as the cleaners finally leave, the lights go out and the door is locked. You alone are still there, sitting before the silent, empty stage? That is Immortality. That's the 28th Siddhi. It's there all along, it's there when we begin our life, it's there as we grow, learn, fall, rise up, fail, laugh, weep, and meditate. It's there when we die. It's there after we die. The only purpose of life is to reveal this presence to itself. It's there all the way through the Transformational journey from the Shadow to the Siddhi. It simply watches, listens, and breathes. It's our essence. It's beyond life and death. It's beyond time and space. It's beyond all drama, it's even beyond love.

The 28th Siddhi does however awaken through drama, through totality. It demands fully embodied human beings. If we're miserable but totally miserable, the 28th Siddhi may still awaken inside us. If we're ecstatic totally, the 28th Siddhi may awaken inside us. If we go out into our life and look death squarely in the face and learn to know fear as an illusion, then the 28th Siddhi will reveal itself inside us. It doesn't matter what our life looks like from the outside. It only matters that we play our part, the part that belongs only to us, and we play it willingly and with an ever deepening sense of trust that life always, always knows best.

I'll finish this Gene Key with something out of science fiction - inside our body lies a great secret - mystically speaking, it's found in the 2nd line of the 28th Gene Key. These lines are the coding patterns of all creation. In the original I Ching this line was represented by an old tree putting forth new roots or an old man taking a young wife. It represents a place within our DNA that will one day switch on a gene sequence that causes the body and its systems to replenish themselves. I said it was out of science fiction! The Siddhi is always about the fruit, so it always contains the seed of the future, and we have this potential for an immortal physical body. Of course physical immortality has been a theme embedded in all our great myths and stories - it's the central motiv of the most ancient stories we know - the epic of Gilgamesh. Myths always contain the codes of life.

But we needn't get too excited yet. This is a secret that will only be unlocked through the very highest frequencies of Grace. It is beyond our striving. The most we can do is quietly trust that it's there and that one day the secret will be revealed. The beauty is that immortality is guaranteed anyway, whether we are in a physical body or not. Consciousness does not need locality in order to experience immortality. Immortality is simply the air consciousness breathes. It's not even unusual. All you can say is that it simply is.

THE 29TH WAY

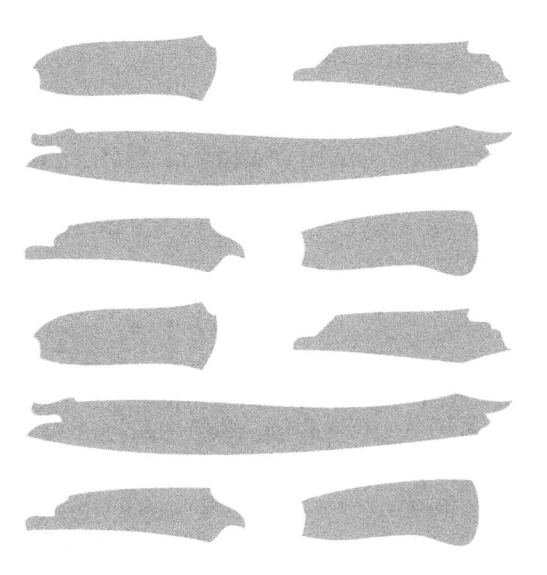

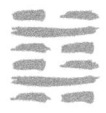

Gene Key 29

THE WAY OF COMMITMENT

The Transformational Way of the 29th Gene Key moves from Half-heartedness to Devotion, and it's the Way of Commitment.

This Gene Key is about the power of commitment. Postponement is when we have a mental idea or expectation about ourself or our life, and if life doesn't appear to be moving in the direction of that mental construct, then our energy withdraws from the present moment. This is the Dilemma of the 29th Shadow. It's about the use of energy and our life force. The withdrawal of life force can happen in a number of ways, depending on our character and conditioning.

If we're a repressive type of person, then most likely we'll postpone our own dreams out of fear of letting someone else down or out of an addictive pattern. We just go on doing something that hurts us (emotionally, physically or mentally), because we don't know how to stop. We get locked into a pattern, a life choice, a relationship, a career, whatever it is, and become a victim of our own choice. Perhaps we put our own heart on hold for another. We're a mouse in one of those spinning wheels. If we're more of a reactive type, the chances are we'll quit what we had begun or not even begin it. Either way, the Shadow, Half-heartedness, means we don't take the plunge into true commitment, the great fear of this Shadow. It's funny how some people who're afraid of commitment often lead such over-committed lives!

True commitment can only be to one thing, the present moment. I know that sounds mystical, but it's actually very profound. Life is all about making decisions, small and big decisions. It's about staying true to the cycles that come from those decisions. The ancient Chinese referred to this Gene Key as The Abysmal. It's of deep relevance to us all; the bottom line is we don't know where our decisions are going to lead.

Shadow: Half-heartedness   **Gift**: Commitment   **Programming Partner:** Gene Key 30
Dilemma: Postponment   **Siddhi**: Devotion   **Codon Ring:** The Ring of Union

---

The 29th Shadow is not happy about that! We have to listen to the Yes inside ourselves, and trust in it above all else. When we say yes to something, we embark on a journey of surrender, especially in relationships. Half-heartedness is when we're not honest with ourselves and others, and that's when our life force withdraws. We postpone our life, because we're not living it fully. We're trying to run ahead in our minds, and we're missing the moment. True commitment involves a deep trust in where we are right now. It involves a turning inwards, a slowing down inside. We don't postpone our life, hopping about on the surface. It's now. We can only be a genius now.

This 29th Shadow has much of the world in its thrall, and it robs us of our true joie de vivre. So many relationships end before they've finished their natural cycles, and much of the wisdom of the world is missed because people don't know when to stop doing something that's hurting them. This 29th Shadow is about the fear of commitment. Whatever we embark upon in life, what is the point of holding anything back? Yet this Shadow will have us hold some part of ourself back, and then we postpone our true destiny, which is to give of ourself completely, without expectation. Oh yes, how deeply we fear the abyss, and what a tragedy it is that we miss the magic, while we go on postponing the only thing in life that's essential, our presence in every moment.

THE 29TH GIFT - COMMITMENT

We've seen how this 29th Shadow has great collective power, we're each geniuses, and genius always breaks new ground. Life is dangerous and risky when viewed from the mind only. This Gift frequency is about living life from the heart, which means risk is inherent. This is what makes it fun, and its Programming Partner is lightness. If we have this Gene Key in our profile, one of our greatest lessons in life is to give ourself totally to every experience. This is the Gift of Commitment. People use that word a lot. I think many of us don't fully understand it. As I've already said, there's only one true commitment, and it's not to the future. How can we commit honestly to the future? It's not here. Our energy is not available to respond to it now, so how can we be authentic? We can only know the truth in the now.

Commitment flies in the face of social expectations and morality. Commitment has its own wild morality. When our energy says YES to something or someone, it's showing its readiness to engage in a cycle of learning and evolution. That doesn't mean we have to jump right into the abyss straight away! There are inner cycles, particularly of desires. When the 29th Gift makes a clear decision, it doesn't make an emotional decision, or an excited or nervous decision. It makes a decision from a place of profound and quiet inner certainty.

This Gene Key has a certain genius, and it's a funny kind of genius. It's about making luck. It's true. When we aren't drawn into emotional or desire decisions, then we create the conditions for good fortune. We have an inbuilt barometer for where good fortune lies. We have no idea how it works or when it will come, we just know that life is our greatest ally, and our life force knows when something is right. This is a genius that extends itself naturally into an innate understanding of all relationships and their possible dynamics. Once we're free from the postponement trip, we see how deeply it disturbs all relationships. This naturally makes us want to help others, not through interfering, but through direct and heartfelt reflection, coming from our own natural, non-judgmental and rather amoral wisdom! So much of the genius of this Gene Key is about letting go of expectations. We are all on a mystery ride. We may think a decision will lead in one direction, but it ends up leading in another quite different one.

All humans have this 29th Gene Key inside us that's attuned to our level of commitment, and that fluctuates. The more we're anchored in the higher frequency of our heart, the less we need to think our way in or out of situations in our life. There are no incorrect decisions in life. The 29th Gift inside each of us knows this above all, and it gives us a vast sense of inner freedom. The funny thing is that as we begin to taste this freedom, we realise how little external conditions have to do with true fulfilment. When we realise that, we no longer postpone our lives either by hopping from one thing to another or by staying somewhere that no longer serves us. We simply smile, and give ourselves continuously to every living moment. That is true commitment.

I'd like to finish this Gift by saying something a little risky. This is the abysmal after all. This may come from my own agenda, that I have learned throughout my life and in particular through my relationships. This Gene Key is part of the Codon Ring of Union, which means that it is a key to unlocking the power of love through relationships. Here is what I have learned, and mostly I have learned it through pain, through my own foolishness, my own fear and my own half-heartedness: relationships blossom only through 100% commitment. It seems like a simple statement. But it's amazing how much fear and wriggling that statement can generate! I have mentioned somewhere before that commitment cannot be 99%. 99% commitment is no different from 1% commitment. 99% is half-heartedness. It's amazing how many of us keep this little tiny part of ourselves secret in our relationships. I'm not talking about verbal communication here. This is in our chemistry, so it runs deeper than words. We hold a little bit back from our partners and we do this deep inside because of our fear. We can ask ourselves if we have done this, or if we are doing so now. Just the asking can be a revelation. It took me several emotional crises to see this pattern inside myself, but once I released it, everything changed. Relationships remain challenging, but the feeling of 100% commitment is so terrifically powerful that it will ride out any storm. It's not even about the other person - it's about leaping into the abyss with eyes wide open.

So I strongly recommend to anyone working with the Gene Keys to try and stay in their relationships, rather than jumping out when it gets too hard or too heavy. We've become a lazy generation. Stay and be surprised. We need to hold our nerve through the challenge. We can use the circumstance to learn how to keep our heart open. Once we've learned that trick, we are master of the universe! The only circumstance in which we absolutely should leave a relationship is in the case of physical abuse. Otherwise we should give it everything until we have mastered the art of returning non love with love, which is the art we will bring to perfection in the 29th Siddhi of Devotion.

GENE KEY 29

The 29th Siddhi - Devotion

I love the 29th Siddhi. It's where all human beings are ultimately headed. It's Devotion. We're all devotees of something. We just have to see what it is, and transform it inside ourself until that something becomes everything, or that someone becomes everyone. This is the deep secret of the guru/disciple relationship. We have to surrender ourself to the guru and let them become the conduit of our higher commitment. They don't even have to be worthy! Sometimes disciples of false gurus have attained through the innocence of their surrender! Ah, don't you love life!

The 29th Gene Key contains one of the highest teachings concerning relationships, and is deeply connected to the spirit of tantra, the surrender of lover into beloved. As I said, we're all devoted to something. Such a truth! The egoist is devoted to his ego, the salesman to his profits, the mother to her children, the murderer to his victim, the seeker to the Truth, even the depressive is devoted in a slanted way to their misery. This is the great mystery of the Gene Keys – that the Siddhi is present even in the Shadow as a seed. The journey is to allow that seed to sprout and grow, until it finally flowers and bears fruit. Half-heartedness causes suffering, and that realisation leads to commitment. At a certain level, commitment itself becomes more and more internalised, until its true nature is revealed. This is when commitment transforms into Devotion. The leap to the Siddhi can never be predicted; it's an act of grace, an acausal event, meaning that it occurs outside of time and space.

This Gene Key, this particular code in our DNA, is activated through a consistent deepening commitment to the present moment. It manifests as Devotion, which is the profound heartfelt knowing that love is the root-nature of all reality. Love is known as percolating everything, and this insight moves deeper and deeper into our being, until it detonates within. Usually, the journey to the 29th Siddhi takes the form of a devotional path, in which the devotee fixes his or her longing onto an external form, in the full knowing that this form is really a representation of the universal love principle. Nonetheless, the absolute worship of the object, whether guru, god, or loved one leads to a series of inevitable breakthroughs. We are not much of a devotional culture in the West. Since the middle ages we have taken a more scientific path - an intellectual path, and we have consequently lost our devotional qualities. We even tend to look down on devotional cultures as backward. Islam for example is deeply devotional, as is Hinduism.

Christianity used to be so, and still is in some places, but it has lost some of that early ecstatic quality that was carried by its best known mystics. The problem for the modern human being is that devotion appears to be blind. We even use that term 'blind devotion'. We all know its extreme manifestations as well, so we have learned to distrust it.

What we need is a rebirth of devotion. And nowhere is this more needed and more possible than in our relationships. There are few spiritual teachers in this realm, and I mean real teachers - people who have learned from and transformed their pain through their relationships. Devotion is blind. Only a blind one would be mad enough to jump into the abyss of the human wound. But the blind one is not really blind. Their eyes are the eyes of trust - that leaps and goes on leaping because their love is returned in every situation, and it is returned magnified.

Our frequency rises whenever we pour out our heart unconditionally to another in service of the highest. We move in this Gene Key from Half-heartedness to full heartedness. The more we love in this way, the more pressure we create within the atoms at the heart of creation. Eventually, all that love ruptures the time space continuum and the inexplicable event occurs, subject merges with object, and the one principle is all that is left. It's an old Sufi equation: Lover merges with beloved and all that is left over is love. That's the 29th Siddhi. Here is a story/poem that often makes me weep. It's by Hafiz.

Bring the Man to Me

A Perfect One was traveling through the desert.
He was stretched out around the fire one night
And said to one of his close ones,

'There is a slave loose not far from us.
He escaped today from a cruel master.
His hands are still bound behind his back,
His feet are also shackled.

I can see him right now praying for God's help. Go to him.
Ride to that distant hill;

About a hundred feet up and to the right
You will find a small cave.
He is there.

Do not say a single word to him.
Bring the man to me.
God requests that I personally untie his body
And press my lips to his wounds.'

The disciple mounts his horse and within two hours
Arrives at the small mountain cave.

The slave sees him coming, the slave looks frightened.
The disciple, on orders not to speak,
Gestures toward the sky, pantomiming:

God saw you in prayer,
Please come with me,
A great Murshid has used his heart's divine eye
To know your whereabouts.

The slave cannot believe this story,
And begins to shout at the man and tries to run
But trips from his bindings.
The disciple becomes forced to subdue him.

Think of this picture as they now travel:

The million candles in the sky are lit and singing.
Every particle of existence is a dancing altar
That some mysterious force worships.

The earth is a church floor whereupon
In the middle of a glorious night
Walks a slave, weeping, tied to a rope behind a horse,
With a speechless rider
Taking him toward the unknown.

Several times with all of his might the slave
Tries to break free,
Feeling he is being returned to captivity.
The rider stops, dismounts—brings his eyes near the prisoner's eyes.
A deep kindness there communicates an unbelievable hope.
The rider motions—soon, soon you will be free.
Tears roll down from the rider's cheeks
In happiness for this man.

Anger, all this fighting and tormenting want, O beloved,
God has seen you and sent a close one.

Beloved, God has seen your heart in prayer
And sent Hafiz.

The 30th Way

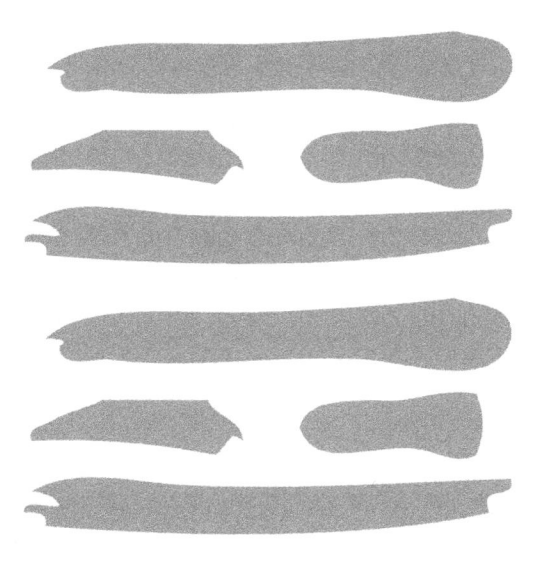

Gene Key 30

THE WAY OF LIGHTNESS

The Transformational Way of the 30th Gene Key moves from Desire to Rapture, and it's the Way of Lightness.

Here we have one of the juiciest of Ways and Gene Keys in the whole matrix. The 30th Shadow of Desire. It says something about all the Shadow states, doesn't it? Each Shadow lends its teaching to the whole. Every Shadow is rooted in unfulfilled longing or desire. Each Shadow is a pattern that emerges out of this unfulfillment in an attempt to try and fix it or do something about it. Desire is a component of being human, so we can let go of thinking that we don't have desires if we don't have this one. That kind of thinking doesn't last long when we come deeper into the Gene Keys. The ones in our Profile simply show us a pattern that we can follow that will help us to transform the Shadows into the Gifts that lie hiding inside them.

Desire can be so many things and take so many forms. No matter which form it takes, it has this single similarity - it's a projection that moves from our centre outwards. It's a seeking, a request, a leaning outwards, whether through our heart, mind, or body, or all three. It's a longing, an ache, a yearning for something that we feel we're lacking.

If desire is because of a lack we feel, then what is the most fundamental lack? If we can find the deepest source of our desire, then we have the best chance of understanding it. Is it the desire to feel whole? To be somehow complete? To know who we are or what we are? Is it a genetic imperative to bond and evolve? Is it the desire for freedom? The desire to be free from suffering? The desire to find peace? Perhaps it's all of these things. In its purest sense, I think we can just accept it as a state of longing that's built into the machine. It comes with the body, but it doesn't come with an instruction manual.

Shadow: Desire **Gift**: Lightness **Programming Partner:** Gene Key 29
Dilemma: Temptation **Siddhi**: Rapture **Codon Ring:** The Ring of Purification

---

I was in the supermarket yesterday at the self service counter, you know how most supermarkets have that now? As I was scanning the items, I rested my hand on the counter, and the machine suddenly spoke to me. You won't believe what it said: *'Unexpected item in the bagging area.'* I looked down and it was my hand! This is the problem with desire, it happens so unexpectedly. We see something and we want it. We weren't looking for it, but suddenly there's the desire. When we really look deeply into this situation, it was actually us, not the object of our desire. It was our hand all along! So we get hooked by the temptations of the world, of the senses. Here we have the Dilemma, Temptation. I can resist everything except temptation. That's what Oscar Wilde said. It's true. Temptation is a tough cookie. The more we try and resist it, the more powerful it becomes.

Every Gene Key is a Way (or path so to speak). We have to remember this. These are ways through transformation. This 30th Gene Key is the Way of Desire. We have to give in to temptation. We have to yield to it in order to transcend it. Now I know this is dangerous talk, and I have no wish to be sued by anyone now or in the future, so I'll say that this is all fuel for contemplation. If we have the 30th Gene Key in our Profile, or if we're drawn to it, then we need to contemplate desire and temptation. We need to really watch it, learn from it, and grow through it. It's just a lens. Not everyone has this as a lens. When I say yield to temptation, I don't mean it literally. I mean trust in it, but we don't have to act on it. Desires are all from the source, but that doesn't mean we have to act out every one that comes along. That's the root of selfishness.

We have to see that desires are not the enemy. They're guests. They come. They go. The contemplative approach is very generous. It allows things in. It listens to them. It gives them space to stay or to leave. It observes. Sometimes the desire does indeed get played out externally, but also the desire simply falls away, returns back to the nothingness. The wider our awareness becomes, the more room we give desires. Above all we're here to learn from them. The biggest problem with desire is the mind. The mind can get hold of a desire and blow it out of all proportion. The mind can also fan a desire as a wind fans a flame, so we need to be especially vigilant as concerns our mind and desire.

There is a great difference between a desire and a need. The body has needs such as food. Desire is a craving for something that we don't really need. Buddha suggests honouring needs but lessening desires. If we really watch our mind carefully, we'll see that it's always the culprit. Without our mind there would be no desire that lasts. Something to consider and contemplate.

The 30th Gift - Lightness

The Gift of Lightness. We're blessed if we have this Gift. Following desire and giving in to temptation is so deeply human and humbling if we're on a spiritual path. Desires come and go in cycles. We can have a period in which we feel quite calm and things seem to be going well, and then all of a sudden a cycle of desire springs up unexpectedly. How we deal with such times dictates the flow of our destiny. I'm no expert in this, please understand. I'm as influenced by desires as anyone. The thing I have learned about desire is that although it isn't bad, if we constantly follow our desires without restraint, we often end up feeling bad. Part of this may be guilt, which comes as a deep self judgment, and part of this is actually the very chemistry of desire.

Desire is a fire in the body. The 30th Gene Key, the 30th hexagram, is famously called 'The Clinging Fire'. When we entertain desire, it enflames and engulfs our lower bodies - our physical, emotional, and mental bodies. If we've been doing refined spiritual practise, for example, and then give in to a deep desire, it tends to really lower the frequency of our being. Again, this isn't bad. It's just a part of our path. The 30th Gene Key, along with the 13th, forms the Codon Ring called the Ring of Purification. There we have the real purpose of desire - to purify us!

Desire itself obviously doesn't purify us. It reminds us that there are higher dimensions by standing in the way of those dimensions. There's a process of purification in this Gift. It's called the Gift of Lightness, because that's the quality we need to begin transcending and transmuting desire. We rise and we fall in life. Sometimes we're flying and sometimes we're dragging. We have to see that desire isn't 'unholy'. There is no holy and unholy. That's what creates heaviness and guilt. Lightness is when we can look at desire with equanimity. If we follow a desire into the world, realise that it hasn't fulfilled us, and that we've actually lost something through following it, then that's not something to worry about. We just have to see that it was a part of our journey and we needed it. We needed to be reminded. Lightness is that reminder - it's the field that lies behind desire. It's generous, it's accepting, it appreciates the juiciness of desire, and also sees the futility of it.

As we embrace the Gift of Lightness, we become less caught up in the desire game. We begin to purify our nature by releasing ourselves from the mind's influence. The desires emerge but are simply fuel, and our awareness begins to refine that fuel. As it becomes refined, it becomes like rocket fuel. It's a higher version, and instead of feeding our lower bodies, it begins to feed and fuel our higher subtle bodies. This is alchemy. We begin to feel lighter. We're able to release the guilt around temptation, and we can begin to use desire to serve a higher goal, a higher purpose.

The Gift of Lightness comes on gradually. It may even take lifetimes. If we come in with this Gift, it means we have deep work to do in this area. We have to understand and transmute our desires. That's work that leads to an interesting and colourful life, so we'll likely need a dose of self-forgiveness and compassion. We'll need to learn the Gift of Lightness, and we will learn it. It may take a while but over time we'll feel lighter, we'll be able to see the futility and beauty of desire. Then we can be more refined in how we approach desire. It won't rack our body. It won't steal all our energy, and make us feel depressed or frustrated or guilty.

Purity is not what people think. Purification is seeing that we already are a pure soul. It's about self-forgiveness. It's also about being responsible for our own behaviour and its consequences. Following a desire to its conclusion may cause others a great deal of pain, and this will create a wave of crisis in our own life. We'll then have to process that, and see deeper into ourself. It can be a revelation. I can't say it's an easy process. I personally have found it one of the greatest challenges of my life. I suspect many of us are the same. There are great Gifts that come from it. We do eventually feel a lift from this Gift of Lightness. We begin to realise that what Buddha said is good advice - simply to lessen the influence of desire in our life. We shouldn't try and do it all at once; it's just a long term goal. Gradually, over time, we feel the lightness coming, and it begins to lift us up onto another plane. From there we begin to really serve and create something of enduring value.

The 30th Siddhi - Rapture

Of course we all know where this is heading - one of my favourite words for the enlightened state of all the 64 Siddhis - Rapture. The 30th Gene Key is paired with the 29th, which is a really great story - at the Shadow level we have Desire and Half-heartedness. So often we begin something, then desire sways us off course, and we lose momentum and stay half-hearted. There are so many people in half-hearted relationships, half-hearted jobs, and all because their desire just keeps pulling them out towards something else, something new, something with the promise of fulfilment. Then we have the Gifts, Commitment and Lightness. How light we feel when we know we're committed. We know we can stay the course even amidst the desire field. That's empowerment.

Finally we have Devotion and Rapture. What a pairing! It's a vital pairing. Rapture can't exist without devotion. Rapture comes when all our desires have been purified into a single over-arching desire - the desire to return to our source, the yearning for the light - freedom from suffering. This is after all what all desires really are - the desire to be free from suffering - the desire for God. Sometimes I just have to use the G word. I mean let's be honest - you're here listening to this because we're all seeking God. We're seeking the source. We're yearning for that source.

The Sufis are good in this area. They know all about the clinging fire. They know about devotion. They say to become your longing, realise how deep it goes, and then let it burn you and burn you until you're on fire with it. We can choose an external figure if we wish - our lover, our guru, our god. It can be any deity. The figure becomes the symbol of our longing, and we pour that longing into the symbol. Maybe it's because they came out of the deserts, out of the fire and heat, maybe that's why the Sufis and the Arabic cultures resonate so much with these Siddhis…

Rapture is to become possessed by our longing, our love. It's to become drunk with it. It's to let it burn us clean. We offer up our every desire to God or the guru. We see everything that captivates our desire as a mirror of the one we seek. Because we offer it up and forgo it on the external plane, the fuel elevates our consciousness.

One of my favourite 'rapture artists' was Ramakrishna, who lived in India in the 20th century. One of his disciples fervently wrote down everything he said, and described in detail his conversations and actions with his devotees. This man was so on fire. He'd be in the middle of a philosophical conversation, and someone would speak a sentence like, 'Krishna was so devotional', and Ramakrishna would just get hooked by it. He'd instantly get swallowed by his samadhi, his rapture, and would be transported into another world. It might take an hour or more before he came back to reality, and then resume his conversation. Can you imagine that? It's good to imagine these things. The more we do so, the more attuned we become to such energies. It's like my series I do on the Ecstatics, when I pick these extraordinary people from history and explore their consciousness. I get so high from doing that. That's a spiritual practise. Anything that gets us high like that is a preparation. Of course we also have to function in the physical world, but I recommend anything or anyone that transports us naturally into higher states.

I often think of a woman who came to one of my Venus courses a long time ago. She was and is an influential woman. She has these codes, these Gene Keys in a very prominent place in her Profile, and for four days she resisted what I was saying. She fought against the transmission. On the fifth and final day, unexpectedly (it's always unexpected), she cracked. Her heart just peeled open, and in place of this impressive, dignified, but closed exterior came forth a woman of sensual wonder and open-hearted devotional depth. She was a child and a Great-Grandmother all in one. She was a courtesan and a nun, a wild lover and a devoted wife all in one package. The power of her love embraced all paradoxes. I remember feeling it vibrating in the air around her. The rapture.

However it happened, she returned to the world, her heart closed off, and she became that important respectable person again. I wonder how that sits inside her. I wonder what it takes to hold that love underwater like that? And I can't judge it. I've known it too - my heart closing down for one reason or another. But we have to honestly ask ourself, what reason is there that we can possibly justify closing our heart? Look at your life and realise that everyone around you is God in a disguise. They're here to teach us, remind us - that beneath our veneer, we are one rippling field of love, of Divine rapture. To let that in is our highest purpose. We need a new wave of ecstatics in the modern world. The materialists need to be challenged. They need to be taken on. I don't wish them ill. I wish them to awaken, like that woman, so that we can embrace each other, so that we can repair the world, so that we can all be unified in the Rapture.

Supplication of Divine Rapture

Shatter my heart, O rapturous God
Crush me in the infinite softness of your embrace.
Lead me gently to the sacred shore
And hurl me into your glittering depths.

Let the sword of my longing
Pierce the rough hide of the Great Illusion
And may the blood of my life pour out
Into the Sea of Eternal Creation.

By your Holy Grace,
May the Red Buddha sweep me clean
Leaving me stainless, pristine as diamond
Empty and Silent as the spotless sky.

O most Serene Lady of Limitless Bliss!
I court divine annihilation in your arms.
Pulverise my soul into luminescent dust
And scatter my dreams among the stars.

I bow to your thrust, to the Divine Rapture
that swells and wells in my breast
As you carve and shape my yearning soul
In the immortal fires of the Fervour of God.

THE 31ST WAY

Gene Key 31

THE WAY OF LEADERSHIP

The Transformational Way of the 31st Gene Key moves from Arrogance to Humility, and it's the Way of Leadership.

The 31st Shadow is all about seeking recognition. That's it in a nutshell. Why do we seek recognition? It seems a very human thing to do. Nowadays we can see how this Shadow has gained more momentum than ever through the internet and social media. The more unsure we are of ourselves, the more we look for affirmation from the outside. Now we have a generation of uneasy, insecure youngsters desperate to be recognised and they don't even know for what. It's rare to find a young person these days who doesn't either want to be rich or famous. The unspoken question at the root of modern culture is 'how can I feel secure?' Yet it's the wrong question that only leads to sickness. The right question is 'how can I best serve the whole?', a question that modern culture doesn't yet ask, at least not at a collective level.

We can see that the root of this Shadow of Arrogance is insecurity; individual insecurity. There are layers in every Shadow. There is the traditional notion of arrogance - the egotistical kind of macho posturing - look at me - I know best. The bullies are always the most insecure ones. That's the brute form of arrogant behaviour that we all know, but there are also subtle levels to this Shadow. There's a spiritual arrogance. Spiritual arrogance is rooted in a deep belief system that we've found 'the way' - that our path is the best path, and that those who don't know are in the Shadow. We see this a lot across the great religions, and we also see it in the New Age. We see it wherever there's a loss of touch with our essential humanity.

To be human is to be fallible. A lot of the time it's to be wrong! To be human is to fall. To scale the heights and then to plummet. Arrogance is a kind of blindness that we all have,

Shadow: Arrogance **Gift**: Leadership **Programming Partner:** Gene Key 41
Dilemma: Choice **Siddhi**: Humility **Codon Ring:** The Ring of No Return

---

and we have it until life exposes it. Arrogance is especially tied to leadership, the Gift, so all people who have this Gene Key have some kind of potential as leaders, as influencers of culture. They also carry the seed of arrogance, because that's the Shadow.

To be arrogant is to act without realising that there are consequences. There are laws built into life. These are the laws of karma. Once we've acted or spoken out, our action stands for eternity. That's why this Gene Key is part of the Codon Ring called the Ring of No Return. Every action carries karma. Arrogance always ends with some form of humiliation. No one gets away. This is why the Dilemma is Choice.

When we act as though we're in charge of our destiny, we'll be disappointed. There are forces beyond our lives that set the rules, that choreograph the tapestry of our lives. The Indians call this dharma, the unique flow and pattern of our destiny. Our dharma unravels as we live. It brings us good fortune. It brings us challenges. The only choice we have is in how we respond to our dharma. When we act without integrity and out of insecurity because we're trying to control our lives, we're acting arrogantly. Some may say that this makes us seem powerless, that surely our destiny is in our hands. Well it is and it isn't. Our karma is in our hands and our karma is how we respond to our dharma. If we respond with cruel words or with complaining or blaming or assuming a victim stance, then we create the very thing we've put out. Whereas if we respond with acceptance, with love and humility, then we create that energy in our environment.

So who is choosing? In your life, are you the chooser? Do you make your life happen? Spiritually this is very subtle. We say that we create our reality. Even I say that. You are the architect of your evolution. I say that often. But it isn't wholly true. I'm sorry.

I say it because it's the first stage in stepping out of victimhood. But it isn't the whole way. It's actually a pretty arrogant thing to say. We do have a say in the script but we don't have a say in the storyline. That's why the Dilemma is Choice. We have to learn to let go, over and over. The thing life wants us to let go of is us. It's the you. The me. Arrogance is all about me. It's about caring what others think. It's about trying to please. Or it's about trying to provoke. It's about attention. It's all me, me, me.

There's a deep moral aspect in this Gene Key. It's actually really, really beautiful. It creates all kinds of leaders, from the Shadow all the way up to the Siddhi. The further the leader appears from being human, from being fallible, from being imperfect, the closer they usually are to the Shadow. This is how arrogance manifests - as people who behave as though they're beyond reproach, who aren't able to see their own behaviour honestly. Arrogance cannot see itself without a breakthrough. It's blind. That's its core nature. The Shadow Programming Partner is the 41st Shadow of Fantasy. Arrogance lives in a world cut off from the human heart.

We see this very clearly with some spiritual people. This is what's known as the 'spiritual mistake' - when we get fixated on the highest frequencies, the Siddhis, and forget to bring them down into the form, into the mess of humanity. That's the greatest challenge. That's what makes a true leader. It's not someone who's beyond us, in a rarified world of bliss and radiance. How can such a person be a role model? They can point to our eventual potential, but they can't really help us practically, not if we can't relate to them. In a way such people have moved beyond leading. The spiritual mistake is to opt out by going for those higher frequencies and then being unable to integrate them in the world. That makes one spiritually arrogant. In any teacher we can sense automatically where they are on this spectrum. Humanity can feel humanity. Beware of the lure of the higher frequencies and those who claim them. We can be inspired, absolutely, and let them lift us and open our heart up to greater potential, but we need to maintain our connection to the human, to the mundane, to the grit. There are a few people who have genuinely transcended the grit, but they're always the most human ones.

Let's contemplate this Dilemma of Choice. We begin by feeling that we have no choice. We're a victim of our suffering. Then we decide that we do have choice and we break out of that victimhood and carve a new life for ourself, an empowered life. Then we come full circle to the realisation that we have no individual choice, that the whole is choosing through us and that our only option is to surrender and keep opening to the unknown. We can't skip the middle step. We can't go to the Siddhi straight from the Shadow. We're suffering, so we try and escape into the higher realms. It's just an escape - that kind of arrogance, spiritual arrogance. This is Shadow, Gift, Siddhi. We only get to the Siddhi by beginning with the Shadow and working deeply into it. We need to find the place where each of us is arrogant, our blind spot. If we listen to our life it will tell us where because it will arrange a 'humbling' for us!

The 31st Gift - Leadership

What makes the true leader? Let's contemplate that - humanity I would say, and vulnerability, but vulnerability as a strength because it has awareness. What other qualities are essential for the true leader? I would say patience, one of my favourites. We need to be patient with ourself to move through our own arrogance and discover the true meaning of humility. That takes patience and courage. Courage is another quality of leadership, not the courage to run headlong at the enemy or do something externally impressive. It's the inner courage to stay absolutely centred in our own Truth, in the truth of our heart, even when others may not understand and may project all kinds of things onto us. It's about standing firm in our own self-love.

It's virtually impossible to see our own arrogance. I truly believe it is. What I mean is that we can't go looking for it. We can try, but our ego won't let us see it. It's easy to see other people's arrogance, but our own? Not a chance. The only way we're going to see it is by making a mistake. We have to fall. This Gene Key is about learning humility, it's about learning to fall with grace. That's what makes a good leader. At least in my eyes. I'm not so impressed by the impeccable saint. I'm more impressed by the fallen saint who picks him/herself up after they've fallen, and still keeps their heart open. These are the leaders. Those who can fall and lift themselves back up again. That takes a special kind of strength.

GENE KEY 31

It's the path of a true human being.

You know that wonderful poem by Rudyard Kipling - it's called *'If...'*

> *If you can keep your head when all about you*
> *Are losing theirs and blaming it on you,*
> *If you can trust yourself when all men doubt you,*
> *But make allowance for their doubting too;*
> *If you can wait and not be tired by waiting,*
> *Or being lied about, don't deal in lies,*
> *Or being hated, don't give way to hating,*
> *And yet don't look too good, nor talk too wise:*
>
> *If you can dream—and not make dreams your master;*
> *If you can think—and not make thoughts your aim;*
> *If you can meet with Triumph and Disaster*
> *And treat those two impostors just the same;*
> *If you can bear to hear the truth you've spoken*
> *Twisted by knaves to make a trap for fools,*
> *Or watch the things you gave your life to, broken,*
> *And stoop and build 'em up with worn-out tools:*

and he goes on, and it ends *if you can do all of that, then the world is yours...*

That's what I'm talking about here. Leadership requires we stick our head out way above the parapet and face the stuff that others throw at us. We trust in our own inherent virtue. That's the 31st Gift. The greater the challenge life throws at us, the greater our potential for transmutation. We have to remember that the Programming Partner of the 31st Gene Key is the 41st Gene Key, and the 41 is unique. It's where all great new breakthroughs hurtle out of the void into the world. These two Gene Keys are all about bringing the new into the world, and the new always meets resistance. It isn't always recognised in its own time.

If we have this 31st Gene Key in our Profile we'll have to face these things in our life. Leadership sounds all very impressive but it comes with a great responsibility. Nowadays there are all these people telling us we're all leaders, and there are all these leadership courses and trainings and conferences. It's a big buzz. Everyone wants to be a leader. But the truth is that leaders are rare. This isn't everyone's calling. The true leaders, at least the new leaders, they're forged by life. This isn't something we decide. It's something that's thrust upon us. It's something that our dharma decides long before we become an adult. To be a spokesperson of the new, we'll have to learn the language of the old. These are our revolutionaries. We can't throw the old away. Many new thought leaders have tried that and it never works.

Leadership has great respect for the past, for tradition, and for the ancient ways. It also brings a new perspective with it. Leadership grafts the new onto the ancient rootstock. This is wisdom in action, using the lessons of everyday life as a means to resolve the deeper questions that haunt us - why things happen in certain ways, why fate sometimes deals us a challenging card out of the blue. The true leaders have lived these trials. They continue to live them and learn from them. Yes, the true leaders are the most human people among us. They aren't unreachable. They aren't ungraspable. They're here on the ground among us. That's real leadership.

The 31st Siddhi - Humility

Here we come to perhaps the most misunderstood of the Siddhis - Humility. It isn't what we think. It's not about self effacement or hiding our ego. It's about egolessness. What does it mean to transcend the ego? Is that something only great masters and saints can do? Not at all. It's something life leads us to when we surrender deeply enough. Life will strip us to the bone when we follow our destiny without question, when we submit to our dharma.

The Siddhi is not about self empowerment. The Siddhi is all about surrender. Surrender isn't just bowing before an altar. Surrender is hardcore. It's about letting go of all definitions of ourself. At the Gift level, we play the game of self empowerment, but we can become righteous.

We try to live with integrity, but the Siddhi demands an extra leap. It demands that we even drop our sense of external goodness. It demands that we step out of the game of good and evil. It may even ask us to play the very role we fear the most. Think about Judas. History has branded Judas the betrayer. He betrayed Jesus for money. That's a heavy burden. To be the one who betrays the Son of God?! And yet imagine if Judas were utterly aware? Maybe he knew that was his role. Maybe he loved and trusted in Jesus so much that he gave himself up to that role. Maybe his trust in God was even greater than Jesus'. Is that sacrilegious? The point is that we don't know. If this were the case, then Judas would be the humblest man who ever lived - to play such a role and be remembered as the worst betrayer, but to know that inside he would never choose such a thing. That's humility. To let others think what they will, but to know our own heart above all else. I'm not saying by the way that this is how it was. I'm just taking a charged example, as a metaphor, an allegory, to demonstrate what true humility looks like.

The Christians in fact have a very beautiful term - penance. It comes from Repentance, to be sorry for our sins. The penitent one willingly receives the dharma and lets it purify and absolve him or her. In Hinduism a similar thing is known as tapas, which has multiple translations one of which is penance. Life brings us these golden opportunities to surrender our attachments. We're asked to surrender our goals, our views, the very constructs of our identity. The beauty is that life brings this to us if we're listening. If we're listening. Most people aren't able to surrender at that level to the external drama. Most people are caught in the net of the drama, so that when things go a different way from their hopes, they aren't able to let go cleanly, and they cling.

All arrogance is clinging. That's all it is. The penitent one trusts in every situation that occurs, and they trust so entirely in it that their action emerges correctly. Others may not like us. They may not agree with us. They won't understand us. Who understands deep surrender? Only another penitent. I wrote a poem once after I received a humbling; it's very short and simple. I hope you'll forgive me including it, it's called 'the Punch line':

The Punch Line

Everyone... everyone here is lost, and looking for home.
I fell on my arse
And everyone saw!
Once you've fallen down,
As long as you don't get up again you can't fall again.
For pity's sake, just stay down!
It's so pleasant down here,
It's so nice and quiet.
I can see up all the girl's skirts!
I can see in all the boy's hearts.
We are all just wandering children.

The only time we actually really talk
Is when two of us happen to fall on our arses next door to each other,
And then, from our new vantage
We look up together laughing,
At ourselves, at our good fortune,
And the irony that those above, pity us!
And we pity them, that never fall
For they will only ever hear
The beginning of the joke,
And miss the wonderful news
That our suffering is the punch line.

Life is about letting go, the spiritual life even more so. To live life right out of the fires of our heart, we'll be humbled and humbled over and over. This is the beauty of a life lived at that level of consciousness. We enter another dimension. We learn to bow to life, not out of resignation, but from deep trust. It's important to understand the difference between surrendering out of resignation and surrendering out of trust. We resign with reluctance. We accept the situation but it never penetrates our heart. Trust includes regret but it also transforms regret.

The regret becomes a part of us. A life with no regrets is a life lived without risk, without totality. Regrets become a part of the sadness that our heart contains.

The heart contains sadness and joy in equal measure. This Siddhi, this Gene Key, asks us to reconsider our life from the deepest place. This is the Codon Ring of No Return. We can't turn back. Regret is part of the journey. We have to make difficult decisions and they're a part of our dharma. We must learn to make them in the spirit of surrender, of deep listening and trust. Then we'll learn what it means to be truly humble, because life will have given us the gift of penitence, through its Grace. Sometimes Grace is gentle and sometimes Grace is fierce. We must bow to both cuts and trust that the spirit inside us will not only prevail, but will thrive and dance and soar as we learn to live without expectations and without fear.

THE 64 WAYS

The 32nd Way

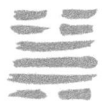

Gene Key 32

THE WAY OF PRESERVATION

The 32nd Transformational Way moves from Failure to Veneration, and it's the Way of Preservation.

This Shadow is a contemplation on failure, and what is failure? It's an interesting question because it leads in two directions. On the one hand we need to see that there's no such thing as failure, that what we perceive as failure is always a gift in disguise. It can be a revelation, even showing us a new way to freedom. We can also look at failure in ever widening circles. There's individual failure, the failure of a specific endeavour that we usually associate with the word - a business that fails, an exam that we fail, an attempt that fails. There's also collective failure, a kind of social failure associated with the whole, for example our human failure as a species to eradicate poverty or war. Our failure to be perfect is the kind that brings with it a great deal of guilt. There's biological failure, the failure to survive. In many instances, we've come to see dying as a kind of failure. So we battle against failure; it's a very human thing.

It's clear that failure is something that can teach us a great deal. Along with the 28th Gene Key, this 32nd forms the Codon Ring called the Ring of Illusion. It might be interesting to look at the connection of these two Shadows - the 28th Shadow of Purposelessness and the 32nd Shadow of Failure. That gives us an interesting avenue for contemplative insight. Is failure a missing of purpose - to live a whole life without a true sense of purpose?. To die without fulfilling our highest purpose? What is our highest purpose? That's the great Gene Keys question. It could create a great deal of pressure that we must fulfil our highest purpose, as though there's something specific we must do. If we don't achieve it, then we'll have failed.

Shadow: Failure	**Gift**: Preservation	**Programming Partner:** Gene Key 42
Dilemma: Panic	**Siddhi**: Veneration	**Codon Ring:** The Ring of Illusion

I've just completed writing and recording the Pearl Sequence for the Golden Path program. It's a deep contemplation on Prosperity. One of the insights it's left me with is this clarity around higher purpose. I've come to realise that the highest purpose we humans have is to live well. That's all. If there's such a thing as failure on an individual, metaphysical level, I would say it's this - the failure to live well. I think that's a place where failure can be a positive thing.

How do we live well? Another great question. Let's go to the Dilemma of the 32nd Shadow. Every Shadow throws us into a Dilemma. The Dilemma is like a nut we have to crack open. The 32nd Dilemma is panic. Panic is a subtle vibration that emanates from fear, from a deep forgetting of who we are. Panic and purposelessness come together. Panic leads us down the road of failure. We might think of panic as a kind of manic energy, a rushing, reactive, frenetic quality. It goes deeper than that on an inner level; it's about how we make decisions. It's about how we go about our daily life. Look back at your yesterday, and be absolutely honest with yourself. When did you panic? Perhaps panic was there all along, the whole day - a subtle undercurrent - a kind of anxiety - you trying to get through the day - trying to reach a place of rest or some kind of completion, some kind of peace. And did you ever find that peace?

Most of us have a few moments in the day where we aren't panicking, where we're actually pausing to enjoy life. If we look at this tendency in our life, and slow down inside ourself, we might see the panic at work. We can see the panic of the world and how we rush headlong from one thing to the next. Most of the time it's without any real deep consideration of why we're trying to achieve a certain thing. If we're following the Golden Path, then we're taking time to contemplate and hopefully learning a new way.

To live well and savour more moments, to sip from the arc of aeons, to revel in the riot of colour that's our life, to see the poetics of nature and not pass them by. That's such an art. All the money in the world isn't worth the ability to learn the art of living well.

At the Shadow we forget what it means to live well. We panic. We move too fast. We live in an intense time. If we want to be different from the crowd, if we want to stand out and be a true rebel, then we have to slow down the pace of the Shadow inside us. Be a contemplative. Let others see the radiance of the river of our life as it meanders rather than rushes. Take our time with things. Be passionate, but not panicky. Then we're outside the loop of failure. Failure also creeps in our relationships. We talk about failed relationships, but no relationship can be a failure. It's simply a mirror of our tenderness, our wounding. A relationship is something so precious. In many ways it's the most precious thing we humans are given.

The only failure is to miss our higher purpose. Let your relationships move you closer to that. And be careful. There's a reason why we think that relationships that end have failed. It depends upon how they end. If they end with graciousness on our part then they haven't failed. If the other can't manage graciousness then that isn't our concern. Our job is to live well and that means to honour ourself and others. An ending is not a failure. If there's such a thing as success, it's this - to live without panic - to let life in. Sometimes that means letting another human being hurt us, at least at an emotional level. That may be unavoidable. It also makes us stronger. If it opens us, then it means we're prospering. If it closes us, then we're poor. Failure can be a portal to many possibilities. It's really an illusion of our perception. It's also very human to see things in terms of success and failure. It's a habit of ours. Shall we contemplate what it means to succeed?

The 32nd Gift - Preservation

It's an unusual word for a Gift this - Preservation. I can imagine someone getting their Profile, and asking 'well what the hell does that mean? I have the Gift of Preservation, and you have the Gift of Totality or Imagination, yours sounds better!'

As always with the Gene Keys, we have to penetrate them to unlock their secrets. If the secrets weren't hidden, where would the fun be? Preservation is about continuity. It's about protecting the things we value. We preserve the thing we love. We can see this at the Shadow frequency - our panic about dying drives us to try and preserve our life through selfishness. We try and cram our life with activities in the desperate bid for happiness. We unconsciously try and preserve our identity. Our identity is nothing but a dream. I am not Richard Rudd. All the things that my mind associates with 'me-ness', my belongings, my home, my family, my friends, my job, my lifestyle, my gifts, my body - none of that is really who I am, so what is it that I'm trying to preserve?

The Gift frequency always describes an inner turning. It describes the field of transformation and creativity. At a certain point in our evolution we realise that the thing we've been trying to preserve is not the real thing. In trying to maintain this illusory thing, this ego, this web stitched together by our thoughts, we're only really preserving our suffering. We're a dog chasing its own tail. The great inner turning comes when the shell of our self-obsession cracks. Remember that this 32nd Gene Key is part of the Ring of Illusion, along with the 28th Gene Key, and illusions are here to be shattered. If we have the 32nd Gene Key, our life story, our dharma, will always bring us to the threshold of this shattering at certain points. The question is, will we allow ourself to be shattered? It's like the film 'The Matrix' where we're offered the red pill and the blue pill. The red pill will shatter our illusions and the blue pill will let us forget everything and go back into our illusions.

When we trust in life enough, we begin to trust in the events of our lives too. We allow them to shatter us and that reframes our view. We realise that this impulse to preserve what we love has a whole new field to live in. The great inner question becomes what is essential and what needs preserving - love, truth, virtue, forgiveness? Just pick a Siddhi. This Gift of Preservation is all about grafting. The strongest plants tend to be when we graft a young bud onto an old rootstock. The 32nd Gift is drawn to the old, the traditional, the ancestral, not in a staid way, but because there are things that have deep value from our past that are really worth nourishing for future generations.

To create something of value, or to preserve something of value for future generations is the most wonderful way of spending one's life. Maybe we take a piece of land and nurture and beautify it, like this wonderful story by Jean Giono, 'The Man Who Planted Trees'. Sometimes a story can say more about a Gene Key than anything, so this is a fable for the 32nd Gene Key and its Gift. The hero is a simple peasant living in an arid area of France where nothing grows and people are poor and wretched. He goes out each day of his life and he plants trees in ever-increasing circles around his home. People come, people go, and still he goes on planting trees. A lot of the trees die, but he just goes on planting regardless. The years go by, the war comes, and still our man continues planting trees. The war ends, the new government arrives, and they realise there's this big forest. They claim it and begin logging there, cutting down the trees. The peasant ignores it all and just continues planting trees. He's miles away from his original home now since the forest has continued to expand and grow far beyond the place where he started. The government falls, and once again the trees are left alone. Now he's an old man, but still he continues. Now there's a vast forest grown up, a whole rich eco-system where people are making all kinds of new livings, and more people are moving to the area all the time. The soil has improved for miles around, the trees have brought life with them, birds, wildlife, water, and all manner of plant life. Villages spring up, new communities which flourish as the land flourishes. The old man goes on planting, until he's just too old anymore. He dies peacefully, with the sounds of the forest and its life in his ears. No one knows who he is. No one knows what he's done. But he knows.

Isn't it a beautiful fable? That's the 32nd Gift. It brings transformation, but first we have to find the essential. What is our essential? What are our trees? What is our fable? What will we preserve for future generations? Think about this Gene Key. It contains one of the more precious transmissions of the whole pantheon. You see how far we've come from failure, from illusion, from panic? We humans have incredible capacity to transform the deserts around us into rich, flourishing oases. One day the whole earth will become an oasis. We can think about our lives. Regardless of our Profile or whether we have this Gene Key or not, we can contemplate the fable of our existence. What will we leave behind? What will our legacy be?

The 32nd Siddhi - Veneration

Veneration. Another beautiful word, and not one we hear much nowadays. Where do we hear such a word spoken? I looked up its etymology and had a lovely surprise. It's derived from the Latin word for Venus - love or beauty. The honouring of the beautiful, the essential, the feminine. It's also a word used a lot in connection with Saints - the veneration of past Holy people, a tradition in almost every religion. This 32nd Siddhi has a lot to do with our ancestry and our lineage. We also see this in the great traditions around the world - the transmission of the lineage. It's quite mysterious.

The Programming Partner of the 32nd Gene Key is the 42nd, which is about detachment and Celebration. These two Gene Keys have a deep focus on death and letting go. If we have them in our Profile, these themes will be especially important in our life. We may work with the dying, or the other side, with birth and the young, incarnation and excarnation, involution and evolution, invocation and evocation. Life is a breathing-in and breathing-out. A child is born, an old one dies. It's a chain, a living, rippling, sinuous, serpentine ladder. Our genes are a holographic depiction, a biological reflection of the great chain. DNA is a ladder of lights, folded and crimped, twisted and twirled like a living ivy around the great tree trunks of our cellular life. It's funny how I keep turning to trees for these metaphors in this Gene Key. It's the tree of life - that shamanic bridge between the realms...

Our DNA is that living cellular ivy and our consciousness travels along it, through it. We're transferred along it like a skybridge inside the body. It connects us to our ancestors, way back through our mitochondrial DNA. This is how the shaman can contact the ancestral spirits when he or she goes into the trance-state that allows access to the inner bridge. We'll find that the shaman always venerates the ancestors. They always ask permission before entering a sacred place, whether that's outside or inside, because at the more sensitive levels of consciousness, everything is animated. Every place, moment, part of the body, event, person, creature, stone or plant all represent a part of the great thread, the great chain of being.

The 32nd Siddhi has a great sensitivity to these things. It enters into the great interconnectedness of things. It also understands the power and mystery of lineage. Wisdom is a strange thing. By wisdom I mean the living transmission of the mystery, not knowledge, which is different and of the mind. Many people don't understand what wisdom is - it's the living spirit of Truth. When we hear it, see it, or witness it moving through someone, it's unmistakeable. It conveys something intangible, something almost hypnotic. One picks it up and travels with it, then dies into it, but it travels on, finding another host. It's just like the ivy I mentioned earlier that needs the host tree. We're the hosts for wisdom. It's why I keep calling the Gene Keys a transmission.

If we can feel or sense the transmission, if we can feel our DNA expanding, responding, opening, then we're imbibing the living wisdom. If we continue to let it in, it'll become strongly entwined around us, and we'll carry it on. The 32nd Siddhi responds to a lineage, the lineage that resonates the deepest inside the body. If we're ready to be the host, then the wisdom will come and live with us. We become a lineage holder, a guardian, a chodak in the Tibetan tradition, and mutate the wisdom as it mutates us. We become venerable, because others see that the wisdom has taken up residence in us, and they come to us to sip of that nectar.

It doesn't set us up higher than anyone else. In fact the wisdom will put us through a very rigorous series of tests! If we're not able to surrender and be humbled, then the transmission will not be able to stay inside us. It's not an easy business this veneration. We have to learn to venerate everything, to embody the principles that come with the wisdom. It takes a lot of self-discipline. This 32nd Gene Key requires a great deal of self-discipline.

We live at an interesting junction. The various lineages are moving in a new way. They always used to require that the living master had to pass on the transmission to the devoted disciple. Now the lineages are criss-crossing, as though they have a new kind of network, a kind of wisdom internet to travel through. It's as though underground springs are popping up in the collective gene pool and suddenly a lineage arises in someone who never had formal spiritual training. It's probably why the Dalai Lama suggests that there won't be another Dalai Lama, because the lineage is branching, opening, widening.

The only essential is the self-discipline, and it's not necessarily about doing anything formal. It's more to do with our ability to listen inwardly to the Truth inside us. The real discipline is to pause. We have to learn how to pause and listen inwardly to life. Without that discipline, we can't really get anywhere at all.

Veneration is a result of preservation. Veneration is something we discover at the heart of life. It's the quality we feel when we pause at a crossroads, at a branch in the tree of life. We're a part of a vast mystery. Ours is a vital life, a precious life, a delicate thread between the past and the future. Follow the gentle pulse of Truth inside you, the higher purpose hidden in your DNA. Lassoo that Truth, and ride it like a wild stallion out across the great plains and meadows of the world…

The 33rd Way

Gene Key 33

THE WAY OF MINDFULNESS

The Transformational Way of the 33rd Gene Key moves from Forgetting to Revelation, and it's the Way of Mindfulness.

In the genetic code there are three markers that act like punctuation marks in the vast biological text that is DNA. If we didn't have these markers, known as Stop Codons or terminators, it would be virtually impossible to read the code. The Gene Keys are a wonderful mirroring poetry of DNA, a holographic story that tells the tales of evolution hidden in these 64 secret archetypes. Coming to a Stop Codon, and the 33rd Gene Key is one of the three, is like coming to a clearing having wandered for months in a dense forest. It's like coming up for air. In the clearing there are always clues hidden in certain places about how to find our journey out of the forest.

The 33rd Gene Key is all about paying attention. That's the Dilemma of the Shadow - we forget to pay attention. We miss the vital clues, the pauses, clearings and opportunities. We don't learn from life. This Shadow of Forgetting actually unites all human beings as one. We're all in this forest but on our solitary trajectories. Sometimes in one of these clearings we meet another lost soul, and suddenly before us lies an opportunity to grow, to change direction and connect. Life is made up of Trials - the three Stop Codons form a group called the Codon Ring of Trials. But how will we fare with these trials?

There are trials in our relationships - like learning to forgive. There are trials in our daily life - like balancing enjoyment with responsibility. There are trials in health - like learning to care for our bodies correctly. Everything is really a hidden trial. But the trials don't have to be overwhelming. They're only overwhelming when we aren't paying attention to them.

Shadow: Forgetting **Gift**: Mindfulness **Programming Partner**: Gene Key 19
Dilemma: Attention **Siddhi**: Revelation **Codon Ring**: The Ring of Trials

---

When we blunder on across each clearing without pausing to see where we are or stopping to have an exchange with an animal or a sunrise or a stranger, then our lives seem intolerably hard.

The 33rd Gene Key teaches us something awesome. It teaches that life is a myth. Our myth is rich with characters and twists in fate. There are those who represent evil, those who represent good, those who turn from good to evil or from evil to good. There are backdrops that change, new characters that enter and characters that leave or die. The whole tapestry is so colourful and exquisite if we're paying attention. If we're paying attention. That's the key. The original name for this hexagram is 'Retreat'. It's all about withdrawal. It's about pausing in the journey. We have to stop and have a cup of tea. If we don't let our awareness come to a rest, how will we see what's really going on in our life? How will we learn what's being offered to us?

In the modern world we've become a rush of forgetting. We've become obsessed with movement, with evolutionary change. We've become immersed in the plot so that we see nothing. We're so absorbed in the screen, in what's rushing towards us, that we don't engage with what's gone past us. The 33rd Gene Key is adept at drawing sustenance from the past, from our mistakes, from history. It's a master of reflection and retreat. These days we rarely pause to reflect or contemplate where we've just come from. In Chinese culture there's a wonderful term called Hui Gan - which means to reflect sweetly on a past event. Time is given over to this custom, and it's part of the teaching of the ancient tea-drinking tradition.

To reflect on the past requires time put aside. It requires attention and focus. If we don't give ourself these moments each day, our life will be exhausting. It will be a life with no harvests. This is the terrible condition of the 33rd Shadow. If we don't pause to reflect, we can't come into the present moment and gain any perspective or wisdom. There are vast reserves of natural wisdom in this 33rd Gene Key. It's fizzing with secrets and revelations, but until we give it and ourselves time and prioritise the inner life, our lives are really unlived and unloved.

The 33rd Gift - Mindfulness

I'd like to talk a bit more about this concept of Hui Gan. Here we come to the Gift of Mindfulness, and I don't want us to misunderstand this word. Mindfulness is a word that may mean many things to people. It's a word used commonly in Buddhist practise. It's a central technique of the dharma - the Buddhist way. It concerns gently bringing ourself into the moment, simply observing our inner and outer environment without any expectation or personal judgment. It's about being in the clearing in the forest.

I'd like to add a whole new layer to mindfulness. I'm going to give us a very practical technique to do. Mindfulness doesn't have to be only about looking. It can also be about creating. It can be about the active imagination. The 33rd Gene Key is a lover of story, song, myth, and archetype. The 33rd Gift is adept at rituals, and rituals automatically bring presence and mindfulness. When I say ritual here I don't mean ceremony, I'm talking about making the mundane magical. For example, drinking tea can be a ritual. Eating can be a ritual. Working can be a ritual when done with imagination. This Gift can turn the whole of our life into a blaze of presence and peacefulness. Retreat doesn't have to be something we do after we've been in action. The retreat can be in the action itself. That is a Gift from heaven.

I'd like to be a bit heretical here and bring in the past. The future we know, because we're always worrying about it, planning it, and rushing towards it. The past we have less time for. This Gift is about turning around and looking out the rear window. Hui Gan involves seeing our past as it is, seeing the mistakes we've made, the hours we were simply in forgetting mode, and it's about seeing the moments when we were aware and bringing those sweet moments back to life. When you sit down to meditate or contemplate, I invite you to bring this into your practise or into an open dialogue with someone. Think about the magical moments, the transcendent moments you've had.

Think about what was best about yesterday and bring it back into your memory. Bring it into your body, your cells. Let your DNA become flooded with the serenity and sweetness of such memories.

Don't focus on difficult memories. Let those go into the stream of the past, let the ocean of life consume those. Forgive yourself those moments of forgetting. But harvest the fine moments. Harvest the very best of yourself and others. We will imprint those moments over and over. This is Hui Gan - to savour the sweetness of the tea in our mouth, to let it wash over our whole being. It's a wonderful, rich practise. It will change your mindfulness from being rather dry into a deep, glittering pageant of colour and inner light. When we do this practise with others, it's like rain from heaven. We sit and dialogue about that which fulfilled us the most - it can be from yesterday, from last year, from our childhood even. We just conjure it up and let it swirl around us. Contrary to what we might assume, we don't leave the present moment when consciously conjuring the past. We're simply making a ritual, a cosmic dialogue with ourself.

When we do this practise with others, it can also be so precious and uplifting. It reaches across the space between us and brings increased intimacy. It softens the edges between people. It creates openings. It's all about stepping into the clearing together. Just for this short time, we are creating a space in which we agree to step out of samsara, out of the drama. The space can fill with laughter or tears. When we recall that which is most precious and sweet it often reminds us of what we've forgotten, and that can bring release, sweet release. This practise can be very simple, without formality. For millennia friends have gathered around the fires, in the clearings, made tea or coffee, smoked something, eaten together, shared their stories, and talked of good times. That's really the simple heart of the practise of the 33rd Gift. I hope you find it inspiring.

The 33rd Siddhi - Revelation

There will come a time for all of us when the trials are over. It's of course written into the script that the story must come to an end one fine day. The curtain will fall, the audience will leave and the stage will once again ring with the soft emptiness of silence. Revelation always comes as silence. It always comes as an ending - this is the cosmic Stop Codon.

All bad things must come to an end. All good things will live forever. Am I an idealist? Certainly, but I am also a deep realist. I have studied the great myths, seen them playing out, travelled far and wide. The news I bring is only good. One day our trials will be over, and we'll reap the harvest of all our good thoughts, deeds, and yearnings.

We all must move through the trial of suffering. Suffering is the tool that life uses to hone us, to make us into who we could one day be. One day we'll graduate, after much sorrow, after much seeking, after many trials and tribulations. Revelation is Light. It always comes through silence and light. The light of Revelation lies within us right now, as a seed growing quietly inside. It exists on a higher plane of being, the causal plane. The causal plane, and our causal body is that part of our being that outlives death. That part of us that still doesn't remember our eternal nature must come to an end. It must awaken fully so that there's no longer any doubt, not even a shred. We'll face some final tests to ensure that our remembrance is unwavering.

We cannot die. The truth of this statement will one day change and reshape the world. The great Masters and teachers come intermittently and remind us of this truth. Our karma follows us everywhere. It follows us beyond death. Take heart then from all your good moments.

Let the not-so-good moments fade into the river of the past and cultivate the beauty you've sowed. Tend that garden with care so that all these beautiful flowers and trees grow up around you, and you become an oasis for others. We have to purify our karma. Suffering is sweet nectar, because it allows us to do so. Sometimes when life brings us a difficulty, it's a great opportunity for us. We must bow to it graciously and let it clean us out. Illness too can be such a gift, if we see it in this way.

We've seen that this Gene Key loves to reflect on the past. It remembers the very beginning of the journey - that Golden Age when we lived in heavenly certitude merged with the creatures and beauties of nature. In early forms, simpler forms, before homo sapiens, before measurable history we lived in simple splendour, and our hearts were one in that wilderness. These early memories of our Edenic being linger in our DNA. The masters rekindle them and rest in them, bringing them into the age that they temporarily inhabit. Revelation also triggers these cellular memories. Revelation therefore connects us to the future as well. We can't remember the past without remembering the future, because the beginning and the end curl around into each other. This is the deep Revelation of eternity.

So there one day comes an incarnation in which we awaken. To do so means that the memory that all we have been must drift up from the depths of time. We'll remember all our incarnations. We'll see the whole glittering sweep of our inner story and we'll marvel at its perfection. Revelation will flood us with these gifts and we'll realise that our story is approaching its end, just as we piece together the fabric of our beginning. When we come to see that we're soon to come to an end, that our being is preparing itself to merge again into the eternal, into a higher evolution, we may begin to prepare ourself for this. We start to pack away our belongings. We do an inventory of our journey. Perhaps we write our autobiography - not literally - it wouldn't be possible to encompass all those lifetimes, but we begin to empty ourself out. We begin to detach ourself from the familiar sights and sounds of the form of this planet - Gaia.

Revelation prepares us for this closure. It's a bittersweet letting go. A part of us doesn't want it to end. But the greater part is now ready to let go of suffering. We realise that the world takes care of itself. There's nothing to worry about anymore. We begin to inhabit a world of peaceful surrender. This Gene Key has such an autumnal flavour. The leaves of our lives begin to fall. The light turns inwards to prepare for its journey into the darkness, into the emptiness from which all things are born and reborn. All around us, there's the quivering beauty of letting go. The colours intensify. Our heart opens and opens in wonder at the beauty and slowly, slowly, almost imperceptibly we allow death to cradle us in its infinite compassion.

This is Revelation. All Siddhis signal this death and the following resurrection. They invite the ultimate sacrifice as we bow and entrust our souls to the deep. Eventually we must even surrender our causal body - that repository of all human memory that has travelled with us all these aeons. As we give up the soul to the Divine, we enter into a being that's so vast in scope that words are swallowed in its fathoms. We become One. We pass through our final trial and take our place around the council fire of the elders, our soul finally able to retreat and rest in the soul of God.

THE 34TH WAY

Gene Key 34

THE WAY OF STRENGTH

The Transformational Way of the 34th Gene Key moves from Force to Majesty, and it's the Way of Strength.

The Gene Keys are a true synthesis and thus they draw their wisdom from as many diverse fields as possible. This next piece of wisdom comes from a contemporary sub-culture that has spawned a great deal of timeless archetypal wisdom, Star Wars. In the first film, always the best, Yoda the Jedi Master is training young Luke Skywalker, his protégé, in the art of mind over matter. Frustrated because he can't do it, the young man protests to his Master, 'I'm trying!', to which Yoda utters the immortal words, 'Do, or do not. There is no try'. Wonderful. That's the Shadow of Force. Its Dilemma is Trying. Trying means not doing or forcing. Listen out in your vocabulary for when this little word 'try' appears. It's always interesting, and it's often when we're unsure of ourselves and have lost our self-assurance, the 20th Gift, which happens to be the Programming Partner of this 34th Gene Key.

The 34th Gene Key is fascinating; it holds so much history inside it. As part of the Codon Ring of Destiny, along with the 43rd Gene Key, it has a powerful hand in shaping the destiny of humanity. Because of the raw primal power within this 34th Gene Key, our mammalian spine was literally forced upright through the currents of evolution that lie inside it. In this sense the 34th Gene Key has already done its greatest job in the human genome, it's created a human being. We will see in the future what its Codon Partner the 43th Gene Key will do to complete the story from the other side, but as I said, that story is for another time…

Shadow: Force **Gift:** Strength **Programming Partner:** Gene Key 20
Dilemma: Trying **Siddhi:** Majesty **Codon Ring:** The Ring of Destiny

---

The Shadow of Force can be brutal it's a primal evolutionary force. All Shadow states are states of force or forcing. At certain stages in evolutionary history we need this power. In plants, the 34th Gene Key provides the thrust that cracks open a tiny seed and forces its way up through the soil and into the air above. However, we humans have come a long way and this Gene Key has other higher attributes hidden within itself waiting to emerge. Even so, the 34th Shadow is always there, whenever we forget to open our hearts and trust in life. It's a state of stress we get into when we think we have to make our own destiny. Our mind has its ideas and we try and make events move according to those ideas. The problem is when life doesn't want something to happen a certain way and we try and force it to go that way. Then we create enormous stress in our body. Our DNA starts screaming at us to stop, but the Shadow of Force isn't good at hearing. It can be very dumb like that, and humans can keep trying until we fall down exhausted or dead. One day we realise there must be another way, there must be a better life than this.

Most humans actually live like this a great deal of the time. When I was introducing the Gene Keys recently, I did a little visualisation into our DNA and I used this Shadow as an example. The image I used was that of trying to force a round peg into a square hole. Go on, do it in every cell of your body for a moment. Let your DNA feel that. That's how many of us live life. As we'll see, there's another way, and boy is it easier and more enjoyable.

This 34th Gene Key can be pretty painful at the Shadow level. It has a great deal to do with our spine, our breath and the way we move. Our spine is an amazing thing. It holds all the tension of our life. Every time we move out of universal harmony our spine compresses somewhere. We literally grind ourselves down. We end up stooping, hunching, with backache, leg ache, any ache. It's all in the spine. We can't be aware of the spine without being aware of the breath. That's the secret of hatha yoga, and other forms of yoga. As we breathe and move, the fluids are pumped along the spine. It's the master communication channel in the body. A spine with no tension creates a feeling of utter buoyancy and joy in the body, as if one is floating.

Most spines are filled with ancient tension, and this is conveyed holographically into the body. Every point in the spine has a relationship to every organ and system in the body, and an aspect of our life. We're so used to forcing our lives we've forgotten what it means to take the easy path. It doesn't even occur to most of us and it takes such a toll on our body. We go on doing things we don't love, we go on living with people without really telling them the truth. We fear change, thus we force ourselves to stay in loops that give us the illusion we're safe and our bodies register the frozen pattern through illness and pain.

If we want to understand the 34th Shadow, we can go into our body to the pain inside and be with it. Listen to it. Stop avoiding it or trying to fix it externally. It's there because of something we're doing or not doing. The deeper we learn to listen to this Shadow, the more attuned we become to where life wants us to go. Finally we let go of trying and what a difference that makes!

The 34th Gift – Strength

The difference between the Shadow and the Gift is summed up in one of the sweetest pieces of wisdom ever uttered by any human being. This one is from a Chinese sage, Chuang Tzu, obviously an old friend of Yoda. Take these words in deeply – Easy is right. Wow, what do you think of that? Forget the Gene Keys book with its hundreds of thousands of words. Just take these three as your creed, and you need nothing else. Easy is right. This was one of Osho's favourites. It's my favourite, and like any great wisdom it takes some penetration. It's not just a light piece of hippy wisdom that means sit back and spend your whole life surfing, even though that doesn't sound at all bad, come to think of it…It's about strength. Here in the West, we've really misunderstood what that word means. All our martial arts and most of our sports are built around the notion of force. Yet when we go to the East, we see that the Oriental mind, always more feminine and more intuitive, has grasped the truth of what strength is. Strength is effortlessness. Remember the 34th Gene Key is all about movement and breath, so in the East they've learned to listen to the rhythms of life inside the body. They look to the animals and birds and insects for inspiration. When creatures move, they actually don't move. They are moved. There's a difference. It takes a lot for the Western, logical mind to understand this. Strength lies in flexibility, flow, and receptivity rather than force, muscle and aggressiveness.

Often strength is about not moving at all. It's about waiting and flowing, like in Aikido or Tai Chi. When we apply these teachings to our lives it makes a huge difference. At every level, Strength comes through the feminine. The easiest fight is the one we avoid in the first place. We simply don't provoke through force. If we do have to make a stand, our spine is flooded with Chi, prana, and our inner strength radiates from our centre. This is the difference between inner and outer strength. The Shadow consciousness always has its focus on the outer, on display, on domination or control, but true strength arises from the core and moves towards the periphery. It emerges and emanates.

This is what our Radiance is. When we first come to the Gene Keys and hear about our Prime Gifts, we learn about our Radiance. This is the emanation of our inner strength. It's rooted in core stability, in how rooted we are in our life purpose. The moment we're in alignment with life purpose, higher purpose, we can access unlimited inner strength. Then we have the weight of the whole cosmos behind us.

Everything to do with transformation has to do with awareness. These Transformational Ways are all catalysed through awareness of the Shadow. Once we identify force, where we're forcing, where we're trying, then the miracle happens and we begin to let go. Force lets go of us. We move away from the collective conditioning. We move onto a higher frequency. It's a breakthrough. It happens every time we remember our heart. The heart knows only the easy. It loves the easy. Core Stability is all about complete relaxation, complete trust. Force was needed. In the beginning it was natural. It was needed for survival. It has to be trusted as well.

Something remarkable happened when our spine became vertical. Our brain developed differently. We suddenly opened up to a new geometry, to celestial forces, and we developed our mental awareness. In a way we also lost something. We lost our innocence. We lost our self assurance. So the phase of evolution we're in now is about opening up to our hearts, to our feminine side, to the part of our nature that is holistic rather than behaviourist. Holism isn't a science. It can't be a science because it includes intuition. It includes the irrational, the illogical. It's about direct inner knowing that comes from inside the body. When we're aligned with our core stability, through our spine and breath, we're deeply anchored in our belly, our centre; we just know things. It's a mystery. Our knowing is vast. This is the kinaesthetic knowing of the body. It feels truth in every cell. That's strength. It's not about display, although it can't be hidden. A person moving from their centre, talking from their centre, has a palpable field of strength around them.

Strength lies in self-assurance. When we know at the physical level, the answer is always so simple because it doesn't come via the mind. It emerges from our centre as effortless knowing, or flowing movement. This transmission about inner strength and the breath, the belly, and the spine can be applied to absolutely anything, from sport, music, art, business, to parenting, and it changes everything. I mean everything. We no longer have to force anything. We already know everything.

The 34th Siddhi — Majesty

Well, here we go again, diving into another Siddhi…I'm going to tell this one through a little story. It's an old story, and some of you may have heard it before, but I like it, and like all stories, every time, it gets better in the telling, so here goes…

The story is set in Japan about a young man who's riding on a train, and he's a student of Aikido. He's been studying it for a long time. The true spirit of the word Aikido can be translated as the art of reconciliation. This is what the story is really about. This guy has learned all this stuff and he feels strong – like in the 34th Gift. He's strong, he has this inner strength that radiates from him. He's riding on this full train, and everyone is sitting rattling around. The doors open and this tramp gets in, and he's drunk and dirty and provocative and looks kind of mean. He starts sort of bawling and shouting at the passengers, abusing them. This young man is all on alert – he's ready, waiting, he can deal with this guy. The tramp starts abusing this young couple, having a go at them and taunting them. They're really upset about it. The young man is just on the edge, he's about to jump in and get involved and lay this guy flat. Suddenly there's a little call from the other side of the train, the carriage, and it's a little old man. He calls out "Hey!", and the tramp stops in his tracks and looks around. There's this little old man sitting there in his kimono, immaculate, and he says, "Hey, come here". The tramp says, "What do you want?" He says, "I want to tell you about my garden". The old man is chatting away to this tramp telling him about his garden, how he loves his garden, how much time he spends there, what a great life he's had, and that his whole life is about gardening. He laughs, and the tramp is taken aback and doesn't know what to do. He's been completely outdone by this little old man who won't stop talking, and is sharing in such a sweet way.

Eventually the old man says, "You know I have this wonderful Persimmon tree. Do you like Persimmon trees?" He stops a minute and pauses, and the tramp who's just standing there lolling in that 34th Shadow-type way says, "Oh yeah I love Persimmon Trees. I used to have one when I was a kid". The little old man says, "Oh that's great, my wife and I sit out there by our Persimmon tree and drink our tea, and it's so wonderful". The tramp says, "Yeah Yeah", and the old man says, "Do you have a wife?" The old tramp says, "No I ain't got no wife, I ain't got no job, and I ain't got no nothing". "Oh", says the old man, "that's too bad, that sounds terrible". The tramp starts bawling, he starts crying, and before you know it, his head is in the old man's lap. He's weeping, telling him how much he's suffered and about his pain and everything. The young man who was about to take him out at the beginning, gets off at his stop and looks across. There's the tramp weeping with his head in the old man's lap, and he's stroking him. The young man realises that he's just witnessed Aikido in action. He's witnessed the art of reconciliation.

This is what the 34th Siddhi is – Majesty. Majesty is beyond strength. It's not to do with the maya. It's not to do with strength or weakness, it's beyond those. The 34th Siddhi, like all Siddhis, brings reconciliation. They all repair the world in some way. In the 7th Gene Key, I wrote about this catalytic concept called the Tikkun Olam, which is translated as 'repairing the world'. This is what the Siddhis do. The Siddhis are binding forces. They bring harmony wherever they go and they bring it through Majesty. Majesty is not display. Majesty is hidden. It's mysterious, humble, subtle. Like all the Siddhis whether it's movement or stillness, it always brings reconciliation – that is Majesty. It always finds the easiest way. In fact Majesty is beyond easy, because easy is a concept in the maya. Majesty just is – it's our true nature. It's what we each are. We are Kings and Queens - we're royalty. We're Divinity in movement. We're consciousness at play, without agenda, without anything added. We're an embodiment of joy. That's the true meaning of Majesty. We're joy itself expressed through a human body.

THE 64 WAYS

The 35th Way

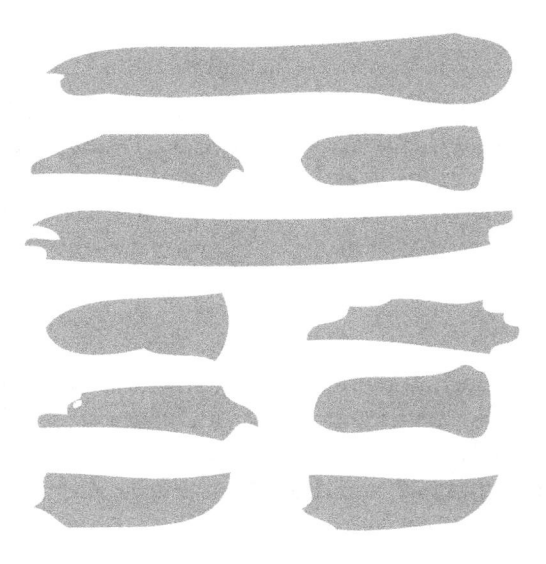

Gene Key 35

THE WAY OF ADVENTURE

The Transformational Way of the 35th Gene Key moves from Hunger to Boundlessness, and it's the Way of Adventure.

There are some Gene Keys whose Shadows just seem ancient, that stretch back into the animal kingdom, rooted in primal urges that have dominated our human planet for aeons. This 35th Gene Key has such a Shadow. Hunger, fear, lust - these are the drivers of the beast, the primal life urges that lay out the field of the Shadow. Hunger to eat, thirst to drink, hunger for power, hunger to escape and forget what we've done, hunger for warmth, love, connection. Hunger for Truth, unity, culture, beauty - hunger for God. Hunger, raw and pure. It lives inside each of us. It won't let us alone.

The Shadow isn't all about suffering. Here's a new truth for some of us. Hunger can also be sweet. It can be savoured. It can be drawn out. It can be appreciated. It can give us a sense of perspective. Hunger makes us human. It can bring us together. Every Shadow contains a Gift, if we learn how to tailor that Gift and mould it to our advantage. This is a trial and error process because it's all about balance. The balance is between appreciating our mortality, our vulnerability and our tendency towards excess. A little bit of Shadow is good for us. Without it we would be lacking in fibre, in backbone, in humanity. Excess of Shadow leads to pain, stress, exhaustion, and excess also becomes addictive. When we flood our body with hormones, an excess of food or drink or anything, we always pay the price.

There's an exact measure for the Shadow. We have to learn the art of homoeopathy - how to take the smallest dose of the Shadow so that we don't get trapped either by excess or starvation. The other route is to starve ourselves and go the way of the puritans, the ascetics. Often that path also leads to addiction and worse, to superiority. My friend, Hamvas Bela, a Hungarian writer, philosopher and genius, who's dead by the way, says there's an exact measure for

Shadow: Hunger **Gift:** Adventure **Programming Partner:** Gene Key 5
Dilemma: Self-Indulgence **Siddhi:** Boundlessness **Codon Ring:** The Ring of Miracles

---

drinking wine. The wine should take us just to the edge of intoxication. We shouldn't feel it hardly at all, but just the smallest push like a laugh or smile from someone we love will become that extra sip that intoxicates us. This is of course a wonderful metaphor for life. Can we live our life like that?

This Gene Key is about being filled with life. It's about stretching out into new experience. Life provides us with an almost infinite set of possible new experiences. If we draw a circle of just half a mile around our home, we'll find enough experience within that circle to last us an entire lifetime. We have to be careful about becoming trapped by the same old ways of satiating our hunger - the same patterns that exhaust us, the same ways of talking, of acting and reacting, of eating food, the same way of looking at life - the same mindset. There's a beauty in repetition. Repetition is essential to a balanced way of living but not repetition of awareness. The awareness should always be fresh, open, zingy.

Life can easily become stale through repetition, (the Programming Partner here is the 5th Shadow of impatience), but that's only because of our inner attitude. If we aren't doing things with presence, then we don't notice the subtle changes and differences in things. The same thing is never really the same. The planets are in different places, places they've never been in before as they wheel through the cosmos. Every challenge we face is really a new opportunity to respond imaginatively, to see things from a new perspective, to evolve.

The Dilemma is Self-Indulgence. You can see why. Just a little too much satiation and it becomes self-indulgence. A small amount, a measured amount of indulgence is actually healthy so long as it doesn't harm another. We know when we've lapsed into self-indulgence because it leads to us feeling bad about ourselves. It leads to sickness.

The secret of mastering this Shadow is knowing when to stop. Stop just before the edge. Leave a little hunger in the bank. Try not to satiate it completely. If we do, that's fine. Be forgiving of yourself. Be understanding of those who're driven by hunger, who do terrible things in life because they're driven by this hunger for power, for territory, for food, for revenge. We don't have to forgive them right away. That level of forgiveness takes mastery, but try and understand the world through this Shadow. Try and see how we each are driven by this insatiable hunger. We will fall, we will forget. We will make the mistake countless times.

That's the purpose of life - to grow in awareness as we ingest the Shadow, as we learn to let it become transmuted inside our very chemistry. Let the Shadow thus become your friend, rather than making it your enemy. Learn to drink tea with it. Learn to unlock its secrets, its Siddhi. That's the lesson in this Gene Key.

The 35th Gift - Adventure

There's a wonderful practise that comes from this Gift - I call it 'silo busting'. You may have heard of the expression. A silo is a self-contained enclosure that doesn't connect outwards but only serves itself. Silos are everywhere. Our thought-patterns are silos, our behaviour patterns are silos, our homes can be silos, our relationships, jobs, cultures, beliefs, languages, lives. It can be a very exciting thing to look at our life through the lens of this Gift - the Gift of Adventure.

Listen to life as it comes to you. It's constantly presenting you with new opportunities to bust open your silos. There's this mad film I once saw called 'Yes Man' about this man who follows this teacher who advocates saying yes to everything and everyone that comes our way. So if a homeless man asks you for all your money, you have to give it to him. Once this man starts to follow this teaching his life changes in dimensions that were previously unthinkable. Of course he meets all kinds of new people and activates synchronicities that are miraculous. It's a silo-busting film.

We don't have to take it to that extreme - that's inadvisable. But if we're listening to life we can take more of the many opportunities she's offering us. One of the things that will really change is that the various spheres of our life will begin to connect to each other in a new way. Our working life and our relationships will begin to dovetail, relationships in one area will cross over into other silos. We may find ourselves doing things in completely new ways. A mundane example might be that we start putting bird food out in our garden, and then all these new creatures visit us. Perhaps we bother to find out the name of the man in the grocery shop who always serves us. And another silo opens up.

The Gift of Adventure isn't about going out far and wide, though it may be; it's really about sampling the incredible diversity of life experience that's offering itself to us. So consider your silos. Read a new kind of book. Listen to your kids' music instead of trying to get away from it. Step into someone else's silo. Build bridges. Everywhere we go, we can build bridges. See how many new bridges you can build in a single day. Get your hands in the soil if you don't already. Go visit the city if you don't often. Move through the silos you tend to avoid. Bring your awareness deeper into the world, into life, and discover what an extraordinary place this earth is. Take tiny doses of the Shadow. You don't need to avoid it but just sample it. This can be even allowing a new kind of thinking in your life. Reach out across the chasms and see where life really wants to take you. This will make every day of your life a new adventure.

You need to understand me here. This isn't necessarily about doing new things. It's about doing the things that we already do in a new way, with a new kind of openness, a new kind of awareness not driven by hunger alone. The hunger is there. We acknowledge it but we also allow it to reach out inside our lives and move us closer to things, to create a greater intimacy within the circles of our lives. Since this Gift is allied with the 5th Gift of Patience, that gives us another clue - learn how to pause, wait, converse, exchange, pay attention. If someone starts talking to us in the middle of something, stop what we're doing and give them our full attention, at least for some moments. That pause may prove magical.

Patience and adventure. Two words twisted into a wonderful paradox. Patience with the Shadow, adventure with the Gift, and adventure with the Shadow and patience with the Gift. They underpin each other. Let adventure be our way. It's why we're here -

to move closer to life, to build bridges, to be present with the many fruits that lie littered all around us.

The 35th Siddhi - Boundlessness

The 35th Siddhi is a truly crazy Siddhi. I don't know how I know these things. I don't really. They just emerge out of my unknowing. I also love to read the patterns and this 35th Gene Key is unique in that within the Codon Rings - the genetic families of the Gene Keys, the 35th Gene Key stands alone like an island. All other Gene Keys, with the sole exception of the 41st Gene Key, which represents the Start Codon, are grouped in families. What are we to infer from this? Well, for one, it's why this Gene Key is hungry. It drives us to connect because it's alone.

It also sits there like a wormhole. That's what these connections are between silos - they're wormholes that connect different universes. It's through this Siddhi that bizarre things can occur - time may be bent, the future meets the past and the laws that govern one universe meet the laws that govern another. Higher beings can use this Siddhi wormhole to move in and out of our world. I have no idea what that really means or looks like, but it feels to be an intuitive truth. The ancients called this hexagram 'Easy Progress' - and it's generally seen as highly beneficial or signifying the emergence of heightened consciousness. Its image is connected to a radiant sun, which feels very appropriate, since the sun itself is our wormhole to higher consciousness.

This Siddhi is also connected to the possibility of Flight. It's about flying. When we dream of flying in our physical bodies, it's because we've done so in another dimension. One day these dimensions will interconnect again, and we'll experience that for real. It's a future memory. Flight is the terrain of the Boundless - our hearts are the wings that will one day make that possible as we move toward our ultimate adventure. This sounds quite mad to many people, but we humans are in fact obsessed with the idea. No one really talks about it. I mean our younger generations are obsessed by all these super-heroes who can fly, but we consider it fantasy. One day we'll see for ourselves what truly lies inside our DNA.

I'll be taken to task for my flights of fancy. Scientific types will crucify me for saying such things. I accept that. It won't happen for a while probably. In evolutionary terms it may be thousands of years, I don't know, but it will happen because it's already happened.

This 35th Gene Key is a relic from an earlier evolution. It sits there in our DNA like the appendix in our gut. It's from an earlier epoch. In that epoch it was once our Start Codon. In other words the 35th Siddhi dictated everything. Those magical Chinese films where the characters fly across the rooftops, that was us. We lived in a more merged time, long, long ago before the Great Flood. Our DNA was different then as well. Now we've become more complex as we've diversified. We've progressed. This Gene Key has assured that. It's driven us with its hunger for progress. And our deepest hunger is to fly once again, to sail up into the sky and become one with the Divine, to be a bird in the skies of existence.

Easy Progress. That's us. It may not feel like it now, but there are twists written into the plot-line of our evolution. There will always be unexpected wormholes that open up before us. If we can remember the grand adventure we're really on, our lives will become easier and more detached. Individual lifetimes will seem less important. Then we can enter into the timeless and boundless dimensions. Knowing that one day we'll fly means that right now we can silently smile and flow with the river in its current form. The river will reach the ocean, so just relax, sit down, and enjoy easy progress. Let go of the sound and fury of our life and its desperate quests. Settle down and look out the windows. Look to the birds in the sky…listen to this advice from Mary Oliver:

You do not have to be good.
You do not have to walk on your knees
for a hundred miles through the desert, repenting.
You only have to let the soft animal of your body
love what it loves.
Tell me about despair, yours, and I will tell you mine.
Meanwhile the world goes on.
Meanwhile the sun and the clear pebbles of the rain
are moving across the landscapes,

over the prairies and the deep trees,
the mountains and the rivers.
Meanwhile the wild geese, high in the clean blue air,
are heading home again.
Whoever you are, no matter how lonely,
the world offers itself to your imagination,
calls to you like the wild geese, harsh and exciting –
over and over announcing your place
in the family of things.

THE 64 WAYS

The 36th Way

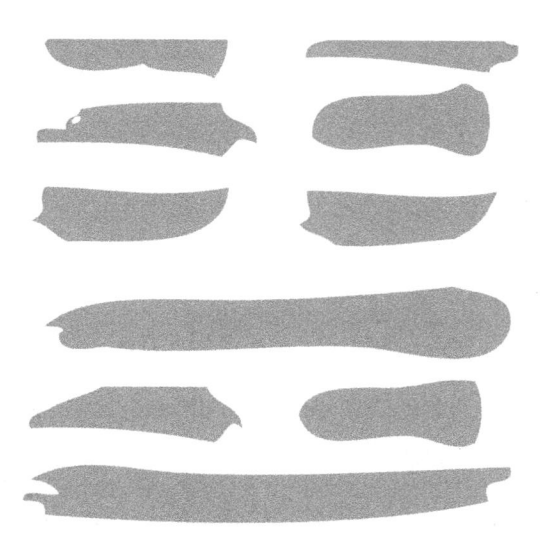

Gene Key 36

THE WAY OF HUMANITY

The Transformational Way of the 36th Gene Key moves from Turbulence to Compassion, and it's the Way of Humanity.

This is an amazing Way through the 36th Gene Key. We have to remember with the Gene Keys that they have this dual component. They are present as collective archetypes that govern all of humanity, being present as vibrational codes inside every molecule of DNA inside every cell, inside every organ and system within us. In addition to this we all incarnate with different sequences of Gene Keys that relate specifically to our unfolding destiny and evolution.

Because of the 21 Codons Rings, which contain the grid of all the Gene Keys as they impact us collectively, we all have contact all the time with the Gene Keys through our relationships. I don't have this 36 anywhere in my own sequence for example, but I have watched it move in and out of my life through friendships, loves, and most recently through the arrival of my young daughter. I'm saying all this here because the 36th Gene Key in particular comes to us as a reminder of the sometimes extreme suffering we humans have to undergo. The original name of this 36th hexagram in the I Ching is the Darkening of the Light. This name may sound frightening, so let me assure you that the embodiment of Compassion is the sweetest journey of all. Whenever I come to it there's always a part of me that wants to do it in reverse. It's one of the most grounding journeys of all the 64 Gene Keys.

The Shadow is turbulence. Don't you love what that word has become most associated with - being on an airplane when we suddenly hit those air pockets, the plane lurches, and our stomach shoots up into our mouth. The next thing we hear is a calm voice saying, 'ladies and gentlemen, please fasten your seat belts…'

Shadow: Turbulence **Gift**: Humanity **Programming Partner:** Gene Key 6
Dilemma: Overwhelm **Siddhi**: Compassion **Codon Ring:** The Ring of Divinity

Well, this 36th Shadow is about putting on our seat belts and making sure we have a life jacket. Turbulence can be physical, emotional, and mental. More often than not, it's all three. When we watch the news or listen to the media, this is pretty much all we see, the turbulent collective field of our planetary Shadow frequency - wars, conflicts, hunger, death, violence, blame, guilt, victimisation. On and on it goes… When we look at this beautiful peach of a blue green globe from space, it hangs there so serenely like an Eden adrift in the ethers. We come down through the planes until we land in a body and what do we find? Suffering. Who would have thought?

This is why the Dilemma of this 36th Shadow is Overwhelm. This is what happens when we exist at a Shadow frequency rooted in fear. We feel overwhelmed by life. Our mind is overwhelmed, our emotions are overwhelmed, our body is overwhelmed. The Shadow frequency itself is nothing but overwhelming.

No one escapes the 36th Shadow. If we have it imprinted in our Profile, then we've taken on an adventurous curriculum. We'll meet suffering at the deepest level. That may not be inside our being but it will be at some level. It often comes through our relationships, through those we love or our choice of work. The thing with this Gene Key is to not be afraid of it. The Shadow invokes the fear of suffering, and it's the fear that's so overwhelming. Were we to have known this when we were younger, how different our attitude might have been. Instead of being a victim of suffering and being overwhelmed by emotional turbulence and drama, we would have understood it as an integral part of our life's journey. Turbulence has a particular affinity with the emotional, astral plane. At some point in our lives we're invited to support another as they move through the Darkening of the Light, as they go through a period of intense suffering.

GENE KEY 36

This is where the 36th Gene Key is designed to shine. When the light darkens in another, then we light up. At the Shadow frequency however, most hearts close down as the turbulence increases. That's the Shadow response, to repress, cave-in, close down, or react through rage and blame.

Yes, at the Shadow frequency this 36th Gene Key is all its name is cracked up to be. It presents a vision of the world that is ever-pessimistic, always struggling, always a victim, always overwhelmed by life and driven by a huge reservoir of unconscious ancestral fear - not a pretty picture.

The 36th Gift — Humanity

This has to be the most incredible Gift of all - the Gift of Humanity. It doesn't sound like much, does it? but what a secret it contains. Part of the Ring of Divinity, this Gene Key has some hefty partners, the 22, 63, and 37, Grace, Truth, and Tenderness. It gives us a clue about who we humans really are. Suffering by design is for only one reason, to crack us open. To reach into our innermost recesses and shatter the patterns that keep us apart. We've seen how the 36th Shadow of Turbulence overwhelms us, so that we enter this collective state of stasis and shock and close our hearts and feelings down. It's a learned genetic response to freeze like this whenever we feel overwhelmed.

The 36th Gift doesn't freeze. It doesn't close down. It stays open. Wow! Do you know what that entails? Someone or something completely threatens to overwhelm us and we stay open. Our heart may recoil for a few moments, but then we breathe deeply into our chest, anchor ourself in the belly, and look the experience right in the eye. We meet it with an open heart, and let the turbulence in all the way. It will shake us up, toss us about emotionally, physically, and mentally, but we stay with the process. Above all, we don't close down.

Oh yes, this 36th Gift is a roller-coaster. With our heart open it isn't possible to be overwhelmed. The heart can open infinitely to accommodate anything and everything. Only the mind and emotions can be overwhelmed. Our soul, our whole being at a higher frequency, can't be overwhelmed by life. As we settle into the higher frequency other things begin to happen. Every Shadow contains a Gift. Grace begins to show itself. Our openness has a deep healing effect and others begin to open, to share their deepest fears, to let go, to heal.

Dying is of course the greatest challenge for us all. Dying, and the pain of the process and the loss that comes with it. Yet what does it do to us? It makes us human. It makes us realise what's important in life. It gives us a whole new perspective on life, sharpens our senses and opens us to the wonder and possibility of transcendence. Ahh, to be human. The dream of the dolphin is to be human - to be transformed in the fires of this suffering, to stay open, to embrace our humanity, our mortality, to trust. This is the 36th Gift. Forget whether we have it or not in our Profile, it's deeper than that. The Gene Keys provide a universal teaching. To move through turmoil and remain open is the quickest way to be transformed and realise the higher frequencies.

This is one of the very few Gene Keys that illuminates the essence of what repentance is. This Gene Key allows for massive transformations. It puts people through the most intense fires. Through this Gift we hear stories of really evil beings repenting of their sins and suddenly realising higher states.

To be human is to forgive oneself. Whatever comes our way in this life listen to the transmission contained in this Gift - practise humanity. Stay open to everything. It's OK if we close momentarily. That's human too, but then forgive yourself, forgive the other, and gently coax your heart back from the dead, and do it again, and again, and again. That's what the Gift of Humanity is about – it's about having the courage to be vulnerable, exposed. We can then discover the grace that eventually nothing can wound us, because nothing can wound a healed heart.

THE 36TH SIDDHI — COMPASSION

Finally we get to the prize, Compassion. I always see and experience this word like a fragrance. It's the natural radiant emanation of a pure human aura. It's a fragrance given off by our DNA as it activates its highest components. If we've ever been around a being of pure grace, an enlightened one, we might pick up this fragrance. It's not olfactory, it's the higher octave of our normal sense of smell. It's the aroma of grace, the smell of the pure light, and once we've remembered it, we can never, never forget it.

Compassion is divinity embodied in humanity. Compassion is the seed that exists within turbulence. The whole transformational journey through this Gene Key culminates with the release of this fragrance from our essence. This is where humanity and divinity become one. This is where the current of evolution meets the current of involution. This is the highest manifestation of humanity - this is compassion. What does it mean to be compassionate? We tend to think of it as a motherly kind of tenderness, and that's certainly one of its qualities, yet it's more. Compassion is a mirroring of the whole sweep of our true nature. It's an energetic torrent of truth that rushes through our being when we meet suffering in another. When we meet compassion, we meet God within a human being. When we look in the eyes of compassion, we'll see the only force within the universe with no agenda. Compassion may carry great ferocity in that moment, or it may brush our heart with the lightness of a feather.

I'm reminded of a story of the Buddha. Since compassion has so many faces, stories convey it the best. There was the Buddha, magnificent, tremendous, the fragrance of pure consciousness wafting all around him. His closest disciples are all about him as he receives the public one by one to offer them the blessings of his compassion. One man comes and asks him, 'Is there a God?' 'No', says Buddha, 'there is no God'. The man leaves, desolate, crestfallen, in tears. Another man comes, 'Is there a God?' 'Yes', says the Buddha, 'there is a God'. The man stands there stunned, confused, and turns away, his mind working, a deep frown furrowing his brow. A third man comes, 'Is there a God?' The Buddha looks him right in the eye, and says nothing. The man nods in silence and turns, a huge smile bursting out across his face.

After the day's darshan is over, and all the people have left, one of the Buddha's disciples asks him directly, 'Master, the three men who asked about God, why did you answer each one so differently?' We don't understand. 'Well', said the Buddha, with a glint in his eye, 'the first man was a believer. He wanted to believe and yet his belief was preventing him from experiencing directly. So I told him no, there is no God. His disappointment will shatter him open. The second man was a cynic, a skeptic, a man whose mind had proven to him that there is no God. He came for confirmation, so I naturally told him there is a God, and now he's in turmoil. Because he can feel it in me, he can no longer only trust in his mind. He too will be shattered open. The third man, he was close to the

Truth. He had looked within. He was right on the edge, all he needed was a little push, and so I gave him the transmission through silence. He was able to receive it. He too was shattered open to a far deeper level.'

These kinds of stories give us some idea of the mysteries of how compassion works. It mirrors our suffering, it shatters us open. Whatever state we find ourself in, compassion supplies its equalising force and creates an opening, a wormhole, and we have no choice but to pass through that wormhole and enter deeper into our essence. Yes, the Darkening of the Light. Compassion is the great and mysterious fragrance, the first fragrance, even there within the Shadows, deeply intertwined into the coils of our DNA, waiting for the right moment, waiting for the right geometry, waiting for destiny, waiting simply for us, waiting for us to let go and rediscover the piercing blade of light that hides within those darkest inner reaches of the void that we all fear. And when we jump, when we do let go, what do we find there? Not emptiness, but compassion, the aroma of truth, grace and tenderness, in everything we touch and everywhere we go...

THE 37TH WAY

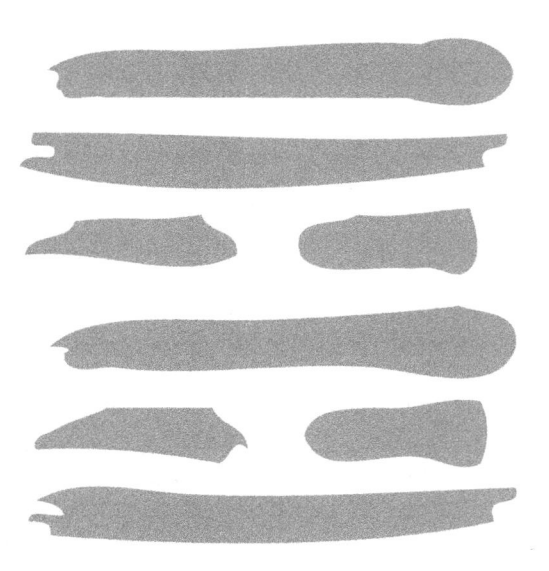

Gene Key 37

THE WAY OF EQUALITY

The Transformational Way of the 37th Gene Key moves from Weakness to Tenderness, and it's the Way of Equality.

This Gene Key has some really interesting insights for us to ponder. In many ways it's driving a lot of the social changes we see occurring in our modern civilisation. As individual freedom breaks out and basic human rights are recognised as more and more important, we're seeing a shift in the balance between the masculine and feminine poles. The feminine is reviving itself after many long centuries of neglect, and the masculine is softening and transforming at a whole new level. This process is discussed in the 37th Gene Key in the Gene Keys book, but it's also taking place inside each of us, and that's what I'd like to get into as we explore this 37th Transformational Way.

In the West, it was Carl Jung who really opened up the notion of the individual having these two male and female poles inside us. He called them the animus and the anima - the inner male and inner female. A healthy life is about maintaining a balance between them. Weakness, the 37th Shadow, is what occurs whenever we lose this balance. Essentially, weakness is the result of an unconscious belief that we're powerless. The fact is that we're not all born equal but we are equal. This is a paradox. Some are born with physical disability or illness that seems to set them apart, others are born into lives of severe lack, into oppressive cultures or poverty and then there are those of us born into lives of privilege, with opportunity, freedom, and choices. When we look at the world, it doesn't seem that fair. It doesn't seem as though we're equal.

Yet the Gene Keys are all about genius. This is where we're equal. We're equal to the task we're given, but only if we don't cave in. The Dilemma of the 37th Shadow is Submission. We have to learn that we each have a different route towards discovering fortitude, towards the embodiment of our genius. We have equal opportunities in consciousness.

Shadow: Weakness   **Gift:** Equality   **Programming Partner:** Gene Key 40
Dilemma: Submission   **Siddhi:** Tenderness   **Codon Ring:** The Ring of Divinity

---

Wherever we are and whoever we are, we always have this opportunity to overcome the Shadow inside that believes we're weak.

The real question is are we living a life worth living? Are we taking the bull by the horns and meeting life halfway? Or are we submitting to the victim inside us? Have we given up on ourself, on our great inner dreams? Have we settled for less than we're worthy of? It's been said that genius requires boldness, and this is absolutely true. Are we proud of the life we're living? This isn't about achievement. It's important not to make that mistake. Outer achievement doesn't necessarily denote a life of genius. Genius is rooted in self love. It's rooted in surrender rather than submission. We might think these two terms are the same, but they're worlds apart. Let's think about ourselves. Where would we say we're weak? Where are our weaknesses? We're only weak through our own perception. What we see as weakness is really an opportunity - for growth, maturity, prosperity. The very area of our being that we consider weakest is actually the place where we can be the strongest, where we can thrive the most.

I'd like us to really think about ourselves and our lives. This Gene Key is all about the archetype of the family. Well, who's the most troubled or troublesome member of our family? Who's the weakest link? We have this cliched saying that any group is only as strong as its weakest link. Well, I'd like us to consider the reverse - the perceived weakest link in the group is actually the binding force of the group. We can apply this to our own life. Which area do we struggle in the most - money, relationships, health, family? Well, that's the area that can potentially bring the whole of our life into a higher harmony.

But it takes work! We have to be equal to the task. The 37th Shadow gives up, submits to fate, bows its head and succumbs to what it considers the inevitable. It's a victim stance. People all over the world are addicted to their victim beliefs. They'll even fight to stay a victim. This Shadow runs deep in the genome. Genetically we're used to submission. Our cultures have bred this fear of independence into us. When we submit to our own weakness we collapse into exhaustion, the Shadow of the 40th Gene Key, the Programming Partner of the 37th. There's healthy exhaustion, and then there's fatigue. Healthy exhaustion is the fulfilling feeling we have when we've thoroughly expended our creative energy on a worthwhile task. Fatigue is the sapping of our life force due to a loss in enthusiasm and a lack of higher purpose.

The answer is to fight for our genius and not give in to our inner demons. Find our weakest link and instead of pushing it away into some dark corner we need to face it, accept it yes, but not assume it's a dead-end street. Assume the opposite. Assume it hides a great power and give our awareness to unlocking that power and potential. This is the true way to deep self-love.

The 37th Gift - Equality

What happens when we unlock this hidden power? This is the domain of the Gifts. The Gift frequency always brings balance and equality. We witness the animus and the anima within coming into balance. They begin a courtship. We really have to look at ourself as a relationship. We have yin and yang aspects. We have a sharp intellect, that's yang. We have an intuitive heart, that's yin. We have determination and resolve, that's yang, and we have flexibility and openness, that's yin. We have a fathomless inner well of silence and depth, that's yin, and we have a vivacious, rebellious enthusiasm, that's yang. Sometimes our life energy dips, and we feel withdrawn and perhaps melancholic, that's yin, and sometimes we're happy and crazy for no real reason, that's yang.

We're a rippling field of contradictory forces. We are male and female. Just as with outer relationships, we need equality. If one pole is oppressive and the other submissive, we're out of balance and weak. If one pole is wounded and repressed, then the other will carry the weight and again we're weak. The poles have to be brought into balance.

The Gift of Equality is a genius for facilitating balance. When we manifest inner equality, we also bring it into the world. The 37th Gift will always find itself in the heart of communities or families, bringing cohesion to some weakened strata of society. The 37th Gift helps others overcome their weaknesses, and helps them towards greater independence and freedom. This is why the 37th Gift is such a healthy energy for any community.

It's a strange paradox that we come to equality through inequality. By catalysing others towards greater rebelliousness and independence we actually create a more powerful linkage in the world. This is the secret to good parenting - we help the child become independent, unlock their Gifts, and in doing so it seems we're helping them move further away. But the opposite is true, freedom engenders loyalty. Sometimes the Gift of Equality has to step back from a relationship in order that the other becomes stronger on their own.

The core of the 37th Gift is about support. We support the tree when it's young and then it stands strong on its own. It may not formally thank us but it will always, somewhere, feel grateful to us. I have this memory of my English teacher when I was young. He was a hard man. He was a real disciplinarian in the old style. But he loved his subject and his love was evident. He sparked my love of language. He provided the structure and support I needed even though I didn't realise it at the time. I often think of him and feel gratitude towards him. He taught me an invaluable lesson; I've tried to pass it on to my children and have encompassed it in these teachings. This is part of my gratitude in paying it forward. The 37th Gene Key is all about paying it forward. This terrific force of goodwill lies in every human being. The enthusiasm, the optimism, the warmth of human beings. The 37th Gene Key has these qualities in spades. It's connected to the archetype of the goddess, the hearth, the home, but it's not only about women.

This Gift is about supporting oneself and others in excelling. To excel we have to break out of our own self-indulgent 'I'm not good enough' belief structures. We have to snap out of our victim frequency. That takes some inner strength but it also often needs support. The 37th Gift is never too proud to ask for help. It knows that there are others who have gifts that it doesn't, and it calls upon them when it needs them. This is the foundation of any healthy community, but it doesn't lean on others beyond a certain point.

It's like these therapists who want us to keep coming back. A good therapist wants to get rid of us! They may have to put us through a program but at the end of that they'll encourage us to go back into the world.

We have far greater strength than we realise, we human beings. Most of the time we're just too scared to pull ourselves up. We become too conformist. We get stuck in processing our 'stuff', instead of getting on with the job of being a creative rebel. Genius has boldness in it. To live a worthwhile life, a life we'll be proud of at the end, we'll have to transform our weaknesses into our strengths. We'll have to overcome our tendency to believe that we're incapable, and we'll have to join in with the human race. Life is a race. It's a race for higher consciousness, and our opponent is time. We can't win the race, but we can let it fill us with vigour, with the urge to help others, with the enthusiastic surge of wellbeing that comes from living a life with true purpose and deep inner equality.

The 37th Siddhi - Tenderness

The purpose of all life is to come to rest in our essence. Everything manifests its own unique obliqueness - the creative edge that sets it apart from all else. Life is a celebration of difference, of the unpeeling waves of consciousness as they break upon the soft shores of the earth. There must always be an earth. Even when the physical shell of our earth is long gone, folded up into the chrism of the sun's passionate fire, the essence of the earth will remain. The earth is an archetype, a resonant symbol of home for all that appears to be separate. When we die, we fall into the earth's embrace, and in the very split second that we die, another version of us reemerges to follow the same curving mystery of life.

Always there's the essence, and the 37th Siddhi stands as a reminder of the essence from which we emerge and into which we shall one day fall. Tenderness is the heart of the universal mother. In the original I Ching, the 37th hexagram is seen as representing the archetype of the family. There's a natural equality that holds a family in resonance, and there's an over-arching intelligence in the family that goes far beyond the individuals present. At the heart of the family is the mother. The mother is the earth and the ground that allows the father to expand his influence outwards in service to the world.

The mother is also the place of infinite tenderness where all members of the family can return to rest and remember their essence and purpose. More even than a single person, the mother is a feeling of safety and trust that allows all human beings to excel. The 37th Siddhi speaks into this great mystery of the mother essence.

The family also is a great symbol of the future possibilities of humanity. When we come together as families then we have enormous strength and potential. A single unified family could bring down a government! The beginning of collective consciousness will spring from the unit of the family. The interconnecting of integrated families all over the globe will generate a wave of tender power and love whose force will be unstoppable in its transformative power. Family is symbolised by blood, close genetic relationship, but that's just a symbol. We're all related genetically. It doesn't matter how immediate that relationship is. True family can spring up in any small group of people, no matter how diverse their DNA. It's a collective essence that through its suffering finds a common bond.

In the time to come, these small units of people will begin to emerge all over the world. Our future consciousness will begin in small groupings of people who are mysteriously drawn together for some form of higher purpose. The Siddhi of Tenderness can only really be felt through this group consciousness. It can't emerge in isolation, because it's the glue that brings us together as one. As individuals explore their genius, so they engage the universal force of synchronicity, which places them in a greater context alongside the allies of their genius. One kind of genius usually requires others in order to complete its highest potential. Even a small net of genius can change the whole world.

If we're contemplating this Gene Key and in particular its Siddhi, think about your greatest potential - your higher purpose. How can it best be of service? What qualities does your genius need to come to its zenith? What qualities complete you? Somewhere out there are your blood brothers and sisters. We can only come together when the male and female poles inside us come into balance. In the Gene Keys Golden Path, this is what happens as we transition from the Venus Sequence into the Pearl.

GENE KEY 37

The Pearl is the goal of consciousness, it's our harvest. We unite our Siddhis in a creative explosion of higher consciousness, but first we have to come into our own tender heart. That is the importance of the Venus Sequence, to ignite our mother essence, our Divine Wound.

The 37th Siddhi is one of four Gene Keys forming a Codon group known as the Ring of Divinity. Its partners are Compassion, Grace and Truth, the 36th, the 22nd, and the 63rd Gene Keys. Quite a package! This Codon Ring orchestrates our higher evolution and will take us to our final evolutionary zenith. It will do this through uniting us in creative service to the whole. The 37th Gene Key is made up of two trigrams, sub-symbols represented by elements. These elements are fire and wind. These are the ingredients of a forest fire and this is what the Siddhi of Tenderness is. We began with the Shadow of Weakness, and to many, tenderness seems to be a weak force. That's because it isn't designed to manifest in isolation. Tenderness is a collective fire, engendered through mutual compassion, fanned by the winds of Grace and carrying the transformative power of Truth. The future will emerge in such a subtle way that we won't ever notice it's happening. The world is already changing, as powerful pockets of Tender Truth place themselves in service to the whole.

One more thing I came across in my contemplation of this 37th Siddhi. I was walking through a Saturday market recently, and found myself just looking into people's eyes. Wherever I went I just looked only into people's eyes. It was a beautiful morning, the sun was shining, the market was alive and murmuring with trade and friendly chatter, as markets around the world are. What I felt was this Siddhi. I felt the tenderness passing from person to person through the eyes. Of course not everyone was carrying it at that moment, but as a whole it was moving through the community.

I followed my contemplation of this afterwards, and this is the insight that dropped in. These Siddhis are so near the surface. All it takes is the right environment and up they come. The problem is that we've created an environment based on fear, greed, ambition, hunger and lack. Imagine if we took money away from humanity. Imagine if we found a way to feed ourselves through small doses of highly nutritious nano-pills. Imagine if we didn't need to worry about food, energy, or money. Imagine that we've created an environment based on beauty, relaxation, and creativity. I tell you, the Siddhis would just bob up to the surface. Imagine everyone was able to simply live out their higher purpose without stress or compromise. The Siddhi of Tenderness would spread like wildfire throughout humanity, re-building bonds of long-forgotten trust and healing the rifts between races. It wouldn't take much for these higher qualities to emerge. They're already our nature. So this Codon Ring is really waiting for its time. In the end, grace will have its day.

It's extraordinary what we find when we look deeply into the codes within our DNA. We really never stood a chance against such higher forces. The Shadow was just the beginning. It's only a matter of time. Who knows how long this will all take to work itself out? Does it really matter? I don't think so. When something is inevitable, all we have to do is align ourself with it then get swept along by the tide and our life will be a whole load easier. If we're reading or listening to this, why don't we just let go and enjoy the ride!

The 38th Way

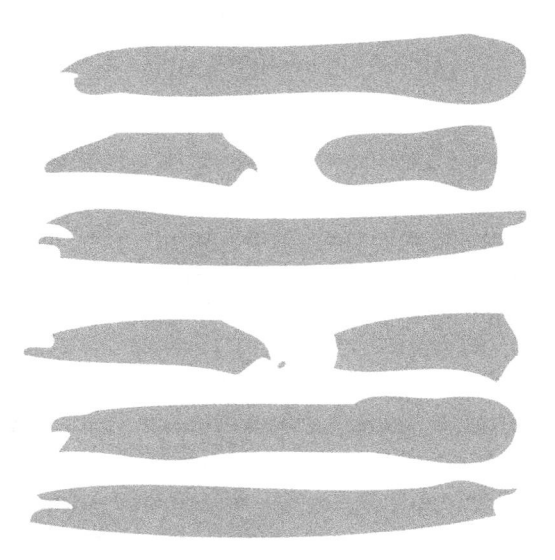

Gene Key 38

THE WAY OF PERSEVERANCE

The Transformational Way of the 38th Gene Key moves from Struggle to Honour, and it's the Way of Perseverance.

This Way through the 38th Gene Key is really pivotal in our lives. When we understand this one, immediately our life will begin to change. This is the pattern of struggle. We don't like the idea of struggle but still in life we always struggle at some level – whether it's the physical struggle for survival in the developing world, or the emotional struggle as we learn the meaning of love and loss, or the mental struggle with just about anything. The revelation of this 38th Shadow is its Dilemma – Habit.

You see we're born to struggle, to fight, to move ever upwards. We're form forced from within to try and free ourselves, to learn to fly, to be free from struggle, to be effortless like the birds in the sky or the dolphins leaping through the ocean waves. But these creatures also struggle. Everything does. It's the nature of evolution to go on expanding, reaching, surmounting itself. In humans, struggle can either free us or trap us. It traps us when it becomes a habit. At low levels of frequency we get so used to struggling that it becomes our daily norm. It's there when we begin our day with a mental list of all the things we have to do, and before we know it the day is over. We may or may not have done all those things, but what's important is that the day itself was lacking. It wasn't in any way memorable because we were trapped by our habit.

There is a lot of sadness in this Gene Key. It's sad because it doesn't get to fight the real fight. I travel around the world now and again. I love to travel. One of the things that always takes me by surprise is that most of the people I meet, after I get to know them a little, aren't doing what they would love to be doing. They're stuck in a habitual lifestyle

Shadow: Struggle **Gift**: Perseverance **Programming Partner:** Gene Key 39
Dilemma: Habit **Siddhi:** Honour **Codon Ring:** The Ring of Humanity

---

that they think they can't break out of. Habit can give the illusion of security but it's a clear illusion. We can't be secure if we're unhappy. How can we feel secure? Security is a feeling in the cells, a sense of higher purpose. We don't have to know how to get there, but we have to begin. We have to break our habit.

How do we do that? Break the habit of a lifetime? Well, it helps to be honest with ourself first. Where are we unhappy? In our job? Our relationship? Our body? Where do we struggle? We can begin with self honesty because we can then put that struggle to better use to serve a higher purpose. Imagine if we could use the consistency of the things we struggle with on a daily basis for a higher purpose. Imagine something we've always wanted to be or do, in our heart, and then put all our struggle into that. That's what will change our life. We have to break the habit and move it onto a higher plane.

Many of us think or hope that we will one day transcend struggle and that somehow when we reach the highest consciousness, the Siddhi, there will be no more struggle. But we should be aware of the difference between the cessation of struggle and the end of suffering. It is suffering that we transcend, not struggle. We need struggle. Struggle defines us, sharpens us, hones us. It is a gift from the higher realms. Even the most illuminated beings struggle, but they do not suffer as they struggle. Struggle is their joy because they know it is testing them, polishing them and refining their awareness. Begin then by accepting this plane as a place of testing and education. The earth is a school and we are here to learn. Rest will come later, when we have earned it. In the meantime, let's use the struggle to raise our awareness, to elevate our frequency and to bring us ever closer to the Gift and the Siddhi.

The 38th Gift – Perseverance

In the original classic translation of the I Ching by Richard Wilhelm, there's a very common phrase that repeats throughout the text – Perseverance furthers. It used to drive me nuts when I played with the I Ching. I'd ask these deep questions and I'd get this flippant impenetrable response, 'Perseverance furthers!' At a very deep level I think I know what it means now – take a pause, take a breath, take a rain-check. Because this is the Dilemma of our habits – they run our lives, they run us into the ground. We just can't seem to stop. So we need to pause. All of nature pauses. Animals pause for no good reason. Watch a dog or a cat or any creature and I guarantee it'll pause in the time we're watching it. It'll suddenly just stop and be, without any reason. It might only 'be' for a few moments, but it's always there. Think of a fly landing on your arm. Why does it do that? It annoys us, but why shouldn't the fly use our arm for a pause?

The seasons also have pauses. Winter is a big pause. Night is a pause, twilight is a pause. So is the day for all the nocturnal creatures. But there are many, many little natural pauses that run throughout our day. If we're caught in our habit of struggling, we won't take a single one and we'll miss the magic of the day. Because a day filled with pauses is a day with awareness, and a day with awareness is an extraordinary day. It's not ordinary, relentless, another day to get through. With pauses, our days become extra ordinary.

Listen to this Gift of Perseverance because it's about all of us. Pause. Stare out the window. Close the laptop, switch off the phone for 5 minutes. We need to let life call us to our pauses. This is the first thing to do and what comes out of this awareness is some kind of shift in our behaviour. The 38th Gene Key is not about thinking. It's dynamic, and the Programming Partner is the 39th Gene Key with its Gift of Dynamism, which is all about action. How will we use our precious life force? What will we do with each precious day of our life? The 38th Gift tells us - find a fight worth fighting for and then pour our energies into that. The human spirit is indomitable. It loves to reach and stretch and break new ground. We won't be happy in life unless we too reach and stretch and break new ground. No matter who we are.

We're built to persevere. We are designed to find our genius and follow where it takes us. We only have to begin. Love carries perseverance hidden within it. And life loves a challenge. Where would the fun of life be without challenges? When we begin to activate our higher purpose then we'll continue to meet challenges but we'll find the appropriate way through or around those challenges. Our perseverance will guide us. Sometimes we need to go for it and meet the challenge head-on, other times we may stand by the side and wait until a more natural way presents itself. What's for certain is that every challenge we meet in life is an opportunity to learn to love and honour ourself more deeply.

One final thing, the Gift of Perseverance is an archetype of what it means to be a true human being. We are warriors. Life calls the inner warrior out of us, and when we answer that call such a shout of joy emerges through us. When we do meet someone living according to their higher purpose what a difference it is. They shine. They're simple. They don't carry the same baggage or anxiety as the rest of us. They're still human and have their Shadows, but they tend to smile and have open hearts. They know what it takes, so they understand the basic suffering we all feel. They've made the great leap – the leap into their heart. Everything they do now serves the love and joyousness that keeps flowing through that heart.

The 38th Siddhi: Honour

It's a great truth that every Siddhi is to be found inside every Shadow. We just have to dig around a bit. We have to honour the struggle as well. The journey always begins with struggle, with the realisation that we're in pain. I was talking with an old friend recently about what happens when we reach into the Gift frequency, and in some ways it's even more uncomfortable than the Shadow. I was talking about Dante's Divine Comedy, and how he divided his allegory of consciousness into these 3 levels called Inferno, Purgatorio, and Paradiso – hell, purgatory, and paradise. The basis is hell. Hell is hell, it's always a struggle, we're stuck in it, and that's the way it is. Then comes purgatory when we get a glimpse of something else, a glimpse of paradise. And it's just a fleeting glimpse, a moment of transport, of possibility, of pure happiness. Then comes the ruin – we still live in hell, but it can never be the same hell again.

This is why the Gift can be like a purgatory, because now we know that the struggle has a higher purpose, that it conceals a secret. The Siddhi is in there, and now the work truly begins. Awareness enters. Now we know we're in hell, which is purgatory. It's midway. At least in hell we were asleep. Now a part of us is yearning for transcendence. Every mistake we make in life, every time we dishonour ourselves or another, we have the potential to learn something and we touch the potential for transformation.

Honour is also in the struggle. It's there as a seed. Every time we find ourself struggling with a challenge, especially an inner challenge, try and remember to honour the moment. We can trust the discomfort not for what it is, but we can trust our awareness of it because that awareness carries a whiff of the Siddhi. It gives strength to the Gift – it fuels the perseverance. With these Gene Keys we have to hold it all in our consciousness – Shadow, Gift, and Siddhi, all at the same time. If we just hold our awareness on the Shadow without remembering that the Siddhi is also there, we'll truly struggle and become weighed down by our life. But feel the field of honour behind life's challenges, feel it driving our evolution forwards and upwards, and our life will feel very different. It will have a certain buoyancy, an uplift.

Honour transforms difficulties into opportunities. It's the hallmark of all great human lives. Honour turns surrender into victory. It's all about surrender. We have to surrender to our Dharma, to what the "Fates" deliver to us, our challenges, setbacks, failures. It's all part of our training for a higher kind of being. To enter into the Siddhi of Honour is to enter into an energy field – a field of knowing, of great human dignity. Honour swallows suffering. With honour, we can say no as powerfully as we can say yes. It's pure and free from all guilt. It doesn't worry about perception.

It takes feelings into consideration, but it will not compromise the deep love within. Honour is a spontaneous response to life and it's rooted in unconditional love. Although it may often go unseen, it also captivates the human imagination, because it's found in the most ordinary and simple places, in the least expected situations. This is a Siddhi that few may embody, but anyone may partake in. It's dynamic, transformational, effervescent, and above all, honour is humble.

People make a lot of fuss about honour. All manner of terrible things are done in the name of honour. But the real thing eludes us. Like all Siddhis it is inherently mysterious and eludes easy definition. True honour comes as a knowing, as an indefinable gratitude to life. It may be inspired by a person or an action or a story, but the honour itself is the uniting force, the blending field, it is the transcending factor that connects the one heart to the many and that brings us closer to life and to each other. Honour is something so quiet and yet it elicits such a burning fire when we hear or see or feel it.

When I think of honour, I think of my Uncle Brian, who was killed in the second World War. Often honour seems to be connected to the theme of death. He was a young Lieutenant and was awarded the Military Cross for Gallantry for leading a raid in Italy. But it is his death that triggers this Siddhi in my heart. He was leading his men up a steep hill against a fortified position, when the Germans started shelling his position. It was a disaster and many brave young men were killed or maimed. I actually went there to the very place where he was killed. It was deeply emotional for me, and for my mother and father who were with me. In the regimental diary there was a rare account of how he died. The medic found him wounded and started dressing his wounds, but he turned the medic away telling him to go to his men first. By the time the medics had returned, my Uncle had died.

He wasn't thinking about his actions, but for whatever reason they live on. If they hadn't been written down I wouldn't be telling you now. In this way I am honouring not just his memory but the memory of all those who died for a higher cause. So many other brave men and women have died in similar circumstances, but their stories remain secret and untold. Honour is like that. It lives on eternally in another higher dimension. That is something worthy of deeper contemplation.

And let's go further even than this, because we often think about honour as connected to death - to die with honour is a great thing, but perhaps equally powerful is to live with honour, and how relatively rare that is. Let's think about our own lives as we contemplate this Siddhi, and may each of us find the insight to live our own life with honour, no matter what the fates bring us.

The 39th Way

Gene Key 39

THE WAY OF DYNAMISM

The Transformational Way of the 39th Gene Key moves from Provocation to Liberation, and it's the Way of Dynamism.

Everything about this 39th Gene Key is about clearing blockages. It's one of the very powerful dynamic Gene Keys that we all have to pass through before we attain any kind of higher frequencies. The ancients evidently knew this since they called it obstruction. In life there will always be obstacles. The only question is: how do we cope with them when they come? The way we cope is what defines our frequency and the level of our evolution.

At the Shadow frequency, we are chock full of blockages. Our very life force is blocked up. We block it up the moment we begin shutting down our higher faculties and our heart as children. Most people are so blocked up that they aren't even aware of a spiritual reality. This is why life constantly offers us opportunities to awaken and unblock ourselves. Life is constantly provoking us to either grow or wilt. The deeper we go into our suffering, the more aware we become of the blockages inside us. It's a very uncomfortable place to be in. There are two types of blockages I'm talking about here. There are the blockages that we carry in our DNA, that we're responsible for. Those blockages and obstructions are self imposed, even though that may be an unconscious thing on our part.

Then there are the blockages and obstructions that we aren't responsible for (at least not directly) - karmic events or situations that arise in our daily lives that come to challenge us unexpectedly. One is an internal blockage and the other external. At least that's how it seems to us, but there's a direct connection between what occurs to us externally and our inner blockages. External blockages arise out of the compassionate, intelligent evolutionary force that wishes us to be free, to become liberated. Think about that the next time something stressful occurs in your life. It has a higher purpose. It may take you a while to get there, but if you open to it, to the karmic teaching, then eventually you'll make a breakthrough.

Shadow: Provocation	**Gift:** Dynamism	**Programming Partner:** Gene Key 38
Dilemma: Blockages	**Siddhi:** Liberation	**Codon Ring:** The Ring of Seeking

The 39th Gene Key is very physical, very energetic. I often contemplate it as the meridian network that runs through our etheric body - our subtle energy field. Our health is built upon that matrix of forces. Blockages in the flow of our meridians cause physical health issues, but blockages in the etheric body are rooted in deeper blockages in subtler fields, like the astral, emotional body. An emotional issue shows up as a blockage in the meridians, so even if we have great acupuncture or tai chi or whatever healing, if we don't find the source, the blockage simply returns. All long-term health issues are rooted in the subtle bodies. They can also be deeper than the emotional. They may be in the mental body, which is even subtler. They may be a belief system or unconscious attitude that we have inherited - a glitch or blind-spot that we never realised we had.

This 39th Gene Key is all about searching. It's a part of the Ring of Seeking, so it's about searching for answers, for the heart of the problem. Each of the Gene Keys of the Ring of Seeking are about finding the source of our suffering. The 39th Gene Key always has a lot to do with our health - physical, astral, and mental. You see, a blockage isn't a bad thing - it's an area of focus for transformation. But it takes some courage to go there. We have to be ready to deal with these things and we can begin by looking honestly at the outer circumstances of our life. We need to look at the way life is coming towards us. What is it delivering to us? Why is it delivering that experience? What are we missing? What haven't we been honest about inside ourself? When we allow our intuition to contemplate the outer events of our life, we'll soon see that they're arising because of inner blockages, patterns of denial that we're not wanting to change.

The 39th Gene Key is very powerful and its Shadow of Provocation is about life provoking us, making us feel uncomfortable so that we'll have to look deeper into ourself. We can never escape this Shadow. It's relentless. It will go on pursuing us, whoever we are, wherever we are. It doesn't matter if we have it in our Profile either. It will still find us through the consciousness field of the world, of someone else.

Whoever disturbs us will bring it to us. So how about doing something radical? Instead of running from it, why not let it in? Look at the things that wind you up. Look at the obstructions that life places in your way - along your destiny, in your relationships, in your work, in your body. Take courage and look into yourself. Which pattern or habit is it connected to? Our intuition will tell us. Our body will tell us. And then don't doubt what you hear. Contemplate it and maybe you'll find yourself doing something about it.

You see, we all do things that are bad for us. We get locked into patterns and habits that undermine our health, our love, our higher purpose. Once we begin to see the obstructions as Gifts, as stepping stones that lead inwards towards deeper blockages that hide wonders, then our whole life will begin to change. We'll actively seek the source of these obstacles. We'll appreciate them, signposts as they are, and then we'll feel more and more healing energy coursing through our body, more love running through our relationships and more ease in our work. Our life will become clearer and easier. There - the 39th Shadow doesn't sound quite so bad now, does it?!

THE 39TH GIFT - DYNAMISM

One thing I should have mentioned in the Shadow, but it's also very applicable to the Gift - in fact at all levels - is the breath. This 39th Gene Key is a breath key. Blockages in the subtle bodies result in blockages in the physical musculature that governs the breath. So provocation is also about coming into awareness of our breath. The place where the deepest repression takes place involving the breath is along the length of the diaphragm. Tightness develops there due to blockages, and again here's the problem - that we can't release it only from the physical structure. But working on the physical structure may well bring something to the surface. Whenever we work with our physical body through exercise, bodywork, massage, we open up the possibility of changing our breathing.

The Gift of Dynamism isn't just increasing our lung capacity; it's also about enthusiasm and optimism. Dynamic energy is uplifting energy, and as we release blockages within our system, mental, emotional, or physical, then our breath returns a little more to the breath pattern that we had as a young child. And so does our attitude. We become more open, we feel more joyous, more exuberant. Young children breathe right into their belly - the breath moves effortlessly down to the base and back again. So the 39th Gene Key responds well to exercise and to gentle, well delivered bodywork.

It's a journey, coming back to our original breath. This is why meditation focusses on the breath - because when we do that - slowly, slowly, our breath deepens until it hits the source, our centre, our Dan Tien. There are many ways other than meditation as well, that encourage the breath deeper into the system through the blockages that we've developed.

In the Golden Path, the Venus Sequence explores the stages and phases of these blockages as they occur through our childhood and even our conception. The important thing is to realise that blockages are not the enemy, even though they're very uncomfortable. The blockages are our greatest allies. Every blockage is a hidden breakthrough, an epiphany, so we must pay attention to them. The 39th Gift is all about unlocking freedom at all levels. These people are either utterly locked, or they're the great unlockers and unblockers. Once they've learned the art, they become expert at helping others. They can apply this Gift into any field we can imagine, because ultimately they know how to release stagnant energy through a system. They are very valuable people.

If we have a Gene Key in a prominent place, let's say our Life's Work or Purpose, then unconsciously we know it's there. We know we're meant to be dynamic but probably we don't feel it a lot of the time. We may be the opposite. We may be exhausted most of the time, so we seek the dynamism. We try and force the blockage open - so we become maybe addicted to exercise, or cocaine, or something that creates an extreme state inside us. But because it's forced, it isn't the natural Gift, so it becomes depressing and painful and ends up making us even tighter.

The real thing is the real thing. The 39th Gift is joyous. I tell you these are the most joyous people. You should see them when they laugh, and how that diaphragm pumps the nectar of that life force out through them. If we're working with this Gene Key, then we're working with enormous life force, with the very jet of freedom. It takes perseverance - that's the Programming Partner, the 38th Gift of Perseverance. To unblock our inner vitality, our chi, is a lifelong mission. If we persist and follow our heart and the life force then eventually we'll succeed.

This is an explosive Gene Key. It's about a system under huge pressure. Our longing to release the pressure drives us to find ways to unleash it, and then it pops. Anywhere we see this Gene Key we're looking at a latent explosion. It could be a Shadow, Gift, or Siddhi explosion. This is a wonderful Gift, the Gift of freeing blocked energy. Once we begin to free our own, it becomes kind of addictive and it's way better than adrenaline. Adrenaline is an attempt to get there, to find the spirit, but it's a pale shadow of the real thing. Dynamism shouldn't be confused with an adrenaline buzz. It's a joy buzz, a freedom buzz, but true freedom - the kind of freedom that only comes through steady, sustained inner work. The release of dynamism is release of the energy of nature itself. We can look at children if we want to know what this Gift looks like; they have so much energy. A child is never satisfied unless he or she is exhausted, then they eat or sleep, and it all just comes back up again - the energy I mean, not the food!

So work on your breath, stretch it, soften it, pump it, tend it, love it, follow it, trust it. Your breath is the greatest key - so listen to it…and listen to those blocks…there's gold hidden inside them…

The 39th Siddhi - Liberation

I love doing these contemplations on the Gene Keys. We can feel the momentum building as we move through the frequency bands. I can almost feel the anticipation for this 39th Siddhi in my bones…Liberation. Such a beautiful word, such a dynamic word. These words are precision frequencies. Even though every Siddhi is the same essential state of consciousness, it comes through our DNA in different ways according to variations in the alchemy of the enlightened process.

One of the things people report as they approach enlightened consciousness is changes to the circadian biorhythm of their sleep and waking. At high levels of consciousness, the mind becomes self illuminated and remains awake even as the body sleeps. The astral process of dreaming ceases as the lower subtle bodies are purified. Whenever we turn our awareness inwards, it sinks so deeply that the physical body is refreshed much more quickly than ever before.

The body is wheeling through the field of dynamism. Vast reserves of energy become available. For the most part this energy is internalised and powers the ultimate breakthrough into the state of full realisation. It can also be tapped instantly whenever one turns inwards.

In the East the word for liberation is called Moksha. It's not a kind of coffee by the way. It's interesting how this term has developed in relation to the term Nirvana. Both terms point towards the same essence, but Nirvana has come to be associated with the realisation that there is no self, whereas Moksha has come to be associated with the realisation that there is nothing but self. Thus flow the politics of enlightenment!

Well, let's explore Moksha through the relationship between the Siddhi and the Shadow. I'm always really interested in that connection, where the Shadow is the seed, the Gift the flower, and the Siddhi the fruit, which contains the seed but has evolved to another level. Liberation then is about being free from provocation. Nothing can provoke us. Imagine that. Nothing can provoke our awareness to change from its self-realised state. That's why it's utterly peaceful. This 39th Gene Key is particularly responsive to sound, to the audio environment - how we're really provoked more by tone than content - the child that whines just at the right pitch, or the wrong pitch, or our partner who uses that subtle tone of guilt that just catches our breath…you know what I mean. Anyway, Liberation is about hearing without following the sound. The sound of a word enters the ear and although the brain may translate that instantly into a concept or memory, the inner awareness is unaffected by this process. In fact the inner awareness can selectively switch off the neurological process, so when we are in deep meditative absorption all sound is simply frequency, without neurological activity, without thought. That is *Moksha*-Liberation.

This 39th Siddhi has some other secrets as well. I usually don't talk about Human Design, because, well, I don't wish to confuse people who have come to the Gene Keys without coming through Human Design which is a related system. My friend Werner Pitzal and myself created Integral Human Design, a version that integrates the Gene Keys seamlessly. You can check it out if you're interested, but beware - you need a lot of time. If you don't have a lot of time in your life, I can't recommend you go into two systems at the same time.

GENE KEY 39

Likely you'll be overwhelmed, but Integral Human Design can add insights to the Gene Keys if you like that kind of extra detail. Anyway, in Human Design, certain Gene Keys are linked to other Gene Keys through things called Channels (specialisations). Those connections aren't always explored in the Gene Keys. In IHD, the 39th Gene Key connects directly into the 55th Gene Key in a channel called the channel of Romance, its highest keynote being the channel of True Love. There's obviously a connection between the 55 and the 39 through these two words, Freedom (the 55) and Liberation (the 39). They sound like they mean the same thing, but it's not so much about their meanings, rather their processes. The 39th Gene Key is a trigger for the 55th Gene Key at a collective level. If you've read the 55th Gene Key, you'll know it's a massive prophetic transmission that sits at the heart of the Gene Keys, and it involves a huge change that's coming to humanity. It's the story behind the symbol of the dragonfly. You'll remember that at a certain point the dragonfly nymph begins to climb up out of the water towards the sunlight, and then in the sunlight it undergoes its extraordinary transformation. Well, what is it that makes it do that? I mean it's a successful underwater predator. It should be quite happy with that. But no, some hidden force inside provokes it to do something utterly dangerous, something absolutely out of character. It's the 39th Siddhi that does that.

The collective consciousness of humanity will be provoked. It will be dynamited - dynamised. The new awareness will arise out of the blue, out of this provocation. The 39th Siddhi, operating through certain awakened individuals, will provoke others, those who are ready, to make radical new changes in their lives. The 39th Gene Key begins things; it initiates and catalyses processes. It unblocks things suddenly and leads to dramatic shifts in consciousness. The 39th Gene Key loves a good drama! This Siddhi will pop up all over the place and wherever it pops open, things are going to be unblocked - systems, energy fields, psyches, all kinds of things. Wherever a major blockage is released we see unusual behaviour! What the 39th Siddhi does, is combines with other awakened Siddhis and exacerbates them.

For example, if we have the 36th Siddhi of Compassion combining with the 39th Siddhi, then that compassion is going to be very provocative. It'll make us see something through the eyes of compassion. It's blunt like that. Whereas if we have the 36th Gene Key without the 39th, then the compassion will be the gentle kind. It may even be invisible to us.

The 39th Siddhi is here to heighten frequency, to cause a stir. It's intriguing how it seems to need to create a cocktail with the other Siddhis to do this.

It's the same at the Shadow frequency. The 39th Shadow provokes our Shadows. At the highest level it provokes our Compassion, or Purity, or Beauty. The 39th Siddhi is going to liberate humanity. It will blast us into Freedom.

It's funny how divine timing works. This morning I had to unblock a blocked drain. Have you ever done that? You stick your hand down and pull out all this stuff, this morass of decay and bacterial gunk. It's not a pleasant experience, but when we wash everything out, blast through the fresh water and watch and see the water flowing freshly again, it's such a great feeling. These Siddhis require that we do that. There's no other way. Collectively that will be ugly, all the bacteria of all our Shadows, our ancestral karma and our violence that hasn't been purified. We're going to have to purify it. The 39th Gene Key will manifest the Obstructions we need in order to go through that process. We'll have to go through a period of intense chaos - this whole planet will. It's unavoidable, but we don't have to be afraid. We have to get good at unblocking things. The more we do that on ourself, the safer our life will become. Liberation requires that we honour our karma, that we clean up our own mess. This is why its Programming Partner is Honour, the 38th Siddhi. We have to honour life, our heart, our past, and the path of our destiny. That's the way of Liberation.

The 40th Way

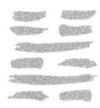

Gene Key 40

THE WAY OF RESOLVE

The Transformational Way of the 40th Gene Key moves from Exhaustion to Divine Will, and it's the Way of Resolve.

Here's a great Gene Key for all modernists. We live in the time of exhaustion. We live in a time of excess, which is the Dilemma of this Gene Key. I think of other times in human history, well European history, when excess ruled - the French Revolution or the collapse of the British Monarchy in the 17th century. These were times in which those in power like Charles I became so self-indulgent that they ignored those at the other end of the spectrum. The gap between rich and poor became cataclysmic and well, the rest is history. Thousands of years of monarchy were brought to a bloody end.

History reflects these patterns so clearly. Today we live in a more civilised society than these examples but the patterns are still the same. These are times when morally questionable people often rise to power. Excess breeds lack, which leads to scant resources, which leads to starvation - not just of food, but also of values, which leads to exhaustion, both individual and collective. This is something to contemplate - the notion of collective exhaustion. We tend to think of exhaustion as an individual phenomenon, but I'd like to extend it here to encompass the whole planet. We're exhausting our resources, our fossil fuels, our morals, our souls.

I wonder how many of us have felt this exhaustion down to the level of our souls. The fabric of our civilisation leaves us parched, thirsty for meaning, for something nobler. This Shadow stalks our communities, our daily lives, and most of the time we don't even realise how thirsty we are. This Gene Key is a special one, it's a direct route to the Divine inside us. This is why it's the Shadow of Exhaustion, because when we cut ourselves off

Shadow: Exhaustion   **Gift:** Resolve   **Programming Partner:** Gene Key 37
Dilemma: Excess   **Siddhi:** Divine Will   **Codon Ring:** The Ring of Alchemy

from our own source, our divinity, then we begin to die. We work to excess, we travel excessively, we think and worry excessively, we even become excessive seekers. We can't rest on a single flower long enough to drink of its nectar.

I want to issue an invitation to everyone drawn to the Gene Keys, and those listening to this Gene Key or reading it now - if you're drawn to this wisdom, then consider staying with it. Make it a permanent part of your life. Don't dilute it with lots of other systems and teachings. Integrate those other paths, yes; they're all here anyway. Have the courage to stay with just one and dig deep and it will nourish you. You'll find the nectar coming right from the heart of the wisdom.

That's my invitation. If you're more drawn to another teaching, then leave this one and stay with the other. The important thing is to stay consistent - to put down roots. If you feel exhausted to the depths of your being, this is the answer to your prayers. Stay with a single thing. The 37th Shadow, the Programming Partner, is weakness. We're weak when we spread our energies too wide. There's strength in focus. This Gene Key is about learning not to waste energy and time. Look at your life, see how widely you spread your energies. Can you be so many things to so many people? How can you encompass that much?

There's a ruthlessness needed in tackling this Shadow. We're going to have to cut out some deadwood in our life. We'll need to get rid of some things, some commitments. Consider this carefully then. We need to take our time - not rush - rushing is the whole problem. We need to slow down and be considerate of our own energies. We need to let the God inside us decide what's truly meaningful to our soul. Excess is a pattern that we'll find is rife in our life. We do too much in certain areas and too little in others.

Perhaps our working life is fulfilling but our relationships are suffering. Perhaps we give too much time to our spiritual path and our family is parched by our absence. Only we know where the excess lies. When we begin trimming off the excess in our life, things soon find a healthy balance. It's like eating less. Our body breathes a sigh of relief. We're finally giving it a break so it begins to readjust itself to the rhythms it yearns for - to be in harmony. Excess also commands our senses - we taste too much, we watch too much, we listen too much, we speak too much - we overwhelm our senses with stimulus. We've forgotten how to do nothing. We've forgotten how to be quiet, how to be simple. How often do we go out into our garden and light a fire and sit by it? We may not even have a garden. How often do we take a bracing swim in a wild river? How often do we wake early and let the sounds of the birds just tickle our eardrums? How often do we go out at night and consider the stars? How often do we sit in silence or candlelight with the one we love, or read a book aloud to a friend or a child, or go for a walk without a purpose?

Do you see what I'm driving at? These are the good things of life. Our life can be filled with such things if we just make room for them. So get busy trimming. Trim the fat off. It's never too late to be reborn.

The 40th Gift - Resolve

Perhaps you can see how the Gift of Resolve works. I've almost covered it in the last part. It takes resolve to stay with something that feeds our soul. We have to change to habits that fuel our soul rather than excessive behaviours that drain our soul. I'm not a puritan. I'm in no way an ascetic. That too is excess in the direction of spirituality. The secret is in the balance, in the subtlety. To come close to God, we have to learn subtlety and refinement. We can imbibe the fruits of life, but with measure. There are even times when we can have more than we need. Life allows that. Life encourages that, but again, at the right moment, in the right circumstances.

The Gift of Resolve is our genius. It's to fix our eye on a mark and bring it into being. It's to follow something through all the way. Resolve is to propel our life in the direction it's designed to go. There's a thing we're here to do, and only we can do it.

Our job is to find it. It's probably already in front of us. We already know what it is. When we finally decide to do it, then we'll flood with the Gift of Resolve. We'll find the energy that sustains us in our task, and it won't drain us - rather it'll keep filling us, replenishing us from within. To do the soul's work is to be filled with life, with enthusiasm, and to place ourself in the exact position to garner support. Everything will simply come to us.

If we only knew how much the Divine is seeking us. When we sever the connection, the higher impulses pursue us relentlessly. They do everything at their disposal to get our attention and correct our course. That's why we suffer, because we're not listening. The 37th Gift of Equality is a mirror to this 40th Gift of Resolve. They're opposites that complement each other perfectly. Equality is about harmonising - finding balance - between the many spheres of our life. Resolve is about our single-mindedness to bring about that equalisation - to feed our community in equal measure to ourself, to feed our body and its needs as much as our soul, to feed the inner and the outer in equal part.

The 40th Gift is resolved, but again not to excess. A part of resolve is to flow with its various nuances. Life provides distractions. It provides breaks, natural breaks. We can do what we're intent on doing, but when life calls us away for a moment, especially a human moment, then take the break. This is the Gift of taking breaks! The breaks need to be balanced with the work otherwise our life is over and we have had no time for enjoyment, for savouring its beauties. It's like holidays - don't get me started on holidays! We work for forty eight weeks and holiday for four. What kind of a balance is that? What kind of a life is that? But don't get caught at the other end of the spectrum either. Nowadays so many people are content to live off the state and they spend the lion's share of their time drifting, seeking, travelling, watching TV. Of course there are times when that's in our flow, like when we're young and in our twenties, or old and in our fifties or sixties. There are natural cycles of rest and exploration, and there are cycles of work, when we're called to fulfil our mission in life. We have to attune to these things. It's a constant flow, and we have to be so alert to our tendency towards excess. Resolve gives everything a perspective. It drives us along the trajectory that's natural for us.

This Gift is the gift of relaxation. That's interesting because how do you bring together resolve and relaxation? Not by taking short cuts, but through balance - between our need for rest and our need for work. What's restful for our soul? Really? I don't mean watching TV! I mean for our soul? Meeting someone who absolutely loves us, honours us for who we are - that's restful. Being with our children, or our cat, or in our garden - that's restful. Doing the work we love with the people we love - that's restful. Rest can be everywhere when we're resolved not to give in to excess. Having this Gift also means that we can inspire others. When a stressed out person meets a deeply fulfilled person, a powerful exchange takes place. We can be that second person and the world will begin to change.

The 40th Siddhi - Divine Will

Behind this whole Gene Key lies something extraordinary. I have done well to contain myself this far. This is the Codon Ring of Alchemy, a group of Gene Keys that we might describe as the guardians of Divinity. These four Siddhis are the 6 - Peace, the 47 - Transfiguration, the 64 - Illumination and the 40 - Divine Will. Alchemy means that we have to transmute the Shadow frequency - the darkness - into light. These four Siddhis all describe direct paths to the Divine. This is why the Gift here is resolve, because this Gene Key carries grace. If we have it in a prominent place in our Profile it can signify that in this life we have a rare opportunity to achieve transcendence.

The whole way through this Gene Key, we're tasked with the job of saving precious energy. One path of alchemy is all about this - simply not wasting energy in excessive behaviour. If our dharma, our destiny, has cleared the space for us then we can give ourself to the path into this Siddhi. Divine Will means that we'll need only one quality - surrender. Our path to the Divine will revolve around this quality. Whatever happens to us we must surrender to it. And we must surrender peacefully rather than forcibly.

If it's our destiny to travel this far in this lifetime, then grace will make all the arrangements for us. A space will appear for us to go within. Support will come so that we can take the journey without distraction. We'll not have to force any of these things. They will simply appear. Perhaps a teacher will also appear. If these things don't come our way then please don't try and make it go that way. It may be in our next life, and if we don't surrender to that then we'll cause all kinds of problems for ourself. The deepest surrender we can come to in life is that we can't choose. We'll have to let go of our individual will and trust in the will of the whole. We are not the chooser. This is our alchemy - to be in the hands of a force that's far beyond us.

It's a delicate realisation, this. If we force or pretend that we've surrendered, then we may be trapped in a spiritual labyrinth. Many seekers make this mistake - exhausted from seeking, they find a teaching which gets them off the hook. Advaita is a case in point. Advaita says that there's no choice and no chooser, so whatever we do it's not in our control. This is true, but it's a Truth that must come through seeking - it must come naturally. It's easy to take this truth into our mind. It gets us off the hook of having to seek anymore. It can give us the illusion that our search has come to an end. It provides relief. It also can have a subtle superiority in it - a spiritual ego - that all other seekers have not yet realised this. They will get here one day.

It's the Will of the whole that we seek until we're found. When we're found, there will be no mistaking it. Don't be fooled. There are no shortcuts. The 40th Siddhi is also extraordinary because it's one of the Seven Sacred Seals, a portal to planetary healing and Grace. If you have this Gene Key, I recommend a deep study of the Seven Sacred Seals. The 40th Seal represents the healing of the base wound of humanity - fear. It doesn't get any deeper than this. It takes resolve and courage to get right to the bottom of our deepest fears. The power of the 40th Siddhi is that it will never give up. It's not programmed to give up. It'll take us right down into the depths of hell, and it will transmute the deepest ancestral fears inside our DNA.

The 40th Siddhi is allied to Archangel Mikhael. He's said to be the Archangel of our current Age. We live in the time of the transmutation of the Shadow, symbolised by the dragon. If we carry the 40th Gene Key, then we are a dragonslayer. Nay, we are a dragon-healer. We don't have to slay the dragon - we're here to transmute it.

For humanity to truly be healed, in order for us to enter into the next epoch, we have to look into the eyes of death. We have to slay death, our deepest fear. Only when we've seen through the illusion of death can the New Age truly begin. This isn't something light I'm saying here. This isn't some new age angelic thing. The 40th Siddhi will put us through the gutsiest, most horrendous challenges. We'll have to prove our courage over and over again.

The 40th Siddhi is a path of aloneness. It's an inner path. We may need a living master to stand beside us, but we'll have to travel this path on our own. We needn't be afraid. Everything that happens to us or around us is the Will of God. Divine Will is here to help us relax so deeply in these bodies that we begin to shine with light. Divine Will is within every other Siddhi. Divine Will is all there is. Whoever we are and wherever we are, one day we too will have to surrender our individual ego into the whole. This is a path of divine alchemy, and we are the base matter and God is the gold.

THE 64 WAYS

THE 41ST WAY

Gene Key 41

THE WAY OF ANTICIPATION

The Transformational Way of the 41st Gene Key moves from Fantasy to Emanation, and it's the Way of Anticipation.

The 41st Gene Key is quite unique. In the pantheon of the Gene Keys, we can relate each Gene Key to a place in the structure of the genetic code. Each Gene Key, through its resonance and numerology, relates to a specific codon group that codes for an amino acid in the body. The 41st Gene Key however is an exception. It relates to the Initiator Codon, which is like the capital letter in every genetic sentence. In our trillions of cells, lying crimped and twisted like a magical serpent, the DNA molecule is the code for who we are. It's made up of codes within codes of base letters, chemical signatures, all arranged in triplets and coding for all the processes in our biology and beyond. The 41st Gene Key is sprinkled liberally throughout the genome. Every time there's a string of codes, for say building a liver cell, each code begins with the 41st Gene Key. Over and over, we'll find it beginning new codes. That makes it unique because it doesn't actually relate to an amino acid. It signals the beginning of a process. When we apply that as a living archetype, it says a lot about us.

The Chinese called this hexagram 'Decrease', and the shape of its character denotes an empty cauldron. It therefore became associated with the cycles of decline, when life empties itself out and returns along its downward arc.

We'll find this Gene Key riddled with paradox; it seems to be about beginnings on the one hand and endings on the other. It is the Shadow of Fantasy, and that is its danger. It is filled with dreams, but those dreams aren't grounded and therefore never come to fruition. Each Shadow is a root cause of human suffering, and here we have a common root - our attachment to our mind's eye of the future. The Dilemma is Planning, in that we plan things in our heads in a certain way. For example, we dream and fantasise that a relationship is going to deliver such and such a feeling

Shadow: Fantasy **Gift**: Anticipation **Programming Partner:** Gene Key 31
Dilemma: Planning **Siddhi**: Emanation **Codon Ring:** The Ring of Origin

to us, or lead to a new direction in life, taking us closer to our dreams, only in the end to see it fall apart and lead somewhere entirely different.

The great teaching in this Gene Key is about letting go of our plans. We can plan, and we must plan in small ways, such as what to eat the next day, or when and where we'll meet a friend, or go on a holiday. These are small plans. Then there's the big planning of fantasy. We fall in love, get married and fall victim to a fantasy of the perfect life with the perfect person, and it doesn't turn out that way at all. In a year it's all changed, they aren't who we thought they were, and instead it's difficult and painful.

Decline comes unexpectedly. It comes often to test us. It comes to lessen our attachments to this world. Like the 41st Gene Key, it's riddled throughout our lives. Along with this Shadow can come deep disappointment, pain, sorrow, grief, resentment, depression and all the sinking feelings that take us away from our joyousness. Our lives are often dominated by our unconscious fantasies, like the marriage/perfect partner dream, the money dream, the power dream, the enlightenment dream. They all haunt our inner lives. One by one they'll be crushed by life, and this is good news, which we'll see when we go deeper into this Gene Key. We're called upon to become naked, like that empty cauldron. Wherever we have a fantasy, it'll be wiped out.

This is why plans can be dangerous. We can plan, but we must hold lightly to those plans because change is all around us. Death is a part of life and it may intervene at any moment. The problem is really our minds. Our minds love to dream and hope. All these people dreaming of a better life with more money, doing the lottery, fantasising about how it could be better 'if'.

The 'if' is the killer, the fuel of our fantasies. Wherever we have an 'if', there we'll suffer. Over the course of our life, one by one, our 'ifs' will fall away. Whether we struggle or let go graciously the result is the same, we all leave as we came, empty. The emptiness can be filled, but not with any achievement or form of the world. It can become filled with love, connection, joy. That's surely the key. What we're really seeking isn't a result, but a surrender into the stream, a sense of deep trust and fulfilment through being a part of a whole.

Let's consider our 'ifs', our fantasies about our future. Each one is destined to decline and fade into nothing. The best is to let them go before they naturally wither. We must prune back our inner life so that the plans we have are held much more lightly. They're simply markers, way-showers that lead us onwards along our path. If they don't happen the way we dreamed them, that's ok. They're the impulse of our spirit. They're the little lights we throw ahead to help us see the path. I recommend we do an inventory of our fantasies, and see how we're setting ourself up for disappointment. Even if we attain our fantasy, we won't be fulfilled because another will simply spring up in its place. This Gene Key is all about seeing through the tricks our mind plays with us. The fantasies are in no way bad, in fact we can use them to our advantage. It's just a matter of seeing through the game.

The 41st Gift - Anticipation

Many people have wondered what it means to be a genius of anticipation? Well. fantasy can be used as a fuel when we correctly understand it. We can also see through this Gift's Programming Partner, the 31st Gene Key, that it has the capacity to have great influence through leadership. Leadership is often rooted in fantasy; the promise of a better way, a better world. We can see clearly how leaders use this as spin to get them into power, but then it all just falls apart from there.

To use fantasy, we have to see into its roots. Let's take the case of sexual fantasy. Even though it's a bit controversial it's also very common. Sexual fantasy dreams of a certain experience, an experience that takes us away from the mundane. When we look deeper it's actually a yearning for a more transcendent experience. At its core it's a wish to escape our current suffering and stimulate an orgasmic feeling. No matter what form fantasy takes, it's really the ache for love, the yearning to be filled or emptied, to connect, to merge. If we really know that, then our sexual fantasy can rise up inside us. It doesn't have to be fixed in the lower centres but can fertilise the higher centres inside us. This is the true tantra that coaxes those earthier energies upwards. There isn't anything at all wrong with them, but it's about seeing what lies beneath them.

We can do this with every kind of fantasy we have. We can do this with every dream inside us; we can look deeply into it and unlock its higher yearning. We can use its energy to uplift our consciousness, raise our frequency and connect with our heart. In this sense the Gift of Anticipation is an alchemical Gene Key. Fantasy can either be an escape or alchemy. This is the gift of anticipating where an energy really wants to go, and that also means where it goes in others. Can we see where their fantasy, their dream is really heading?

If we've found the roots of our own we'll be able to see it in others, which means we can help them move beyond their suffering. The Shadow frequency is marked by the feedback loops that keep us in states of suffering. We get stuck in a certain pattern of doing things and this goes on feeding the same behaviour. Anticipation looks and senses the time and place for the breakout. It can therefore provide completely new experiences and entirely new cycles for people.

One of the contemplations I've done with this Gene Key is ask myself the question, 'What is there that we humans can create that truly lasts?' Everything we build decays; buildings crumble, laws and rules fail, empires fall, even art and music become lost to time. After some time I came up with two things that last: children and stories. These are the two that stood out. We will always create children, and they continue the process and create their own children. Stories, oddly enough, also last the test of time. Songs or poetry may be the way they're delivered, but the thing that endures is the tale. There are stories and myths in the world that are as old as we are and have been here since we began to talk.

What our story and place are within the fabric of destiny are the great questions for this 41st Gift. It knows how to tell a story through whatever medium it adapts, and it knows where stories come from and their importance. A story bypasses the logical brain and goes right into our core. As children it's the first thing we learn. As old people our own story is perhaps the last thing we consider. Stories are holistic and transcendent. They smash down walls and boundaries and divisions. They even transcend language. If we have this 41st Gene Key or are drawn to it, we can consider the power of story in our life, and find a way to weave it into whatever we do. It will revivify and enrich our whole world and the world of others.

Stories are all about anticipation. That's their whole reason for being. We love to listen to them as children and adults because we know what the ending's going to be. There's really only one story circulating in many forms - the story of human evolution. There are those who can see through the story and anticipate what's coming. There have always been such people among us; they become our sages and prophets. They live their lives simply, less attached to the outcomes of our individual lives than the rest of us. Though they may not share what they know with us, they do share their love of the moment and their joy of simply being a part of the script. These are the people of the 41st Gift.

The 41st Siddhi - Emanation

The deeper we go into this Gene Key, the deeper we go into the mysteries of existence. This is the Start Codon. It's the beginning. It begins with the words, 'Once upon a time', where all stories begin.

This beautiful word emanation alludes to that which emanates from the source. We have to follow the emanations back to the beginning. Our lives really are a journey, an odyssey in time back to the place beyond time. That's the only story, the ultimate story.

In the mystery of the Codon Rings, every genetic family (and there are twenty two of them) relates to one of the symbols of the Tarot. The Tarot, despite its fortune-teller's reputation, represents some of the oldest story symbols in existence. The 41st Gene Key relates to the very first of the symbols in the Tarot, the Fool. The Fool represents the beginning and the end of the story, the alpha and the omega. The beginning contains the seed of the end and vice versa. The Fool begins as a mortal who knows nothing, the innocent, the child.

Through his long journey with its many travails, he gradually becomes wiser. His number is usually zero, the circle, and often he also appears again at the end, as the number twenty two. The final story, depicted in the twenty first card (the universe) is that the Fool, having realised the secrets of the universe, reaches enlightenment and immortality. He remains the Fool because he attains his or her realisation through knowing nothing. But his nothing at the end is different from his nothing at the beginning. I'll leave it for you to figure that one out!

When I come to these Siddhis I love to use stories. Last week I took my boys to see a film at the cinema, one of those Marvel films, Dr. Strange. As is often the case, these kinds of films hide coded truths with which the younger generations deeply resonate. They go for the Emanation because in their cells they're anticipating the Siddhis, our collective future. There were several very deep truths in this film. My favourite was that the hero, Dr. Strange has to do a deal with the devil at the end. I'm paraphrasing here. He manages to lock himself into a time-loop with the devil in order to bargain with him. The devil refuses to bargain and kills him. Dr. Strange keeps returning and the devil keeps killing him. He's effectively caught the devil in a trap because he's willing to keep coming back and lose to the devil, which makes the devil his prisoner. It's a beautiful paradox and reminds me of Chuang Tzu the ancient Chinese sage, who says similar things, such as, 'we win by losing'. This teaching then is about surrender. We have to give up our power, our identity and every attachment we have to the outcome of the story. The story can then use us to find its own perfect ending.

We're all in the story, in our stories together, living out our tales. I can't offer any advice but I can tell the story as I see it. That's what the Gene Keys are, the story-codes of creation. They all begin and end in this Codon, in this Gene Key. One day we'll return to the source. It won't happen because of anything we do but because our particular story has found its way home. All we can do is follow the emanation. We think we're travelling into the future, but we're really travelling back to the beginning.

This isn't a tale told by an idiot, full of sound and fury, signifying nothing. Hamlet was in some serious Shadows when he said that. This has an exquisite ending. The 41st Siddhi is about the fulfilment of our wishes, our dreams. All our dreams will come true, just like in the fairy tales. The powers of grace will ensure that our dreams come true, but only when we've discovered what our highest dreams really are. All those fantasies we began with, like the dream of higher things or an escape from our suffering are all impulses seeking the source, emanation, our immortality.

One of the oldest stories known, as far as we know, is the epic story of Gilgamesh. There's an intriguing character in this story who the hero Gilgamesh meets; he's known as the Flood Survivor. He's the only human to have survived the flood along with his family, and he's been granted immortality. Gilgamesh wants desperately to know how to get this secret, as do many heroes in our myths, but his karma doesn't allow it. So here in this story, there's a being from another age, another epoch, and he testifies to the fact of our earlier immortality. The notion of the flood is also universal to so many myths. Scientists and geologists look for localised floods, but perhaps they don't realise that the myths speak of a global flood, a flood that wiped out all humans. What remains is the only thing that survives, the story.

One day we'll return to our immortal nature. We'll come to the end of our human evolution. On that day the tale will end. Outside of time, there are no longer any stories, and when there are no stories, there are no children either. The two come together. We can allow ourselves to be a child and remember that this will end well. If it doesn't appear to, it's because we're still in the part that's working out the drama. People enter the stage and leave the stage. Life and death are a part of the drama. One day though, our dreams will come true, and all those we've loved will become merged within our heart. We'll realise that we've never died, nor has anyone. It's all been the most wonderful dream, and the greatest paradox is that if we hadn't been asleep in the first, we would never have even heard it!

THE 64 WAYS

THE 42ND WAY

Gene Key 42

THE WAY OF DETACHMENT

The Transformational Path of the 42nd Gene Key moves from Expectation to Celebration, and it's the Path of Detachment.

In the Gene Keys at a mystical level, there are alchemical paths, Christ paths, and Buddha paths. This 42nd Gene Key has strong aspects of Buddha's teachings. As we move deeper into the Gene Keys and the Codon Rings, we'll notice aspects of each of these paths in the individual Keys. The 42nd is in the Ring of Life and Death, with teachings about living and dying and birth and death.

As I've been contemplating this Gene Key it seems as though it contains the complete works of Shakespeare! - all the great human dramas, tragedies, comedies, histories, and tragicomedies. Here we have the Shadow of Expectation and the Dilemma of Disappointment. It's about life as a story and our attachment to that story. At the Shadow frequency we're so immersed and involved in our story that we identify fully with the character and cast in our lives. It's really valuable to think about our cast - our family, friends, lovers; all the people who for good or bad, have helped shape our life. It's also important to contemplate all our disappointments and regrets, the hurt we've caused others at times and the paths that didn't turn out the way we wished. If we're young, time contemplating our future is important too, and we can consider our dreams and aspirations and how attached we are to their outcomes.

None of this is wrong, in fact it's all perfect, this human drama. If we have the 42nd Gene Key we're here to really know the human drama. The central player in this drama is always the same character for all of us - death. All roads lead to death. This Gene Key is all about our relationship to death.

Shadow: Expectation **Gift**: Detachment **Programming Partner**: Gene Key 32
Dilemma: Disappointment **Siddhi**: Celebration **Codon Ring**: The Ring of Life and Death

---

The Eastern cultures have a huge advantage over us because most of them have figured out the secrets of incarnation and reincarnation. It's a part of their culture and this makes a huge difference to the drama and their relationship to it. If we know that we're just an actor and will return again to play another role in another play, then detachment will be much easier for us. Without this key insight we can really suffer more. If we believe, as the materialists, that when we die it's the end, that can lead to one of two possibilities. One is that we make the most of every moment and create our life as a work of art, a life dedicated to beauty. The other is that we decide to be selfish and get what we want for ourself because there isn't anything else. The former scenario is rare, and the latter is a hallmark of our modern worldview.

We're setting ourself up for disappointment at every turn. We all begin life with hope, and hope can be a beautiful thing until our mind gets a hold of it. Hope is the energy of evolution at work in us, the impulse to improve our lives and help others. When our mind starts to shape that hope into specific ambitions and ideas and those outcomes don't play out the way we wish, it engenders huge disappointment. Disappointment can become a worldview, and the world is filled with disappointed people who have stopped trusting in life, in their hearts, and in others' hearts.

We really see this in our relationships. We have this romantic dream of the One, the perfect partner, and it just never lives up to our dream. As we get older we tend to give up on our purest dreams. It's also here that we come across the victim, the victim of fate. There are two levels of victim. The first is we let life pummel away at us until we've given up on our dreams because nothing works out the way our heart really wishes.

The second is that we believe we're in control of our life and can therefore direct it through pure force of will. Both are doomed to disappointment. Whichever way we turn we'll find disappointment, and then we run out of energy and time.

The Shadow can sound so depressing because it's hooked into the drama, but it's all for a good purpose. The true purpose of expectation and disappointment is to teach us the rare art of letting go.

The 42nd Gift - Detachment

The Gift of Detachment is a huge Gift that may not sound like your average genius, but we can't rise to our genius without it. No one has ever managed to unlock their genius without this quality. If we define genius as the creative explosion that comes from an open heart, we'll see the uplift that comes from this Gift. To be detached means to not worry about outcomes. It means we begin to trust in life. At the Shadow, we're not trusting in life and hoping that things will go the way our mind wants. At the Gift, we're learning to surrender to life.

This is one of those Gene Keys that touches on the subject of free will. Free will, that precious pearl of the western mind where life is ours to do with as we wish. It's an open book where we write our own story, and it's very captivating. It makes us feel excited to have choice like that, and so we set off to create our life. A funny thing happens though; it never turns out the way we intend. Unpredictable events happen and people let us down. There is deep disappointment. If we're listening to life, we learn to let go of our expectations but we never let go of our hope. This is detachment. Detachment actually begins to open our heart. It sounds like being detached might make us more distant and objective, but it doesn't mean that at all. It means that we begin to accept life. We begin to realise that life knows what's best for us. When we hit a big obstacle, instead of seeing it as an obstacle, we see it as an opportunity for growth. That's the Gift of Detachment. It turns Shadows into Gifts. We begin to realise that in the drama of life there's a beautiful choreography that's beyond our control. If we surrender to that, life will be easier, even more mysterious and exciting.

Isn't a life where we aren't in control ultimately more exciting than one in which we are? If we go to a movie and know what's going to happen, where's the adventure in that? The Gift of Detachment becomes a master of letting go. To do something with detachment is to move into a really deep flow with the universe and the harmony in the greater pattern. It allows us to adjust instantly to unexpected changes in the flow and really enter into our mortality and the bittersweet moments of life. We begin to become more and more fearless and trusting in the great flow. This is the essence of the teaching of the Buddha - to let life pass us by and become the witness to our own story. To simply sit by the side of the river and watch the way it flows around us. We become so soft and yielding on the inside. The more we evolve in life, the more feminine we become. To be feminine means we don't react to the drama or fight with others. Women have had such a hard time over the generations that they've had to dig deep into their psyche to find the yang. They need this yang to demand their independence, to protect their honour and integrity and to bring back the power of the yin, and that's beautiful. The next stage is to once again soften and return to the Mother and that Divine tenderness.

When a woman unites that inner courage with tenderness she becomes whole again. Detachment means that we even surrender to our gender. Man or woman, we have to one day transcend our gender and its issues and traps. There are layers and layers of attachments we carry. The Indians call these subtle ones skandas. As we continue to let go of these skandas, our consciousness rises and our heart opens to wider and wider vistas. Imagine your heart being that open that even the issues of your gender mean nothing to you any more.

Detachment is all about desire. We have subtle layers of desire and we have to move through layer after layer and let go of each one. We begin to use the props that nature supplies to increase our love. That's the upper level of detachment, and detachment is a long road. The Gift frequency has many layers of subtlety to it. When we reach the Siddhi, it's basically an ending, but the Gift is a journey of refinement. As we become more detached we ironically become more playful with the Maya, the drama. We engage more with life and its richness and become a whole human, loving life, loving the mystery, loving whatever life delivers because we know it's all for our highest purpose.

To know that everything that happens is for our further refinement is a magical and beautiful stage to reach. We become a master of letting go and nothing clings to us. We become joyous and more human and loving and compassionate.

The 42nd Siddhi - Celebration

Eventually there must be a complete letting go. This is what initiation calls out of us, and there are levels of endings as well. The big ending is when we let go of death and dying. The Ring of Living and Dying contains the codes to unpick the mystery of how and when the spiritual essence, the soul, enters and leaves the form, the maya, the body. It's funny that we generally only celebrate things at the beginning or the end. We don't usually celebrate something in the middle, but this Siddhi is about celebrating in the middle. It's about every moment becoming a celebration.

Because of death coming, we have these two possibilities of either leading a selfish life or a beautiful life. The Siddhi is about living a perfect life. *Carpe diem*, "seize the day", means to not miss a single moment, to make of your life a work of art and celebrate every beautiful, aching moment. This has everything to do with the breath. We can't be that present without being deeply relaxed in our body so that our breathing emerges from our belly without any resistance. This means that we have to let go of all our fears, one by one, until there are no more fears left in our system.

Can you imagine for a moment your body without any fears?, to live permanently without fear? We can close our eyes for a moment and conjure up what that might feel like, what that blissfulness feels like. We can touch the ecstatic realms where the mind lets go and thinking comes to an end. And when thoughts do come, they're the thoughts of God so they only engender more bliss. We become like a child again and life becomes heaven on earth. These six Siddhis of the Ring of Living and Dying really describe what the building of bliss feels like. The 3rd Siddhi of Innocence brings this eternal child, the 'puer eternis', Adam and Eve naked in the Garden. The 24th Siddhi brings Silence, not a deathly silence, but the silence of Light and Illumination. It's the silence of Quintessence, of reaching the heart of hearts, the 23rd Siddhi. It also brings vast caring for everything, the kind of love that's selfless and unconditional, the 27th Siddhi. Finally this Ring brings the 20th Siddhi, pure presence, a resting in the eternal now. When we discover this, we realise that we're eternal and can't die. The body may die, but the indwelling quintessence can never die.

The body may even not die, because when we break down the illusion all manner of things become possible within the field of Celebration. A part of Celebration is to pierce the veil of the possible and access the seemingly impossible. Siddhis sometimes bring superpowers! The body can be made to live to a great age.

The cells of the body can be transfigured back into their quintessence and literally cause us to ascend. The 42nd Gene Key is about letting go at so many levels. As the Maya, the Grand Illusion of life and death is shattered, eternity lies before us. Higher realms and evolutions beckon. The celebration is that there's been an end to death and our spirit is finally released from its self-imposed prison.

This 42nd Gene Key is like the punch line to the great cosmic joke. Celebration always comes with laughter - the laughter of angels, not a cruel laughter but the laughter of relief or release, of utter joy. In the 'Hitchhiker's Guide to the Galaxy', it's funny when he's finally able to ask the supercomputer what the secret of the universe is. The computer falls silent for a while, and then comes back with a single number. The secret of the universe is 42, it says. Only the one who's transcended death can get this joke. To do that we have to have already surrendered everything. This is what the mystics call the Second Birth, what Christ referred to as being 'born again'. It's a complete rearrangement of our atomic structure. There are no endings. As the poet Wordsworth said, 'hills peep o'er hills'. We never get to the top.

This revelation of the 42nd Gene Key also brings an end to all our myths and stories. At the beginning I said that all the complete works of Shakespeare are in this Gene Key, all the world myths and stories. They all come to an end here. The story either traps or frees us. We have to celebrate our story and every twist and turn of fate. Celebrate the Shadow, Gift, and Siddhi. We're entering an era when the great world myths will all come to an end. It's the time of 'happily ever after' - the ending of suffering and the ending of time.

The 43rd Way

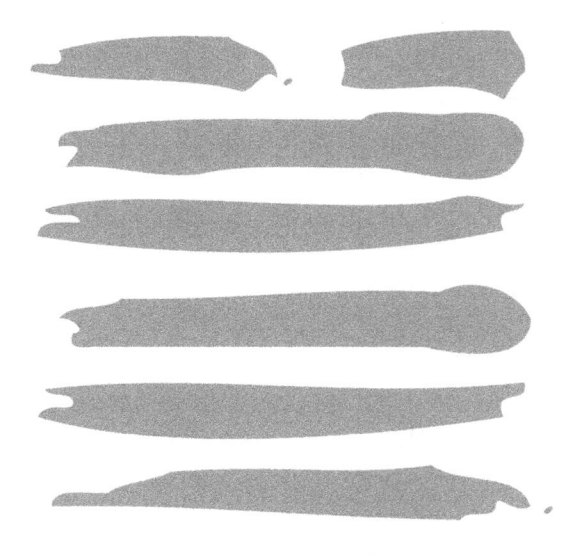

Gene Key 43

THE WAY OF INSIGHT

The Transformational Way of the 43rd Gene Key moves from Deafness to Epiphany, and it's the Way of Insight.

In the original I Ching, the masters of old used the 64 hexagrams to track and harmonise with the forces of nature. Like the Gene Keys it's a book we have to let live inside us. In the cosmic drama the 43rd hexagram was named Breakthrough because it represents a repeating phenomenon of life. Life frequently and sporadically achieves breakthrough. Evolution itself has made so many genetic breakthroughs in order for us to be here. The mystery of our being here seems so random it sometimes overwhelms us. That's why we think we have to know why, as if in knowing why we would have an answer.

This is the Dilemma of Knowing and the Shadow of Deafness. We're deaf because we can't handle the silence of the question without an answer. This Shadow can lead us into psychotic waters and may be responsible for a lot of difficult mental states. Worry and not knowing can lead to these states, like when we wake up in the morning and don't know what we're supposed to do that day. It can make us worry, where we give way to our mind and over time develop a habit of living that way. We fill our lives with the activities of our mind and live inside an endless list of things we must do. The day is gone before we get there and then we're too exhausted to appreciate its beauty.

All this activity makes us deaf. We need to allow a little more not knowing into our lives, since it's our true nature. Then our genius and breakthrough can arise out of that kind of fertile soil. This Gene Key can easily turn into breakdown, physical exhaustion, emotional overwhelm or mental obsessiveness. We often think of deafness as silence, but it's not. It's noise and activity, *'a life of sound and fury signifying nothing'* (Shakespeare's *Macbeth*). This

Shadow: Deafness	**Gift:** Insight	**Programming Partner:** Gene Key 23
Dilemma: Knowing	**Siddhi:** Epiphany	**Codon Ring:** The Ring of Destiny

Shadow can be depressing and make us into lemmings, hurtling towards oblivion, chasing our tails and goals in the future or haunted by our regrets.

The 43rd Gene Key loves a joke, and in it lives the Divine Fool. It's a joke because we can't escape oblivion and always live on the edge of it. In the ancient Tarot, there's a wonderful symbol of the Divine Fool. He's always depicted dancing along the edge of a cliff with a dog biting his heels, but his head is thrown back and he seems blissfully unaware of the danger he's in. This Gene Key demands honesty of us. We're mortal. We'll die. Life is inherently unpredictable. Since we can't know the future, we might as well surrender. That little dog biting our heels is our fear driving us round and round in circles. If we let the uncertainty in, breakthrough might happen and it's a lot better than breakdown.

We can't escape breakthrough. Death is a breakthrough. We just have to give up our knowing - a life of knowing, of knowing what to do, how to behave, knowing where we'll be, how we'll get there. We can dream and cast our pennies into the well, but we can't know if our dreams will come true. They probably won't, so why burden ourselves with all this knowing?

Knowing not only makes our lives more boring, more monotonous, but it also keeps us from others. Our knowing prevents us from truly loving others. How can we love someone if we think we know them? We don't really know anyone. Others will always remain a mystery if we're honest. There's a beautiful mystery that the closer we come to another, the less we seem to know them. That's why we drive each other nuts. Our potential is that we can love completely even if we don't understand completely. Our knowing just makes us deaf and dull. Nobody likes a know-it-all.

The Gift of Insight

There are certain conditions necessary for breakthrough to occur. In life we can always maximise those conditions but we can't force a breakthrough. It can only occur spontaneously. In many ways, the Gene Keys Golden Path is about creating the conditions for a quantum leap to occur in our lives. One of the main conditions is to dwell more frequently in our not knowing. We have to pause more often and inhabit the uncertainty. A true pause is always this, and it has no purpose; it's a gap.

Our habits desperately want to fill the gap - quick! turn on the TV, check our email, put on the music, do something to drown out the silence!

The 43rd Gift is a Divine Fool. It's a fool because it embraces unpredictability. The best comedians are the ones who completely ad lib; they stumble across the most ridiculous ideas and word combinations. Genius is always unstudied. Just imagine living more of your life like that. I'm not saying we have to give up our jobs or make big changes. I'm just saying that breakthrough demands an environment of not knowing and mystery. In the beginning that's uncomfortable but it's also something we can get used to. It's what meditation and contemplation do, where we don't know what will emerge. The foundation of the practise itself is uncertainty.

This is what the Gift of Insight is. Insight as a word is understood more clearly in the Eastern traditions. In the Buddhist tradition it's called insight meditation. We stumble across a satori, an insight, a breaking through from within. There's a lovely word in English, incandescence - to be lit up from within. This is the core of the Gene Keys, that the light is buried in our DNA.

The 43rd Gift must be a rebel. Its nature is to rebel, not so much as a social or political rebel, but a rebel on the inside and a rebel from the mind. Whatever the mind tries to tell us we don't buy it or let its expectations deafen us. We run along the banks of life with a smile, and accept the little biting dog, who's just doing his thing. Insight is always an incendiary event, a flash. It usually comes from the very direction our mind hadn't considered.

The creative rebel thinks outside the box, plans for breakthrough, makes a space for it to occur. We don't carry preconceptions around with us everywhere. It doesn't mean we aren't intelligent, in fact our intelligence is dazzling since it emerges from our insight. Our insight is also wild; our mind isn't a neatly tended garden without a weed in sight. It's a wild jungle filled with wonder and unpredictability. It has its own kind of wild order.

This is the mind of the 43rd Gene Key, the heart-mind. The breakthrough is really of the heart, not the emotional heart, but the heart of our being. Insight is always of the whole being because genius is inclusive rather than exclusive. The creative rebel isn't afraid of society or its projections. The creative rebel breaks through the niceties but is still courteous and respectful. This isn't an angry rebellion. It's a rebellion of delight, a glittering pair of eyes. This is vulnerability without being sappy. It's feisty without being provocative. It's royalty without pride.

Maybe we can feel the transmission pouring through these words. It's eloquence without wastage because the 43rd Gift of Insight is all about efficiency. This kind of efficiency isn't the dry, soulless efficiency that we find in so much of modern life. It doesn't take us away from our roots. It comes out of our roots, from our connection with nature. That's why we're wild, because that's what nature is. Nature is all efficiency; she's a quest for efficiency. Whatever your purpose and life's work is, you already have the ingredients to fulfil it. You don't have to build something on top of yourself, or master spheres that lie outside the domain of your needs.

Think of a cheetah. Its sole purpose, besides beauty, is to catch and eat the impala. It comes with the equipment needed to do that, a flexible spine and breathtaking acceleration. It doesn't have good night vision or stamina because it doesn't need them. It has exactly what it needs. The lioness on the other hand doesn't have that kind of equipment. She has a specially adapted eye that gives her incredible night vision, so she doesn't hunt during the day but at night. We don't get the qualities that we don't need in life, so there's no reason to waste energy chasing them.

The efficiency of the 43rd Gene Key is based on Simplicity, the 23rd Gift, which is its Programming Partner. True insight makes life simpler, not more complex. The more evolved we become the simpler we make our lives; it's a mystical equation. When you contemplate the meaning of breakthrough, it opens you up to more of yourself, but perhaps closes you off to the wastage in your life. It makes you deaf to those things that used to matter to you, but that you now realise are inessential.

The Siddhi of Epiphany

It doesn't matter whether we have this Gene Key in our profile or not; it really doesn't. Part of our insight may be to realise this about the Gene Keys. They sneak up on us in their own mysterious way. We have deafness, then we have insight, and finally we have epiphany, and all these words have a connection to something acoustic. Deafness is about trying to escape the silence. Insight is about listening to the inner ear, which gradually allows us to adjust to the silence by cutting out the noise wastage from our lives. Epiphany brings us back to the silence once again. Finally we're ready to embrace it, and wow is it loud! Have you ever heard deep silence? I was alone in a cave once deep under the ground. I sat there in the darkness for a good hour listening to that silence. It filled my whole being, my every cell.

The Sidhhis move beyond the Gifts, and in this one there's no longer a need to be a rebel anymore, or for that level of creative self expression. I mentioned the Fool earlier, and in the original tarot, the Fool was the first and last card, the alpha and omega. There were two Fools, which is the origin of the jokers in a pack of cards. They aren't part of the pack, but they can be used in all kinds of interesting ways. In Shakespeare's play *King Lear*, the character of the Fool holds all the secrets. He's the opposite of the King, a man with no ideology who rejects all appearances, all human attempts at understanding or order. As the King descends into madness the Fool doesn't desert him. He goes with him, because he knows what true madness really is - to see the world as rational.

We can't know anything - this is the epiphany, and in knowing nothing, we rest in the everything. This 43rd Siddhi is part of the Codon Ring of Destiny, and as in the tarot, the epiphany is beyond destiny. With the Siddhi we again become ordinary. We know that the universe is a hologram and that everything happens according to its own nature in its own timing. We no longer think about the future. We might make a plan to meet someone on a certain day but it's not something that we take seriously. A breakthrough can occur at any time and change our destiny, not that it changes it either. It's just a paradox. Fools and Kings. The 43 is the Fool, and the 34 is the King, the Siddhi of Majesty. I love these patterns - the 34 and the 43, the alpha and omega. It's also illuminating to consider the Christian epiphany with its archetype of the three Kings or the three wise men kneeling before the baby Jesus.

What could be more emblematic of the meeting of knowing and not knowing, the old and wise kneeling before the newborn and innocent?

There's one more special thing about this 43rd Gene Key. A nice finale. Humanity is pre-programmed to undergo a collective breakthrough. The 43rd Gene Key is one of seven Gene Keys known as the Seven Seals, written about in the 22nd Gene Key. Each of these Keys is a Seal that holds back an element of divine truth. At a certain point in time (maybe), the Seal is broken and a massive process of breakthrough occurs. The 43rd Siddhi of Epiphany has a design to heal the great cosmic wound of rejection, an expression of fear held in the DNA of all human beings. It's this fear that keeps us from trusting each other, that keeps our hearts closed, our borders closed. It keeps us separate. It's the fear of nations. As the 4th Seal opens, humanity gets to experience itself without fear. Our borders open, immigration officers and passports are in rapid decline, and the true human spirit is born. If you'd like to know more about that, you can explore my teaching on the Seven Sacred Seals.

The true human spirit is that of friendliness. This is the special destiny of the 43rd Gene Key, to cure humanity of its deafness and make us truly efficient as a species. Friendliness alleviates the need for defences, borders, laws, fears. It's just gone from the human genome, but not overnight; it will likely take many thousands of years in genetic terms. If it happens, it'll happen from the inside, from within our biology as we mutate to the next level. This would be the mass breakthrough of the 43rd Gene Key, even though it sounds futuristic and romantic. This Gene Keys transmission is ahead of its time, encouraging us towards a day when people may actually experience this. You might have noticed I'm using the words 'would' and 'could' and 'might' and 'if'. I have to because if I knew, I'd be a fool, and if I didn't know, I'd be a wise man. Or is it the other way around?; I guess I'll never know. Such is the Dilemma of Knowing.

The 44th Way

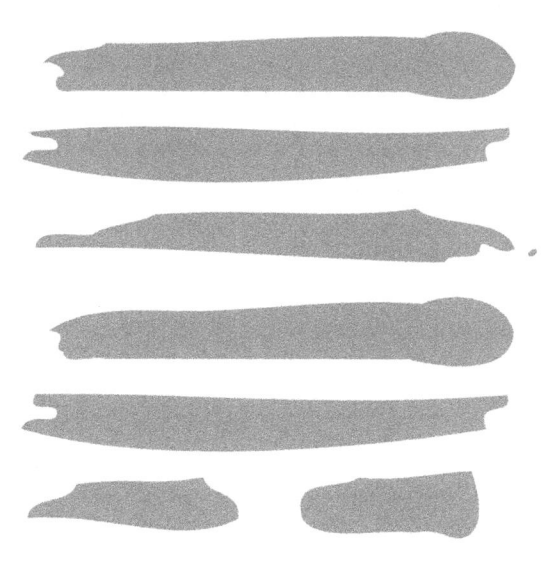

Gene Key 44

THE WAY OF TEAMWORK

The 44th Transformational Way moves from Interference to Synarchy, and it's the Way of Teamwork.

Hierarchy is a theme that's so obviously a part of our human history, through our evolution as a species from ape to homo erectus, from our hunter-gatherer roots to modern day civilisation, with all its advantages and challenges. As any social scientist or systems analyst will tell us, hierarchy exists everywhere within the universe. It seems to be a part of the way nature organises herself. Everywhere we look we see evolving chains of consciousness and awareness, all interconnected and all involved with each other, from the microcosmic to the macrocosmic. It's important when considering the Shadow awareness to realise that hierarchy isn't a bad thing. In effect, it is an inescapable principle written into the very structure of the universe.

In the Way of this 44th Gene Key, evolution is a passage from Hierarchy to Synarchy and the only difference between them is perception. It's all a matter of where our awareness is based. At the Shadow frequencies awareness is still rooted in survival and fear, whether that's on an individual or group level. On the group level this is the fear that drives the most powerful and liberal nation on our planet to spend the same amount of money on their defence budget as the rest of the world combined. It's all about hierarchy and competition rooted in fear. It's not healthy competition, which is rooted in excellence or service.

The Dilemma of Hierarchy is only a perceived dilemma. Anarchy is the great fear, the fear of what might happen if we all let go of the reins. It's the fear of going backwards to a more primitive way of life. If we carry this Gene Key in our Profile, this fear is deep within us as a theme we'll grapple with throughout our life. At the Shadow frequency we're always either overwhelmed by the fear or in reaction to it.

Shadow: Interference
Dilemma: Hierarchy
Gift: Teamwork
Siddhi: Synarchy
Programming Partner: Gene Key 29
Codon Ring: The Ring of The Illuminati

We either accept the hierarchy's laws, try and escape them or we learn to manipulate them to our advantage.

Let's bring this down to grass roots. This Gene Key is about relationship dynamics, and particularly group dynamics. We can think about how the fear frequencies operate in our own family. There are those members who are always submissive and just go along with things in order to try and maintain a sense of peace - these are the repressive natures. Then there are the stirrers, the reactors, nuclear reactors, where the fear is externalised through anger. It comes out more often as irritation and the need to control everything, from the tiniest movement our body makes to the way we dress and act. It's also not always cut-and-dry. Sometimes we can be both and as we shift our pattern, the patterns around us shift in reaction to that. This is the interference frequency at work and its job is to maintain misery. The overall frequency this creates in any dynamic, whether it's a family constellation or a business structure, is resentment. Resentment inevitably leads to break up. In the individual it leads to breakdown, and in relationships to break-up. It splits apart families, causes businesses to fail, divides communities into factions or gangs, and eventually drives countries to revolution if it's internally expressed, or war if the interference is externalised.

Peace is in the cells. All fear creates interference throughout any organism. It begins inside our body, deep in the DNA. When fear is provoked, our DNA will output chemical signals that cause us to repress our individuality and our genius, or our DNA will output chemical messages that excite us into reaction. It's water or fire, and one way or the other fear will trap us.

The Dilemma isn't really hierarchy but our response to it, and our perception of it governs that response. Hierarchy offers us a mirror. It asks, 'Am I allowing external forces to shape my reality, or am I a victim of something that appears to be outside me?'. Hierarchy can only take away freedom if we think freedom is something external. If we find true freedom then hierarchy can't touch it. Nothing can touch true freedom. It's all about how we respond to the Shadow consciousness of the world. It's inside us, downloaded at conception, and life places us deep in interference frequencies, dysfunctional families, challenging hierarchical dynamics and groups that split apart, all in order for us to learn this great lesson. It isn't about the others. It never has been. It's about us. The interference begins inside us, as a perception of the outer world that's rooted in fear. When we see through that illusion, everything in our life begins to change.

The 44th Gift — Teamwork

Embrace the Shadow and release the Gift. That's the central and simple Gene Keys formula. As we embrace the interference frequency we're emanating, it can bring about transformation in our lives and open up the Gift of Teamwork. Teamwork means drawing in the right groups of people in life, and working with healthy group dynamics. When it comes to our biological family we don't get a new one until our next incarnation, but we're really talking here about our fractal family, our soul group, our true allies in life. As we begin to raise the frequency of our DNA, many things begin to happen in our life. They may not happen right away, but when we stay with the process our outer life does begin to self-organise at a higher level.

This 44th Gene Key is so central to the Gene Keys synthesis. It's one of the core teachings of the whole Gene Keys and really deserves our attention. As we may or may not know, it has to do with fractals - self-replicating harmonic patterns found throughout the universe. When we talk about fractals, in particular concerning group dynamics, we're describing the principle of hierarchy at a higher level. As we awaken to a higher potential within ourself, we begin to activate our inner genius, our higher life purpose, and simultaneously we come into alignment with others doing the same. We move into a higher hierarchical gear, but instead of this hierarchy being based on control, manipulation, and fear, it's based on creativity and service. Oh, and how different that feels!

This kind of creative, expansive hierarchy I term heterarchy. Heterarchy means that the individual elements within a system are given their freedom. In a heterarchy, individual uniqueness or genius is paramount, the prefix hetero meaning different. In a heterarchical system, control is distributed organically and horizontally, as opposed to vertically like in a hierarchy. In fact these two terms are mutually inclusive, because hierarchies can contain heterarchies and vice versa. Again, it's all a matter of perspective.

Inside our being, as we raise the frequency of our DNA we naturally move beyond the traditional hierarchical way of processing information. Our mind begins to lose its power and our heart explodes into action, working alongside our brain. It's a known fact that heterarchy processes more information more effectively than hierarchical design. Science has utilised these breakthroughs in understanding how the brain works and in the creation of artificial intelligence. Our cells begin to operate as a team, but it may appear a lot more random than the old hierarchical model. In the old model we knew where we were. In the new higher frequency model, control is placed in the hands of the creative, evolutionary impulse itself. This is why our life changes so much and so quickly once we leave the Shadow frequencies.

Life begins self-organising and its true intelligence is freed to operate at a higher more synthetic level. Genius rises up into the holographic quantum field and downloads truth, which then emerges as breakthroughs in understanding.

Although this 44th Gift of Teamwork is about operating in much more efficient and exciting group dynamics, it presupposes that we've first unlocked Teamwork within our being. Our inner hierarchy begins to function at a whole new level. We have increased vitality because all the energy that was going into survival and defence is now liberated through our body. Our true fractal begins to show up, and teamwork is not really work at all, but play. Once we find our true human fractal, we'll begin to find more and more support for our higher purpose. Higher Purpose is not intended to operate in isolation. This is how we have traditionally viewed genius, as a few special individuals dotted around the world working in different fields. That's not the vision of the 44th Gene Key. Imagine what will happen when we have a whole connected field of creative brilliance working cooperatively in service of the whole!

That is where the 44th Gift is leading us as a species. This is how we're going to build this Eden, and it's not that hard. All it takes is a few people operating at this new, higher level, interconnected, and all serving the same higher vision. The Gift of Teamwork is the genius of drawing together such a heterarchy and empowering it to find its own direction. If we have this Gene Key in our Profile, our destiny is to be this kind of a hub for all manner of creative people. We're their common denominator and they come together around us. It's effortless, magical, and will save the world, if we ever think the world needs saving, which it doesn't!

THE 44TH SIDDHI — SYNARCHY

I love the paradox of the Gene Keys. We go on these wonderful, colourful transformational journeys through the Shadow, releasing the wonderful tide of energy and optimism of the Gift, and somehow, mysteriously, we arrive at the Siddhi. This is a strange place because it always somehow brings us back to the place where we began, but it completely reframes the Shadow at a whole other level. We began by seeing how hierarchy is natural to all universal systems. The origin of hieros means 'sacred', so hierarchy was originally understood by theologians as the way angelic beings were arranged beyond our human evolution. You see now how darkly coloured this Gene Key has become?

This Gene Key is coupled with the 50th Gene Key in a Codon Ring known as the Ring of the Illuminati. This Illuminati concept sounds mysterious, almost sinister. As the Shadow consciousness would have us believe, we might wonder if they're a powerful group of tycoons, media moguls, and freemasons, who are secretly controlling the direction of the world. They may well be, there are such groups and they probably do think they're controlling things, but come on. If we're learning anything from being around the Gene Keys we'll have learned that all systems are interrelated. Nothing exists in isolation. Our breakthrough is the world's breakthrough. That's basic chaos theory.

This time we're in now, this transitionary era, this Great Change, is a breakthrough at every level within the universe. The sun is involved, the galaxy is involved, and the entire cosmos is involved. Awareness is opening up within the living chain of being throughout the universe. The hierarchy is becoming aware of itself at another level, and as it does so, its behaviour will shift. This is what is meant by this wonderful word synarchy. Synarchy means that we all lead together. It doesn't mean that we're all the same at all. It means that our uniqueness has a place within the orchestra, and instead of just playing a nice tune and being oblivious to all those around us, we begin to play in harmony with everyone else. When we get to heterarchy, it's a bit like finding our section in the orchestra. We find all these other people playing the strings, we start jamming with them, and this amazing music comes out.

When we get to synarchy, it's a whole other level. We realise that our section is playing in concert with a whole other universe of sections, and they're all coming into symphony. We become aware for the first time of the conductor, and the conductor is inside every single individual part. This is the great revelation of the fractal universe. Inside every single molecule of our DNA is a conductor, the conductor, who's waiting for us to follow their lead. It's us following a higher harmony, the 50th Siddhi, that includes all elements within the world hierarchy. There are those who still operate at the Shadow awareness and they too are simply aspects of the higher harmony. In time, their awareness will evolve.

Synarchy is not an individual phenomenon. This Siddhi is one of the great collective Siddhis. It can only blossom in a collective, as a collective. If we have it within our Profile, that's really something to contemplate. We saw that the Shadow is interference, but the Siddhi is about non-interference. We see everything as it is, and leave it where it is. We know all life to be self-organising, even the Shadow. It eventually organises its own breakthrough. Once we've banged our head against that wall enough times, we begin to realise that it hurts and maybe we might like to stop doing that. This is the great story of incarnation here in this Gene Key. Eventually all humanity will realise its true nature as one cosmic harmony.

Our underlying nature is synarchy. Synarchy includes hierarchy and heterarchy, oligarchy and shmologarchy, and any other archies we might like to make up. It transcends and includes all evolutionary levels and steps. It's the realisation of perfection in all things. It's freedom.

Here's a mystical addendum, which is about the difference between synarchy and THE Synarchy. THE Synarchy is different from all this. It's specific to this time of the Great Change. It's the name I give to the group incarnation that's coming to catalyse the next phase of human evolution. It's the collective genetic instrument in which communal awareness will begin its breakthrough into humanity. Synarchy is a living spirit that's waiting to be unveiled within us, and THE Synarchy is where that spirit will first be experienced and demonstrated. Our role is to be the threshold for the breakthrough and establish the physical manifestations, the systems that will allow more and more members of the synarchy to come into its living quantum field. This isn't an illuminati based on power; it's based on nothing more than perception. Once this eye opens, the sight will spread like wildfire throughout humanity. Over many generations it will allow us to perceive the truth of our synarchy, and then recreate our world in its image. Just like wot it says in that there Bible! How's that for mysterious!

THE 64 WAYS

The 45th Way

Gene Key 45

THE WAY OF SYNERGY

The Transformational Way of the 45th Gene Key moves from Dominance to Communion, and it's the Way of Synergy.

The 45th Gene Key has held our planet in its thrall for aeons, especially the Shadow. It's about dominance - dominance of the male over the female, of the teacher over the child, of the left brain over the right. It's also the dominance of the few over the many. When we're all caught up in the game of dominance, it's always the few who will rise to the top. This one is such an obvious human dilemma, and it's about insecurity. We've fallen out of trust. Sometime in our early childhood we get the distinct impression that this isn't really a very safe world, and our whole being contracts and constricts. It's a learned reflex.

The Shadow frequencies are all connected to the old parts of our brain, the animal part of us. When we look at nature, we see how all animals have to compete to survive. That's what it means to be an animal. If we're a gazelle, we compete with a lion, but we humans are no longer animal. We still have those memories, but we've also evolved a completely new and more advanced operating system. We're only just learning that there are other ways and that perhaps we needn't compete with each other to survive. The Shadow frequency and its fear doesn't see any of that; it only feels unsafe. Safety is a feeling in our cells, and when we give in to fear we lose touch with the whole and start feeling deeply unsafe and insecure. We cave in to the weight of the Shadow and forget that we're supported by the whole.

It seems like a long way from dominance to communion. We can see the story of this written everywhere. No matter how hard we try, the old patterns creep back. Because of the way we've set up our modern world it's become the norm to compete with each other. It begins the moment we step out the door. For many it's there before we step out the door; it all begins inside us. It begins whenever we allow the fear in, our fear of lack and

Shadow: Dominance **Gift:** Synergy **Programming Partner:** Gene Key 46
Dilemma: Insecurity **Siddhi:** Communion **Codon Ring:** The Ring of Prosperity

---

mistrust in the whole. We have to remember that we are safe. That's what maturity means, remembering how to breathe again, remembering what it really means to be human. We have to overcome our insecurity in a world run by the frequency of dominance. The challenge is how to feel safe in a world that doesn't easily let us relax.

We rarely feel truly secure in our skins. If we did then we would feel safe even in our suffering. Our suffering is the place where the journey begins. It's supposed to be there, to wake us up. When we listen to the feeling of unsafeness inside our body, our attention to it dissipates it, melts it. The Shadow is a good thing because it leads in the direction of the heart. Many don't want to own their own fear so they externalise it as dominance. They try and take over a part of the world, own it, hold onto it. We all know this urge. Life is slipping away so we want to hold onto something. Much of this Shadow is about ownership.

Here in the UK almost every acre of land has a piece of paper attached to it with laws, decrees, disputes that are all part of its history. We really feel the need to own our territory. We can look into our own life for this pattern. How deeply do we hold onto the things in our life? Do we feel we need more? There's nothing wrong with owning our own piece of space to call home, but it's only temporary. We all know this, but we don't act like it. We act as though we could take it with us. It's only as we approach the end that our grip begins to slacken. Of course some of us live more lightly. We have to learn that in a masculine dominating world. We've really set ourselves up for stress. I'm sorry if I appear to be painting a negative view of the world, but it's because I'm aware what lies at the other end of this rainbow at the Siddhi.

How do we overcome our insecurity and remember that we are truly safe? It's the same answer in all the Gene Keys - face the Shadow, feel it, embrace it. Know the nature of the fear that lives inside us. When we feel it, we can give it the space it needs inside us and it'll be transformed. Behind it lies trust, an expansive feeling that everything is fine, that life is still beautiful even amidst difficulty. The game of dominance runs deep but one day it may give way to something marvellous. Shall we see?

THE 45TH GIFT - SYNERGY

Synergy is a beautiful word. Like many of the Gene Keys' terms, it can be applied across many dimensions and has many meanings. We come into synergy when we're in a state of trust. All the codons within us create a harmonic resonance. It's like when we put a magnet beneath a piece of paper that's covered in iron filings. They all form beautiful organised patterns, but the magnetic field itself is invisible. The universe is like that; trust is like that. We just come into alignment with the whole cosmos, and we feel calm and ease, no matter what we're going through. Synergy takes place like this at an individual level, within the chemistry of our DNA. It also takes place collectively as we come into alignment with others.

Synergy is a word we often apply to a group dynamic that's functioning smoothly, that's buzzing and creative. Once we realise that we no longer need to compete with each other to survive, the next stage is figuring out how to work together. This is a great challenge and the 45th Gene Key is adept at this. It's not so much about teamwork as facilitation. The 45th Gift knows that any group has its own self-organising principle and that if it's given enough time and space, it'll eventually find a natural higher harmony. Every group has its own identity, chemistry, and higher purpose but it's quite a journey getting there. We have to navigate the collective Shadow, which often expresses through an individual or certain individuals. Those individuals are simply carrying the Shadow for the whole group, so the group has to work through that. It can be a very creative and empowering process for everyone but it requires commitment, empathy, patience, and of course, trust.

Synergy is like a healing wave that rushes through the human genome. It balances and equalises different chemistries, making a higher group awareness possible. This is our future awareness and any group that comes together for a higher purpose can experience this transformation. The wave of synergy is an aspect of the evolutionary impulse at work; it's the creative field of transformation as the old themes of dominance are set aside in favour of a new awareness. This self-organising principle exists at all levels within the cosmos. It's even there within the Shadow frequencies.

For a long time, scientists thought that life moved from order towards chaos, until a man named Mandelbrot discovered the existence of universal patterns called fractals. He noticed that even within chaos certain patterns could be discerned. Life creates itself in wild, organic patterns; it isn't a neatly clipped rose garden. When we allow life, it naturally tends towards evolution and seeks a higher manifestation. This is where trust stems from and synergy comes into play. It uses the interference patterns of the Shadow to create the higher order.

The amazing thing is that this higher order already exists in another dimension. It's behind all the world events. It's what Heraclitus, a Greek mystic, called the hidden harmony, and when we find it, we've found gold. The hidden harmony is synergistic, bringing things and people together and catalysing their various counterparts, making the whole exponentially more powerful.

As I said earlier, the ultimate synergy takes place within our DNA as different chemical components are fused and combined to create a higher functioning with capacities that transcend the parts themselves. This is what genius is, a higher cohesive functioning within human DNA. It's the phenomenal power that's locked up in each of us.

The 45th Siddhi - Communion

In approaching this Siddhi, I'm aware that I could easily jump in and talk about its mystical side and capacities for initiating a collective transformation throughout the whole of humanity. I've spoken of these things in the Gene Keys book and mentioned the power of communion as a mystical initiation in the 22nd Gene Key. I'd like to approach it a bit differently here, and talk about Sundays - Sunday, the 7th day of the week. In almost every religion there's a tradition of having a day or two of rest. On this day we put aside our business and either pray, eat, sleep, fast, or spend time with our family. Whatever we do, it isn't supposed to be about work. This is the origin of the word holiday - the Holy day, the day set aside for contemplation, for the essential. I find Sundays fascinating! If you've ever got up early on a Sunday morning and gone outside, there's this aura hanging over the land. It seems almost as if even the birds are in on it. There's this Sunday consciousness, a descending silence that sets the day apart. It feels as though the world has just been born. It's really a special feeling, because there's no humming, no buzzing from the busy human bees.

The funny thing about this feeling is that it's a total illusion. It's fake, fabricated. We made up the days of the week. They aren't natural rhythms, they're purely social. Sunday consciousness does give us a glimpse of something else, of a possibility. What if the world were more like that all the time? I often think about what life might be like on other planets with more evolved species. I wonder whether they would spend six days a week working and one resting. I wonder whether a more natural balance might be the other way around; we're just so conditioned by our world, our world of domination.

The 45th Siddhi concerns the true nature of prosperity, and what a prosperous civilisation could look like. Money is our great symbol for the value of time. Money makes the world go round, gives us only one day a week off, and three or four weeks in a year. We don't often think about these things, but does that sound natural? I like the idea of Sunday consciousness, and having a lot more resting days. We might ask what we would do with all that time, but we only ask if we don't know how to pause and let life in. Our world is almost unfeasibly beautiful. People see that on their deathbed. How and why can we not let that level of beauty into our souls? It's the only essential thing, and yet we give all our time to the inessential.

This Siddhi represents a quieter world where we all live in Sunday consciousness. Imagine what it would be like to be born into a world like that - the silence, the spaciousness, the trust. No 'why am I here?', no 'what do I have to do?' Just being here is enough. Imagine dying after a life like that. It would be no different from living. We just drift in, and drift out; no need to even miss each other. We're just coming and going, coming and going, for millennia and millennia. Timeless.

We might ask about food and energy, and if we don't work, how will we live. We'll have to think differently about the world. I often wonder about the food of the future and if it will be nano-food. We could have our entire life supply of nutrients in a suitcase. They would just circulate in our bloodstream, releasing nutrients when the body calls for them, no need for farming or eating. We might enjoy growing vegetables and harvesting fruits because they need us to do that. The rest probably isn't necessary, and we may think it sounds dull or boring. I'm with you on that; I love eating meat, but it isn't necessary. The level of sensitivity we could have on a diet like that would be amazing. I've experienced the Siddhic state and it's very far from boring. It's blissful. In fact I don't think dullness exists at those frequencies. Imagine what we might do with all that time, such as become a polymath whose genius is spread across multiple fields. Everyone might have an intelligence like that, and there would certainly be no need for money. We'll have figured out energy by then too; we'll have discovered the secret of free energy.

So I reckon Sunday consciousness would be pretty damn good; it would certainly allow for a greater communion. We would feel the seasons in our bones, know each other's innermost awareness, and enter into harmony with all the creatures and elements. I don't think that's an idealistic dream; I think it's a logical outcome. Remember those iron filings? The hidden harmony is already there; it's our inner nature. It's hidden in our DNA, just waiting. Waiting for its time.

The 46th Way

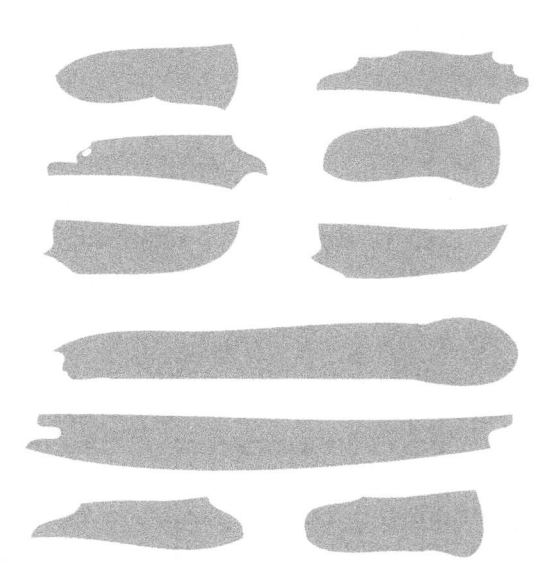

Gene Key 46

THE WAY OF DELIGHT

The Transformational Way of the 46th Gene Key moves from Seriousness to Ecstasy, and it's the Way of Delight.

The 46th Gene Key contains a delicious teaching about luck - good luck and bad luck. The Dilemma of this Shadow is Fortune, and the Shadow is Seriousness. Seriousness is connected with luck. What do we mean by luck; it sounds like a Western word, the roll of the dice. In the West, we've inherited this modern scientific worldview that sees life as random, as chance. If we go back just 500 years that worldview didn't exist and everything before that we now tend to consider naive.

It wasn't so long ago that we all believed in God. Granted, we didn't understand much of our world, we were pretty violent as we still are, but we did have a deeper understanding of fortune. If we go to India we'll find a very ancient and mature understanding about these things with a long tradition of sages who've embodied the principles of Divinity. The teaching of karma, through Buddha for example, gave us much understanding. There's a veil between life and death and the soul transmigrates from lifetime to lifetime, through age to age, and one day matures and learns what it is - a piece of God submerged in matter. Fortune is connected directly to our behaviour over great spans of time and there's justice in everything. That's a nice story, and rather logical in fact. The cherry on the cake, the trick, however, is that we don't always remember the reasons for the karma because we don't remember our lives beyond the veil.

That little detail is what makes the drama and what makes us serious. If we could see that every thought, word, deed, and act we make has direct consequences for our future, the world would clean itself up really fast. We create our own good or bad fortune and this Gene Key will show us that. Seriousness is about how deeply submerged we are in the drama. To glimpse the other side is to spoil the game. It's like someone telling us the

Shadow: Seriousness **Gift:** Delight **Programming Partner:** Gene Key 25
Dilemma: Fortune **Siddhi:** Ecstasy **Codon Ring:** The Ring of Matter

---

outcome of a great story before the storyteller has reached the end. Sooner or later, when our fortune dictates it we'll see the joke. We may not share it, because how can we share it easily with others who are submerged in the seriousness and suffering?

There's a path out of the pain. Seriousness is all about attachment. The deeper we're in the Maya, the illusion, the more attached and constricted we are (the Programming Partner here happens to be the 25th Shadow is constriction). We can't breathe with that constriction. To forget our eternal nature is to really take on a deep level of constriction. This Gene Key is also part of the genetic family called the Codon Ring of Matter, which reinforces the belief that the material world is all there is. So the question is how to move out of seriousness, which is no joking matter, excuse the pun.

We can loosen our attachments, beginning with our mind and its beliefs and opinions, which are based on good and bad. There is no good and bad. There's only the playing out of the mechanics of fortune. Bad behaviour simply leads to a consequence, which takes us deeper into matter. Good behaviour loosens the grip of matter. I leave it to you to figure out what good and bad behaviour means, and life will show us, all on its own. It's like this game I play sometimes with my young kids. You grip them really tight and the more they struggle the tighter your grip becomes. When they remain still, you make your grip gradually looser and begin to open. They suddenly try and break free and your grip instantly tightens. It's a great game. Kids love it because it's a universal law. They eventually figure out how to escape by doing nothing!

We're so serious, and the spiritual people are the most serious. We get locked into these tight little systems and then play out our politics within them. A system should be loose for it to be truly transformational. I meet so many serious Buddhists, Lightworkers, Human Design believers, whatever raiment they've put on. It becomes a layer of constriction for many, not all, but many. If they can sit and be human with me, laugh at their own system, then I know they're wearing it lightly and that it's just a way for them to move beyond the matter. Most of the time, we become stuck and ossified in these things. For many people it's science, for others it's politics, and for others, it's service or religion. We get bogged down in our own seriousness. Fortune favours the fool, the one who can see the joke but still respects the drama. Suffering is suffering. People are dying, being raped, life is horrible, and the world is filled with corruption. Yes, and it's no joking matter. Behind all that though, there's a reason for everything. We're here to learn, to loosen our grip within the illusion, to realise that death is a falsehood. As we do, we begin to reshape our own fortune. We can do it right now, and that's exciting. We can change our view, begin to act and think selflessly. We can change gears in our life and things will slowly change around us. It takes time. We may not see the impact until our next lifetime, but know that karma is real and that Justice lies behind everything. We're all in such an adventure.

THE 46TH GIFT - DELIGHT

The magic of the Gene Keys is that it isn't just knowledge. It shows us this very simple truth which anyone can try any time. Be nice for a day and see what our next day is like, then be nasty for a day and see what our next day is like. It couldn't be simpler, and it's not a head trip, it's just learning from life. The 46th Gift is the Gift of Delight. It's what happens when we discover the secret - that our acts, thoughts, and words really do have an impact that returns to us. Very few people actually live with delight; we've mostly forgotten what life is for.

Delight comes only with a beginner's mind, a certain innocence. When we've realised the truth of the principles of karma, everything becomes simpler. There's a stage where the negativity of the Shadow has to be challenged inside us. It has to be transcended and replaced. A new part starts growing in that space as we empty ourself out. As we unlearn knowledge and discover the living wisdom of life, our body starts to zing with life. We reset our body clock, maybe start waking up earlier with the sun, or finally sleep a truly deep and restful sleep. We cultivate habits that our body enjoys rather than those fleeting pleasures that we have to pay for later.

Life is a box of delights, too many delights to name and number. This Gene Key governs the key development stage in our childhood between birth and seven. This is the foundational stage of building the physical body and internal organs. Through the Gene Keys, particularly the Venus Sequence from the Golden Path, and deep contemplation, we may re-experience some of the challenges of that time in our childhood as our contemplation deepens. We get to re-imprint the way our cells were first imprinted. We get to lay down a new copy of ourself in our DNA, and the key building block is the energy of delight.

Matter doesn't have to be heavy. It can be very refined and wonderfully sensual. The 46th Gift is a very sensual Gift, but not in the sense of sexuality so much as physicality. This is like a child's sensuality, the way they taste everything through their body and senses.

We might wonder how a genius for delight has use in the business world, the modern world, and what it means. It means that we're desperately needed, that we bring perspective to everything. Wherever there's deep attachment and seriousness our presence and wisdom brings things down to the heart of the matter. Why are we here? There are many possible answers to that question, but surely one of them is to appreciate life, to enjoy ourselves.

A master of living life well is a rare phenomenon. How often do we meet such a person? We're so focused on task-oriented living, on skills and projects and endeavours, but the 46th Gift isn't focussed there. They may be involved in all of those things, but their priority is to bring a light touch to everything they do, and good fortune into the world. The 46th Gift is a great Gift of love, and lives through the heart. It's fluent in the language of emotion but never overwhelmed by emotion. It loves dialogue, connection, touch, laughter, good food, and good living. It loves wine. I mean that. A 46th Gene Key that cannot enjoy the fruits of the earth, even in very small measures, is no true 46th Gift.

THE 46TH SIDDHI - ECSTASY

In these Transformational Ways I keep coming back to the figure of Dionysus. The new paradigm coming into the world is one of fusion, of the melding of heaven and earth, of the spiritual and the material. For the great mutation, the Great Change, to impact the whole of humanity the spirit must become human. This is what the Siddhi of Ecstasy is. We might have thought that ecstasy takes place only in some far-off spiritual dimension. It takes place right here among human beings. We're natural-born ecstatics, but to allow that level of beauty into our inner being we have to unlearn many of our masculine traits.

To court ecstasy we have to become contemplative. We have to slow down. We have to pause so that we come once again into communion with the elements, nature, and each other. Ecstasy is a swell that grows inside our breast. We can actually cultivate ecstasy like a gardener. We just have to tend to the garden of our inner being. Ecstasy is like a garden where the gardener has just done enough to create the feeling of natural order. In such a garden, plants are allowed to dance, but no single plant is permitted to dominate. Wildness is crafted and respected. There's no dominant human ego projecting itself into the garden. The garden sings, because it's tended always with a light touch.

We can design such a life for ourself. It takes care and time like any garden and it takes deep sensitivity. We need to go out and sit in such a garden and listen to its inner world, frequencies, and vibrations. Wherever a part of our being is expressing a little too violently, a little too brashly, we go in with the pruning shears and reshape that area. Our awareness does the pruning; we don't go in with heavy machinery. We tend to little corners of our being, and over time we'll reshape every aspect of our life. When our inner being is at rest or play, then ecstasy can come. Only then can it visit us, and it will play inside us in soft zephyrs, swirling subtly at first. We'll experience times of intense softness, when it seems light is flowing all around us.

This is how grace visits us, it swells. Ecstasy swells and dips, it isn't a consistent energy. It's like the wind, so we have to give ourself to it. Many people in today's world are visited by this grace, but are too busy to recognise it, and don't realise that the angels are all around us. Each Siddhi is a different kind of mastery. The master of delight becomes the human teacher and this 46th Siddhi loves the human body, its movement, delicacy, and ability to taste the essences of life.

We humans have no real idea of the capacities of this body in which we live. It can sip the nectar of a star when it's correctly attuned. It can make sweet love to another person just from thinking about them. The body is a mirror of the macrocosm. It has so many jewels and treasures within it that we couldn't explore them all if we had aeons. Our bodies are the great untamed wilderness. They're the frontier, not the final frontier, the only frontier. We'll never exhaust their abilities, their capacity for love and ecstasy.

Ecstasy begins with the breath. When we learn to breathe deeply, not in a forced way, but in a relaxed and open way, then the softness of life can approach us. There are ways of living that we've forgotten. We used to live like this - just sitting, just having enough to provide for our simple needs, just being together drinking tea, talking, laughing, and being silent under the stars. One day we'll return to those times when ecstasy is allowed back into the garden and life becomes a gentle festival. Listen to this from the Tao Te Ching:

> *Imagine a small state with a small population*
> *Let there be labour-saving tools*
> *that aren't used*
> *Let people consider death*
> *and not move far*
> *Let there be boats and carts*
> *but no reason to ride them*
> *Let there be armour and weapons*
> *but no reason to employ them*
> *Let people return to the use of knots*
> *and be satisfied with their food*
> *and pleased with their clothing*
> *and content with their homes*
> *and happy with their customs*

GENE KEY 46

*Let there be another state so near
people hear its dogs and chickens
but live out their lives
without making a visit*

THE 64 WAYS

The 47th Way

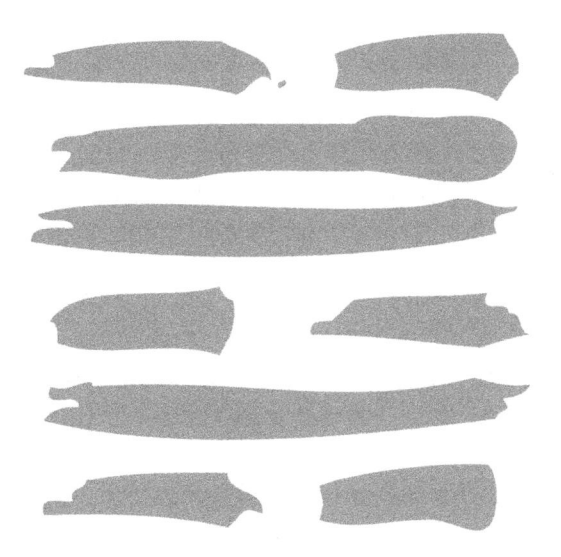

Gene Key 47

THE WAY OF TRANSMUTATION

The Transformational Way of the 47th Gene Key moves from Oppression to Transfiguration, and it's the Way of Transmutation.

In the original I Ching, this 47th hexagram had to do with how we face adversity, and one of its images was a dried up well or ditch. The suggestion is that when we face adversity in an open way, we eventually find the hidden meaning in it. Hence the following hexagram in the sequence is the 48, the Well. The way we face adversity gracefully is through owning it rather than denying or deflecting it.

This 47th Gene Key is really fascinating and points towards one of the greatest problems of humankind – the issue and purpose of suffering. Many people live their lives without even realising they're suffering. We unconsciously try to escape feeling it in so many ways through work, the many distractions of our senses and the multitude of projections of our mind onto the world and those around us. Rare indeed is a human being who finds the courage to look deeply into the nature of his or her suffering. The fact is that we can only come face to face with our suffering when we embrace our aloneness. We have to look within and when we do, we meet the 47th Shadow. We begin to claim ownership of our suffering. It's wired inside us, and is connected to what the ancients referred to as our karma.

Let's explore this for a moment, because karma is such a misunderstood term. It belongs to the collective and is both individual and collective in nature. As we go through our lives we accrue positive and negative karma. Positive karma gets drawn up into our higher subtle bodies and negative karma flows out into the world of manifestation. What we call negative karma is really only low frequency vibration, the Shadow quantum field.

Shadow: Oppression **Gift:** Transmutation **Programming Partner:** Gene Key 22
Dilemma: Ownership **Siddhi:** Transfiguration **Codon Ring:** The Ring of Alchemy

---

It's actually imprinted in our physical DNA as memory, ancestral memory, and that ancestral memory is then passed on through the bloodlines. Every human body comes wired with ancestral karmic patterns that are collective in nature rather than solely personal. Our body has its own karma but that has nothing to do with our essence, which is pure. The essence inside us simply requires that kind of karma in order to live out our incarnative drama. We each get to write a word or a few lines in the great story. A great life maybe has a whole paragraph, and a life where we're a victim of our own Shadows might be just a punctuation mark.

What I'm driving at is that oppression is universal - it comes with the vehicle. It's not possible to find a vehicle without a history yet, but that's what is coming. Our history is exactly the one we need for our script. We have to own it while we're here. It contains just the right ingredients and challenges to match the amount of positive karma we've accrued throughout all our lifetimes. I'm feeling slightly uncomfortable because there's this deep knowing inside me that knows the relativity of what I've just said. Even at subtle levels of being, there's still separation. There's a plane, the causal plane, where great light and purity resides and there's still delineation in consciousness. This is the level at which incarnation occurs, and yet it's only a half-truth. At the more expanded levels, there are no levels and there aren't even individualised souls or causal bodies. The bottom line is that our oppression, the particular nuances and flavours of our suffering and karma during this lifetime are exactly equivalent to the greatness of our inner light. Their purpose is to awaken that light.

The final thing about this 47th Shadow is it's always externalised through our life until we turn inwards. Most people manifest their karma externally and wonder why it's happening to them. They don't own their karma and therefore they become a victim of it. Some people carry such powerful collective karma in their DNA that it has to manifest in order that their journey through it can be of inspiration to others. When we turn inwards and meet it as a seed before it externalises, then our awareness can disable and transmute it before it manifests. This is why it's said that our meditation, awareness, breathing, or presence can burn off karma. This is the great mystery of Alchemy, and we have to own the Shadow we carry, even though it's not really us at all. It just comes with the vehicle.

The 47th Gift - Transmutation

This 47th Gene Key really captures the essence of the transformational journey through the frequency bands so profoundly. Every Shadow contains a Gift. The Gift of Transmutation occurs more and more as we enter into the present moment more fully. In the 15th Gene Key I talk about Dante's Divine Comedy, an allegory which like the Spectrum of Consciousness in the Gene Keys book, has three levels of consciousness. Dante calls them Inferno, Purgatorio, and Paradiso. The Gift frequency is Purgatorio, which is funny! Once we become aware of our oppression, our suffering, it becomes more and more acute. Wherever we go this divine ache is within us, a deep restless longing to remember something.

Such creativity lies in purgatory. In Dante, purgatory is represented by a mountain with terraces, and souls are either ascending or descending these terraces into heaven or hell. The Gift level is where karma is transmuted and we gradually rise up. Dante, genius though he was, missed this part in his allegory but like all of us he was heavily influenced by the times in which he lived. It's true that at the Gift frequency we rise and fall in and out of the Shadow as its karma becomes transmuted. The heat released from that transmutation gives us the lift to raise our frequency onto higher and higher terraces. The terraces are like the subtle bodies, as they become gradually purified and refined.

Transmutation is an ongoing process that has plateaux. These are called the Initiations, and many mutations make up a transmutation. Many small breakthroughs lead to bigger breakthroughs as more and more trapped, oppressed light is released from within our DNA. This is how our Shadows drive our Evolution, which shapes our Life Story, our Life's Work. More and more radiance breaks through from within. Each of the Gifts has this ongoing process underlying it. As our contemplation moves deeper inside us, it begins to reach out into the Siddhic realm. It then transforms into absorption, an ongoing chemical and molecular process that's irreversible as the Siddhis begin to suck us into their gravitational field.

The genius of the 47th Gift is that it thrives on adversity. At its higher reaches, it really embraces challenges with glee. We know when another Shadow appears, that that Shadow contains more light for us. We welcome them and draw them deeper and deeper inside us with graciousness, the Gift of the Programming Partner, the 22nd Gene Key. Transmutation takes place in the belly, in the cauldron. Here all karma is burned from our DNA and transformed. This is why we keep going down into the belly over and over again when we work with the Gene Keys.

If we have this 47th Gene Key in our Profile, we have some really interesting scripts hidden away in our DNA. We have some work to do. We've inherited a vehicle that is designed to overcome adversity by drawing it inside ourself, owning it fully and finally releasing the light inside it. One key to know is that adversity is about time. It takes a long time to burn all that ancestral anguish. Our body and life may even become the battlefield for it to play out in, but we can trust in the process. What film or book or good story about overcoming adversity doesn't take almost forever to conclude? That's the fiction, and like Dante's comedy, our lives are an allegory for the playing out of consciousness as it burrows into the form, transmutes and digests it before its true nature can be realised. Ah, such great stories we write…

The 47th Siddhi — Transfiguration

All great stories, true stories that is, end in redemption. There's always the period of innocence, the great trial where we're tested to our very limits and then finally there's the atonement, the victory. So it is with all the Gene Keys. With this 47th Gene Key, all those little mutations that occur as our awareness transforms the shadow on a daily basis lead to the great transmutations. Those are the special times in our lives, or the special lifetimes when we break through to another level and achieve stability at a higher frequency plateau. These great transmutational periods are usually very intense and they become more intense as our frequency rises into the Gift frequency and beyond.

At a certain stage as I mentioned earlier, contemplation, that state in which our awareness is turning inwards on a regular basis, gives way to absorption. When this stage is reached, we know. Our whole frequency begins to move into another realm. The intensity remains, but our life becomes at the same time softer, quieter, and our effort begins to drop away. The Transfiguration actually begins at the higher reaches of the Gift frequency, as our aura enters the state of absorption.

What is occurring is that our genetic memory is being cleansed, purged, expunged. As it falls away, a new being emerges in its midst and our karma becomes so purified that our biochemistry goes through some radical alchemical changes. Combinations of hormones are synthesised in our brain stem that were never possible before. They were waiting for the right genetic environmental signals. Now the DNA can release those signals because the frequency of light that is hitting its coding catalyses them. These hormones allow us to enter long periods of pure being, in which greater and greater gaps open out between our thoughts. We become suffused with our own presence, with our essence. Our awareness is now so inward that it comes to a point of complete rest. Then the magic occurs and we reach the centre.

Of course we don't really reach the centre. It realises itself inside us. The 47th Siddhi is rather extraordinary. The word transfiguration obviously refers to Christ's ascension on the cross, and it's more than just symbolic. This is the phenomenon known as the rainbow body in Tibet or China. People with the 47th Gene Key at a particular position in their Hologenetic Profile can physically become transfigured. This only occurs in specific pre-destined vehicles - just having the 47 is not enough. We have to have a certain combination of Gene Keys, but in a way, physical transfiguration is not the point. All Siddhis bring about transfiguration because they each show us our original face. They mystically change us at such a fundamental and genetic level that we're permanently altered.

The 47th Siddhi has a wonderful mythology to move from *inferno* to *purgatorio* to *paradiso*. It's about victory, redemption, the sun coming out after the storm. It's the great leveller that only those who really own their suffering and destiny bring their life to this kind of a peak. It only happens rarely. At least that has been the case in the past, but with the advent of the synarchy coming into form and the Great Change, this Siddhi is sure to pay this planet a more regular visit. Even now, vehicles are in the production line with the right ingredients for physical transfiguration. The world is getting ready once again to embrace the magical realm, the state we originally came from. All it takes is a few transfigurations and the game is up. Life is not what our scientists and popes and moralists would have us believe. As the bard said:

> *There are more things in heaven and earth Horatio,*
> *than ever your little philosophy dreamed of...*

The 48th Way

Gene Key 48

THE WAY OF RESOURCEFULNESS

The Transformational Way of the 48th Gene Key moves from Inadequacy to Wisdom, and it's the Way of Resourcefulness.

Wisdom is rooted in not-knowing. That's the one-liner I'd like to use to begin and end this contemplation. Not-knowing as a Shadow pattern is very different from not-knowing as a Gift or not-knowing as mastery. As a Shadow pattern, not-knowing is experienced as inadequacy, the belief that one can't cope or the fear that one may fail or falter. This is a very human fear, an understandable trait that we humans often experience when facing the unknown. This is a deep fear key and whoever has it in their Profile or as a living contemplation will have to face some deep fears.

One of my favourite places to travel is the Highlands of Scotland. I used to live up there in a small mountain cottage, what the locals call a shieling or croft. I would often go out from my croft, which was halfway up a remote Scottish glen, and run through the forests, sometimes barefoot as the earth is so soft and yielding. I loved above all this waterfall in the forest, and I'd climb up the side of the waterfall. There was this little pool at the top, quite deep, and then the water would plunge off this pool some 60 metres down to a large pool at the bottom. One of my dares was to jump into this upper pool. It was dark and deep, you couldn't see the bottom, and it was cold - the kind of cold that brings up one's fears.

One winter I decided to go out at night into the forest and I reached my pool and stood on the edge and stared down into the blackness. Some insane impulse within dared me to jump into that void, so I took off my clothes in the cold night and stood there on the edge of life. That's how it felt to me. Fear grabbed me like a rictus.

Shadow: Inadequacy	**Gift:** Resourcefulness	**Programming Partner:** Gene Key 21
Dilemma: Not-Knowing	**Siddhi:** Wisdom	**Codon Ring:** The Ring of Matter

It was illogical, elemental, ancient fear. I stood there quivering with the cold and the fear, my mind wrangling with the terror. At a certain point the jump happened. I didn't do it. It just happened. It was one of the most exhilarating things I've ever done. I was alone, but a great whoop tore through me, one of Walt Whitman's famous barbaric yawps!

This is the fear of the 48th Shadow. Our life will bring us this fear if we have the courage to face it, and face it we must. There's no choice. It's the fear of our annihilation. When we do face it, a great energy will come through us and we'll never have to face it in the same way again. We needn't go looking for it either. It'll come and find us when we're ready and it'll come when we feel unready! Perhaps the fear will find us through a relationship when someone dies or leaves, or through a teacher or circumstance that tests us to the limits. No one knows how or when these things occur, but they're defining moments.

Let me reassure you and myself, that there's nothing to fear. This hexagram consists of two trigrams, symbols, and one is called the abysmal, the other the gentle. Isn't that a beautiful paradox? Go gently into the abyss. The abyss will treat us with gentleness. The elements are wind and water, or wood and water. This is why the ancients called this Gene Key the Well. Some think it's because the wooden bucket brings the water up out of the well, but in fact the old buckets were made from clay. The wood refers to the supports that guide the bucket up. We also have this inner support when we relax and find that place of gentleness within.

One of the problems we create for ourselves in life is tension. We have learned tension and unlearned gentleness. Children are gentle, but as we grow, we unlearn that pliancy and softness. Some of us retain it, but it's rare. In ancient Chinese medicine the seat of fear is in the kidneys, but the kidneys are also where we find the virtue of gentleness. Inadequacy is actually a choice. To believe we're inadequate is to allow ourself to become a victim of our fear of the unknown. We truly don't want to give that power of ours away. Here in this Gene Key is the antidote to fear - gentleness, so be gentle with yourself. Always remember that.

One final insight for us from the 48th Shadow is that this Gene Key governs our developmental cycle from the age of eight to fourteen. This is a stage of massive growth as we move through puberty. It's the stage when the golden child finally leaves Eden and crosses the rubicon of innocence, never to return. What this means is that there's a very challenging passage we must go through in this cycle and it always concerns our emotional life.

This seven year cycle dictates the growth and development of our emotions. We become emotionally imprinted by what happens to us during this phase. There's always some great emotional trial that we face. It's kind of written into our dharma, our destiny. Whatever it is, it doesn't have to dictate the rest of our life. We'll have to face the root fear and disentangle it inside ourself. It'll always involve our ability to love, both others and ourself. If you have this Gene Key you can give yourself the gift of the Venus Sequence. It's a contemplative journey using the Gene Keys that allows us to understand what happened to us during this difficult period in our life, and helps us transform what sometimes seems to be the curse that dogs our relationships into a blessing. This is the only time I've ever used one of my contemplations to recommend such a thing, but for you with the 48th Gene Key, I would say that this is essential.

THE 48TH GIFT - RESOURCEFULNESS

Out of the well, the emotional depths of our psyche, comes forth all manner of fruits. What a beauty we are when this 48th Gift transmutes the fear…what things we can achieve in life. How sought after we might become…

We need to ask not what we might do, but what can't we do? We can do anything we put our heart into, anything that we feel passionate about, anything that has a practical impact on improving some part of the world or elevating some part of society. If we've been given the Gift of Resourcefulness, it's for a reason and we'll require it. The 48th Gene Key lies at the heart of the Ring of Matter and it's about impacting the material realm. It's about bringing resources to people. It's about connecting others with their own depth, or helping them find whatever's missing from their lives, whatever brings them into balance.

The 48th Gift is good with money. We may be surprised to hear this but of course it must be, since it's about inexhaustible wealth. Deep within the form, the atomic structure of life, lies all this untapped energy and the 48th Gift knows how to release it. We can apply this to any sphere of life. There have always been those in the world who see things, who know things. They don't know how they know - that's the nature of not-knowing. They can use this Gift to their advantage and the advantage of others. It's a felt gift, an intuitive gift, a magical gift. If it's channeled into service it even increases, whereas if it's used for solely one's own benefit, it will eventually dry up.

There's such a thing as natural wisdom and it's rooted in common sense, but more than that it's rooted in a connection with the natural world. This is a Gift that needs to be outside often, under the sky, in the woods, by the ocean, in the ocean, connecting in with the source of power. The 48th Gene Key lost behind a computer screen - nothing is sadder. God weeps to see such things.

With so much potential to connect people, things, animals, plants, this is a waste. Be careful with this Gene Key not to squander the goose with the golden eggs. This is a Gene Key that can hit many health problems if it isn't out sharing its Gift of Resourcefulness. It doesn't necessarily mean that we're some kind of social natural, but it does mean that we need to stay connected to the earth.

With the 48th Gift, the Gift is in what we don't know. Always remember that. Others are defined by what they know. We alone are defined by our willingness to approach the unknown with confidence, openness, and a sense of adventure. From this open space we'll become the field through which knowing arises, of its own accord. This can become a blissfulness for us, and an inspiration for others. 'How did you know that?' they will likely say…and we don't know, but that's ok. It's simply how it is. It also means that we need to keep moving. We may not succeed at the same thing twice. Our Gift is with the unknown, not the known, so we must be wary of repetition. If we decide to bake the same cake again, we must do it differently - if we try to repeat what we did before, it probably won't work.

Of all the Gene Keys this is the one with depth, the deepest. It's the most yin, along with the 2nd Gene Key. Here we find the true place of the Goddess, the unknown, the unknowable, the eternally abundant, infinitely unpredictable - the mystery of mysteries. Woman. This Gene Key is all woman. If we're a man, don't fret; this Gift is the Gift of appreciation of the ways of the woman. We may love woman more than any woman can. We may see the nature of the feminine more clearly than any woman can. If we're a woman, we're here to embody these qualities of womanliness, above all gentleness and the unfathomable, the wind and the water.

The future healing of the world will come out of the feminine, not from women, but from the feminine, the honouring of the feminine. This means the love of curves, the love of slowness, the love of the subtle and the supple. There's not an ounce of showiness or ego in woman, not in true woman. There's only the smile, like the smile of Mona Lisa. People have wondered for hundreds of years about that smile. There's no reason for that smile. It's the smile of the yin, that knows all is held within the lap of the Divine, surrendered and accepting of everything, that can be passionate and on fire, but also knows that the greatest power is in stillness and water. Resourcefulness thy name is woman.

The 48th Siddhi - Wisdom

We come to the Siddhi of Wisdom, which perhaps we've felt already as we've explored the Gene Keys. Wisdom is not the same as knowledge at all. They're diametrically opposed. Knowledge comes from knowing and wisdom comes from not-knowing, from innocence. Similar to Revelation, wisdom wells up. Revelation floods and wisdom wells up. It wells up gently from beneath the waves. It requires deep unlearning of knowledge. It requires a radical Valour, the 21st Siddhi and its Programming Partner, to let go of what has come before, to be that open, that naked, that vulnerable.

Wisdom lies between the words, behind the concepts. It's older than the mind. It may be reached through the mind, like sunlight through a prism, but it doesn't attach itself anywhere. It emerges spontaneously, right from the heart of creation. It's alive, intelligent, and it lurks in our DNA. It's hard to explain this to people with a strong mental polarity in life. Our body contains great wisdom. The sun contains vast wisdom. Whenever I'm challenged by a masculine mindset, someone with a greater intellect than mine,

I think of the sun. The sun is inexhaustible in its intelligence. It's always been seen as a masculine principle but it also has a feminine aspect. Like all living wisdom, it draws its energy and light from the darkness of deep space.

Thus wisdom comes into the world. It's perennial. Many teachers have carried it. It comes to roost inside certain people. Regardless of our Gene Keys, it will alight on us if that's our karma. The Gene Keys are a living wisdom, a terma, a treasure, a transmission of light refracted through word and shape and concept and person, but the wisdom is simply using us as its hosts. The words are its host, I'm its host, you may be its host. After all this is gone, after you and I and the Gene Keys are gone, the wisdom remains. It's the only thing in the universe that will survive the end of the universe. The only thing that survives death is death. That's deep, I know. What it really means is that unless we can become empty like this, we can't realise our eternal nature.

We can't grasp onto wisdom. It will elude us like a slippery fish, and if we make it into knowledge, it'll no longer be wisdom. It'll have become ossified and only have limited use. Wisdom is endlessly useful. We speak about pearls of wisdom, and that's what they are - endlessly dripping from the heavens. The beauty of wisdom is its very ephemeral nature. Because it detonates like soap bubbles it can't be trapped, caught, or materialised. This is the Ring of Matter, but its greatest secret is that it's not permanent. Nothing material lasts. It can't. Wisdom emanates from everything, even the very smallest things. A snail has more wisdom than the greatest logician.

This is why wisdom has long been the domain of woman, of the wise ones. Because the woman brings the child into the world. She alone knows the mystery of birth, of something coming from nothing. We can study this as a man but until we experience it we can't know what it really is. This isn't to say that man can't be wise; most of the Masters throughout history are in fact male. There are two reasons for this; the first is because the feminine pole can be developed within the male in a way that makes it very visible and easy to understand.

This is not-knowing shining through knowing. The second reason is that the female Masters are not really masters in our understanding of the term; they're usually mothers or grandmothers, so their responsibility has been to bring masters into the world, and remain hidden because of that. We don't even have to give birth. If we're born a woman, then the transmission of wisdom is latent within us, within our aura. Until I met my wife, I never wrote anything. The Gene Keys couldn't come. The future of wisdom therefore is not only with the woman but with the male and female working together. This is where the transmission of wisdom is now seeking to come through, in the magical exchange, the fluidic emanations that lie between the male and female poles.

We live in a fascinating time when the wisdom termas, the wisdom streams, are seeking synthesis. They're seeking partners with a yin and yang pole to manifest through. That's the future of our coming awareness, the collective awareness that's coming. It means that we need to take deep responsibility for our emotional cleanness, have great patience and love to stay in a relationship and allow the living wisdom to give birth to itself while we take the background role. To do that, both partners have to surrender their agendas and let go of what they think they know, because wisdom, as we have now seen, is rooted and will always remain rooted in not-knowing.

THE 64 WAYS

THE 49TH WAY

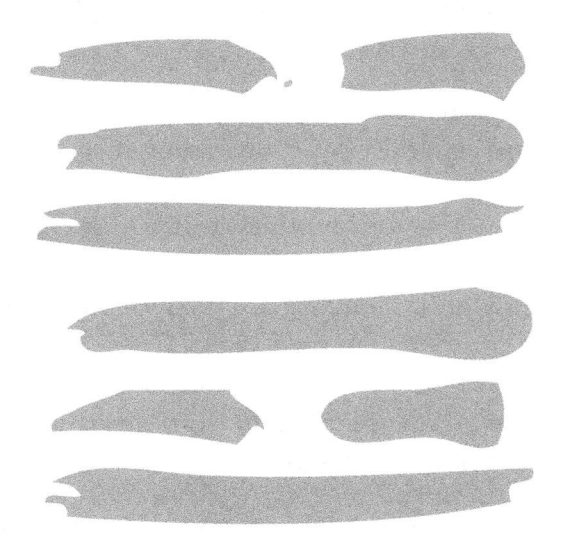

Gene Key 49

THE WAY OF REVOLUTION

The Transformational Way of the 49th Gene Key moves from Reaction to Rebirth, and it's the Way of Revolution.

This Gene Key has taken some penetration to get to the bottom of it. I had to contemplate it for a long time to really understand what it was doing inside me. After some time it just immediately became clear. It's particularly powerful because it's part of the histidine codon, the wonderfully named Ring of the Whirlwind, which connects it chemically to the 55th Gene Key. It's the coalface of the big mutation that's occurring right now in our solar plexus centre. It's about ethical cleansing. That's my inner joke, and you'll see why. This 49th Gene Key is highly emotional. At the Shadow frequency it's about reaction, and the reaction patterns that govern our relationships and keep us fighting with each other. Its Dilemma is needs and these needs are different from the habits of the 38th Gene Key, which are more to do with our human habit of struggling.

The needs of the 49th Gene Key are deep physical needs, urges that arise constantly from our desire nature. They're so embedded in most of us that they literally run our lives. They give us an illusion of consistency, as in our needs for food at a certain time of day, or to put our makeup on, or have a bath. If we don't have them met, we feel like something is wrong. We're so often a victim of our needs. Let's say one of our needs is to have a coffee every morning, which seems normal enough. Everyone else does it, surely we're allowed that I hear you say? Well, let's say one morning we miss our coffee because of some unforeseen circumstance. We find that for the rest of that day, nothing quite goes right because we didn't get our morning fix. We're trapped by these needs. If we weren't trapped, missing our coffee wouldn't have registered or set off a mood in us.

Shadow: Reaction **Gift**: Revolution **Programming Partner:** Gene Key 9
Dilemma: Needs **Siddhi**: Rebirth **Codon Ring:** The Ring of The Whirlwind

---

That's a very mundane example, while the deepest ones are food and sex and external love. If we don't get those met, we really react! This is a subtle tapestry inside us. All these hidden needs are like secret tripwires crisscrossing our being, all across our solar plexus. Every time someone or something triggers one of those needs, we lose our centre, because the solar plexus is our centre. We're like a minefield of desires and we're a victim of every one. We don't stand a chance for finding any kind of freedom with all that going on. This is why the mystics have always said we have to pull out our desires.

When I was younger I went on a work exchange in Poland, and it was kind of an interfaith thing. I won my place through writing an essay and I was the representative of the UK. We were all under 30, of different religions and from all around the world. It was an amazing experience. I was basically a mystic and shared my room with this crazy Buddhist monk from Bangladesh, a real character. One day I came in from working; we were digging ditches to bring water to a remote village. I came in in the evening and ran myself a bath. I really needed that bath. I was hot and sweaty and muddy from a hard day's labour. I came round the corner with my towel and there was Sibu the monk sitting happily in my bath! I was so annoyed with him, but I didn't say anything. I'm English, and he was a monk, but I was annoyed to say the least. For him it was just a bath. He came in, saw a bath running and got in it. For me, it was my bath. It didn't take long for me to get the joke. This is what we do, and it's how we react. We set ourselves these tripwires and invite people to provoke us. Our needs create expectations and those expectations often lead to disappointment. It's all a sham, an illusion. All these emotional reactions are placed there by us!

The 49th Gene Key is bringing a new awareness into us that's digging into these needs. Those who're working with the Gene Keys or other spiritual systems will know what I mean. As we clear our solar plexus, we see into the true nature of our desires and these networks of needs become clearer inside us. We go through a kind of ethical cleansing in which the needs, which are pure (I'll explain about them in the Gift) are sorted from those which are impure, inessential, and detrimental to our health and wellbeing.

It doesn't mean we can't have that coffee every morning, but it does mean that we probably won't need it every morning. That's a huge difference because our needs aren't really the problem, they're the Dilemma.

The problem is our emotional reactions, when our needs are unexpectedly unmet. Freedom, which is moving through this Gene Key because of the 55th Gene Key, is to not be a victim of our needs but to accept them and our relationship to them in every moment. It's only when we don't accept our relationship to our needs that we find ourself trapped. This Shadow demands that we look deeply into our daily needs, our need for food, for sex, for attention, for things to be going in a certain way, for certainty. These are deep needs we feel, but we must eventually yield to them. Uncertainty is magic when we embrace it, but hell when we don't.

We need to examine the world of our needs. Whenever we find ourself emotionally reacting or feel emotional discomfort of any kind, we need to look immediately at the source need behind it. When we see it, our awareness will pull it out from the base like a weed, and though the need may remain, our reaction will come to an end. That's our work - alone, in relationships and in community. We need to be vigilant and hunt for our reaction patterns. As soon as we see them, we must cut them off and dig out the roots. We'll gradually find ourself tasting a new kind of life and a revolution will occur in our being.

The 49th Gift - Revolution

We have all these needs inside us. Some come from below, and some from above. The 49th Gift is a sorter, a sifter, and it filters our needs. The new awareness coming through this Gift is magical. It sees a need arising from the body, watches the body address the need or not and remains non-judgmental. It just waits and watches. Was the need essential? If the body needs food, it seems essential, but often the body doesn't actually need food, yet still we eat. The awareness notices this and it makes us uncomfortable. We realise we've gone against the body and harmed it. Some needs are essential and some aren't.

Our soul or higher self also has needs. It needs self-love, awareness, inspiration, wisdom, beauty. We often don't listen to these needs, especially since they're quieter in the beginning.

The 49th Gift begins to sort them and puts the essential ones in the in-tray and the inessential ones in the out-tray. This is the revolution inside our being. It's a process that's going on in many of us now, making us more and more uncomfortable, and that's a good thing. It's a mystical cleansing of the emotional system and it's why many people who begin working with the Gene Keys quickly lose a lot of weight and others fill out to just the right amount. We're coming into balance, because we're throwing out old genetic patterns. It's about pruning back our desire nature because the solar plexus centre needs a new kind of environment. It needs a cleaner, more open environment, less cluttered with old frequencies.

Some needs are really addictive and it takes a lot of awareness to drop them. It's a revolutionary process. I have this image of us holding up a voodoo doll of ourself with all these pins in it, and one by one we're pulling them out. Each time one comes out, our breath sinks a bit deeper into our belly, into our being, and a bit more freedom opens up inside us, a bit more inner space.

I really want to give us the experience in this Gene Key of what exactly is going on inside us as we're awakening right now. It's especially acute in our relationships. They've become harder. I wonder if you've noticed that? They aren't really harder; we're just more aware of the wound patterns. The more we let them go, the more subtle ones take their place. I know it sometimes seems like an endless process and it requires a really deep sense of forgiveness, of self-forgiveness. The Programming Partner of the 49 is the 4th Gene Key, and this is the Siddhi of Forgiveness. It's one of the agents of Grace, the 22nd Gene Key, a really important one to read. In our relationships whenever we do or say something that causes hurt, our awareness shows us that we've actually hurt ourselves. It's so important to give ourself the gift of forgiveness, and really let it in. Yes, we were cruel, reactive, insensitive, but we're human. We can learn from it. The more aware we become, the more we'll have to forgive ourself.

The 49th is a new cutting-through awareness and it's ruthless. In Human Design, it's known as the gate of the butcher, and that's what it's like. It becomes more and more accurate with its cuts. It's a really, really good thing; it's revolutionising humanity. It's creating a new inner environment for something extraordinary to occur. If we have the 49th Gift or are contemplating it, its Gift is to show others what they don't need and help them to see what they do need. It's a Gift that could turn a person's life around or make an ailing business suddenly successful. As we give ourself over to this mutation, we'll become much leaner. Our body will become strong, translucent even. We'll become immune to society's many tricks. Modern society in the West is so chock full of distractions and marketing, and most of it is utterly inessential. The 49th Gift is saving us time, money, and making our lives so much simpler and more beautiful, and then we're in a position to really enjoy life. We aren't a victim of our needs so we can choose to eat that cake if we like. It's no longer an unconscious need, but an impulse, a conscious choice. We know we don't need it, but we have it anyway, because it's the right moment and the right kind of cake, and it's fun to share those things with each other. It's what life is all about - to live well.

This is the revolution. To live a pure life and live it well. It begins in the individual, passes into our relationships, and then into our family and society. Each time one person begins to awaken they start to stand out from the crowd. They become a creative rebel, and their transformation is electric and infectious. Some recoil, but others want to know how they can get a taste of that dish. They ask us, we tell them, and then they get on board with us. This is a magical happening at a magical time in history. If we're one of the awakening, and we are, then we won't be alone. We're a whirlwind, and we'll be used as a force to bring others into the same storm, the storm of our future rebirth.

The 49th Siddhi - Rebirth

The 49th Siddhi is revolutionary. How could it be anything else, moving from reaction to revolution to Rebirth? We have all heard many descriptions of the awakened state. The masters will mostly tell us that individual awakening is a process that leaves us utterly reborn. They call it the second birth. It's nothing less than a complete erasing of the genetic imprinting of our birth. It's a reset of our primary purpose, or a reboot of our DNA back to its factory settings before we were born. It's a transcendence of the actual genetic imprinting itself. This wonderful last paradox has always delighted me, that human DNA is actually designed to be self-transcendent. It's the means by which God comes to know itself, so it can't be fixed. It must mutate.

The Ring of the Whirlwind, with the 55th and 49th Gene Keys and its related amino acid histidine, is the place where the mutation first begins. Mutation requires great heat and the greater the heat, the faster and more dramatic the mutation. We can see this literally and metaphorically. The metaphorical heat is the voltage of unconditional love that purifies the structure of DNA so that it must adapt to the new frequencies. It will become a triple helix rather than a double. Since I'm not a geneticist I have no idea how this will work, but it must be so, because all life is a trinity. DNA will use elements of itself already in existence rather than invent something new. It will rebuild itself like the phoenix from the brightening ashes of the old structure.

DNA literally needs heat in order to mutate. The whole planet needs heat in order for this mutation to take hold across the entire gene pool of humanity, and indeed across multiple species. As humanity sits at the crest of the visible hierarchies on our planet, so our Great Change will ripple out to affect changes in all other life forms, so bound together are we all. We are in no way separate but intimately linked and fused together as a single consciousness. We can expect some dramatic changes coming, most probably from the sun. The sun is essentially our father and we're also intimately linked to its higher life. When the sun mutates, so does the earth and all her children.

Little has been spoken by the masters about collective awakening. What is collective awakening and what do we mean by that? How will humanity be reborn? This is the question that involves the 49th Siddhi. The 55th Siddhi is about individual awakening, but the 49th is about the collective version that arises as a chain reaction coming out of the former. In a relatively short span of time, we humanity, and we Gaia, are going to look and feel utterly different. Like the dragonfly or the butterfly, we're going to go through a series of moults that culminate in a complete rebirth. What comes after has very little in common with what went before.

Look at the difference between the butterfly and the caterpillar! We'll exist in a higher element, with a different DNA structure, a collective awareness that will spread like wildfire through our organism. This is the mythical 6th Race, the Trivian human. Trivian refers to the integration of the holographic truth of the trinity throughout creation, of the three paths lead into the one. That's what Trivian means, and this next Age will be about the embodiment of that. It's a process of coming into synarchy. It begins at the core and then it spreads like a Divine cancer. There will be cells that resist it, reject it, fight it to the last breath, but they can't prevent the whirlwind. Those that can't mutate will be hurled out of the whirlwind for another evolution at another time.

Old genetic material is leaving this sphere, even as we listen to or read these words. When the whirlwind has passed, Gaia will be reborn anew. That which wasn't prepared to change will be absorbed back into the sun to continue its evolution from a new kind of beginning. This is Divine Justice. It's the great compassion of life that everyone begins again with a clean slate. It's just those cells that refuse the mutation into the collective that will miss out on the party. They'll also have their day one day in a future now. It's not personal; it's just about universal principles. The 49th Siddhi sorts the human genetic material into fertile and currently infertile, into ripe and unripe. It's really as simple as that.

We're going to see people who cling to the old ways and systems. We'll see those who change so rapidly that the old ones are not able to understand or keep up. It's a fractal detonation throughout the gene pool. There are also those who exist at the edges of the fractal, the cusp-dwellers. These are places where they may either fall inwards, safely drawn in by the centripetal force of love at the core, or fall away to be carried off by the centrifugal force for another day. We'll always recognise these people - they will half-embrace the change, but won't quite be able to change enough themselves. We must always keep the door open for them, as we can't tell which way they'll go. They may just make it through before the door shuts. Part of the compassion of the core fractal is to hold the door open until the last moment because we never know what miracles may occur inside people. If it becomes apparent that they aren't coming into the collective, we need not feel sad. Their time will be coming at another time, and we may bow to them in respect as they leave.

Sometimes I hear people getting nervous around this kind of talk. We hear people say, 'well I'm not a group person' or 'we are not all one'. To say such things is to just misunderstand. We don't lose our individuality in the union, in fact, we become more differentiated than ever. It's only in union that true differentiation can thrive. The two belong together, but our awareness is the union, not the form. The form remains different, unique, varied, beautiful, but we won't be able to hide. No personal thoughts, no personal feelings. Just the pulse of the collective ever purifying us, elevating us, saturating us in waves of blissful wonder.

You can't be a loner anymore. The new loners will be the lovers. The sacred couples will become the fundamental unit of the Trivian human. Two people in love are never two anymore, but three in one. The third is the awareness, the intelligence of the love itself, and it paradoxically melds the three into one. No human is an island and no one can be cut off from the whole. Families will be completely new, and there won't be nuclear families like before. The nuclear family is a fusion laboratory and the new family will become the unit of the collective. It will transcend its genetic ties, so there's no obsession, no sibling conflict, no repeating wound patterns. There's only the flow of love through the unit and its magnification. The family of the future will be the whole community, the fellowship. It will be a welcoming friendliness that pervades all awakening humans. Everywhere we go, we'll find this spirit. If we're working deeply with the Gene Keys for example, we'll discover this rare fellowship wherever we go and meet others working with the Keys in their lives. The love is a deep recognition, a cellular recognition. Yes we're coming into such a time and very few are really aware of how vast it's going to be. The Rebirth at the core of our DNA will of course ripple out into the outer world. I've spoken about this future in the 55th Gene Key and the potential changes to our way of life and being.

The future human, the Trivian human, will look to us like an awakened genius and there will be thousands and thousands of us. Such a fellowship will change structures all across the planet, replanting our world with new systems that are hyper-efficient, that save energy, money, time and needless suffering. The new human is a recycling centre on every level. We recycle emotion, suffering and toxin, and the earth has a lot of toxin. We've created a huge amount of toxic material that won't naturally biodegrade. We're going to find new ways to return these materials back to their natural states. In this sense we'll become reverse alchemists, so that we can clean up the mess we've made of Gaia.

I know this Siddhi is a long one, but I want to really do it justice. It doesn't look as though we can save the world from the direction we're going in now, I know that. As Hamlet said "I know not 'seems'", and nothing is going to go the way it seems. This awakening is coming, it's right around the corner and it's begun. It really took root in 2012, and it'll break forth its very first shoots between 2012 and 2027. After 2027, the Trivian humans will begin to spread all across the globe. It's an inner takeover, a loving takeover. You needn't believe me; time will tell whether my words are true. If we're close to this Siddhi, we'll feel what's coming as well. We can let our spirit rise up to greet this new future. We must let it swell our heart and renew our effort and devotion to our highest purpose.

The Trivian human has a new matrix. It goes from seven centres to nine to three. It's a mystery, and the nine is the transitionary vehicle. It's really a three within a three, and we see that in Human Design. That matrix only serves until awakening occurs, after which it's defunct. The new matrix is only three centres, because of higher voltage and greater efficiency. I'm talking about the birth of the Siddhic human being. It's so fantastic that most people can only assume I'm speaking utter dreamspeak. These movies that the younger generation are all captivated by, they depict humans with magical powers. Why do you think that's pouring into the younger generations?

Siddhis are not all about special powers, but some are. Most Siddhis are simply aspects of deep compassion and clarity, but they still create huge changes in the environment. If we even go to a place where a great master once lived, we can feel a palpable presence permeating the rocks and landscape. If it's there when they're gone, imagine how powerful it is when they're present and in numbers. The atomic structure of the planet will begin to change in response. The hidden hierarchies within the earth, the Devic realms, who've been long asleep, will reawaken and revivify the earth, the elements, the water, and the air.

We simply can't comprehend the vastness of the change that's coming. It comes in us through our hearts, through love. There's nothing but compassion in this universe. It's the breath of God, the fragrance imprinted in every cell by the stars. If we've felt it even once, we can never forget it. I hope we can feel its frequency through these words. There's Truth here. There's Truth being spoken by this voice, and I offer it to any who're listening or reading. Sometimes we just have to come out and speak the great secret. That's what this 49th Siddhi is for. So bless you for listening, and bless all those who can hear the secret and know it themselves. And bless all those who haven't yet heard it but will one day know it. And bless all those who won't hear the secret or know it this time around. Their time too will come. Thank you, thank you and blessings to us all.

THE 64 WAYS

THE 50TH WAY

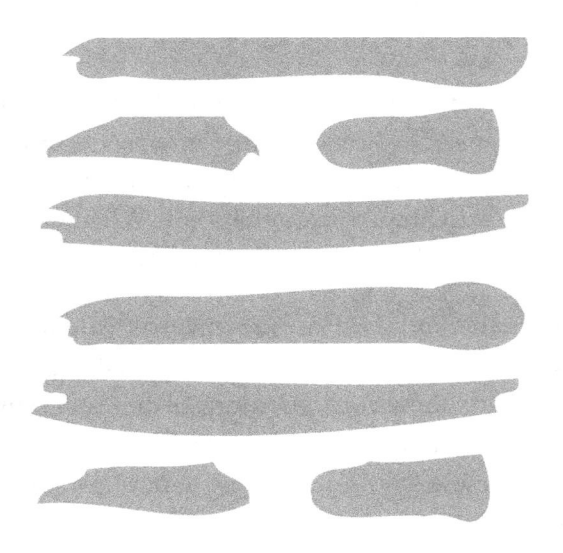

Gene Key 50

THE WAY OF EQUILIBRIUM

The Transformational Way of the 50th Gene Key moves from Corruption to Harmony, and it's the Way of Equilibrium.

The 50th Gene Key has many, many dimensions including being one of the eight musical Gene Keys; that is, musical in the sense of governing an entire realm or dimension of frequency. The others are the 12, 22, 59, 6, 27, 57 and 20. Those of us who know our Human Design will recognise a pattern there, a Divine Circuit for another time. When we explore the transmission known as the Delta Fellowship we'll learn more about these.

The 50th Gene Key is rooted in the Siddhi of Harmony and has to do with the patterns of celestial harmony woven into all forms and realms. It's a potential portal to the Siddhi level, as we'll see. Here in the Shadow frequencies it's about corruption, one of those collective words. When people first see their Profile and have the 50th Gene Key they see this word and are often aghast; 'But I'm not corrupt!', we say. It's one of these words we're going to have to penetrate a bit deeper. In the Gene Keys book when we read about this Shadow, it speaks of the idea of corrupt data, similar to the notion of a computer with a corrupted hard drive. The inner meaning of corruption here is that our hard drive is corrupted. We incarnated with a virus built into the hardware, and from the moment we started growing in the womb the virus began its work.

It's wound around our DNA and it's our karmic legacy. We all come here with karma, with ancestral baggage, genetic patterns that corrupt the true pattern of our nature. Our whole purpose in life is to root out these corrupted programs and reboot the primary hard drive. That's the journey of awakening.

The Gene Keys also have very carefully chosen words. If we have corruption in our Profile,

Shadow: Corruption **Gift:** Equilibrium **Programming Partner:** Gene Key 3
Dilemma: Resignation **Siddhi:** Harmony **Codon Ring:** The Ring of The Illuminati

---

or if this Gene Key comes strongly into our contemplation, then karmically we may well face corruption. We may draw it into our aura. We may have grown up with it in our environment or just be deeply disturbed by it in the world. The Dilemma of this Shadow is Resignation. This is a deep story and if we dig a little deeper, we'll find its roots. We can look at the outer world, at governments, power structures, culture, society, nutritional habits, moral values and we can see that the Shadow of Corruption is like a cosmic weed that's everywhere. It manifests on the outside because it's wound around us on the inside, which means that we can never stamp it out on the outside unless we pull out the root on the inside. That's what it will take to get us to Harmony.

The Dilemma is Resignation because we don't believe we can do anything about it externally, and most of us have quit. We hear ourselves saying, 'no one else fights, so why should I and how can I do anything anyway?'. That Shadow attitude is so self-perpetuating and it can seem equally discouraging on the inside. We can hear ourselves say, 'well we've really tried, we've followed teachings, teachers, meditated and prayed and none of it has worked, not really. We may have had an experience or two but the weed is still there and we're still deeply corrupted.

The Christian idea of sin is actually quite revealing here. We have this original sin and this is the corruption. It's not our personal fault in the way that most Christians make it sound, but we still have it. Most of us are simply resigned to the fact. The world is full of sin, I'm full of sin and that's just how it is.

GENE KEY 50

The 50th Gene Key is a pivotal Gene Key and this is one of its special qualities. In the Wheel of life it actually is a pivot, a breakthrough point. That's why it's the Gift of Equilibrium and it's why its Programming Partner is the Shadow of Chaos. Chaos and corruption. That's what the ancients called the Wheel of Samsara. But there are ways out. The mystics have indicated that there are ways out, but it takes a lot of work. We can't give up, we can't be resigned, even though the Shadow of Chaos wants us to give up and Corruption relies on our giving up. It knows the odds are stacked against us, but there's a tipping point inside each of us. You have to ask yourself how much you really want this? It's just like in these movies where the hero is surrounded by corrupt officials and injustice, and he or she decides to take a stand. There's a huge battle as the weak takes on the strong and finally overcomes impossible odds to win victory in the finale.

That's the 50th Gene Key - the battle against impossible odds. We have to take a stand and overcome the weight of our karma. We have to reach that tipping point and we need courage and real perseverance. The good news is that the odds aren't impossible, even though the Shadow would like us to resign and give up. But as soon as you take a stand to find out what awakening is, a great force comes alive in you. It will wax and wane in the beginning, but over time it will stabilise inside you and things will become easier. It takes self-discipline, but that will come naturally and start flowing from your core. Our longing calls this power for good out, and that's how we tackle corruption. Slow and steady.

We have such a tendency to react to the Shadow, we have an uncomfortable day and then we get all tight inside trying too hard to pull out the weed, which makes us even more tense. This 50th Gene Key is a real help in offering advice on how to approach uncomfortable Shadow states. It's musical remember? We just have to tune those strings better. It's like when a child starts to learn the violin, making this terrible rasping sound. It's agony to have to listen to, but then over time, little tunes start to appear, little riffs that are perfected and integrated. It's all a learning process. Our subtle bodies are like that. We have a lot of habits that undermine us, that create corruption in our aura, and we have to work away at them. We have to identify them one by one and disable them, replacing them with new habits, harmonic patterns. It takes time and patience; it's a learning process.

That's how we tackle the Shadow of Corruption. We have to keep our spirit buoyant and learn the knack of cheerfulness, finding things that keep us moving in the right direction. If we give in to the negative forces of the Shadow we'll quickly return to the place of deep suffering. Life constantly sends us signals and gifts if we pay attention.

The 50th Gift - Equilibrium

When facing the shadow, one of the greatest gifts this teaching will give us is the art of contemplation. Contemplation is the art of maintaining perfect equilibrium.

It's funny how the Gene Keys integrate these two ancient Paths - the Path of Christ - the Path of Love, and the Path of the Buddha - the Path of Wisdom. I've talked about this before, the balancing of concentration and meditation. The Path of Love requires concentrated energy, and we pour all our love, longing, and prayer into it. Everything we do is an effort to reach the higher consciousness. The other way is the Path of Wisdom, which is to simply observe all patterns that come up. We exert no effort whatsoever; we just watch and accept everything as transient, ephemeral and unreliable. Over time, both paths can lead to the goal, to Truth.

The Way of Contemplation is the path of equilibrium. It's about threading the passage between these two Ways. If we go too far in one direction, we tense up or give up, which keeps bringing us back to the centre point. It's such a powerful thing. It does take some time to master this and we'll probably keep forgetting and take the extreme. But because the extreme hurts, it'll keep bringing us back to the point of balance. This 50th Gift therefore has a lot of power and can be hugely creative. It uses the corrupt energy to create balance. If we have this Gift, then this is our energy, our Genius - to go into an environment that's dysfunctional, where the music is awful - a cacophony - and use our inner power to reunite the elements and recombine them so that harmony is once again possible. We can apply this metaphor to any social sphere from business to the arts.

As we discover the inner Gifts that equilibrium brings us personally, we become an agent of equilibrium in the world. We can also see this in nature. When natural systems move out of balance, they right themselves. Humanity can only do that when we've found the internal equilibrium, so that whatever we do on the outside reflects what we embody on the inside. With this 50th Gene Key, we'll be called upon to tackle corruption at one level or another, and that could be anything. We'll just find ourself doing it. Whatever job we have, this Gift can be applied in that job now, as soon as we discover it on the inside.

In the Wheel of Life there are many patterns and sequences. One of them begins with the 3rd Gene Key in the Wheel, and if you follow it all the way around, you will see that it ends with the 42nd Gene Key. That's the evolutionary sequence that governs all cellular life on our planet. If we look at that in the Wheel, we'll see that the 50th Gene Key is in the exact centre. It's the tipping point, the fulcrum, and it's actually the 50th Gene Key in the first line, giving this Gene Key a unique power. It holds all life in the balance. When we begin that process of awakening, our spirit recalibrates itself in stages, incarnations and initiations. The greatest of these is the one when we come into inner equilibrium. We learn to trust in the Truth inside us. We balance the paths of love and wisdom, and begin to travel the central path - the path of Truth.

We are all on the Path of Truth, and it's the new path of the new human because it unites left and right. It avoids the extremes; we can't all be renunciates anymore. This path is for modern life, for a viable way of modern living. Buddha said 'don't pull the string too tight or it will snap. Neither let it sag too loose or it will lose power'. Christ said: 'unless ye come to me as little children, ye shall not enter the kingdom of heaven'. They were both saying the same thing - don't be too extreme, be playful and disciplined, be open and soft. Be balanced. Let the music of life dance through you. Let life live itself beautifully through your life. Cultivate awe, cultivate peacefulness and cultivate Truth.

The 50th Siddhi - Harmony

We move from Corruption to Equilibrium to Harmony. Equilibrium is the flowering and Harmony is the fruit. When the process of flowering into equilibrium has become so deeply ingrained in our nature, then at the perfect time, when we're ready, the fruit drops to the ground and we find ourselves inhabiting a permanent state of inner harmony.

The Gift of Equilibrium isn't just a balancing act of left and right. It's not just a tightrope walk. It's about constant readjustment to the rhythms and events that our dharma, our destiny brings us. Life tests us over and over to maintain our inner equilibrium. We have to keep on innovating, meeting each challenge with creative adaptation, as in the 3rd Gift of Innovation, its Programming Partner. At the Shadow state we spend most of our time out of balance, hurled by the currents of pleasure and pain from one side of chaos to the other. We're caught in the net of the Maya, but as our inner life opens more we begin to realise that equilibrium lies within. It takes a lot of work to maintain it because there are so many things to be balanced - inner life and outer responsibility, social and financial commitments, relational challenges, daily decisions about our diet, health, and wellbeing.

It's interesting that our sense of balance is connected to the ear, the inner ear. In the ear there's a pool of fluid and in that cavity float crystals that relay chemical information to the brain and nervous system. That's how we stay physically balanced. It's like a liquid crystal compass. At at a higher level that's also what our DNA is. The liquid in every cell of our bodies is constantly attuning to the frequency field we're aligning with. If we align with the Shadow of Chaos that the human world puts out, then that's what our body feels like. We're like one of those early planets that's constantly being hit by meteorites every few seconds, and there's no hope of relaxation at that level.

As we align ourselves with higher frequencies and learn to balance our emotions, use our mind creatively and our physical body wisely, so our DNA attunes us to a deeper harmony that lies behind the world that our senses can see. The inner world, the spiritual world lies beyond the five senses. To pick up its frequencies we have to develop what the Buddhists call equanimity, such a wonderful word. It means two things - to see from a higher view and to rest in the middle. That's the challenge of the Gift and Contemplation constantly brings us back to the higher view. That view allows us to stay in the centre and become more anchored in our Core Stability, no matter what life throws at us.

Life initiates us and tests our equanimity constantly. It is in fact very compassionate and generous in this way, if we can view life from that level. Everything that happens to us is for our higher benefit. We're here to learn to live with equanimity.

Even shock has the capacity to lift us with Grace to another level of consciousness. As our equanimity, our equilibrium becomes truly stable, we become unshakeable. We become truly peaceful and our life opens up to a higher reality, a harmony that lies hidden from view but is communicated continuously to us from every cell within our DNA. As this harmony expands inside us, we begin to function through our higher bodies. Most of us only know our lower vehicles of the physical, emotional, and mental bodies. We think that's all we are, but our higher trinity - the causal, buddhic and atmic bodies are our hidden instrumentation. It's through them that we pick up the higher harmony. They are like our spiritual antennae in that way.

As we attune to the higher harmony, so all our subtle bodies come into harmony. The inner light that they emit is communicated through resonance through our lower vehicles, and we experience transformation. As I said, we're musical beings. We're built like an octave, and all those notes need to be plucked in the right way through our opening up to love. Then the emotional system is transcended, the mind falls silent, the physical body becomes radiant and we enter the state of self illumination.

One final insight is from the Codon Ring. This Gene Key is bonded musically to the 44th Gene Key through the Codon Ring of the Illuminati. At the level of chaos and corruption, we find ourselves among a very different Illuminati and we're a victim of that lower world. At the Gift level, our allies become fellow seekers, carefully treading the narrow path to Truth, sometimes falling off, then resuming, then falling, then resuming, but always learning, growing, and expanding. The 44th Gift is Teamwork, so we have to learn from each other, in our relationships, families, and communities. The teamwork is also in our cells. Our cells have to learn to work together as a team; we're their captain and we have to guide them to work at higher levels of frequency.

The finale is our awakening. As we awaken to the higher harmony, we become aware of the eternal hierarchy of higher consciousness. The universe is peopled by entities from the lowest, densest frequencies to the most rarified beings of light. We enter a vast inner world where for the first time we become aware of the principle of synarchy, the 44th Siddhi. Synarchy is the awareness that all consciousness follows a higher order. There is a centre of centres, and it's everywhere and in all things. Everything is knitted together in this grand harmony. All beings are caught up in the great drama and the higher we go, the more unified the field becomes, until finally we disappear into the whole. That's synarchy.

The 50th Siddhi brings awareness to our role within the hologram of the cosmos. Every planet, star, creature, and blade of grass has a corresponding place within us. The entire cosmos is reflected in us. As above, so below. We become the ocean in the drop. We become everything and nothing. We become God.

The 51st Way

Gene Key 51

THE WAY OF INITIATIVE

The Transformational Way of the 51st Gene Key moves from Agitation to Awakening, and it's the Way of Initiative.

I've been circling around this Gene Key for ages now, and it's a strange one. It's almost as though it's dormant a lot of the time, at least its potential. Agitation, which is the Shadow, is ever-present. Until we begin to look within we never realise the depth of our agitation. It's like when people first begin to meditate; it's such a shock. It's not like we close our eyes and find it easy, peaceful and calm inside. Usually we suddenly realise the terrible truth about how screwed up we are and how crazed our mind is, leaping from one thing to the next, never giving us a break. If we're brave enough to stay with the process and explore deeper, we'll find the same frequency extends into our emotional system. After some time, we'll hit these inner walls of anxiety and fear. We don't even know what they are; they seem to be so primal in origin.

Sometimes when I go within, I hit one of these walls. It's like a wall of frequency that towers over us like a wave. We can sit and sit with it, and it's just there, immobile inside us. Our agitation runs deep, and it's a tangled web. It takes some courage to plumb the depths of our discomfort. This is where the Gene Keys really begin. The 51st Gene Key is part of the Codon Ring of Humanity, and this inner darkness is a part of our humanity that we have to explore.

When we say that every Shadow contains a Gift, it may sound simple, but the reality is that the process of getting the diamond out of that coal face is pretty intense. Not everyone is ready for it. This Gene Key and its Shadow really give us some good tips about how to deal with the Shadow and its discomfort inside.

Shadow: Agitation   **Gift**: Initiative   **Programming Partner**: Gene Key 57
Dilemma: Harshness   **Siddhi**: Awakening   **Codon Ring**: The Ring of Humanity

---

One of the keys to help us understand this Gene Key lies in the Dilemma of this Shadow, - the Dilemma of Harshness. When we face discomfort, this tends to be our immediate pattern - to meet it with harshness. At the Shadow level, we do one of two things - we either turn and run, distracting ourselves and diving back into our denial in some way, thus repressing the pattern. Or we try and correct and fix the pattern. We tense up and start trying to resolve it. Maybe we go to therapy, try yoga, meditate even harder! It's a natural human tendency to want to be free of something uncomfortable and try and shrug it off. It's like that lovely fable by Aesop about the competition between the north wind and the Sun. They decide to see who's stronger by getting a man to take off his coat. The north wind blows and blows, but he just pulls the coat tighter and tighter around himself. The Sun says, 'ok, now it's my turn', comes out from behind a cloud, and the man gets hot and takes off his coat.

We're like this, because we tend to take the harsh approach. However, this Gene Key will teach us how to turn these Shadows to our advantage instead of being their victim. There are two ways through this Dilemma - we wait it out, sit and watch the pattern, like vipassana meditation, and observe ourself observing it. We watch our mind struggling and struggling until eventually our mind gives up, the Sun comes out, and we're through. The Buddha taught that approach.

The other approach, and it's the core of this process with the 51st Gene Key, is to use creativity. We use the energy and direct it outwardly in a creative direction. We'll see what that looks like when we get to the 51st Gift, but for now we just need to come to deep clarity around the nature of this Shadow.

Let's look at this Shadow in relationships. Relationships also play out the agitation. Two wounded human beings come together and fall in love. Let's say they get married. Once the honeymoon period is over, the chemistry of the underlying agitation will come to the surface. Because of its deep-rootedness it will always surface, and now we have two states of agitation interacting. What it takes to ride this wave and stay together through the process! If we haven't some experience with meeting this state inside ourself, we don't really stand much chance when it arises, because we just project it onto the other person. We blame them, they blame us, and we know the mess that causes.

It's all because we most often resort to harshness. We snap at each other and then blame ourselves. We feel bad because we've been harsh, and then we propagate the harshness inside ourselves and the relationship. Most people never really stood a chance in the first place. Incarnation on this planet is quite a trip. We're not taught these basics.

I'd like to take a pause from this idea now and introduce another idea. The 51st Gene Key is very powerful and is represented in the I Ching by sudden flashes of thunder and lightning. It can be deeply disturbing but it also bring huge possibilities with it. The idea I want to offer is that agitation is not only inside us, it's also outside. It comes from the frequencies - the cosmic and celestial frequency field. Our solar system moves through space. It's on the move, and as it does so it moves through fields of cosmic frequencies. It actually describes a vast spiral arc through the galaxy. Everything in life spirals and the solar system moves out of one field of energy into another. The stars and Sun do this too, everything does. The I Ching and Astrology are based upon this ebb and flow of celestial patterns. Our planet is moving into a new field right now, a shift described through the precession of the equinoxes. The whole solar system is caught up in this change, and new energies and currents are available now that can take us out of the state of agitation.

I'd like us to know that there's great hope coming to our species. I don't say this to make us dream of a new world or to take our awareness away from our discomfort, but as a counterforce to the Shadow. Behind our agitation lies a huge energy of great potential and light. It's as though our entire solar system has been moving through a long period of galactic eclipse. As we move out of eclipse, for the first time in millennia the light of the galactic core is coming back into view. The light from that core is already starting to stream back into our consciousness, and it's driving a new inner revolution. We can see this as a metaphor, but it's also true. It's what is happening externally and internally right now.

Externally, this will take hundreds, even thousands of years as the eclipse reveals the true light behind the new form. Internally it can be instantaneous, depending on how we approach the Shadow. We must watch ourself carefully and beware of our tendency towards harshness. At times of intense change the quality most needed is gentleness. We'll see this through the Gift in a moment, but the Gift is something we also have to claim. It doesn't just happen to us, we have to move towards the light as well as it coming down into us.

The 51st Gift - Initiative

Sometimes to really understand a Gene Key we have to look first of all at its Siddhi. If we can see where the energy is all heading, then that can be a point of illumination. That's what these Transformational Ways are all about. It's why I introduce each one as the Way from the Shadow to the Siddhi - from Agitation to Awakening, in this case. How do we make that huge transition when agitation and awakening seem such a long way from each other? We're talking about a Gene Key whose primary word for the Siddhi is Awakening, so it'll be able to tell us a great deal about what awakening really is.

Awakening is like an hourglass. At one end we have the Shadow, at the other end, the Siddhi and in the middle we have the narrow neck of the Gift. From the perspective of the Shadow we appear locked into the glass, trapped by the endless cycles of our agitation. But when we look at everything from the perspective of the Siddhi, time itself dissolves. We experience the boundless dimension, so there's no end to that end of the hourglass. It isn't really an end at all; the sand just goes on forever and ever, it's infinite. What's interesting here is that the two places where the Way to Awakening is the same for everyone is at the Shadow and the Siddhi. It's only unique in the middle, at the Gift.

I'm obviously speaking metaphorically, using an image for our mind to play with. When we experience the Shadow of Agitation, no matter who we are, it's the same - uncomfortable and persistent; it's human suffering. It's universal and we're all born into it. From the other end of awakening, it's also the same - freedom. When one person experiences that freedom, it's the exact same freedom as another person's freedom. No matter how they got there, no matter what expression it takes, no matter what Siddhi it's refracted through, or what language (or not) they chose to frame the Awakening with, it's the same experience, it's identical. Isn't that a nice symmetry? The Shadow and the Siddhi are the same for us all.

What about the Gift? The Gift is the way, the path. It's the neck of the hourglass. It's a narrow path, our path through our suffering. It's utterly unique and it's our path because it's virgin, untrodden. It heads out into the wilderness of the inner planes. Guides can sometimes be a distraction, and it's tricky to walk our own path because there are so many unconscious influences. That's why this Gift is called the Gift of Initiative. Every Gift has this same urge to break new ground. Every Gift is inherently creative and original, so how can we follow another? What about the words of the Buddha for example, or any other great teacher, the great indicators of Truth? Can't we follow them? Can we trust the paths of others? Well, yes and no. They can be an inspiration and provide impetus. They can encourage and enthuse us, but can they lead us? I would say no. No external teacher can indicate the way for us. That's what the Gift of Initiative is about. It's about having the courage to trust in the direction of our own feet and it's about how we deepen that trust.

What about teachings like the Gene Keys, do they offer us a path? They don't really. They lay out the whole matrix, but they don't say, 'well you have the 51st Gene Key as your Life's Work, so you have to do this meditation or take that path.' They simply offer us a mirror. That's what the master is. He or she is a mirror of Truth, but they can't direct us. They can only encourage us to find our own way.

The 51st Gift is a great invitation to each of us, and it's Programming Partner is the 57th Gift of Intuition. Only our intuition can show us the way forward, and intuition requires subtlety and softness. We can't fall victim to the harshness. We have to have courage and practise following our intuition. There will be many mistakes when we don't.

The mind wants the security of a defined path. It wants a fixed teaching and technique. The Gene Keys don't really give us that - no trainings, no teachers, not even me, I'm just a fellow traveller. Even contemplation is hard to define; the Tao can't be defined. There are indicators though, and gentleness is a great indicator.

We can each take heart from this Gene Key; it supports the unknown. Our correct path in life can't be copied, and we aren't going to get the answers out of any Profile. Taking the initiative means we find our own interpretation; we find our own creative way through the minefield of the Shadow. We must go into the agitation and get to know it. We need to create a softness around it, a spaciousness, and trust in the discomfort. We need to learn to yield to the energy. It's like in martial arts, Tai Chi for example, when our opponent comes at us, we energetically lean into their thrust rather than opposing it. It's counterintuitive. Only when we go towards the obstacle can we find its correct relationship to us. We can redirect it in a spontaneous creative way, and the other guy flies across the room. We don't really know how it happened, and if it happened again, it would never happen in the same way, even though he'd still go flying across the room!

What the 51st Gift does is asks us to approach difficulties with creativity. Instead of giving in to harshness and propagating the agitation further, we create our way out of the situation. I want to urge us to just try this in our lives. Go inside yourself, locate a problem in your life, and find a source of agitation. It won't take long; we all have them! Instead of worrying about it, lean into it with softness. Trust it. Feel the energy of it. Let it flood your DNA and listen to it. We can then allow our intuition to penetrate the problem. We can be creative and allow possible solutions to emerge. One of the things we'll notice is that it's usually the way we've been thinking about it that's the problem. Now we can find a new way of thinking about it, letting our intuition guide us. We can soften into it and let it glide past us. What does your life feel like without this problem?

It's a process. The Gift is all about transformation, the transformational field. It's alive. It's wonderful. It's alchemy. It's also a knack. We have to take the initiative.

The definition of being a victim is someone who doesn't take the initiative. As long as we take the initiative, the energy moves. It has to. The external may not change so much, that may take a bit longer, but the internal completely changes. That's how we deal with the Shadow. This 51st Gift is the key to Awakening. It's a knack. It's the root of genius. That's what initiative is - it's genius. Creative thinking, creative acting, creativity at every level. No use looking outside for an answer. Look inside. The depth of beauty and originality we'll find is infinite and astonishing.

Finally, the word initiative happens to be the same word for one of the Pathways in the Golden Path, the Pathway that leads out of the Core Wound towards the Sphere of Culture in the Pearl Sequence. It's about Vocation, which is about taking creative initiative. In business, initiative is essential for ongoing material success. At a higher frequency, it's also essential for awakening. As we start to transform our wound into creative opportunities, we change the way the world spins around us. We change the pattern of our destiny. We no longer trap ourself in a narrow set of parameters or remain stuck in the narrow neck of the past or the future. We imbibe the living energy of the present, the wonder of the ever-changing present. The Siddhi feeds us with its boundlessness.

This 51st Gift is an essential one, and it's so important to take some time and lean into our problems, issues, worries, agitations, and create our way out of them, breathe life into them and learn to love them. The better we get at this, the more we'll relish opportunities for transformation. We'll come to an obstacle in our path and smile. We'll listen to it, appreciate it, and when ready, give ourself to it and unlock its incredible gift. Every Shadow contains a Gift; we just have to unlock it. It's that simple.

THE 51ST SIDDHI - AWAKENING

Every Gift in the spectrum of consciousness is a Gift of Initiative, of Creativity. They all lead us out of or through the Shadow. They take the energy of the Shadow and make it work for us. I like this word 'initiative', because it hides another word inside itself, 'initiation'. The 51st Siddhi and in fact every Siddhi is about the secrets of initiation.

The definition of initiation is in the Glossary of Empowerment at the back of the Gene Keys book:

At certain points in our journey we move through 'initiations' — periods of intensity in which we undergo huge transmutations. True Initiation is not something that can be predicted or ritualised. It is a natural part of life itself as it evolves. Neither does it require any learning or religious or spiritual affiliation. True Initiation is a rare process that one always undergoes alone. The great Initiations are upsurges in the frequency of our subtle bodies, and when we pass through them, they are often dramatic and challenging to integrate into our lives.

This is what Awakening really is, and there are layers and levels to it. When we read this Siddhi in the book, it actually says the opposite. It says there are no levels; there is only awake and asleep, and no middle ground. That's true, but there's also another Truth, and it doesn't contradict that. I'll try and explain.

If we read the 22nd Gene Key, we'll learn about the nine Portals of Initiation, major shifts in consciousness that we undergo periodically in the narrative of our evolutionary journey. From the evolutionary human perspective we could say that the whole process comes to an end at the Sixth Initiation, which is called The Communion. This is what most masters are referring to as awakening or enlightenment, when the separate self dissolves and life sees itself as everything or as emptiness. That's awakening, and before that realisation has occurred we're missing a vital aspect of Truth. Because after this initiation we can never be the same again. All the Initiations prior to this Sixth Initiation are preparations that lead us to this vast experience.

There are awakenings before and after that, so it's not quite true to say that this is the only awakening. I'd like to open up another understanding, which is far more important than understanding what awakening is or which one we've had and where we are in all of this. None of that really matters; it's all just semantics. It can be useful for the mind to grasp so that we can relax a bit more deeply into the process, but the most important thing is to develop the qualities needed to integrate these awakenings.

No one knows when an awakening or initiation will sweep through our being. It's always a shock, and this 51st Gene Key is a thunderbolt. In the Tibetan tradition, initiation is symbolised in the symbol of the vajra, a kind of sceptre that the initiate holds in his or her hand which represents permanent and indestructible change. What is the quality most needed in order for us to move through one of these portals - love, truth, or wisdom? I would say yes to all of these, but even more I would say gentleness and softness.

We find this insight in the Programming Partner of the 57th Gene Key. The 51 is the shock of thunder, while the 57 is the softness of the flowing wind. To meet thunder we need to be soft. We need to be pliant and yielding.

Awakening is really a series of softenings. Our awareness becomes more one-pointed, but our heart and mind becomes softer and more open. Whenever we're confronted with harshness, the unexpected, noise, turbulence, and the thunder of life, instead of tensing up, we need to relax and open, soften and become milder. Mildness is the essential quality needed to allow spiritual initiation. In fact, as we become more yielding, so our consciousness expands to encompass wider and wider vistas and possibilities. It's a beautiful paradox, as every Siddhi is. We need never be afraid of initiation or awakening. We have only to let it in, and that requires we cultivate this inner quality of spaciousness, softness, and trust. Then, and only then, the miracle can occur.

THE 64 WAYS

The 52nd Way

Gene Key 52

THE WAY OF RESTRAINT

The Transformational Way of the 52nd Gene Key moves from Stress to Stillness, and it's the Way of Restraint.

This is the Dilemma of Shallow Breathing, and stress is a manifestation of shallow breathing. We can see through this 52nd Gene Key how deeply these Shadows are collective terms. Stress is a frequency that we allow into our DNA. Most human beings forget how to breathe as they grow up; we're conditioned to forget. Because shallow breathing doesn't oxygenate our cells sufficiently, our rhythm moves out of kilter with the whole. We actually create interference with the whole. What a profound thing it is to move out of harmony with nature! The moment we do, we experience stress. The whole body responds by activating neurological pathways in the old part of our brain. Because of our advanced brain development, our thoughts become predominant. We were never intended to run our lives from our heads, even though this is what happens when we activate the low frequencies of this 52nd Shadow.

There is of course a reason for everything in nature. Our body tells us when we've moved out of harmony so we can adapt and find the most effortless way forward, but we aren't intended to live out of harmony. We actually become addicted to stress and the hormones it releases inside us, like adrenaline. No one enjoys stress; it's deeply uncomfortable, but we do become addicted to it. When we only think with our mind, we're operating out of a mere fraction of our true potential.

The ancient Chinese called this hexagram 'Keeping Still', and it's symbolised by a mountain. Its message is that there is no hurry. The fear that we'll miss out comes from this Shadow - the fear that we haven't got enough time. It's all about time and our perception of it. When we're stressed, time is always running too fast or too slow. Stress also has a passive manifestation, which is when we feel stuck or frustrated. That feeling comes out of this

Shadow: Stress **Gift:** Restraint **Programming Partner:** Gene Key 58
Dilemma: Shallow Breathing **Siddhi:** Stillness **Codon Ring:** The Ring of Seeking

52nd Shadow. When we feel stuck it's because our breathing isn't reaching down to our base. We can never really be stuck; we just aren't accepting where our rhythm is.

Every Gene Key has an archetypal association in the structure of the physical body. This 52nd Gene Key is connected to the perineum, right at the base of our body between our genitals and anus. This is where the breath arises from and descends to. This point has a direct connection to the fontanelle on the head, and they bookend the spine. When we feel stressed, this is the place to tune into. As we do, the breath will gradually return there and we will feel at ease.

The 52nd Shadow is also a collective phenomenon. It's generated by the world aura of humanity. The more out of kilter we become with Gaia, the more stressed our physical body is. It's a shadow quantum field. To rise above that field, that victim field, we have to slow down, not our vibration, but our rhythm. The earth, Gaia, has a tempo, a heartbeat called the Schumann Resonance. When we go to the ocean or forest we can feel the true tempo of the earth and it's magical. It's a deep drumbeat sounding in every cell of our being. The DNA expands when it hears and feels this tempo. When we forget this deep, natural tempo, our DNA contracts and sends our body into a stressful state, as though an alarm goes off inside us. The secret of this Shadow, and every shadow has a secret, is to trust that alarm instead of ignoring it and carrying on. Much of the world today is living with the alarm bell still ringing. If we hear it all the time, soon we just get used to it and it becomes normal. The secret is to trust the alarm and our discomfort, stop what we're doing, slow down, breathe, come into our base and tune ourself back into Gaia's heart.

GENE KEY 52

THE 52ND GIFT - RESTRAINT

This 52nd Gift of Restraint is such a great gift, and even though it sounds so unexciting, it's one of the most powerful. If we have the 52nd Gene Key in our Profile, we're blessed. We have the capacity to slow down time and bring others out of stress – what a lucrative life we can lead in this day and age!

The 52nd Gift is about the art of focus. These people are only really interested in the long term view. That's why they know to take their time. Everything in the universe has its natural rhythm and timing; its seasons, ebbs, swells, dips and flow. The genius of the 52nd Gift is to align oneself with such cosmic timing, which will gradually bring others into alignment with their natural timing.

When we meet someone living out of this Gift, we're meeting someone whose breath is rooted deeply inside their bodies. They're really like great anchors, they're so grounded. That's why this is called the Gift of Restraint. An anchor allows an organism to rest, come to a natural pause and regain perspective, clarity, and above all, timing. This Gift has a huge impact on the emotional body. It communicates and exudes calmness throughout the aura. There have always been people in the world who remain completely unflustered by external crises like emotional turmoil or human conflict and war. When we're grounded inside ourself, all of Gaia and her natural rhythmic power are at our disposal. If we have this 52nd Gift in our profile, we're such a person.

Restraint is not as bad as it sounds. The process of transformation through this 52nd Gene Key is one of deep slowing down, and it's also a calming environment for others, both emotionally and mentally. Once we've established calmness, clarity emerges, and whatever situation we're in has an easy and obvious way forward. This is another collective Gene Key and its central question is: how can I be of the greatest service to the universe? This Gift will demand that of its entire environment, whatever profession we find it in. It's therefore highly attuned ecologically to all natural living systems, because it sees and knows how an environment most naturally survives and thrives.

All natural systems require restraint and this isn't about putting the brakes on our enthusiasm. This Gift is filled with optimism, idealism and enthusiasm because that's the dynamic energy of life. It also provides a natural patience, a waiting, an attunement to a deeper flow that lies beneath everything. If this is your Gift or you feel drawn to contemplate it, these are the secrets you'll discover inside yourself – the secret of slowing down and the secret of the breath.

The 52nd Siddhi: Stillness

Even when he is still, the selfish man is busy. Even when he is busy, the selfless man is still.

Ashtavakra Gita

Stillness is how the world will be transformed. Although on a first pass, that doesn't seem to make sense, it's an absolute truth. Deep within our DNA, stillness is all there is. When we enter into the world of the Siddhis, we come into paradox over and over. The ultimate stillness is to be found in movement and our bodies are constantly in movement. At the cellular level, we're being rebuilt over and over every hour we're alive. Yet one day, when our body is dead and gone, there's nothing but stillness. The movement is within the stillness, and the stillness is within the movement.

Stress contains stillness, and only when we slow down do we begin to remember that stillness. Stillness is not death or an icy lifeless world. On the contrary, stillness is bursting with potential and potency. True stillness is about awareness. Only the selfless man is still. He is still because he is not. He's so in harmony that he's merged into the background, and nothing but love moves through him. Stillness is beyond effortless and beyond frequency. It's beyond the mind and understanding.

The journey through the 52nd Gene Key is one of gradual or sudden realisation. Slowly, as the Gift of Restraint turns our awareness inwards to our source, we move out of the stress of the Shadows and come into alignment with our greater reality. This Siddhi involves the release of hormones that silence thoughts. This is Eckhart Tolle sitting on a park bench gazing into space for weeks on end. This is the fury and passion of the dervish disappearing into the dance. Not only do gaps open out between our thoughts, but our emotional field is also placated. An emotion rises up inside us as though in slow motion. It moves so slowly we could reach out, touch it and turn it over in our hands before it breaks the surface. All our inward processes occur as though in slow motion. A feeling or thought is like a precious penny dropped into a pond. We watch and marvel as it spreads throughout our chemistry and runs its course to dissolve once again back into the stillness. Now there's only the breath, silently moving in and out, and the stillpoint at the centre.

When the 52nd Siddhi takes us, there's no more drama in our life. We observe it all from a distance but there's no part of us that's interested in playing the game anymore. The stillness is too captivating. It wells up inside us, breaking over us in wave after wave, bringing such peace that we can no longer put anything into words. Stillness is in every cell, at the heart of our DNA, within the core of each atom, where the mystery of the universe is constantly pouring through us. From within this stillness activity naturally arises and its only interest is to reach out and touch the stillness in others, in all things. Stillness sees only itself. It's the wellspring of joy, the font of bliss, the end of all seeking – it's that most magical of places where everything meets at the end of the rainbow.

THE 64 WAYS

THE 53RD WAY

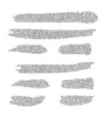

Gene Key 53

THE WAY OF EXPANSION

The Transformational Way of the 53rd Gene Key moves from Immaturity to Superabundance, and it's the Way of Expansion.

The 53rd Shadow of Immaturity points us in a single direction - immaturity is that stage in human evolution where we haven't yet learned to look inwards for the resolution of our problems. This whole Gene Key spans the spectrum from externally fixated to internally grounded. It's actually quite a controversial viewpoint so I'd like to explore it in more depth.

We live in a Maya, an illusion where things are not what they seem. If we've been studying the Gene Keys we'll have come across this idea over and over again. It's like the film The Matrix, a seminal film in which the protagonist gradually comes to realise that the world he's living in is a construct, a mental projection. We also live in that world, that construct, in which we believe what's before us. We become a victim of what life brings us. We become lost in the drama of our lives and the lives of those around us. Of course, we have to be careful in saying these kinds of things because people can get angry when they hear them. What about my friend dying of cancer or those children starving in that terrible place? There's nothing illusory about that, we might say. I'm not trying to be glib about such things. The world is filled with intense suffering. That's an obvious truth, but the question is how do we deal with and meet that suffering. This seems to be the question that dictates maturity.

The 53rd is a wonderful Gene Key that's all about beginnings and the new. It's the energy to start again and at a deep esoteric level it governs the cycles of our lives and our incarnations. I always think twice when I speak about this subject of reincarnation, because I know that it has relative truth to it and will meet with opinion. If we can suspend our opinion until the end that will be helpful. I'm just using this opinion to express a truth.

Shadow: Immaturity **Gift**: Expansion **Programming Partner:** Gene Key 54
Dilemma: Restlessness **Siddhi:** Superabundance **Codon Ring:** The Ring of Seeking

The paradox is that when our incarnations are over, when we're finally free, we come to realise that there actually were no separate incarnations. It was all a game, a film, a Divine play, and once our awareness is released from that drama we no longer need to participate. There's no longer a sense of separateness to incarnate.

In the meantime, it's helpful to talk about these things in the context of this Gene Key and its Shadow. It keeps us coming back over and over. There's immaturity on many levels - in a single lifetime, as we grow up, learn from our mistakes and hopefully become wiser and maturer, and then there's incarnative maturity, where our consciousness increases its light over many, many cycles and lifetimes.

Think about flowers and how different flowers come out at different phases of the season. Some, like the lovely snowdrops here in the UK, come out in the very early spring, sometimes when there's still snow on the ground. At the other end of the spectrum there are flowers that don't bloom until autumn, and they're just as beautiful. I want us to get away from morality here, so flowers are perhaps a good example. There are humans who are immature at the incarnation level, and there are those who are more mature, but there's no judgment in this. Earth is just a school, and once we've taken the classes and passed our exam, we're free, and new pupils are arriving all the time. These new pupils are not really individuals. It's tempting to see them as separate souls, but really they're just consciousness, the same stuff as those who've graduated. It's as though all the background radiation from the Big Bang has to evolve over time. That one aspect flowers early and one late in the game doesn't make the underlying consciousness different.

GENE KEY 53

The Dilemma of this Shadow is Restlessness. When the new consciousness arrives at school it has so much to learn, and the greatest thing to learn is that the outer life can never offer genuine fulfilment. We have many, many incarnations where we seek pleasure or run from pain, until we begin one day to question the whole game of life. We might remember when we first questioned the game, and what it was we were responding to. Perhaps we were drawn to a book or teacher or a bright human example carrying a deeper maturity than usual. Perhaps it was an acute crisis or the death of a loved one that turned us inwards. Whatever it was has also led us to listen to or read this.

The 53rd Gene Key is part of the Ring of Seeking, and it drives us to seek. Our restless spirit has to go through this exhaustive search, this great quest. Eventually that becomes the spiritual quest. In our immaturity we're fixated by the outer world and the events of our life, and it's all brought to us through our karma, created out of our past lives. Everything is linked back to a cause. There's a Divine Justice at work that's utterly invisible to us. There are places of immaturity in all of us, and as we begin to spiritually evolve we have to gradually shake off our immature patterns, and it takes a long time. We all have our blind spots, and it's important to ask ourselves where our blind spots are, and where we're playing the victim. It's likely to be the biggest focus of our life right now. Suffering is like that; it dominates our consciousness.

The 53rd Gift - Expansion

What does this process of maturity look like, and is there anything we can do to speed up the process? That's the question of our era, and it's ironic because the question comes from the Shadow and its Dilemma, Restlessness. The very question is wrong because it's only when we start to understand this question inside us that we begin to slow down and mature. Isn't it funny that maturity always seems to involve slowing down? The mature person is older and slower. The mature river is wider, slower moving. One of the hallmarks of maturity is slowness!

It's also insightful that the Gene Key of slowing down is the 52nd Gene Key, which comes just before this one in the I Ching sequence. Maturity is rooted in slowing down and is a stage in our seeking. Spirituality must always learn the art of meditation or contemplation or prayer or breathing. We have to learn to breathe. When we learn to breathe more deeply, that's when we begin to see things more clearly. We see life as though in slow motion. Our rhythm may slow down, but our awareness quickens, our intelligence heightens and becomes more refined. Our lives become more efficient, more effective. We enter into a period of gradual expansion.

The Gift of Expansion needs to be understood clearly. Expansion can be balanced or imbalanced. For example, we can over-expand our business so that it becomes a liability and a danger to the whole, and this kind of over-expansion is another sign of immaturity. Maturity knows that expansion must be balanced. The Gift of Expansion is about the expansion of awareness, love, and creativity, and those three together create a perfect harmony. Awareness without love can be cruel, love without awareness can be painful, and creativity without love can be reckless.Expansion really refers to a ripening of our spirit. When our spirit ripens, our life tends to move naturally towards balance. Life is a holistic phenomenon, but we tend to compartmentalise our lives. We think of our relationships as one thing, our family, work, and health as another, but these are all one thing. Expansion in one area only creates imbalance. Maturity is to allow expansion to ripple through the whole of our life, and the secret to this is effortlessness. Expansion comes without effort and emerges naturally, slowly, quietly. It brings calm rather than excitement. It brings simplicity rather than complexity, perspective rather than ambition. It all comes through slowing down.

Expansion also takes place over lifetimes. In the esoteric lore, there's an expression I've heard used for the soul. It's called the permanent atom. There's this notion of there being a single atom in our being that's carried over between lifetimes, and it carries the charge of our karma. In the terminology of the Corpus Christi, the mystical side of the Gene Keys, it's called the causal body. The causal body represents all the good that we've learned over the cycles of our lives, and it all gets stored eternally in this atom. Over time, this atom begins to glow. The more it radiates, the brighter the soul becomes. This is the aura of an expanded state of awareness. Such a state has learned that the problems of the world can only be solved within, when we go to the root cause. We can stop a war on the outside, but it will only spring up somewhere else. Suffering is like the Hydra's seven heads; the more we try and cut them off, the more sprout forth. This is not to say by the way that we shouldn't try and help others. On the contrary, one of the primary means to transcend suffering is to serve others selflessly. This selfless service is a part of our expansion. We can't expand without serving others in some way. Service is a by-product of love.

The Gift of Expansion is about turning all that restless energy of the Shadow back towards its own source; it's all about how we deal with the suffering. Can we use it as a means to expand our awareness, or do we let it overwhelm us and crush our spirit? The 53rd Gift uses suffering to expand, and that is its greatest gift. It uses the difficulties and traumas of life as creative fuel. Along with its Programming Partner the 54th Gene Key, the 53rd Gene Key are two of the most driven energies in the whole genetic matrix. They either drive us mad or they drive us towards enlightenment and great wisdom.

The 53rd Siddhi - Superabundance

What on earth does this word superabundance mean? There's a lovely word in English - hyperbole, which means something that is overly exaggerated on purpose. Is superabundance hyperbolic? In other words, can you have more than abundance? I love words, they're so specific. The prefix 'super' is from the Latin meaning 'above' or 'beyond'. This is what gives us the key to the 53rd Siddhi; it's beyond abundance.

In the modern New Age everyone is looking for abundance. Have you noticed we have all these affirmations like, 'may I be abundant' ? There's nothing wrong with that, humans have always prayed to the gods of abundance, like Ganesh in India for example. It's a part of our expansion, our maturity, that we need to experience material abundance to a degree. When we have all our material needs met, we soon realise that having money doesn't make us happy. It makes us comfortable, but it doesn't lead to fulfilment or alleviate suffering. It's important to realise that for most of us, we need to get our material needs met before we can truly turn inwards. It's a practical consideration. Superabundance however is of a different dimension; it's really saying that abundance no longer matters. Expansion is the other side of contraction; the universe expands, the universe contracts, life and death. Superabundance is the state beyond them both, beyond seeking. It lies at the end of the quest, the end of the rainbow. Superabundance is where everything springs from, a mystery; it's The mystery. It's the locus of God. The poet Rilke put it best at the end of his most famous poem, the Ninth Duino Elegy: *'Superabundant being wells up in my heart'*.

Superabundance is Being. It isn't about abundance, nor does it care about whether there's abundance or not. It's beyond all agendas. It's the numinous state. The so-called permanent atom that we spoke of in the Gift is shown to be semi-permanent here in the Siddhi. That atom explodes, incarnation comes to an end and there can be no more beginnings. We can now only say that there's one beginning and it's eternal. Eternity is really that, an eternal beginning without end, as always a paradox. The Gift was ripening, and here in the Siddhi the fruit drops from the bough. Although it's difficult to describe the Siddhis, it's also important for us to have some sense of this superabundance.

When I first began contemplating this Gene Key, it came to me very clearly. It makes us run; it wants us to run, and we humans need to run. Running is good for us; it's healthy, it burns energy, is meditative, rhythmic and feels good. It's funny that a moment ago I was talking about slowing down and now I'm talking about running. Can you contain that paradox? When we run, we can feel superabundance and the world actually does slow down. After a while it begins to fill us. The running runs us, and of course this is a metaphor and also true. I think people with this Gene Key probably do need to run, but it's also symbolic. We're all here running around the wheel of life and death, and superabundance is as much about the dying as it is the being born. The focus is not on the forms that come and go, nor on the waves that rise and fall from the source, but on the source itself.

One day this universe we're in will contract and withdraw into itself. All the matter and story and song - the whole glittering pageant of humanity and Gaia and all her creatures, the solar system, the wheeling stars like tiny birds in the celestial sky, will all return to themselves, to their source. One day another mystery will be born from that source, and that's the only way our mind can handle eternity. We have to say 'one day…'. Of course when space returns to its source so will time, so in that sense the world will end, but it also can't end. It can only keep running and burning and breathing.

Sometimes I wonder if these contemplations are useful. I suppose if I wanted them to be useful I would talk about the glories of the Gift and how to expand your life, how to reach out and embrace wider horizons and touch more souls and open your heart more and more to life. That's the essence of this Gene Key - of every Gene Key. But then there comes a time when transcendence occurs. But we can't force maturity.

We have to relax and simply let it come in its own time. The more mature we become, the softer we become and the easier we are on ourselves. I think that's what superabundance really teaches us - the fine art of letting go…

THE 64 WAYS

The 54th Way

Gene Key 54

THE WAY OF ASPIRATION

The Transformational Way of the 54th Gene Key moves from Greed to Ascension, and it's the Way of Aspiration.

Here in this Way there are many wonderful pieces of wisdom and advice for seekers of the great Truth. This Gene Key is part of the Ring of Seeking, and of the six Gene Keys in that Codon family it represents one of six classic paths to God. Much confusion exists because of these varied approaches. As we ascend the ladder of consciousness we come to a time when sooner or later we will begin a spiritual path of one form or another. This 54th Gene Key can clarify much around which path we choose.

The other side of this Gene Key is that it's really quite base. At the Shadow frequency the 54th Gene Key is a brute energy, after all it's the Shadow of Greed. There's this wonderful anti-poem by Nicanor Parra, a Chilean poet, and it's called 'Oda a unas Palomas' - Ode to Some Doves. Parra takes a big swipe at the sometimes haughty poetry of great poets like Pablo Neruda, a risky thing to do in itself, but I love it because it's so naughty and irreverent. He takes the subject of doves, which for so many generations have been sanctified by poets and mystics, and tells it how it is. He's watching a flock of doves feeding, and he points out some basic truths. They're essentially bottom feeders, living off flies and fighting amongst themselves for who gets which fly. In other words, he portrays their Shadow side; they're just a bunch of greedy thugs, fighting over scraps, none of your dove of peace or Holy Shekinah here!

So this 54th Shadow is base, hungry, driven by greed and the survival of the fittest. This is what Nietzsche called the Will to Power, the driving force in all humans to reach the highest possible position in life. The Chinese also codified this will to power in this Gene Key by naming it the Marrying Maiden. It's one of the most enduring images of the I Ching, this cultural notion of the concubine

Shadow: Greed **Gift:** Aspiration **Programming Partner:** Gene Key 53
Dilemma: Egotism **Siddhi:** Ascension **Codon Ring:** The Ring of Seeking

who rises up in the hierarchy through sleeping her way to the top until she finally gets to be empress.

We can see this Shadow of Greed still at work in the world, both in the developing world, where it's dog eat dog, and in the so-called developed world. Free trade and the modern capitalist approach also encourages the full expression of this same energy. The more money we have, the higher we can rise up in the hierarchy, and at what cost? Here's a statistic I got off the internet recently: Just 62 people, 53 of them men, own as much wealth as the poorest half of the entire world population - or 3.6 billion people - according to a report released by anti-poverty charity Oxfam. And the richest 1 percent own more than the other 99 percent put together. Oh my God. I mean we all know this, but the reality of it is still shocking. We're part of that culture of greed, and it's no good blaming the very wealthy. We also share in this Shadow consciousness and our whole approach is based on rising up. We say to ourselves, I'll just earn enough so I can relax and do what I love, support my spiritual path, get that little house on the beach or in the mountains. We know that that very attitude, though absolutely human and seemingly harmless, has within it the seed of greed.

Greed is when we put ourself first, when we put our wellbeing before others. We may say that that's logical, that it's ok, that if I'm not healthy then I can't help others. I'm not saying it isn't ok, it's just where the journey begins. It also keeps us in a space of lack, and poverty isn't only financial; it's relational, spiritual, emotional. The Dilemma of this Shadow is egotism, an uncomfortable word for most of us. It pursues us all the way through the many layers of this Gene Key - am I doing it for myself? is that ok? should I feel guilty? These are the questions of the 54th Gene Key.

GENE KEY 54

Every Gene Key is simply a mirror. That's all this wisdom really is. We look in the mirror and see the pattern playing itself out. The journey always begins with the ego, the 'I am', 'I need', 'I want'. Children are the most honest, well, children and dogs and the Spanish. Children just say, Mummy I want one of those, I want that sweet. My dogs are great at this honesty. They just come up and ask for love. Actually they don't even ask, they demand it. I want your love and I'm going to stand in your way and look at you with these eyes until you damn well give me some action. The Spanish, well, the expression in Spanish for "I love you", at least one expression, is *te quiero*. I want you. Very honest!

We're also greedy in love. In fact, this is where we're the most greedy. We taste love and want more, so we pursue it, and like a chimera it vanishes. We try another one, and another, and then we blame the other when they can't deliver the love exactly the way we want it, and the mess continues! Those greedy doves. That's us. That's what the poet was pointing at. We need to watch the ego, not try and do anything about it, which is also the ego, greedy for being beyond the ego. It's a trap. All we can do is look and see the pattern driving us and then be honest. We can see clearly that our greed is because of a deep lack inside us, a deep disconnect and loss of unity. That seeing can propel us to a breakthrough.

Still the greed continues and drives us. It's the fuel that takes us onwards. We'll sooner or later realise that our search for fulfilment, or stability, or love, or money, or anything on the outside, is never going to fill the deep hole we have inside. Nothing will stop the ache, nothing external. Sooner or later we have to turn our awareness inwards. This can take many lives but when the turning comes, then things get interesting. Our egotism is not a bad thing; we have to see it for what it is. It's simply fuel, and as fuel it has its use. But without awareness we don't refine that fuel, so we don't leave the trap of our urge to find fuel-filment. Ok, bad joke, but the bottom line is that ego isn't the enemy. It's the booster rocket that one day will launch us into inner space.

THE 54TH GIFT - ASPIRATION

The 54th Gift uses the fuel of our greed to propel us to a higher purpose and vision of our lives and the world. I love this word "aspiration". It's like inspiration, which shares the same root, the Latin *spiro,* I breathe. We breathe in the fuel of greed and begin to transform it inside us, refining the fuel so that it can take us higher and further. Aspiration is a step up from ambition. Ambition is for a particular goal or a thing in the future, whereas aspiration is wider. To aspire means to seek something higher. We don't even have to know what that is, but we sense it exists and pursue it.

Aspiration is rooted in this same honesty I spoke of earlier. We have to see the Will to Power at work inside us. There's a spark inside us that seeks that which is higher, the evolutionary drive to go further. The Programming Partner is the 53rd Gene Key with its Shadow of Immaturity and Gift of Expansion. Immaturity doesn't allow us to expand and we simply stay in the pattern of greed. We may expand our business or our empire but we never expand our consciousness, so we stay trapped in the endless cycle of greed. We see that with business when people become addicted to earning more money, and more and more. What can we possibly do with all that? and still we go on with a new car, a new home, a new wife or husband.

At the Gift frequency, we begin to mature a bit and realise the futility of that cycle of greed. We begin to ask the great question, the grail question: how can I serve my fellow human and how can I serve life? The core of aspiration is to be of service. This question is a diamond. It cuts through our egotism instantly and renews our whole approach to life. All the skills and drive that the 54th Shadow has learned can now be put to a higher use. In the case of the 54th Gene Key, it's always about raising our consciousness. This same energy of greed gets fed back inside and we begin to covet the higher states. This is a healthier use for the energy. It has its dangers, but it's much healthier. We begin a committed spiritual path, and we still have a lot to learn at the Gift frequency.

When we look at the Codon Ring of Seeking, we can see the various ways that seeking can take. Both the 53rd and 54th Gene Keys represent the Path of Yoga, of effort. So we may find a technique or a spiritual teacher or a teaching and we yoke ourself to it - that's what yoga means, to yoke. We pour all that raw greed energy into this higher purpose. It takes commitment and perseverance but the 54th Gift has those in spades. It's driven by the will to power - the most awesome force in the universe! One day, this very force will unite us with the Godhead.

On the other side of the Ring of Seeking, we have the 52nd and 58th Gene Keys, two other Programming Partners. They represent the yin path to realisation, just sitting, watching, allowing the energy to move wherever it wishes. This is a very different path from active seeking. We then have the 15th and the 39th Gene Keys. The 15th is the Way of Service and Love - to serve humanity, to follow one's heart. The 39th is the Zen or non dual approach that uses awareness to cut right through the illusion. These are all very different paths with much scope for confusion among seekers of Truth.

The 54th Gift has to wade through all this, and as it matures, it picks a path. The most natural path for this Gene Key will always be a path with many levels and layers - a progressive path, an alchemical path, in which the base instincts are transformed into higher aspirations. This takes time and effort, and the 54th Gift is more than up to the task. This is the Path of Ascension, of the gradual refinement of our essence, and it's a beautiful path.

So much for the spiritual dimension, now what about the worldly? This is a vital part of the 54th Gene Key's journey to master the material plane. You can't be only a spiritual person with this Gene Key - you have to also be worldly. The 54th Gift has to take the material realm with it on its journey and move through the worldly dimension, which can be a tricky thing for some.

The problem is we're always looking for the short-cut, and that's the greed, making us so crazy that we do things before we're ready. Part of maturing is to make mistakes and try paths that don't suit us or get us anywhere. The problem with short cuts is that they lead to short circuits, and there's danger here in this Gene Key. The 54th Gift uses the raw spiritual energy of the life force, the un-transmuted kundalini force, and has to learn to harness it.

It's a tricky balance when we are too greedy, even for Truth, and it can be dangerous. We can overheat our inner mechanism by doing too much spiritual practise. The intensity of this Gene Key has to be regularly grounded by material reality. This is why the 54th Gene Key often finds itself being brought back down to earth. Grace will do that for us, and help us find the healthy balance.

This Gift is to elevate yourself and others, to bring the mystical into the mundane and give others a vision of a higher reality, of the world of the soul, of love, of a higher potential. This is a Gift especially designed for those who feel entrenched or trapped in the world of form, those countless souls stuck in lives with no purpose, lives of compromise and misery. If you have the 54th Gift, these are your people. These are the people who need you the most, so you can bring hope and radiance and possibility into their lives. That's your service and your path towards the higher worlds.

THE 54TH SIDDHI - ASCENSION

When we hear a word like ascension, I wonder how differently we all think of it. In the modern New Age it's a word that's been rather dragged into the spiritual marketplace and cheapened. The reason I feel this is because ascension has to be earned, and there are people out there toting it as something we can get through a few workshops. Real ascension is achieved only through lifetimes of hard toil, intense effort and sadhana. The Siddhis are all like that. They aren't games. They're hardcore. The intensity of our longing purifies us, and ever so slowly. We have such deep wounds. We don't only carry our own karma but the karma of the whole. All of that has to pass through the cauldron and be transformed.

The process of ascension concerns the highest levels of refinement. Each step along the way is so important. We can't skip a single step. Every difficult experience that life brings us must be passed through and transformed inside us, in our heart. If everything in your life is smooth except one person who always causes problems for you, you can't skip past that person. You have to confront the issue, transform it and only then can you move on. Nothing can be sidestepped. There are no short cuts. This is the language of the 54th Siddhi. As we get more refined and purified, we become more intensely spiritual.

Many great masters had this 54th Siddhi in their Profiles. We can find a place or a community and focus all that intensity into our spiritual practise, but the greed and the will to power remains. This is why most people need a spiritual teacher, a master to keep them humble. If there's someone beyond us, it's a constant reminder of how far we still have to go, so that spiritual ego doesn't get carried away.

The spiritual ego is the worst kind of ego. It's like giving a madman a Lamborghini. We've purified our inner state to a certain pitch and tasted some of the higher states, but we haven't stabilised them. The egotism gets a hold of that and we end up being a false master, addicted to the power that comes from that kundalini we've released. Many times this happens in life - that a gift of grace gets dragged down by the ego, and it's all part of the game of life. Those people are great testers for the spiritually discerning. Many of us have to follow such people and then go through the inevitable crash and disappointment. It's a phenomenon.

There's such an intense beauty in this 54th Siddhi of Ascension. It's a very specific word that doesn't just mean we can reach a higher state of consciousness. It actually means we have the capacity to physically ascend to a higher plane, like Jesus. There are only a few Siddhis that have this miraculous capacity; the 47th Siddhi of Transfiguration is another, but they're rare. Nietzsche called the highest level of his will to power 'the Superman'. His ideas have been dismissed or misunderstood by many down the years, and yet I find his insight beautiful and true. We do all have the capability to transcend this reality and become a superman or superwoman - someone who is destined to attain the very highest state of purification possible in a human body.

To be superman or superwoman is to bring an end to death and become eternal. That's what ascension refers to. It's given only very rarely to those rare orchids that have refined their human energies over much time and along the way lost all their hard edges. The greed isn't transcended, it's simply softened, like wind-blasted rocks that become all smooth and feminine. To ascend beyond the human form is to enter into the Divine Tenderness of the Great Mother. The journey there is so masculine because we have to be a warrior and so determined. We have to sacrifice everything along the way. Finally just before the peak, we realise we've become this pure yin essence. It's kind of a joke that one extreme gives way to its opposite. In so many of the great myths we see this ascension, this resurrection. It happens whenever a form or an idea can no longer be contained in the dimension it appears to belong to. A higher dimension opens up, a wormhole - and a new species reveals itself just as the old one sacrifices and burns away. This 54th Siddhi is also noteworthy in that it contains one of the great mystical lines of the whole I Ching, the 54, line 4.

I rarely mention the lines in these contemplations as they're part of another layer to the Gene Keys, but I'm going to break with tradition here and tell you the story of this one. It's a nice way to end this 54th Siddhi. The 54, line 4 is called The Sin Eater. It's an aspect of ascension. In order to ascend to the highest, one has to first of all make the ultimate sacrifice and descend to the lowest. That's what the whole journey in this Gene Key is about. We see this in the story of Jesus after his crucifixion. He descended into hell and on the third day ascended into heaven. Isn't it mysterious? Why would he do that? The truth is it's a universal myth and it's also more than a myth. As the white light of our Divinity is progressively realised, it becomes almost unbearable for the old being. The brighter the inner light burns, the deeper it burrows into the form principle. Heaven has to come to earth. As this inner light returns to its source, it has to burn through all the collective memory held in its DNA. This will one day happen to each of us listening to this, so get ready!

We have this wonderful image of Christ going down to hell where all the deepest impurities reside, and this white figure touches the heads of those tormented souls. And as he does, they're instantly freed and fly to heaven. This is the final transformation. Every single cell of our being has to become free, thus before we can ascend fully (which by the way happens in the 5th line), we must transmute every being to whom we're connected. It's an enduring image and one that I hope will inspire our contemplation for many years to come....

THE 55TH WAY

Gene Key 55

THE WAY OF FREEDOM

The Transformational Way of the 55th Gene Key moves from Victimisation to Freedom. Freedom is the only Way there is.

This Dilemma is External Validation, the need to know we exist. That's quite a one liner isn't it? This is the Shadow of needing to know that we exist, and yet everything about this 55th Gene Key hinges around this question of 'What is Freedom?' The answer to this question, like all great questions, can only be lived. It can't be learned. Freedom can only come about through unlearning. In this Gene Key lies the secret to all the great teachings, particularly those of the East. Over and over we've been told by sage after sage that we need to drop the ego in order to experience true Freedom. What is this ego, and what does it mean to surrender our self? It seems an obscure and uncomfortable language to the Western mind.

Here in the Gene Keys, we're reframing all this language to suit the modern mind, not even the Western mind, but the synthesising mind, the mind that's evolving as East meets West. Our word is Freedom, and how do we realise true freedom? Whatever we're seeking in life, whoever we are, let's be clear about one thing, we're looking for freedom. We can call it whatever we want - money, recognition, happiness, love; it's all covered by the word freedom. If we're honest, it's freedom from suffering that we really want. The great world teachers have always realised that the root of all human endeavour is suffering. That's what drives us, our search and our quest for perfection, peace and solace. We seek because we suffer.

This 55th Gene Key is obviously unique. Out of all the 64 Gene Keys, it has only two words - Victimisation and Freedom. There always has to be a joker in every pack. We have to know that when we approach this Gene Key, we'll not be able to approach it in the way that we approach all the others. We'll have to approach it sideways, in the spirit of the

Shadow: Victimisation **Gift:** Freedom **Programming Partner:** Gene Key 59
Dilemma: External Validation **Siddhi:** Freedom **Codon Ring:** The Ring of The Whirlwind

---

joker within ourself. When we manage to access its secrets we'll have created the conditions of a great quantum leap in our life. Such conditions are by their nature deeply unstable. Before an atomic explosion takes place, the radioactive elements are in such a deep instability.

Every Gene Key we enter, we're also entering the 55th. The theme is universal and underpins all others. All Shadow states are victim states. Whenever you contemplate the Shadow Gene Keys, always contemplate where the victim is hiding. In the 23rd Shadow for example, the Shadow is complexity and we become a victim of the complexities of life, of our own mind. Everything we do only creates more complexity. Everything we add to our life, from a new car to a new lover, can only make our life more overwhelming and more complex. It's all a state of being. Victimisation is nothing more than a frequency.

The question can be made more practical, instead of 'What is Freedom?', it can be 'Where do I not feel I am free?'. Now there's a question! Where do you not feel free? In your relationships? In your finances? In your living arrangements? In your job? In your body? In your spirit? Where are you trapping yourself? Where are you seeing yourself as a victim? Where are you playing the victim? There's the rub. We probably don't see ourself as a victim but we can guarantee that at some level we are playing the victim. Do we know why we do this, why we play the victim, propagate more suffering, almost wallow in it? In order to know that we exist!

External Validation. As long as we suffer, we're there. We have an identity. If we aren't suffering, we have nothing to hold onto, no opinions, teachings, friends, agendas, nothing. What does that make us? It makes us seem like a shell, true Freedom. To the ego it looks terrifying. *'Every angel is terrifying,'* said the poet Rilke.

The Transformational Way through the 55th Gene Key, and therefore all the Gene Keys, is one of letting go. We have to let go of all agendas, hidden or otherwise. We carry a lot of hidden agendas, all aimed at validating our separate existence. We want others to like us or not like us; no one wants to be unnoticed. Oscar Wilde said, *'If there's one thing worse than being talked about, it's not being talked about.'*

Yet true freedom doesn't care, and so how do we get to that level of inner freedom? Well, we walk sideways! I'm sorry for being so cryptic and playful here, but we can't go aggressively into freedom. We have to allow it to unveil itself and it's already our natural inner state. So we have to answer this question: where do I not feel free?

We have to then live into the answer. The more we contemplate freedom, the more our life will show us where it isn't. Like Buddha, we have to exhaust ourselves in the search. Yet as we search, lifetime after lifetime, in this teaching, in that teacher, in that realm of pleasure, in that realm of pain, something inexplicable and infinitely subtle occurs. We gradually begin to drop stuff, and become more and more open. Slowly, slowly we become lighter. Our search, instead of being desperate, becomes more amusing, more jubilant. Until one day we come to a life where even though the longing is still there inside us, even though it hasn't changed one inch in all these aeons, our relationship to it has changed. We begin to see through the veils, and realise how deep a fool we've been. It is I who have ensnared myself. I make myself miserable. Why do I keep doing that? Why do I keep distracting myself from my own pain?

We can then begin to take the suffering inside ourselves, and we have to take all suffering inside, that of our friends, families, community, country, the whole of humanity, and earth's suffering. Then the external drama gradually dies down. The behaviour, the karma we've been creating for so long, the reaction, the complaining, the blame, it's all drawn back inside through awareness. We can become an audience to our own fate. We stop interfering, trying to add something to ourselves, trying to make our lives go in the direction of our dreams; we simply stop pushing and pushing. We enter the drift. We flow, we allow, we watch, we wait, we drop, we float. We play. We accept, we allow, we love.

To be a victim is to be heavy, weighed down by worries, concerns, plans, memories, life, death. To be free is to be lighter than air. That's why freedom is always associated with flight. It's to be unburdened by agendas of any kind whatsoever. To be free is to live as we're intended. Here's a trick, since this is the joker in the pack. We can't chase freedom. We can't run out and sell everything and drop our dreams and become a monk or a hermit drifting about.

We have no chance of dropping our dreams. We have to be so patient. Freedom will come on its own, without our doing anything. It's Wu Wei – the greatest teaching there ever was. We have to live as a human, with all the trappings and trimmings. From within that our freedom will arise. The 55th Gene Key is all about romancing freedom. We have to romance it; we can't rush headlong at it like a battering ram. Freedom is a feminine spirit. What woman wants that, I ask? The feminine has to be courted, serenaded, romanced. The mystery has to be followed through to its conclusion, wherever she leads us, whatever bizarre pathways she draws us down. We only find freedom from following our nature. There are no short cuts.

I invite all of us to consider our life through the mirror of this 55th Gene Key. Where are we trying? Where is our agenda? Where are we looking for confirmation of our painful story? We all carry these stories. The 55th Shadow has these two dynamics – repressive and reactive. The repressive is complaint. We complain inwardly about our lives, or externally, and then it becomes blame. We pin it on something or someone outside us - it's very clever really, because that ensures the story of our pain can continue. If we blame something outside ourself, we've made ourself a victim.

Any concept we hold has the capacity to trap us. Take freewill. Such a heavy subject. One man believes he's free to do everything and anything. He's responsible for his life. He lives with that. Another man believes it's all the will of Allah, or God, and he's nothing but a puppet. He lives life through that. Both men are standing by the road and a man is hit by a moving bus. The first man takes it upon himself to rescue the victim. It's his responsibility. He feels that. The other man does nothing. It is the will of Allah. It's also the will of Allah that he's standing next to the first man! Who's right, who's wrong? Freedom is knowing that there is no right and there is no wrong. We move out of the drama entirely.

Through the 55th Gene Key we can all take heart. It's where the change lies. All human beings will eventually realise this state of inner freedom. It's about allowing ourself simply to be the way we are, and if that changes, let it change, and if it doesn't, let it not change. We can just be the way nature intended us to be. That is freedom. It's both a being and a becoming. It's the great joker in the pack. I hope you can enjoy and partake of its human humour as much as I do, because it's why we are here.

THE 64 WAYS

The 56th Way

Gene Key 56

THE WAY OF ENRICHMENT

The Transformational Way of the 56th Gene Key moves from Distraction to Intoxication, and it's the Way of Enrichment.

In this 56th Gene Key we can see clearly the connection between the Siddhi and the Shadow. These 64 Transformational Ways are really powerful when we understand them and apply them to our life, but they really aren't very comfortable. They're not meant to make feel us comfortable, just the opposite in fact. How can we awaken to a negative pattern that threatens to undermine us if we're not willing to really own it one hundred percent?

In the world people are already deeply familiar with their Shadow patterns. We indulge them all the time, in our homes, sitting at our computers and out in the world. I could take just about anyone off the street, even the most hardened cynic, and talk him or her through his Profile, describing his or her Shadow patterns in depth, and they would gasp at the truth being revealed. The Shadow we know. The Gift and the Siddhi we aren't so familiar with. When we look at this from the view of the Codon Rings, genetic families of the Gene Keys, we come across some amazing patterns. The 56th Gene Key doesn't code for an amino acid but represents one of three 'Stop Codons', genetic markers that define the endings of chains of genes throughout our body. The Stop Codons are quite special and operate differently from all the other Gene Keys.

This group of three Stop Codons, the 33rd, 56th, and 12th Gene Keys, make up the Ring of Trials, three ongoing archetypal tests that all humans face in their lives over and over. Until we pass these tests, we can't fully transition from the Shadow through the Gift into the Siddhi. The 56th Gene Key is the lynch pin. The 33rd is the Trial of Forgetting, the pressure to remember our true nature and the ease with which we forget.

Shadow: Distraction   **Gift**: Enrichment   **Programming Partner:** Gene Key 60
Dilemma: Pleasure / Pain **Siddhi:** Intoxication   **Codon Ring:** The Ring of Trials

---

The 56th shows how we forget; we become distracted. We're distracted by the many traps and snares of the world, by the cycles of seeking through pleasure and pain. Pleasure and pain we'll note are also the Dilemmas of this 56th Shadow. Finally the 12th Shadow is our deepest trial, even if we've overcome all our human trials, all our forgetting and our distractions, at the end we must give up the illusion of our individual existence through the 12th Shadow of Vanity.

This is all quite a story. Our lives are quite the story. Let's consider for a moment, our Siddhis, our true nature. We're immortal, and we each contain an embryo of immortality. Whether we feed that embryo is up to us. If we forget what we are and feed only our desires, then we're starving our true nature. Our true nature is deeply intoxicating and it's so far beyond our Shadow life that it's hard to even contain it for a second. I was reading recently about the great sage Ramakrishna, and we really get a picture of this intoxication through him. He's sitting around with his devotees chatting about life and someone may casually say the word God, or Krishna, and Ramakrishna would immediately hear it and go into a trancelike ecstasy. God intoxication would take him. I mean it was difficult to have a conversation with this guy! He would be gone for hours sometimes before he just came back into the room, into his local, physical body.

That's what we're distracting ourselves from, the great forgetting, and we all help each other in being distracted. We recreate the distractions on every conceivable level. We forget so perfectly who we are that we fall into the trap of looking for a way out through our distractions. We seek a way out by looking for pleasure, through food, sex, power, trying to recreate a life of happiness constructed by our mind. In kind of a dark way, I particularly enjoy the new 'lifestyle' culture we see on our screens, with people in beautiful homes by the sea, lovely families, faithful partners, great food, all seemingly so perfect. What a false romance. Think of countries like Ladakh in the Himalayas - a beautiful, remote little place where people used to live as recently as the 1960's cut off from modern civilisation. A truly happy, sustainable culture with deep spiritual roots, and in twenty years, as modern culture arrived, how that civilisation has crumbled. People who were perfectly happy, living in harmony, now see themselves as poor and are on the dreaded treadmill of trying to find this pleasure, this wealth and this happy life. Today the distractions are so unsubtle, that's our one great advantage. We can see them so clearly, and they really don't fulfil us.

Then there's the other side of the distraction - the pain cycle. The pain cycle drives the pleasure cycle, and vice versa. Because we feel this deep ache inside, this unfulfilled longing, we seek an outlet through pleasure. The other side is that the pleasure doesn't last and leads to an even deeper ache. We get distracted by trying to fix the ache. The ache becomes emotional, and we give in to it and allow it into our relationships as projections. We blame and persecute others because of the ache. The ache becomes physical and we go to the doctor, herbalist, massage therapist. We try this diet and that diet, but we don't address the fundamental problem. We avoid at all costs the real problem; we're spiritually barren. Our lives have lost true meaning and we've given in to being a victim of the world, our projections and our ideas for the future.

In one of my webinars, I listed out the 64 victim states for each Gene Key, and in the 56th Gene Key, we're a victim of the distractions of the world. They're addictive. They fill us and occupy our minds temporarily with hope so we don't have to feel the ache. When we switch off the computer, the TV, or our phone, there it is, the Stop Codon, and it's actually a great gift. It's the greatest gift we've been given, and we run from it constantly. That's something we can all contemplate - the Shadow of Distraction and how deeply it has us in its hold.

The 56th Gift - Enrichment

Here's the beauty - the moment we stop feeding the beast and stop the cycle of pain and pleasure, whatever we do is by its very nature enriching. This is what these Stop Codons are for, they're gearshifts. They allow us to operate at whole other levels and taste new dimensions of being. Enrichment isn't something we do; it's something we stop doing. This is why the ancient Taoists, friends of mine, called the greatest art of all 'Wu Wei', the art of doing by doing nothing.

It's like modern children. As a father I face one of the greatest challenges any parent can face - how to parent a child in the age of technology. Almost all parents I know have given in; the weight and pressure is just too much. These kids have iPads when they're two or three now. Well I'm a fighter and my wife and I, we're hold-outs, die hards. I don't recommend it, it's a hard path. We don't deny our children access to technology, but we do our best to hold it at bay as long as possible. One of the reasons I give is that I want my children to know what it feels like to get bored. If we can't be bored, we aren't tasting life. Boredom is such an important part of growing up, to simply have to be, without any distractions. If we don't have that being somewhere in our repertoire, we're doomed in later life. That's how I've fallen in love with the art of contemplation, because I was bored as a child. I was isolated, living in the woods, and I had to find things in the trees. I had to look deeper into life, into nature for my stimulation, and it fed my soul. I hated it sometimes at the time, especially when I saw what great lives my friends had in the towns and cities. But now, now I am eternally grateful for those moments of being. They're my references. Enrichment is not what we might have thought it was; it's to learn how to stop.

When we pause, when we find ourselves in the gap, when we're in between jobs or lovers or homes or countries or communities, those are precious times. Those are the times when we can actually bring in the harvest. Our lives move in cycles of activity and inactivity. We must learn to not be distracted from being inactive. Inactivity is filled with magic. When we're inactive, we're fuelling the embryo of immortality inside us. When we stop, that's when we realise we're drunk!

We can use this Gene Key in our life and really allow ourself to taste this Gift. A great French writer and scientist Blaise Pascal said, 'All men's miseries derive from not being able to sit alone in a quiet room'. How true these words are. We need to learn to contemplate, to be alone with ourself, to enrich our spirit with those things in life that are essential for our growth, evolution and enjoyment. We can let our enjoyment be a by-product of our presence, not the goal.

The 56th Gene Key is a great connoisseur of life, of frequencies, tone and colour and taste. Again the secret is not in the taste, but in the presence. When I sit down to drink a rare Chinese Puerh tea from Yunnan, I bring so much presence into the preparing and drinking of it. I don't get all intense though, but just allow the conversation to flow normally. I also love to share the refined frequencies of such a special substance. I love to choose the right tea for the right moment and the right company. The same with wine, it must be drunk at the right time, in the right place. Knowing this is an art. It's part of the art of contemplation, to attune to the naturally arising frequencies of the moment.

This is what enrichment is - to flow with life, sip the seasons, savour the light, joust and tickle with dialogue, and sing out with life. It all flows from nothingness, from the void, the wu chi. Everything great and powerful comes out of nothing. We don't understand how it works, but it does. Enrichment deals in not being distracted, so that we can listen and respond to the heavenliness of the moment we're inhabiting. Life is so filled with poetry, with music. Even in the darkest places and recesses life is still rich and beautiful. To court the 56th Gift is to learn to appreciate all aspects of life, all its myriad layers and levels without judging them, without making any one better than any other. That's the foundation we have to build, the cornerstone of Intoxication.

THE 56TH SIDDHI - INTOXICATION

Intoxication - it sounds pretty 'out there' doesn't it, so I'll try and make it practical. Here's where my contemplation of this Gene Key has led me. When we approach the Siddhi, we begin to work with refinement. We're refining our awareness to a super-subtle pitch, and that means that the distractions become subtler as well. One of the greatest distractions is the suffering of others. As our awareness opens up, so does our heart, and our compassion for all beings swells in our chest and throughout our whole being. We wish more than anything to help others and offer them comfort and solace in their suffering.

This beautiful wish can become a subtle and powerful distraction. In many ways it's a beautiful and noble distraction. It's the basis of the whole Gift frequency, as we move out of our selfish tendencies and into the realm of the selfless. But to really move into the numinous realm entirely, we must let go even of this, our yearning to help and be of service to others. In our relationships we may have noticed that when our friend or partner is suffering, and we want nothing more than to help them. And yet sometimes our help isn't what they need. What they need is our disinterested love, our acceptance of their state as a perfect teaching. This doesn't mean we can't or shouldn't offer help or support. As I said, these are subtle levels and layers. We just have to make sure that deep down inside ourself, we're not coming from a tiny morsel of our own discomfort. We hate it when those we love suffer. This is the greatest test of our faith in a way, to detach ourselves from the suffering of others while still remaining absolutely open and empathic.

There's a story told by Ram Dass about a Himalayan Master who gave his devotee two potatoes and told him to take them down to the river and eat them. The devotee took the potatoes to the river, but when he got there he met a beggar who was starving and asked him for one of the potatoes. The man was torn whether he should follow the instructions of his teacher or his heart. In the end he gave the man one of his potatoes, but when he returned his master called him a fool. One of the potatoes was material fulfilment, which he kept, and the other was spiritual enlightenment, which he gave away. I love stories like this. They can be interpreted in so many ways. I'm not going to interpret it for you. Just consider it inside yourself. There are levels of distraction that are deeply subtle.

One of the great modern masters of Intoxication is Osho, Bhagwan Rajneesh. Through his figure of Zorba the Buddha he coined a new path for seekers, to fuse together the highest levels of material appreciation with the highest levels of enlightenment. To Osho, the likes of Ramakrishna are incomplete, they're from an older time because they're all heart but no intellect. The complete higher being must have both poles, says Osho.

The complete being must include absolute physical enjoyment and embodiment with spiritual refinement. This is who Zorba the Buddha is. Zorba is a fictitious character in a famous novel called Zorba the Greek, and he's a sensuous liver of life. Whatever he does he does one hundred percent with his whole being, with no guilt or self judgment. Zorba on his own has no morality or refinement, and Buddha on his own can seem dry and lofty, but the two fused into one are the ultimate expression of Intoxication.

I'd like to introduce us to another intoxiate - is that a word? It is now. A man, a flame of intoxicated truth, a Hungarian writer called Hamvas Bela, he's a great figure of Divine Intoxication. His philosophy is one of the divinisation of the senses. His greatest love is the mouth. Of all the five senses, says Hamvas, the mouth is the one that takes life in the deepest. The eyes keep life at a distance, the ears allow it a bit closer, the hands reach across the physicality and the nose inhales life into the body. The mouth stands alone, because it has to take life in and ingest it. He says the mouth has three ways of connecting; speaking, eating and kissing, and kissing is the ultimate because it alone gives and takes simultaneously. Hamvas says that the ultimate exchange of life is the kiss. This is both literal and symbolic. To kiss life is to become intoxicated by life. Hamvas adores the senses. He sees them as the vessels of enlightenment rather than thieves that rob us of our energy and awareness. This is a very different approach to the Siddhi than most others. It's life affirming but it also requires a certain self discipline. The self discipline of the intoxiate, unlike the renunciate, is to ingest the minute, homeopathic doses of life's essences, both poisonous and healthy. The renunciate avoids. The intoxiate absorbs, but nothing is over-ingested. Everything is tasted, rolled on the tongue, filtered by the body and the heart until the quintessence is extracted.

By life's essences here I mean experiences as well. Our suffering is not to be avoided either. Suffering is as sweet as pleasure when ingested with openness, love, and without judgment. No doubt few people will comprehend such a foolish-sounding statement as this, and it may sound banal and flippant to say such things, that suffering could be savoured in any way. But that is the intoxiate's task - to transmute the toxins of the world, to extract their pure essence. There's purity in everything at its root. God's breath is to be found everywhere, suffused with creation.

If this is our path, the path of the 56th Siddhi, then we are to celebrate life, to drink life in through our mouth and not be afraid of the senses, not be afraid of meat, of fatty food, alcohol, or wine. Wine is the ultimate symbol of the intoxicate, which is why the sufis love it so. The purer and more refined we become, the less we need to become intoxicated. Even the smallest sip will do, and yet even then, sometimes there are exceptions, sometimes we can drink the whole bottle! Perhaps we can feel from this Siddhi how paradoxical and rebellious it is - drink from life, it says. Drink well and deep, and that totality, that deep trust in the form will naturally lead to its own transcendence. As Hamvas says: 'You are not externally condemned to damnation. You, yourself, keep yourself in a state of damnation. Everything depends on you. Every soul is born whole and cannot lose its health. Be clever, recover your health. Remedy can be acquired anywhere. Drink. What I offer you is the oil of purity, the oil of intoxication. Drink and the wine will take care of the rest.'

The 57th Way

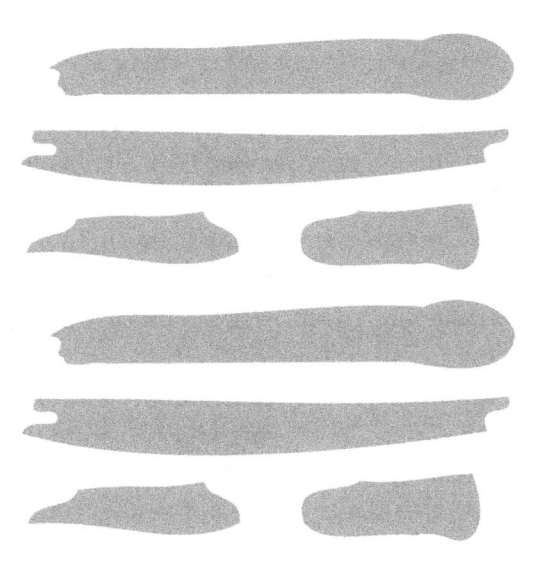

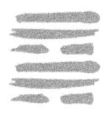

Gene Key 57

THE WAY OF INTUITION

The Transformational Way of the 57th Gene Key moves from Unease to Clarity, and it's the Way of Intuition.

This 57th Gene Key is a fascinating Gene Key. It's the basis of all matter. I'm going to begin it with a story. Back in the ancient times, in the so-called Golden Age, we humans were different. I'm talking before recordable history at a time when the continents were all connected, the time of Pangaea, when the world was fresh and still had dew upon it. At that time, we humans were here in a very early form, not a material form that we could ever know about through fossils, but in a vaporous form, an etheric form. We inhabited a higher plane of reality called the buddhic plane. This was the mythical time of the Garden. As we gradually came closer to the earth in our involution, we began to crystallise more and more. One day something momentous happened. A soft shell of matter formed itself around our spirit, like an eggshell. We began to ingest matter and take it inside ourselves (like Eve eating the apple), and over time this shell became harder and harder until it coated us with skin and flesh and bone. And so we became material, physical.

This is an important myth if we want to understand the Transformational Way through this 57th Gene Key. When considering its shadow, we can begin to see this at work in our lives. I often ask people to simply sit still and close their eyes in a room for half an hour. When we do this, we quite quickly come into touch with the Shadow of Unease. It's a primal unease that comes with these material bodies. It's fear, a basic discomfort that all is not quite as it should be. It's a kind of deep forgetting that sits inside the DNA of every cell of our bodies. It's the very base frequency of mortality. This unease drives all humans, and I want to explore it together. The Gene Keys are a journey into this unease. What is it and what are we to do about it, if anything?

Shadow: Unease   **Gift**: Intuition   **Programming Partner:** Gene Key 51
Dilemma: Trust   **Siddhi**: Clarity   **Codon Ring:** The Ring of Matter

---

When we do the Golden Path, it's a courageous ride into the depths of this unease in our bodies. We have to allow it to move from the background of our consciousness from the unconscious to the conscious. In most of us the unease is unconscious, so it drives us. It powers our desires, hopes, fears and all our endeavours. We unconsciously seek to bring an end to the unease. But we never do so if it remains in the background. This Shadow is paired with the 51st Shadow of Agitation, its Programming Partner. They make a pair of ugly sisters together - unease and agitation. They lie beneath most people's lives.

When we one day begin to truly turn inwards through contemplation, meditation or some other form, we first of all must meet this deep discomfort that's been driving us. We have to turn and face it, which takes courage because we can easily distract ourselves. We don't really want to keep looking at this difficult place. I mean the more we become aware of it, the more it seems to dominate. It's not a comfortable feeling. Nonetheless, the Transformational Way through this Gene Key has to tackle the unease. If we're working with the Gene Keys, every Shadow we dive into is really diving into this unease. However, it's rewarding work, this mining. We'll begin to find some gems if we persist. Shadow work is hard, but it gradually begins to lighten our load. The unease doesn't go away but moving it into conscious awareness prevents us from being a victim of it and chasing our tails in the outer world.

Occasionally if we're lucky or predestined, we meet someone unusual who seems to have transformed this unease entirely in their being. We call these people masters. There's an aura around them, a radiance, a sense of peace that some distant part of us remembers. We know what it was like to live without this unease. Imagine it for a moment - your body with no unease. These people are electrifying to us. We want to know how they did it. How did they transmute this unease? Of course we want that for ourselves. It's a huge turning point when we realise that it's possible.

GENE KEY 57

That's really what this Shadow is all about - getting to the heart of the matter, burrowing deeply into the form, into our DNA, which holds this germ of our suffering. I call it the Sacred Wound, and it's a wound with many layers to it. The deeper our awareness penetrates this place inside, the more layers we discover and the more layers we transmute. This is the journey and it's why we're here. If we know this, then we're blessed. When we know this, our journey has truly begun in earnest.

THE 57TH GIFT - INTUITION

I haven't spoken yet about the Dilemma of this Gene Key - Trust. Let's examine it through the lens of the 57th Gift of Intuition. Trust is a vast energy field. We may not have thought about trust as an energy field, but I'd like us to consider that. If trust is an energy field then it's something we can rise into, something we can inhabit, and it's something we can also fall out of. In the Shadow we fall out of trust and at the Gift level we do indeed rise into the field of trust. We do this through listening to our intuition. Our intuition is magical, and it's the part of us that knows, that trusts in the whole. It's a sacred thread left by God to help us out of the labyrinth.

Everyone knows about intuition. Even the most logical, skeptical being has experienced it. We can't really explain how we know something that can't be seen, but we do. Intuition is a channel inside us and the more we use that channel, the wider the path becomes. The more we trust in it, the more we find ourselves in the field of trust. It's a dilemma because we have to trust in it to find the trust! A great deal of the time we hear our intuition, but don't follow it. That's how we learn and gradually we pull ourselves out of the Shadow.

Another funny thing is that our intuition is only for us and the service of our Truth. Sometimes we follow our intuition and when it takes us deeper into our suffering we begin to doubt again. In time it's revealed why our intuition wanted us to take that wayward route. In the New Age, we have to be careful because many people believe that their intuition is truth for everyone. This is a disaster, and deep arrogance. Intuition isn't the same thing as truth. It's our path towards truth, but it isn't anyone else's path. Of course, our intuition can be helpful to others, but it's really for ourself. The Gift of Intuition isn't to be confused with the 7th Gift of Guidance for example. The 7th Gift comes from a leadership Gene Key whereas the 57th Gift is an inner Guide. Please be careful about laying your intuitive trip onto others or onto the whole world!

So we begin to follow our intuition and we find our way out of the lower frequencies, through a series of initiations, and we find the courage to transform the unease inside. Intuition is a ladder and it ascends in an arc out of the Shadow realms. As we penetrate deeper into the nature of our sacred wound, we begin to unlock older residues of karma, memories that we carry. The ancients call these 'sanskaras', the programming codes of our mortality and of our core fears. The 57th Gift will take us all the way into our deepest fear - the fear of separation, of the unknown, of death. It all goes back to the point of conception. It's at the point of conception that the sacred wound is passed down from the yang sperm as it penetrates the yin egg. Wholeness is ruptured. In the Ring of Matter, the Codon Ring associated with this Gene Key, each of the four Gene Keys represents a key moment of imprinting. The 57th holds a key cycle of unease that is encoded into us, and it's the deepest and oldest of these codes. It literally locks us into the illusion of matter. Because it's a key, like all the Gene Keys, it's also, magically I think, designed to be unlocked.

Our intuition is very powerful. It begins to unlock and loosen our connection to our body. As we continue to listen to it, it becomes subtler and subtler. The ancient Chinese called it 'Yi' - the water eye. It's the subtlest of the subtle, the gentlest path inside us. That's why they called this Hexagram 'The Gentle Wind', because like water it cuts through the very hardest of matter and right down to the core. It always finds the easiest and gentlest route to the core. As we learn to enter into the depths of contemplation and turn inwards, our intuition unlocks a whole new inner world. It keeps guiding us deeper inwards and it systematically loosens our sanskaras and opens us up to a whole new inner world - the world of lucidity. The world of Clarity.

The 57th Siddhi - Clarity

The Way leads on to the Siddhi, but before we arrive at it, there are signs that it's coming. Our awareness penetrates an inner world of the subtlest light and our connection to our body and the world begins to soften as well. It really is a beautiful journey, this journey to awakening. The 51st Gene Key is the Programming Partner, and it's often associated with shock and thunder. The real shock is how subtle it is; it's the shock of gentleness.

Clarity is a new world with no I; it can't exist with a sense of identification. To get to the heart of the matter (I love that pun), we must let go of all that we've ever known. Our intuition will take us finally to a precipice in consciousness. Beyond that precipice lies an unfamiliar world. This is the place inside each of us where the deepest ancestral fears reside. Mythically, it's the memory of when Eve ate that apple. What happens when we take off all those clothes of our attachments and let go again into that most naked, vulnerable place? What will become of us? Often in our inner journey there's a pause here at the threshold. Many mystics have described this place, this dark night of the soul, this meeting with the doppleganger, the dweller at the threshold, the devil in the wilderness. It's here that the serpent lives, and we have to meet the serpent and look it in the eye. Our intuition will desert us at this final obstacle. This is the Ring of Matter, and to throw off this final shell of matter is to court annihilation. At a certain point grace intervenes and gives us a hand. We jump or slip through into the other world, and we shed our skin. We reenter the buddhic and atmic planes, these higher dimensions where clarity resides.

The 57th Gene Key contains the myth of the philosopher's stone. Our body, our DNA is encoded with that stone, that densest form of matter. Deeper in the heart of that density an infinite light lays trapped, and when we finally unlock the deepest layer of that light, a supernova occurs. We discover the Divine. We realise that we're a part of God, that God is in us and in everything. We see clearly for the first time. We're 're-conceived'. Once the bond with matter is severed at its root, the game is over. This is realisation. Clarity is all there is. There isn't intuition anymore. The pathway, the thread has gone. There's no path. We're there. We've realised that we're eternal, so all fear has left our system. From this new space of deep clarity, anything is possible. This Siddhi can do all kinds of things with matter. It can bend matter to its will, control matter, levitate it, even transform one thing into another. It's not that the 57th Gene Key will do any of these things; it probably won't. When we're in the field of clarity, there doesn't seem a great deal of point, unless God in us has a particular reason for doing so.

Every time a human being unlocks the secret of enlightenment, they discover the philosopher's stone. Each time it happens, the whole world is loosened somewhat. All matter is interconnected throughout the universe. Every planet, rock, life form is a part of the ocean of matter, Mater - the mother. When awareness penetrates to the heart of the matter, the Maya, then the whole fabric of reality is shaken. In time this is what will occur. The fabric of the material realm will dissolve and reveal its higher truth - the truth of our immortality. We will no longer die; we'll 'de-materialise'.

Clarity is then the softest and subtlest truth. A final puff of divine wind that pushes us over the edge of reason and into the pool of the great mystery. It's waiting inside each of us. It's a place - a secret glade hidden deep within the forest of our body, our DNA. It's why I keep going on about DNA. It's the higher purpose hidden within that last line of defence of the material realm - the final molecule where all our programming is unlocked, transmuted, and finally transcended.

The 58th Way

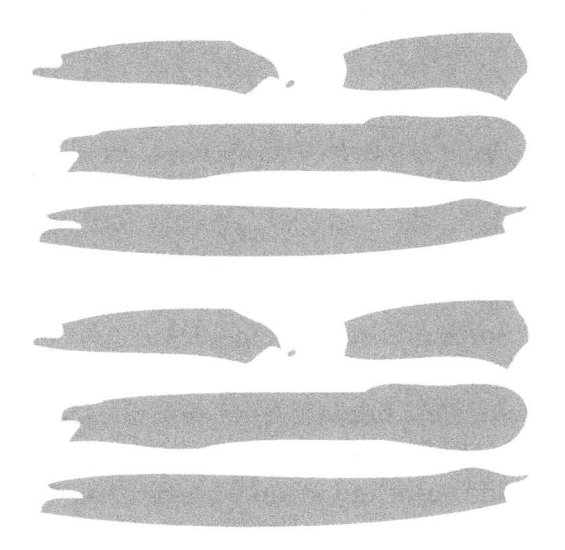

Gene Key 58

THE WAY OF VITALITY

The Transformational Way of the 58th Gene Key moves from Dissatisfaction to Bliss, and it's the Way of Vitality.

Of all the 64 Shadows, to me this is the most beautiful. That may sound like an unusual thing to say, and probably I ought not to have favourites. It's just my way of showing that even the Shadows have their wonders.

Why dissatisfaction? Because it's a propulsion and it draws us ever upwards. It unites all human beings, from the lowliest to the highest. Even the Master has had to move through intense dissatisfaction. Of course in its early stages this energy is not pleasant, whether we're its propagator or receiver. We'll have to go a long way to find a person who isn't dissatisfied in this era. I say this era because it was not always this way. We used to be satisfied, content, happy, peaceful beings, but something happened. What was it? What spoiled those early days of innocence and mellow fruitfulness? A Shadow crept into the garden. We all know the story, and a part of our consciousness mysteriously separated from its source. It became lost somewhere in the void of space and time. An ache began, an ache to return home, and all creatures participate in this ache. It unites all beings.

Look around yourself. Look at the lives of those closest to you. Do they appear satisfied? Really deeply satisfied? Is there anything inside us that feels complete - even the very smallest thing? Can we imagine a state of utter satisfaction? Of course we have had moments. We all have moments - precious, fleeting experiences when our frowns are wiped away by something beautiful, something numinous. Yes those precious moments. Our underlying state is that of incompleteness. Thus we all are seekers by degrees, and there are all manner of manifestations of seeking. This is the Codon Ring of Seeking, and the 52nd Shadow, the Programming Partner, is stress. Stress is a kind of seeking, as is

Shadow: Dissatisfaction　　**Gift:** Vitality　　**Programming Partner:** Gene Key 52
Dilemma: Rhythm　　**Siddhi:** Bliss　　**Codon Ring:** The Ring of Seeking

aggression, and hatred, if we can stretch our awareness to encompass those. Each Shadow state is an attempt to fill the vacuum left by the cosmic hole we feel inside. Seeking can be positive and creative, as we shall see in the Gift, or it can be negative and destructive. When seeking is unconscious, it's destructive. It's very far from beautiful. What is beautiful is the underlying Truth of its energy. The expression however can be horrendous. The 58th Shadow as a field in our world may well be responsible for some of the greatest atrocities and conflicts.

The Dilemma in this Gene Key is all about rhythm. There's a natural rhythm that unites all creatures and leads to joy and peace. When we're not in tune with that rhythm we feel disturbed inside. It's possible to fight against the rhythm and swim upstream against its current. In our frustration, anger, misery, numbness, we'll sometimes decide to do that. We may be bored, empty, lost, depressed, desperate, and so we do anything to get a reaction from life. The reaction usually causes more suffering to us and others. Strangely, at the Shadow frequency, the rhythm of life can be so bent and perverted that it may even give us a strange kind of black relief from the vacuum of dissatisfaction.

I started off I by saying how beautiful this Shadow can be, and now we can see the other side of its expression. It's important to understand how these things work because it helps us to accept the dark side and see it in a more compassionate light. Underneath every human behaviour is the same seed of dissatisfaction, and there's a beauty in that. We're one in that. We're all brothers and sisters on the same journey, and we all share the same ache. We have to learn to put ourselves in the right rhythm to our seeking. We need to learn the hard lesson over many lifetimes that seeking pleasure or relief on the outside can never remove the ache, the dissatisfaction that we feel in our souls.

The 58th Gift - Vitality

As awareness begins to arrive in our life, we see a gradual transformation occurring, the Transformational Way from Shadow to Gift. The Gift is revealed from within, through a series of insights and breakthroughs that come about as we meet life face to face. This takes courage; we have to let life cut us. We have to learn to bow to our suffering. The ancients named this Gene Key, this Hexagram - the Joyous. Yet, how can we have joy without sadness? Loss is a part of human life, and we all lose those we love. How we deal with loss is a deep, deep part of our learning within this Gene Key.

Loss actually contains vast reserves of vitality, and this is the Gift of Vitality. It all depends on the qualities of our soul and how much we've learned over the course of our lives. Everything is there for us to learn and grow and evolve from. Life as we know it has a deep melancholic flavour. Those we love leave us. Our hearts get attached and then broken, and we have to heal over and over again. Yet there is a deep undercurrent of tenderness at work in all of this. We don't remember our other lives because we're mostly still asleep in the drama. We think that lives and souls are extinguished, but life isn't all about loss. We never lose the things and people we love. It's a cliche to say that we carry them in our hearts, but it's true. Everything we touch and everyone we love becomes a part of us and increases our vitality.

All the people we've ever loved through all our lives will all be there in front of us when our heart one day opens absolutely. I mean this both metaphorically and literally. They're there because they're aspects of us and us of them, but we'll also see them reborn in the souls in front of us. The Gene Keys teaches us many things and one of the greatest things it reminds us is that loss is not what it seems. It's actually an opening to greater joy. The one who appears to have left is actually allowing us to feel more whole. That's the sole reason for their leaving. Yes there are other reasons rooted in universal laws, but essentially the whole game of seeking is about moving deeper into joyousness. It's the wound that makes us whole, the dissatisfaction that drives us towards the essential, and the essential is love.

When awareness arrives, it's as though the most beautiful dawn has come in our being. We become a cultivator of seeds, and we use the experiences of our life to bring more light into our heart. It takes time and lifetimes. Sometimes we will spend a whole lifetime just refining a single virtue. Awareness is like soft rain that falls upon our dissatisfaction, which then sprouts into creativity and service. This is the great secret of this Gene Key - service, to serve the whole and to serve others. To use that seeking energy, that precious fuel, and help others - not as a means to escape our own feelings - but as a means to feel human, to feel that we've a higher purpose, and that purpose is to improve the world in some way.

There's a great tradition in almost all religious cultures of service, of serving others less fortunate than ourselves. Why is that? It may have become a stale tradition or a mere custom, but originally it was an impulse from those who had raised their consciousness to great heights. As we refine our life force, our vitality, it becomes benevolence. It becomes a great swelling urge to help others. The more we give, the more our vitality grows. It's an open secret. You can try it out. Go on I dare you. Just do something different one day in the next week of your life - do something unexpectedly giving. See how this Gift of Vitality returns to you and you'll see right through into the heart of the great mystery.

The 58th Siddhi - Bliss

I used to have an expression with my wife, and I called it 'elevening'. We used to ask each other, 'how are you feeling on a scale of one to ten?' Every now and again I'd get a burst of the elevens, so I called it 'elevening'. I'd come in from a night walk with a certain expression on my face, and she'd say, 'you've been elevening' ! I say, 'used to', because I think that was before children came along - 'elevening' then takes a different form!

Let's discuss this word 'Bliss'. Are there levels of bliss? When and how does vitality become bliss? Is it something everyone feels automatically when they attain a very high state of consciousness? I think not. The beauty of the Gene Keys and these Siddhis is that they give us some kind of objective view of the enlightened consciousness. For some, bliss is undoubtedly an aspect of their expression, but not everyone. Also, is there a difference between Bliss and say Ecstasy or Rapture, two other Siddhis?

I don't want this to turn into a weird intellectual discussion of higher states, but I think the key point is to see the connection in each Gene Key between the word for the Shadow and the word for the Siddhi. This is the seed and the fruit. The fruit is there all along right from the beginning. That's when these slight variations of words begin to make sense, so with the 30th Gene Key, Desire contains the seed of Rapture, and here, Dissatisfaction contains Bliss. It's a subtle difference but I hope we can see the subtlety. In any case, let's consider Dissatisfaction becoming Bliss. Can we imagine this inside ourself? All our seeking one day detonates and comes to an end. Our self inquiry, our search becomes so internalised that it has no choice but to return to its own source.

This is our eventual ending. For most of us it may be something of a dream, but the beauty of these Siddhis is that we get to bring those dreams closer. Deity Yoga is an ancient form of spiritual practise. We imagine ourself into the siddhic state. We imagine ourself to be Krishna or Christ, and we walk in their footsteps. We bring the Siddhi into the form of our life.

If we happen to have this 58th Siddhi somewhere prominent in our Profile, like our Radiance or Purpose or Life's Work, then this one will really resonate with our intuition. If you've ever experienced a moment of bliss, you can use that as a seed and water its memory, flood your cells with the memory again and cultivate it until it becomes stronger.

This is a great, powerful and practical practise. This is as practical as the Siddhis get. I recommend it to anyone coming to the Gene Keys. It forms the foundation of my course on the 64 Siddhis - Dare to be Divine. We may enjoy doing some deep research into our preferred Deity, whether it's an abstract form or a personalised form. I mentioned for example, Ramana Maharshi in the text in the 58th Siddhi in the Gene Keys book. He was a man who often exhibited blissfulness, and he had his Life's Work as this 58th Gene Key. Ramana often lapsed into silent blissfulness, sometimes lasting months. There's also a story about his first experiences of bliss when he's sitting naked in a small temple, night after night, and the mosquitos are feasting on him, but his bliss is so great that he doesn't even notice.

It's these kinds of stories that help us prepare ourselves to begin to comprehend these higher divine states of consciousness. I recommend we do some research, either literally or imaginatively or both, into the state of bliss, so that we can begin to relate it to ourself.

We still have to go about our daily lives, but we can layer in this part of the experience. How can we move in bliss and still be able to communicate with others and be useful, be a human. It's all about weaving the state into our life. The moment there's a pause and our awareness turns inwards, the bliss is there, but then life, our responsibilities, others, anything, can draw us back out again into the outer senses. Then the bliss moves to the background as the awareness comes back out.

Seen in this way, the Siddhis can be much easier to integrate in the world. They never leave us. They're always the background state, but our awareness moves and breathes with the flow of life, and so the state becomes a stage. It doesn't leave us; it remains, and only awareness moves. This is what I meant earlier when I asked the question if there are levels of bliss. No, there's only bliss, but there are stages of being anchored in it, and we have to practise it and get used to its frequency. Our bodies have to acclimatise to its voltage, and as they do so, over time the Bliss becomes stabilised. This is why the 58th Siddhi is paired with the 52nd - Keeping Still Mountain, because the bliss has to become anchored in the world. Heaven must come to earth. The mountain must come to Mohammed. Bliss, true bliss, is utter stillness. It's unmoving, unflinching. It is eternal, as we are.

THE 59TH WAY

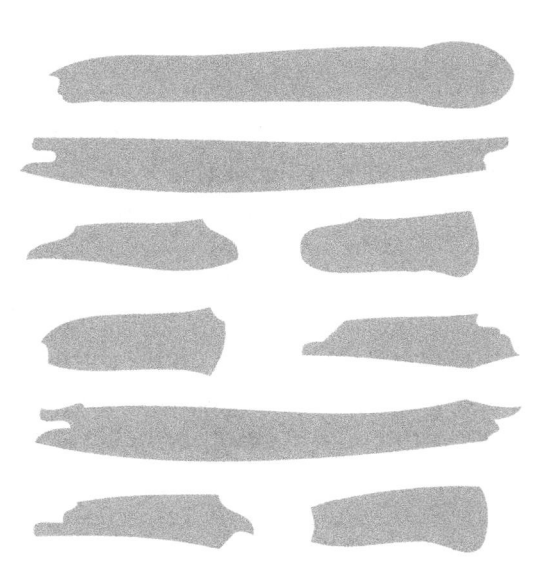

Gene Key 59

THE WAY OF INTIMACY

The Transformational Way of the 59th Gene Key moves from Dishonesty to Transparency, and it's the Path of Intimacy.

This 59th Gene Key is changing so rapidly inside us that it's dizzying. Even now as I speak these words, this is my third updated version of this Key. It is the only one that keeps calling for this…so let's hope that the third time is the charm…

The Shadow of this Gene Key is Dishonesty. 'Whenever a man tells a lie, he kills a part of the world'. Thus spoke the mythical Merlin. The 59th Gene Key is pretty unique. It concerns the ways in which we relate with one another, which is why it is all about dishonesty and intimacy. But dishonesty begins within us. How honest are you inwardly? We tell ourselves so many lies. We often justify our bad behaviour inwardly by projecting our blame onto others.

This shadow demands that we do some deep inner spring cleaning. And it isn't a comfortable process. The dilemma of this Shadow is Trauma. As we clean out our inner life and really look at our own vanity and our dishonesty in depth, we uncover layer upon layer of trauma stacked inside the cells of our body. Most human beings are not yet aware of the trauma they carry - because they are still looking for resolution or some form of escape in their outer lives.

When however you begin to turn within, this is the world that you find - a world of pain. I'm sorry to be so blunt about it. This is why it's a dilemma - because we know we must go in and yet we don't wish to, because of what we know we will find. Where does all this trauma come from? It is ancient. The ancients call it our sanskaras - wound slates from

Shadow: Dishonesty   **Gift**: Intimacy   **Programming Partner:** Gene Key 55
Dilemma: Trauma   **Siddhi**: Transparency   **Codon Ring:** The Ring of Union

---

past incarnations carried in our bloodlines. Every human being carries the wounding of the ancestors in our DNA. The DNA is the code of life, so it contains all the memories of our past experiences.

The depth of the trauma may seem overwhelming and relentless at times. But we have to keep turning inwards. Each time we face ourselves in this way, just by gently holding our awareness on the pain, we begin to transform that pain. Our dishonesty is any part of us that doesn't own our own trauma. It is a pattern of avoidance we play, like hide and seek, we run off into the world, or into a relationship, to try and find some relief, but the trauma follows us and finds us. Maybe we change our partner or we move to another country or we get caught in a relationship pattern that we blame on another - we will literally do anything sometimes so as not to own the trauma. It's understandable. We are human and we don't wish to feel this pain.

Sometimes it's really hard to look at oneself with utter honesty. We can even use our spiritual knowledge to put another down or make them wrong. Anything, absolutely anything inside us that smacks of negativity - it is part of our dishonesty. If we were to own the source of our projection, we wouldn't need to project anything negative onto anyone. We would see through unclouded eyes, with transparency.

Karma propagates itself. We enmesh ourselves in relationship tangles over and over again. Is there anything about any of your relationships that you don't accept? You don't have to like it, just don't get caught in projecting the blame. If this is in your life, it is because there is a contract between you, and you haven't paid off some ancient karmic debt here. How to pay it off? It's simple - be honest with yourself - go into the trauma inside.

You can try and resolve it externally - that is noble, but it won't work unless the transformation of the discomfort has been done inside you. When it has, you will no longer hold any negativity around that person's behaviour. I mean none whatsoever. However they treat you, or see you, you will no longer blame them in any way. You must do your inner work and then you will be free. Then you can see what happens to the relationship. You no longer need anything from the other person. Finally you have rooted out your own dishonesty.

You see how this works? All the trauma your body feels is yours to transmute, and a great deal of these patterns are collective karma. They aren't even ours. The more advanced our spiritual journey, the more we take on this deeper, collective trauma. But it's important to say that there is good news! Every time we transcend and transform one of these sanskaras, we feel an opening, a breakthrough of love in and around our heart. When we have felt the pain deeply enough and wrapped it in self-compassion, then it spontaneously lets go of us. It just does. And then we feel this beautiful upliftment, a spaciousness around our heart.

This is the process of the 59th Shadow and it is universal for all humans. The most important element to take away here is self-compassion. You must treat these wounds as you would treat a helpless, terrified child. Hold the child close. Soothe yourself. Support yourself with your own loving awareness. Call upon the loving awareness of some great saint or figure that touches you. Or ask for support from someone you love and trust. We each have to find our way to care for ourselves as we transform this trauma we all carry.

This is what dishonesty is, and I hope you may see it more clearly now. Dishonesty is when we forget that all the trauma we feel is ours to feel. It has been sent to us by God. It's an envelope of pain but when we open the envelope we find it contains love. A lot of the time we would rather just give the envelope to someone else rather than open it, but then they just give it back again. No one wants to open it!

So take heart, because now is the time of the great cleansing of the human wound. If you are listening to this, you are part of this cleansing. So take heart, find your inner courage and cease all projections. Own absolutely the trauma and the pain that is triggered inside you. Support yourself by all means in this process. Most of us do well with others to support us on this journey. And you will be amazed at where this is heading…

The 59th Gift - Intimacy

Right now in this epoch, even this decade, the 59th Gene Key is mutating. It is paired with the 55th Gene Key, which I recommend you take the time to read or listen to - the 55 gives us the backdrop of these times in which we live. It explains the nature of the Great Change, this transitionary period we are living through, in which humanity is moving through a huge deep genetic change. The 59th Gene Key is instrumental in this process. It is literally tearing us apart from the inside. It is dismantling us, shattering us, opening us up so that we can become an empty vessel for the new, for a new functioning, for a new human.

The 59th Gift is teaching us the true meaning of intimacy. What we currently think of as intimacy is nothing compared to what is coming. We are going to share awareness with each other. Can you even imagine that? The closest we can get to that is the feeling of falling in love, when we utterly give our heart to another and it feels like we are inside them. Even when we are far away from them, we still feel them. But it will be even more potent than this. I know this seems like a fairytale I'm telling. But this is the message and reason for the Gene Keys teachings - to prepare us for this change, so I have to share these things!

The Gift of Intimacy is the process of one heart opening up to the universal heart. All relationships on our planet right now are clearing houses for this collective trauma that we have seen in the Shadow. It all has to come up to the surface to be purged. And as it is purged, so our heart opens more and more widely. Relationships are the field through which humanity will make this great quantum leap into collective intelligence. For so long we have been driven by our desire nature - by our longing for union (this is the codon ring of union) with another. This is the romantic longing to merge with another in love - and of course it has never been able to fully deliver that dream.

This is also about sex. It's about moving from trauma to tantra. Tantra is the sublimation of sexual energy that leads to higher consciousness. But this doesn't mean you have to go and do a tantra workshop or anything - the tantra is in your life. Your destiny brings you exactly the ingredients you need right now.

Look at your relationships right now. They are exactly what you need. Is there any residual, untransformed energy anywhere? This is where your work is. Intimacy is actually a very internal experience, ironically. We become intimate with our own heart, and then we can be honest with another heart. We need to be really careful here because honesty needs to be balanced with kindness. Intimacy is a blend of honesty and kindness. We don't need to pour all our suffering out onto someone we love. Sometimes that is too much. And we don't need to share everything all the time. Sometimes our heart has to decide how much to share. So much of our transformation takes place in the silent chemistry field of the relationship itself. That is the tantra. We have to transform inwardly every piece of trauma that is triggered inside us. This doesn't mean we can't talk about it, of course we can, if that helps us to care for ourselves more. But also intimacy is about listening to the other, really listening deeply through our heart.

Intimacy is really the by-product of inner transformation. It isn't something we do. Intimacy is something that is revealed from within. As we become more intimate inside our own heart, so we let go of needing another person to change. That is the magical moment. That is when unconditional love comes into the game. When the other person feels that disinterested love from you, they are finally free to feel their own trauma. Even if they continue to project it onto you, it doesn't have to affect you. You will then no longer close your heart or be triggered by their projections. Only then can the true healing begin.

This is our inner work in intimacy - to get to a place where someone else's behaviour no longer triggers our heart to close. This is a lofty goal. But that is the process and it is attainable. This is the new spiritual way of relationships. If you are drawn to the Gene Keys, and this resonates with you, I highly recommend you do the Venus Sequence, Part 2 of the Golden Path. It offers an exact roadmap of your personal journey through the terrain of your wounding in relationships.

So this 59th Gene Key is taking us to the bottom of ourselves. Eventually we will have transformed all the trauma. We reach the bottom of the well, and then our heart truly opens, and when it does, it stays open, for ever and ever! The 59th Gene Key creates this interference inside our emotional body in order to empty us out. We are digesting our own past and using it as compost for a higher experience of union. So again, take heart. Your relationships are the path to higher consciousness. This is the way of love and it leads all the way to your heart's highest dreams.

The 59th Siddhi - Transparency

What then of the future human? If I describe it, it will seem like a fairytale. Nonetheless I must go there. The people of the world need a vision of what is coming. And I must say right at the beginning here, either everything about the Gene Keys is nonsense - it's all just the fantastical whimsical raving of a deluded soul, indulged in by other deluded souls, or it has truth deeply embedded in it. If the former, well, it was a nice ride, but if the latter, if there is truth here, then what I am about to tell you is the most true of it all. I feel it in every cell of my being. I would stake my life on it. I have already done so. I hope you too will feel its Truth and that it will become the deep target of your highest aspirations and dreams. All else will pour towards this great vision.

The 59th Siddhi is about sacred marriage. It is the dream of true love, of high romance. The 21st century will see this coming into the form. It won't be everywhere. In the beginning it will appear as do the first early flowers of spring, buds pushing up through the snow and ice of the past…and over time it will spread and flower until spring is truly here… the spring of the new human and the new earth.

However, we should be clear about what is coming, this is a whirlwind. It will uproot us, individually and collectively. There will be chaos as the trauma continues to come up to the surface. There will be huge upheavals and crisis. There must be. But within it all, these new shoots will emerge. There will be new children carrying this mutation in their DNA. You see, fear is nothing but a boundary membrane. We have to pass through it in order to reach the next plane of existence.

The sublimation of the astral body of humanity involves the gradual decline of the sexual urge in human beings. Thus the population will decrease steeply. When you experience dual enlightenment, the ecstatic union you feel is so far beyond anything one can imagine, that physical sex will likely become a thing of the past. Imagine two stars making love. There is no end to their lovemaking. It is infinite and fresh and never ending in its journey. One can never be parted from one's love. Even physical death will be transcended in this next phase of our evolution. Such relationships will endure from life to life, so even though incarnation may continue, the memory is no longer lost since there is no membrane anymore. The fear of death is gone. The love has evaporated it. On an even wider level, a vast individuality is forming that sees beyond incarnation itself. It is part of a much greater timeline that remembers all that came before - the great forgotten epochs of the past - and it also sees where we are going, yet time itself still remains, to a degree. Only in the final epoch will time itself dissolve, and that is still to come…but our next phase will be the penultimate epoch, the so-called 6th Race. A new human will dawn, with a faculty of awareness that travels outside the body and connects us to all other beings…

Into this next epoch the future human will step. It is the phase of enlightened activity and of embodied presence. We, humanity, are a super-cell. We will learn and remember this truth. This is the deepest kind of intimacy possible. All the old cliches are true. We are one world, one people, one heart. The hippies will be happy!

And this Transparency will clean us out, like a great cosmic broom. It will sweep us clean of the past. And we will not only come together as couples. We will also come together in other geometries - threes, fours and all manner of geometries. Our greater body is formed of countless kinds of sacred geometries. And the crystalline structure of our world light-body is mind-bending. You can have countless sacred marriages, all with different flavours and nuances. It is a shared orgy of ecstatic union, not in the physical body but at the subtle level. It's an orgy without sexual desire. We humans are truly the most orgasmic species in this cosmos. As we realise our higher nature, there will be periodic rushes and ripples of awakening that flush through the Whole - these are the orgasms and contractions of humanity's birth into higher and higher dimensions.

Those of you who are nervous about all this, you needn't be. You won't lose your sense of individuality. This is an ocean of drops. Every individual monad retains its creative uniqueness at the same time as being part of a greater union.

This is the meaning of Transparency. I told you it was 'out there'.

So what are we to do with this knowing? Well I hope it puts the trauma into perspective. With every piece of pain or trauma we process and transform, no matter how internal or private, we are clearing more space in the whole. We are opening it up for everyone. And the more we transform, the wider our heart opens and the easier it becomes. At the higher levels, our suffering actually begins to turn into bliss. So the underlying message of the 59th Gene Key is: breathe, be gentle, be compassionate and patient with yourself. See your tendency to project your own trauma as blame, and honestly own it. We are human. We are allowed to make mistakes. So constantly forgive yourself and move on. The whole process is moving so fast. The 59 is very fast and it takes no prisoners! It will deliver us to the other shore. And what a ride it will be!

The 60th Way

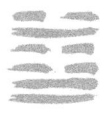

Gene Key 60

THE WAY OF REALISM

The Transformational Way of the 60th Gene Key moves from Limitation to Justice, and it's the Way of Realism.

The Gene Keys are a universal knowledge, a transmission, and they make good use of the laws contained within this Gene Key. Being a holographic knowledge the Gene Keys have connections to all systems, and since they are the codes of life, all our systems have come from them in one way or another. There are 21 groups or families of Keys within the Gene Keys, known as the Codon Rings. These have links to the mystical symbolism of the tarot with its 22 major archetypes (the twenty second is a mystery I will divulge another time). The 60th Gene Key belongs to a Codon Ring called the Ring of Gaia, which relates to the symbol of Justice in the Tarot - the scales.

This is the Dilemma of this Gene Key - it's about Balance, and it's all about maintaining the balance. Our planet Gaia is an expression of divine balance and like us, Gaia is a balancing act between structure and energy, between form and evolution. This 60th Gene Key is also one of the deepest transmissions of the Gene Keys. It's not easy to penetrate and understand and it may take some time when we come to contemplate it. The Shadow is Limitation. We hear that word and perhaps think, oh no, I don't want to be limited. But we are and always will be until we're dead, and even then, who knows!

Limitation is not the enemy; our attitude is the potential enemy. If we succumb to the forces of limitation, we'll find that we can't breathe, expand or evolve. There are forces in the universe bent on pulling us backwards, gravity being one. Perhaps we can begin to glimpse why this Gift is Realism. There's an upward force in our nature, a drive to extend, evolve, stretch, reach, and fly. But there's also a counter-force of constriction, limitation,

Shadow: Limitation **Gift**: Realism **Programming Partner:** Gene Key 56
Dilemma: Balance **Siddhi**: Justice **Codon Ring:** The Ring of Gaia

---

pessimism, resignation and tightness. We're caught between these forces, just as Gaia is caught within the net woven from the darkness of space and the light of the Sun.

We might be asking what does this Gene Key mean for us? Simply put, it means we must keep the balance. Too much Sun and we burn; too much darkness and we shrivel. The 60th Shadow really works through the mind, and the mind likes to builds structures. Think about science. Science uses structured thought to make breakthroughs that propel us forwards. That's an amazing service involving a perfect balance. But it's only a balance when the scientist extends his idea beyond the known. The greatest breakthroughs often come through the wildest thinkers. Science moves at its own steady pace, but reality isn't science. We have to open our mind up. Religion is the same - it's a structure that allows us to go beyond the structure. But most people don't get out of the structure.

The Gene Keys are a classic case, as they provide a structure through our Hologenetic Profile. If we get caught in that structure, worrying about what it all means, then we'll be stuck. The 60th Shadow knows the meaning of stuck more than any other. The structure is there to launch us beyond the structure, and that's the whole purpose of it. Our thinking gets us stuck, - the way we think about our partner, our enemy, our bank account, our government, our future. It all catches us in the net; we get caught by our minds. Language is the ultimate mental structure. Do we think a tree would still exist if it didn't have a name? Of course it would. The child doesn't know language. Language is beautiful but it gets us stuck.

The 60th Shadow is all about finding the balance. We can use the structures, but we mustn't fall victim to them. That's how we find freedom. The limitation is genetic. We inherit this ancestral cosmic wound, and it gets laid down in layers through our biology, our emotional life and finally becomes a great weed in our mind. The question is how to pull out the weed. Contemplation is the ultimate weeding and the first layer is always our mind. Look at the way your mind sees your life and really examine the ways your thinking limits you. That's why we contemplate all these Siddhis; because they show us our potential without the limitation. The 60th Shadow gets stuck by its own self-imposed limitations, but it's also about striking the right balance. We don't throw the baby out with the bathwater. Without the banks there's no river. We need the structures and we need to be free of them at the same time.

We must begin this work with the mind. As we begin to see that we're more than we allow ourselves to often believe, then that frequency, that vibration of possibility, begins to activate something inside us. It's communicated to our DNA and we begin to open. The next layer is our emotional patterns, our deep-seated issues of guilt or rejection or rage or whatever they are. Once we loosen the limited thinking of our mind, these feelings all come up and our contemplation enters a new phase. This is all the Venus Sequence work I'm describing. Behind that early emotional pain, those limiting emotional defence patterns, lies the prize - love. It's our dearest, truest nature. When love comes alive again in us, then finally we begin to crack open the final layer, the physical coding. We actually break the limitations within the DNA molecule itself. It opens, light pours through us, and that's when the Siddhis arrive.

This 60th Gene Key is a very deep journey, and we have to use structures and then transcend those structures. Eventually we have to let go of language itself. The 60th Shadow is well worth our time and attention. If we have it in our profile, our whole life is going to be influenced by this Shadow. We'll have to find the right balance between our expression, and the form we use for that expression, which is all very deep work.

The 60th Gift - Realism

If we want to get something done in life, we really need this 60th Gift. Realism is quite a loaded word and it can mean so many things. In this instance we need to think about it in terms of what we've just discussed. The Gift arises from looking at the Shadow in a new way, which allows a shift in our attitude. Limitation is no longer our enemy; now we use it for our evolution. I'm a good example. I have something to give to the world, which I hope is inspirational and useful, but how do I get it out there and structure it? Before the Gene Keys existed, it was all just swilling around inside me and it drove me nuts - all that juice and no structure. Along comes the Gene Keys, and suddenly I have a vehicle and it's wide enough to encompass my illuminations. Yet the system (if I can call it that) is a limitation, and I feel that all the time. Whenever someone asks me something about their birth time or profile, I feel the limitation. It's not about any of that; that's just the delivery mechanism. The thing is the wisdom - the living transmission, and that we get through contemplation and osmosis.

The Gift of Realism is about being able to take advantage of structures. It also has a twinkle in its eye, this Gift, because it knows that the structure is a means to an end. This is a rare Gift that holds the balance between the forms and structures of the world, and knows the mystery that moves through them - the evolutionary current. The Gift of Realism also may have a dark sense of humour because it sees the paradox of its position. It needs a structure, but knows that all structures are ultimately doomed! All roads lead to death! That is realism. Knowing this can free us from being caught up in the structure itself. The world is full of people wrestling within their self imposed structures; just look at the world economy. We created those structures, and now they've become so complicated they threaten our survival!

Life moves in cycles. Every now and then a transmutation occurs. Something comes along that shatters our vision of reality and the structures crumble and we have to begin again. It's like the decline of the Roman Empire. And one day this world we've built will decline and another will take its place. The Gift of Realism has a natural business sense, a common sense. They know how the world works. They build structures that mutate and don't become brittle, but also move if the earth moves and are open-ended and adaptable. The most successful businesses in the world are the ones that can adapt to change, take advantage of change and make a profit out of it. Change is built into life.

In the text of this Gift in my book, I describe this as similar to grafting a young shoot onto a powerful old rootstock. The 60th Gift realises the power of the past, of heredity and tradition. It incorporates and honours them but it isn't taken in by them. As we've seen repeatedly, this Gene Key is a balancing act - we need the old and the new. We need science and love, and this Gift of Realism unites them in a practical and imaginative way. For the 60th Gene Key, this whole notion of contemplation is vital. In a way it comes out of this Gene Key because we need a form to contemplate but there's a lot more to the form than its content. Our continued interaction with the form ignites a wild wisdom and this emerges in the gap between our intent and the form. It emerges spontaneously, surprisingly and brings with it great rewards.

Transformation always comes in the gaps. This is the teaching of the Gift of Realism; we plan for luck. We set up our easel, start a business, whatever the form may be, and go through the motions. We don't know when or how or what, but sooner or later a breakthrough will occur. We just have to begin, and it has to come from our heart. Sooner or later, because we're doing what we believe in and build a structure, fortune will find us. We're like a spider with our web, and we build the web in the right place and in the right way, and then we wait. Maybe we'll need to adjust the form or change the location until it feels right. Sometimes it takes time. It usually does, but magic is never far away. The trick is not to become a victim of our success; forms trap us all the time. We think we have to go on making more, but the Gift of Realism knows when to stand back and let go. Quite possibly that is its very highest gift of all.

The 60th Siddhi - Justice

I love contemplating these Gene Keys, they're so deep and endless. This one is like a fathomless well. What is Justice? That's such a profound contemplation. Sometimes when I'm thinking of these things an image comes to me, or a snippet of a book or film. With this one I'm thinking about Victor Hugo's epic novel 'Les Miserables'. Everyone has probably heard of this now, as it's also a famous musical. The story is timeless, and I think it contains a powerful meditation on justice. It's about a man called Jean Valjean, and he's imprisoned for stealing a loaf of bread to feed his family. He's a moral man and this was his one failing in life, an act of understandable desperation. His punishment is harsh; he spends nineteen years in the mines, and of course it seems so unjust. One day he's finally released, and he wanders the land trying to rebuild a life. Everywhere he goes he's treated as a criminal until one day a kind bishop takes him into his home, feeds him and looks after him. In the dead of night, Valjean commits the second crime of his life and makes away with the Bishop's silver. The next day he's caught by the police and brought before the bishop. To his surprise, the bishop tells the police that the silver was a gift and Valjean is freed. Here's the pivotal moment in the whole book - the bishop tells Valjean that he's bought his freedom for the price of living an honest life. And Valjean does go on to lead an exemplary life.

I like this story, because for me it epitomises the Siddhi of Justice. Justice is not retribution; it's a reward. It's given as grace, not taken as punishment, and when it's given, freedom flows from it. It isn't an imposition or a limitation. It's an invitation, an opening. One of the hardest things to do is be forgiven by someone we've wronged; it cracks us open. Unless we're in denial it forces us into a transformation. When someone else makes a selfless sacrifice on our behalf, it invokes the power of Justice - of divine balance.

Justice as a Siddhi carries these kinds of stories within it. If we carry the 60th Gene Key, such opportunities will come our way. It's not up to us to punish. Life redresses the balance, and it's always about balance. Our invitation is thus to let go. The Siddhi is always about the quantum leap from the personal dimension to the universal, so it's also about letting go. All the power and glory we've gained in the Gift, we surrender to the Siddhi. All roads lead to death, the great equaliser. We can see here how this Codon Ring links these themes, the 19th Siddhi is Sacrifice and the 61st is Sanctity. These are the three themes of this Codon, this genetic family. The 60th Siddhi holds an apt description of what happens when a human being becomes fully realised. At a certain point our hearts open to our true innocence and we begin to unlock other codes in our DNA that are ancestral rather than personal.

We begin to transmute more global karma, and the more our being opens, the more we're given. We may recall this Gene Key is part of the Ring of Gaia, and it holds the karma of Gaia. When we're ready for that, we get to be an agent of divine justice. We take on the sins of our fractal, our fractal being the ancestral lineage we're born into. All this is in the DNA, and all those acts that came out of fear down the ages are stored as sanskaras, memory imprints, in our DNA. Full realisation means we agree to transmute that on behalf of the whole.

This isn't a destiny that's for everyone! We have to surrender the balance of the Gift of Realism. Love requires that we let go even of that at a certain point in our evolution. It doesn't feel balanced at all to let go into this kind of process, but our love will carry us through. We've seen that language too must go towards the end. When language goes, thought also goes and we enter into the silence of justice. In that silence, all things are justified. All polarities are annihilated. We enter into the sanctity.

Yes there are unusual manifestations through this Siddhi. There have to be, as it's one of the miracle Siddhis. It doesn't come around often; it may only come around at great turning points in evolutionary history. I can envisage a time when this Siddhi will come into the world more frequently and precipitate major changes in the structure of life. We could also see it the other way, that as the structure of life transmutes, so this Siddhi comes into the world as a by-product. Either way, it'll bring big changes. The transmutation of world karma will always bring big changes. It will bring an end to certain limiting structures and redefine the meaning of realism.

I've always seen this Gene Key as intimately connected to gravity. Gravity is the ultimate physical limitation, but surely we're one day going to crack this one. Within the confines of gravity are locked massive amounts of free energy. Once we know how to use this energy the whole structure of civilisation will change and a new era will dawn. I know I'm sounding like a prophet, but assuming we don't blow ourselves up or get blasted by an asteroid, this is fairly certain to be our destiny. Free energy means free resources, which means less need for territory, which means more peace. Of course, the current laws of physics as they're understood will have to be smashed to allow for a new understanding. Then we're also into things like bending space and space travel, because we're no longer restricted by our understanding of the speed of light.

We can see how structures trap us, and even light seems limited in our eyes. The structures trap us until we're ready to smash our way out of them. Light is unlimited because it lies hidden within the formless. We can't conceive of that with our current understandings; we're weighed down by the gravity of our thinking. What we need is levity! Justice is always about the balance.

Levity is what happens when we drop our past, our karma and our heavy baggage, and we become weightless. It's funny how the word light also means light in weight. Justice is levity just as limitation is gravity. Light itself doesn't need to travel. One of my great heroes is a man named Walter Russell, a genius from the last century. I'm certain that one day his theories about light will be mainstream. He famously said, 'Light does not travel'. It's already there. Our current understandings are so far from this truth. Russell also said that the problem with scientists is that they assume from the beginning that consciousness is an effect, rather than a cause of the universe. One day justice will prevail, and he'll be shown to be right. How do I know? It's just a matter of balance.

THE 61ST WAY

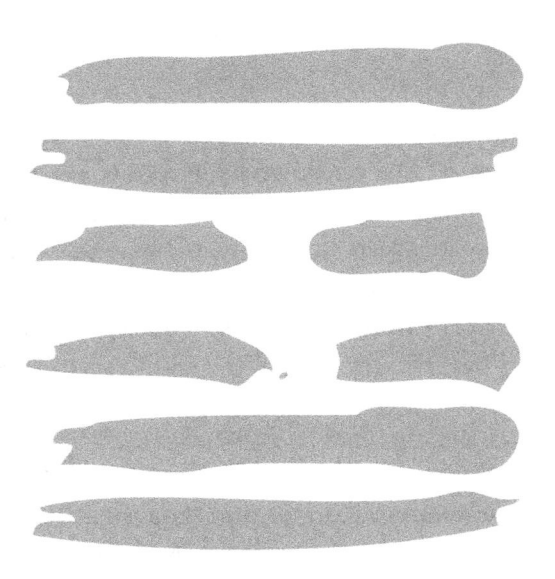

Gene Key 61

THE WAY OF INSPIRATION

The Transformational Way of the 61st Gene Key moves from Psychosis to Sanctity, and it's the Way of Inspiration.

OK so this is the one I am bound to land myself in trouble with. Let's just accept it - people aren't going to be happy when I label all humans psychotic. But you know, sometimes these people who use these words need to be taken on and challenged. It is assumed because they have knowledge that they know more than the rest of us. But there are truths that just need to be spoken even though it will cut those who claim to know. The Dilemma of this whole Shadow is Knowledge. Knowledge that we learn through the mind. Knowledge is always of the mind, and this Gene Key concerns the eventual transcendence of the mind.

For those who don't recognise the existence of a higher world, an invisible world, a divine world, for those who consider all states merely activations of neural pathways in the brain and central nervous system, this will not land easily. We're all psychotic. We are all psychotic in the sense that psychosis generally points towards a loss of touch with ordinary reality. That's why I say we're all psychotic because we're all out of touch with ordinary reality. We think that the world that our mind sees is the world. But the sages of all time testify that this is untrue and that there exist planes of reality that are far beyond what we generally refer to as 'normal'.

In India there has long been a tradition of revering madness, and people who were detached from ordinary reality were not seen as the 'village idiot', as became the way of the West. They were seen as touched by God and honoured for their view. The mad people always bore a resemblance to the wise, the ecstatics, the sadhus whose yoga put them in

Shadow: Psychosis	**Gift:** Inspiration	**Programming Partner:** Gene Key 62
Dilemma: Knowledge	**Siddhi:** Sanctity	**Codon Ring:** The Ring of Gaia

touch with other planes of being, giving them otherworldly behaviours. Such people were once revered. How far we have moved from the magical; magic is now seen as a backward step in evolution. When I use the term magic, I'm not talking about conjuring spirits but the ability to interface directly with the spirit of life, to feel the rush and whoosh of power coursing through your blood, and to know that your underlying being is emptiness.

Where does all that leave the psychotic, and what does it mean for those with the 61st Shadow? It means that there's a precarious balance to be struck. If we go too far from our waking reality and are unable to return and integrate the experience, we may be labelled an unstable psychotic by other psychotics. But if we don't even dare venture beyond the terrain of the mind, but stay couched in the false sanctity of the scientific, religious, or any other mindset, we'll be a stable psychotic.

Are you a stable psychotic? It's good to just be honest; we all probably are, and it's ok. That's where we must begin our journey and the Gene Keys invites us along a path that begins simply enough. However, as we venture deeper and the transmission of the wisdom bites more deeply into us, we'll find ourself transiting some pretty funky terrain. For example, the Seven Sacred Seals is a mystical part of this Synthesis. If we do those invocations for a few months things will get interesting for us, as other dimensions will begin to open up inside.

I certainly don't aim in this contemplation to belittle our scientific understanding of the mind, or the marvellous work done by those whose lives are given to helping people in mental distress. My point really is that mental distress has grown because of the world that our minds have created. Generally, when we look around, we aren't seeing a world created by the heart, but rather one by the mind. This is our civilisation, that has come about through greed, lust for power and fear of death. It's the world of the Shadow frequency, but imagine how different the world might be if we remembered what lay beyond death. We would quickly realise that we're accountable for our every act, thought, word and deed. There's no escaping justice. Justice is the 60th Siddhi, the Gene Key underlying this 61st Gene Key in the great sequence. It's also one of the three Gene Keys in this Codon Ring, the Ring of Gaia - the others being the 19th Siddhi of Sacrifice and this 61st Gene Key.

The most basic etymology of the word psychosis simply means 'a condition of the mind'. When we begin to move into states beyond the mind, we move into territory where the mainstream consciousness, the Shadow consciousness, doesn't venture.

It doesn't go there because science needs to retain its objectivity, and the domain beyond the mind is definitely subjective. Where it gets interesting is when the subjective experiences that lie beyond the mind's three dimensional thinking are reprocessed through scientific thinking. People like Terence McKenna, for example, came back from his inner voyages and then wrote a whole science of what he had experienced. The sciences of the beyond state are quite something, and the Gene Keys is one of these modalities. We'll look more at this when we come to the Gift and Siddhi.

Knowledge can be beautiful and filled with inspiration, but we should beware of it all the same. In the Kabbala, the mystical teachings of the Tree of Life, the Sphere of Knowledge is called 'Daath' or the abyss, and beyond the abyss lies the Sphere of Wisdom, Binah. The message is clear - that to find wisdom we have to give up knowledge. Wisdom is alive, vibrant, wild, spontaneous, illogical, paradoxical. Anyone can gain knowledge, but few become wise. If we're working with this Shadow, we need to look at our systems of thought, the thinking that we hold dear and everything we've learned. This is a journey of unlearning. The knowledge can be useful, beautiful, and take us right to the edge, but it can't take us over the gap, across the abyss of death.

So be gentle with yourself but crystal clear about your mind. It isn't the enemy, but it isn't here to protect you either. We tend to use it to make ourselves feel safer, but if we don't feel safe it's because we aren't accustomed to states beyond the mind. This is why the Gene Keys takes us there gradually, showing us how to open our heart softly and slowly, so that the higher frequencies can change us over time. I know many people who've sought the inner mysteries too intensely, impatiently and with too much fervour, and that's also dangerous. It can lead to chemical overload. Higher states are not the goal. Integration of the higher states is the goal, and that demands we be in the body, healthy and here, in the world, even as we explore what lies beyond this world.

THE 61ST GIFT - INSPIRATION

The secret to this Gene Key is creativity, and it's a beautiful secret. Who thought that the key to higher consciousness lay in creativity? Perhaps we thought it was in spiritual practise, austerities, meditation and prayer, and there's truth in that, but what lies forgotten and for the most part neglected in our modern world is the beauty and wonder - the healing power of creativity.

As I've mentioned before in my contemplations, I love green woodwork. Give me a knife or axe and a piece of freshly cut wood, and I'm in heaven. Generally I like to make eating utensils, such as spoons, bowls and the like, because they're useful and a lovely gift to give people. But I've discovered that when my mind is perturbed or confused, the moment I begin to create, it lets go and enters into a fallow state. It begins to empty out. After a while, all the dross has come out and only the essential remains, and I also have a beautiful spoon in my hands! All kinds of creativity does this - it soothes the mind, and especially music. Music is the greatest salve for a troubled soul - playing, listening or singing. Music allows the mind to find its natural geometry, its harmonic basis within the world. This is the Gift of Inspiration, of being 'in-spired', of listening to that which comes from within, from beyond the veil, and allowing that to re-imprint our awareness with its truth. The layers and frequencies of music all reach different centres within us. For example, Mozart softens the heart, Bach brings order to the mind and Rachmaninov stirs the body with ecstasy. Folk music brings us down to earth, rock music stirs the lower centres, and chants activate the higher centres; the frequencies are endless and exhilarating. There's a piece of music for every moment.

This is what inspiration is - playing with the music of creation. We can do it through dance, art, building, gardening, cooking, any aspect of human endeavour that has at its heart the attunement to a higher harmonic principle. To be inspired means to be filled with breath, with life - spiro from the Latin 'I breathe'. This is the secret to how we can break out of our psychosis, our 'stuckness', our head-trip. We have to experience what it feels like to be God, and so we have to learn to be a creator. In life always try and remember this - if we're feeling down, disturbed, if our mind is pursuing us, we can take up a guitar, a trowel, a pencil, let the feeling emerge and let our soul express its longing.

When I was travelling in Canada a few years ago, I stayed in a beautiful house in the woods. A kind patron and friend of the Gene Keys opened up his home for me to stay for a few days. The house was right in the woods, but out the back he had built this beautiful garden with walkways and temples and seats and ponds and dragonflies right into the landscape. It was beautiful, clearly a labour of love. As I sat with him one evening, he shared the story of how the garden came to be. His beloved wife had died of cancer, and distraught with grief and loneliness, he took up his tools and began this work. He had never given the garden much attention before, but now every day, he rose at dawn and poured his grief into his work. The result was, a year or so later, a beautiful, exquisite garden, a clear mind and heart, and a testament to his beloved. That's the alchemical power of the 61st Gift.

The 61st Gene Key is a key of secrets. We'll see its specialness in the Siddhi, and it's always connected deeply to the theme of death. If we have this Gene Key, our life is a contemplation of death. We mustn't turn away from this work, and it will fill us with life. The answers will come and the memory of the beyond will return in time. We must listen inwardly for the music of life and let it move us in creative work. Being born in a body is to be born wounded. Inspiration is a way of healing this wound, and as we learn to heal it inside ourself so we'll heal it within others. They'll be drawn to us and our work; they'll be drawn to our music.

I have one final thing to say about the 61st Gift - it's all human. It's about the meaning of the word human. I would like to say that the word human really derives from a silent word whose meaning is 'to let go of'. I have however made that up. But letting go is our great theme. It is our sadness, our joy and the source of our depth. There is great grief within humans, in our ancestry, in our forgetting. We are a sacrifice, and no matter how much we run from it, our lives are a sacrifice for the sake of the whole, for the sake of Gaia. This is the delicate fabric of the Ring of Gaia - that we are here to heal our hearts, and to give our breath, our inspiration, for the sake of this beautiful planet.

The 61st Siddhi - Sanctity

This is the Siddhi of Sanctity. How do we approach that which is holy? Some teachers tell us that nothing is sacred or holy, that nothing can stand out from the whole and be glorified above anything else. The non dualists speak this truth, but it's simply one language of truth, and there are other languages. The 61st Gene Key seeks the holy, and looks for the sacred by creating it. Sanctity is another subtle Siddhi. If we look at the chop of this hexagram and its shape, we can see something hidden inside. It's even named 'Inner Truth' in the original I Ching.

The mirror of psychosis is called kenosis, a wonderful wordplay. Kenosis is the emptying out of one's own will in order that the Divine can occupy us. It's remarkable that little is made of this by Christians, because the term derives from a Greek word in the Bible referring to Jesus. He emptied himself out. It's remarkably similar to the Buddhist notion of shunyata, also meaning emptiness. I'm deeply drawn to the word because it's about becoming empty in order that one can be filled with God, with the Divine. In psychosis our mind is also occupied, but with the spirits and nebulae of the Shadow frequency realm.

If we empty ourself out but our temple is not clean we attract disturbed energies. Only if we've cleaned the inner temple can the higher emanations enter in, as even the smallest speck of fear will keep the Divine from entering. It's like the idea of the unicorn, who won't touch anything impure, and if it does, it'll die. If we wish to invite a unicorn into our stable, we can't leave even a speck of dust in there.

GENE KEY 61

To court the Divine is to empty oneself out. You must supplicate yourself before life. You can't hide any part of your soul or your past. We're not here to judge ourself, but to simply see ourself for what we are. Only then can we come cleanly before the altar. The 61st Siddhi uses this kind of inner language; it learns humility and must bow in sacrifice. It understands Divine Justice and knows it must become impeccable if it's to know its highest emanation. The Divine, the higher subtle bodies spoken of in the 22nd Gene Key, have never left us. They can't express themselves through our denser layers, and we have to polish ourselves a great deal so they can.

This 61st Siddhi is a path of prayer, of supplication, of worship. Through its creative living, its inspiration - it remembers the higher world, as flashes, as fragments. You will experience brief moments of celestial transport. And you will then fall again and begin your work again. But the work of being human gives you these glimpses, and the glimpses keep on leading you, encouraging you to go on climbing, to go on emptying yourself out. In this work, lifetimes do not matter. Your love of the pure, of the high places and your memory of the music you have heard, of the voice of God, will all keep leading you. This is a beautiful path to God.

God is also in the geometry. The mental plane is confused and embroiled with the emotional plane at the Shadow level, and the geometry of these planes is chaotic. Each plane of being has a living geometry. When the perfect geometry of the higher planes descends, even for a moment, it instantaneously aligns the geometry of all the lower subtle bodies, like iron filings following a magnet. This is how Christ performed his miracles; that higher geometry worked through his aura on all those present in his field. Many psychotics came to him, people disturbed by so-called demons. When they say that he cast out the demons, it means that the living perfect geometry of truth realigned all those subtle layers, so that those minds were instantly re-ordered.

The mind is not what we think it is, and it exists on its own plane of being, the mental plane. That plane attracts and repels thought forms. The purer the thought form, the more perfect its geometry in your aura, and the less pure the thought form, the more disturbing its geometry is. Our thoughts thus arrange themselves around these forms, and it's all really musical. The music of selfishness is catastrophic in our aura. The music of sanctity is so refined and pure that it can't be missed. The aura of sanctity is a rare phenomenon. If we're able to really attune deeply to a higher being, like Christ or Buddha, or any other pure one, alive now or from the past, we'll pick up the aura of holiness. It's unmistakeable and will change us forever. It's also interesting that many with this Gene Key will live lives of irreverence - the exact opposite of the holy life, and they may even take pride in debunking that which is sacred. But the holy life is not the perfect life.

It begins with inspiration, then it becomes a life of higher striving and finally it becomes the life of self-emptying, in which all that we have learned is released. Death is coming to us all and the 61st Siddhi has to know what that means, not out of fear but out of utter conviction. Once we've sipped the Divine, even for a moment, we can think of nothing else. It takes courage to follow such a path. It's a lonely, but lovely path. Here in the words of the wonderful Chinese poet known as Cold Mountain, named after the mountain where he lived and roamed wild, he encapsulates the searing beauty of kenosis - the art of emptying:

> *I delight in the everyday Way, myself*
> *among mist and vine, rock and cave,*
> *wildlands feeling so boundlessly free,*
> *white clouds companions in idleness.*
>
> *Roads don't reach this human realm.*
> *You only climb this high in no-mind:*
> *I sit here on open rock: a lone night,*
> *A full moon drifting up Cold Mountain*

THE 62ND WAY

Gene Key 62

THE WAY OF PRECISION

The Transformational Way of the 62nd Gene Key moves from Intellect to Impeccability, and it's the Way of Precision.

Quite a few people have been rather shocked to find that one of the Shadows in the Gene Keys is the Shadow of Intellect. It reminds us I think that the Shadows aren't in and of themselves bad; they're just starting places for transformation. The reason that intellect is a Shadow is quite simply because it's rooted in dualism. Duality is such a paradox, not to itself, but to truth. To itself, dualism is all there is, so intellect only sees life in terms of opposites, black and white, right and wrong. Our world is fabricated out of that and we don't really realise it because we're so immersed in it. We grew up with it and it's everywhere, in the structure of our societies, our language patterns, our emotional bodies, in the very way our perception operates.

But it isn't all there is; there are other modes of perception. The world of intellect is a construct and it's what the ancients called the Maya. It's interesting to think about the ancients here, because it appears that the construct of maya hasn't always been as rigid as it is today. There's this persistent intuition in humanity that somewhere, somehow, a long, long time ago we saw things differently, and that there was a kind of Golden Age before our modern thinkers came along. We've inherited fragments of this distant epoch through the ancient texts, the Vedas, the Emerald tablets of the Hermetic corpus, the Orphic tradition, the wisdom of the Cabbalists, the Druids and of course the shamanic elders, some of whom still embody the old wisdom even today.

When we try and look through the eyes of those ancients, it doesn't quite work anymore. How can we look back through the eyes of an earlier evolution?

Shadow: Intellect   **Gift**: Precision   **Programming Partner:** Gene Key 61
Dilemma: Facts   **Siddhi:** Impeccability   **Codon Ring:** The Ring of No Return

---

We can try, but it doesn't quite work since the brain has moved on.

The 62nd Gene Key is special because it has the capacity to see beyond the maya by going through the maya. This is the Path of Jnana Yoga, or what the ancients called Gnosis, to use the mind to go beyond the mind. First of all we need to understand the backdrop, where we've come from, where we are now and where we're going. I can feel this contemplation wanting a bit more detail and a deeper exploration, so that's what I'm going to give it.

Intellect is based upon a single foundation; Number, the basis of the cosmos. I'm not talking about number in the way we see it today, but the way the ancients understood number. Number is the connective tissue that allows the mind to see the true nature of everything. Number today is associated with fact, and we'll get to that in a moment. I want to help us understand what number meant to the ancient world, the world before the intellect took over. Number is the means to see correspondences, and the key to seeing the connectivity of the Holographic Universe. When we hear that ancient statement 'as above, so below', that's the core foundation of the ancient worldview. The means to see it was number, and this is why the ancients used astrology and anthropomorphised their world, because everything corresponds to everything else.

All the old systems are based on codes - the 22 of the Kabbala, the 12 of astrology, the 64 of the I Ching. Everyone used number in order to create the correspondences. Number had quality rather than quantity. Number was spiritual and it became the connecting rod that allowed us to enter into courtship with the Divine. Number was our yoga, nothing like it is now. It was magical, and the way in which we identified with number shaped the way our brains worked. We lived in a more merged existence, because everything meant something.

It's why in all the old stories number is so important, so prevalent, but the modern mind just thinks it's obscure.

I was recently in the Hebridean islands, and I visited the standing stones of Callanish, a truly amazing place. Such places baffle the modern scientific mind. When we read the modern descriptions of such places, it's a non magical mind projecting onto a magical mind. We can hardly imagine this. The brain was different, at an earlier stage of evolution and more merged. There's no way we can understand the minds that built those ancient temples with our intellect. Now number is all about measurement and has become time. After the birth of Christ, more or less, we began using number to create time and therefore history. In the ancient world however, time wasn't numbered. It's hard for us to imagine that now. The people that erected those stones did it for a reason, because stone is a witness to the passing of time. They wanted to have a witness to their passing generations and a way of remembering and ensuring they were remembered, at least energetically by future generations. Now we no longer live in that timeless dimension. Our brains have learned a new way of using number.

I blame Socrates, no, not really; he was a wonderful thinker. He was however one of the earliest examples of the direction the brain took, as it evolved into a dualistic mechanism. Everything became about the dialectic, about identification, opposites, reason and conflict. We went through a process of un-merging. We differentiated, and a new logic was born; intellect and fact were born, and here lies the 62nd Shadow.

When we take the magic away from number, it becomes as rigid as fact. And to build a world out of facts is to build a hall of mirrors, a false reality. This is the modern world. Facts are the Dilemma of this Gene Key and its Shadow, but what are facts? We know that a scientist can prove virtually anything with enough data, regardless of whether it's true or not. As Nietzsche famously said: 'There are no facts, there's only interpretation'. So today's facts are the future's fables - a very quotable sentence, and true. Facts give us the illusion of order, balance and harmony but if we build our life around them, we're building our home on shaky ground. We want to be careful if we have this Shadow; our worldview is very likely built upon sand.

One of the related Shadow Gene Keys here is Arrogance, through the Codon Ring that connects the 62nd Gene Key with the 31st Gene Key - the Ring of No Return, a name I love. There's an arrogance in believing in facts, where we think we've solved something and used number to empirically prove it. But that something can't be proven as truth. Fact and truth aren't even of the same dimension. What I'm saying is that facts shouldn't be trusted. Look at the facts that we assume are real, the propaganda we've swallowed. That's what working with this Shadow is all about. It's all about uprooting our opinions. In Human Design, the 17th Gene Key and its Shadow of Opinion is at the other end of this 62nd Gene Key. Facts may drive us towards truth, but they can't be regarded as truth, or even as truisms. Some of the most important facts that hold up our worldview today may turn out to be absolutely false one day in the future; they're bound to. Arrogance is intellectual certainty, whereas humility comes through cellular certainty, and the only cellular certainty is love.

I'm explaining this in the hope that some small aspect of it we will break through in our minds to demonstrate how utterly intellect has us in its thrall. We've been hoodwinked, and the intellect has become so influential, so useful. The intellect has advanced us so far, giving us all our technology and efficiency. It's helped an awful lot of people move from poverty to prosperity, but it's only helped in one dimension - the external. It's not helped us internally. In fact it's made everything worse on the inside. If we look at all the Shadows of the 64 Gene Keys, we'll see what intellect is really made up of - confusion, agitation, doubt, expectation, chaos, and the 61st Programming Partner of Psychosis. That's what we've become - we've become mildly psychotic - we are split, we are no longer one, and have become two.

How does this relate to us, we might say? I know it all sounds rather philosophical. That's the modern mind and it has us utterly trapped and cornered. We have no idea how to overcome our inner difficulties and we can't go back to how we were. The ancient world and its systems can't help us anymore, not the way they used to, because the brain itself has changed. How do we break the psychosis and get out of the Maya?

GENE KEY 62

The 62nd Gift - Precision

When we're in duality, we can't go back to one. We can't turn back the clocks to timelessness and return to that archaic Golden Age. This is the Ring of No Return. There's no going back. We can only go forwards, and forwards from two leads to three. In the first aeon, the archaic aeon, we were submerged in oneness, in the second, we fell and divided and gave birth to the historical aeon, the aeon of measurement, the aeon of two. We return to unity, to one, by moving forwards into three, trinity.

If you have this 62nd Gene Key or are exploring it through contemplation, look at your life. You may well have an obsession with details, and you may well be the victim of life's endless details and trivia and plans. Look at how your days are numbered. And there's no pun intended here. Your life follows the dictates of numbers and facts, times and dates, lists and accounts, progressions and sequences. Your bank account, the amount of time you spend on this and on that, your cell phone, your computer; all based on numbers. The opinions you have formed as a child, the ideology you have imbibed through your language and syntax, your culture, your political stance, even your health is measured. Everything is held together within this structure we have created. It's extremely hard to step out of the Maya. How do we step out? That's the conundrum and the challenge of the Gift. The first thing we have to do is see the depth of the illusion that surrounds us. The next thing to do is to go on seeing it, in everything, everywhere. This is the value of contemplation. Contemplation begins with the mind. We must see the numbers behind everything, the ordering principles, the laws.

As we see them we'll feel an acceptance slowly rising in us. There's order and perfection in the cosmos. It's also disturbing because we're in a deeply transitionary period between the aeons, a gap between the epochs. We live during the time of the Great Change, and to see the Maya is to step through it and out the other side. We'll become aware of something profound as we keep contemplating this Gene Key - that there are two harmonies, a false and a real one. The false one is the world we've created over the real one. The real one is nature; the rhythms of the seasons, the passage of the stars, the ebb and eddy of the waters and tides, the great rhythms. Then there's our false harmony held together with sellotape. A couple of intense sunspots or a meteorite and it's all gone - no more supermarkets, internet or amazon deliveries to our door.

I'm not saying that's going to happen, but I am saying that the days of our modern society are numbered. A fundamental change is coming to humanity and it's coming from inside us. It may have its reflection on the outside, but it'll change the way our brains operate. Our DNA is mutating, and we're moving from the dualistic life to the trinary life. In three we arrive back at one, but it's not the same one; it's enriched by the journey through two.

The Gift of Precision is not nearly as boring as it sounds. It's about the precision of awareness, the ability to see which patterns are in resonance with truth and which ones are false, paper tigers. Part of this Gift's purpose is to pinpoint that which is false, but the other part is to organise information and structures and people, so that they're in right relationship to the higher harmony. This Gift always involves love. Love is the only way we can dismantle the Maya - the construct of the intellect. And I don't mean yearning love or needing love. I mean Love - unconditional love - love rooted in service of the whole; what the religious people have always called 'the love of God'.

In the old world, every number could be related to a plant, stone or place and it showed us where we were in the space time continuum. The art and science of alchemy, which is the art of using the qualities in the numbers in certain combinations to bring about transformation, shows us that it's us that's transformed. Number and language is the route forwards to paradise. Hermes, as a god of numbers, was also god of magick for a reason. So the Gift of Precision is about aligning our life correctly with the sacred principles. It's about awakening Love.

So we began with archaic number, which was only about quality, and we moved to historical number, which is only about quantity. Now we come to a new age, in which we arrive at unified number, combining quality and quantity and transcending them both. In addition, Unity brings an end to history, which we'll explore more when we come to the Siddhi.

I want to keep making this simple - embrace the Shadow, release the Gift, embody the Siddhi - is what I'm describing in the context of the whole. The 62nd Gene Key sees the entire holographic cosmos. Everything is connected to everything else in perfect harmony. Every experience is perfect, including the timing of our awakening. Precision is everywhere, and the more we start seeing it and imbibing it the more we relax and come into deeper harmony. And this coming into harmony will put us through a few initiations, and they often feel far from harmonious. Stepping out of the Maya is like leaving the earth's orbit, and we have to build up a certain escape velocity to punch through its veil.

The Gene Keys are not facts; they're wormholes that open into love. They're stitches in the holographic fabric of time and space and our awareness can travel along them. This is a magical system, because we live in a magical universe. We can read the book, and then forget what we've read. We won't be tested; this isn't that kind of a world anymore. The Gene Keys will teach us how to use the number to transcend the number. They teach us how to use a language in order to transcend it, and they teach us from the inside. All we have to do is keep contemplating.

It's all about thoughts. Energy follows thought is an ancient axiom. When we change our thoughts, we change our attractor field and our frequency. The Gene Keys represent the language of light, and they elevate our mind up into the causal plane, the dimension beyond the mental plane. At the causal level, numbers exist as pure principles, divine archetypes, and as these archetypes come into our mind they open our mind and heart. It's a precision technology this new language, and we have to learn it as we would learn any new language. The old worldview is deeply flawed and made up of half truths, opposites and opinions. There's not real order, only a false order that keeps our heart and mind closed.

A while ago I coined a new term for this kind of thinking through the 62nd Gift - 'synthinking' - the ability to think across multiple dimensions simultaneously with our heart, the ability to allow a higher archetype - a Gene Key - to descend into our body and illuminate us from within. It takes contemplation and surrender and precision. These new ways and language of seeing the world give us a ladder for our thoughts to become more and more rarified. They then begin to merge with the field of light itself, our thoughts become ecstatic and our words carry fire inside them.

The Gift of Precision is a new kind of precision. It's not a masculine precision, which is how we usually understand this word. This is the precision of the feminine, like how a woman has her own timing, and the men hearing this will know exactly what I mean! The feminine keeps us waiting sometimes because her body is more deeply attuned to the celestial rhythms than the male. I'm talking about poles, and there's a male timing and a female timing. The female version of precision is not about exactness - it's about harmony. Information is more swiftly and efficiently organised through intuition than through any other means. The digital revolution certainly looks impressive in its ability to create order, but it can't track harmony because harmony sometimes has to move through disorder.

The Gift of Precision knows how to move with equanimity through periods of order and disorder. This is our Gift, to navigate these big changes with absolute precision, mentally, emotionally and physically. How we move through transformation with precision and grace, and to inspire others to do the same - that's our Gift if we have the 62nd Gene Key.

The 62nd Siddhi - Impeccability

Finally we come to the Siddhi where everything becomes simple once again. This is the logic of unity, the language of light embodied as Impeccability.

It's always been intriguing to me that the higher we go up the ladder of frequencies, the fewer words become available to us. The tendency is to use those words in paradoxical or poetic combinations, because the words are continually dissolving back into the silence of the unity.

We might have grasped that this Gene Key has a lot to do with words and numbers and Truth, and it's next in the sequence to the 63rd Gene Key of Truth. This is when fact is utterly superseded by Truth. At the Shadow frequency, fact has all the influence, but at the siddhic frequency only Truth has influence, and when Truth is expressed through our physicality it becomes impeccability.

What is this impeccability and what is truth? It's pure authentic presence. It's a single emotion, fully embodied, fully owned. It needn't even be expressed externally. This is what has influence - utter authenticity and utter humanity. Here's a thought for you: there have been so many paintings, writings, pieces of great art and music that have been lost, that never saw the light of day. There have been great masterpieces never seen by anyone but their author.

Perhaps they were destroyed or lost of burned. Think about that - music as beautiful as a Mozart Requiem, art as fine as a Rembrandt, literature as perfect as a Shakespeare or Dostoevsky.... The art itself has no influence, but the act of creating the art as it occurred is what has influence. The art as it came into the present moment is the only influential thing at the Siddhi level. It's never the result, but always the moment. In eternity, no moment of truth is ever lost. It remains always, and it alone survives. A moment of pure awareness is more precious than anything we could ever create.

Those moments are what remain when we die, etched forever in the fabric of our causal body - the best of us, the purity of our hearts, our impeccable moments. An impeccable moment doesn't have to be perfect, in fact if we're thinking of impeccability in that way, we need to let it go. This is a Siddhi, a paradox. Begone intellectual thinking. You cannot enter here. Facts have no meaning here. Words have no meaning. Only the presence behind the words has meaning. This is embodied truth.

The logic of unity brings an end to history, and we enter a new epoch and a new kind of human stands at the door. It's a timeless dimension but one that is also mentally, emotionally, and physically integrated. It's the three in one, the great mystery of the trinity, which I call the Trivian Race - the new human. In the times ahead, we'll let go of history and stop recording it because we'll stop noticing it. It may remain in the records for our interest and inspiration, but we won't keep time anymore. Number in its purest form brings utter synthesis to our lives. We're no longer the movers but the moved. We're no longer the choosers but the chosen. We're no longer divided but whole.

In Japan, there's a certain philosophy that pervades the arts and crafts movement, and in pottery it's called Kintsugi, which means literally 'golden repair'. It's the art of fixing broken pottery with powdered gold or silver. And once it's been repaired in this way, the broken pot actually becomes far more precious than a pristine new one. These pots are so beautiful. The thinking behind this is that every object has a history, and that history is part of its beauty and depth, so why discard something if it can be repaired and made even more beautiful?

We so often try and disguise our wounds and throw away our broken objects. Yet there's a deeper beauty to our wounding than anything because it's part of our authenticity. It can be embraced entirely within us and remain a part of our beauty. When we suck in the golden light from the higher planes and let it remould us, we become even more exquisite. We become imperfectly perfect. We become impeccable.

I'd like to close this extraordinary contemplation by leaving you with one final right brain image. One of the approaches into the Gene Keys is called the Dream Arc, which equates every Gene Key with its corresponding totem animal, bird or underworld creature. It's a shamanic way into the Gene Keys, and the bird of the 62nd Siddhi is the woodpecker. The woodpecker (who likes to pun with the word 'impeccability' by the way) signifies the eternal drumbeat of truth and sees value everywhere, particularly in old dead trees where he draws sustenance and makes his home. Think about the deadwood in your inner life. The parts of yourself you have been trying to escape, the aspects of your past you are running from. Open your heart to your full self. There is great beauty in your mistakes. Breathe new life into your inner being. Gently fill the cracks with the golden light of compassion and self-forgiveness. You are beautiful. Your life is impeccable. Be yourself absolutely, utterly.

Think of the little woodpecker and his bright, proud red throat. Open your heart and serve life, serve others. Remember, the only real influence in the universe is your presence as yourself, inside yourself, in every waking golden moment.

The 63rd Way

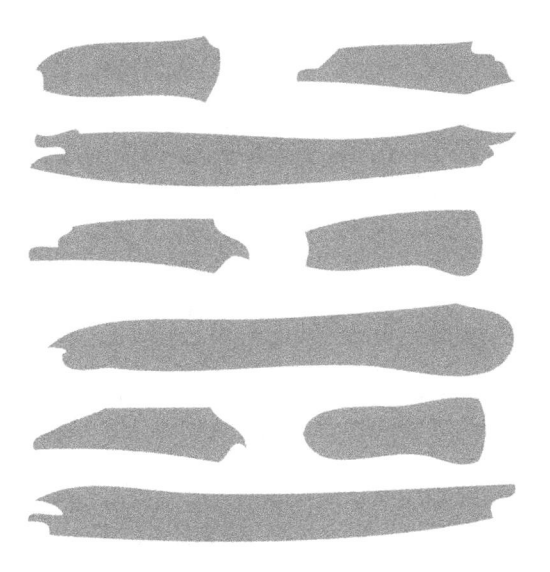

Gene Key 63

THE WAY OF INQUIRY

The Transformational Way of the 63rd Gene Key moves from Doubt to Truth, and it's the Way of Inquiry.

The 63rd Gene Key really holds some secrets. In the original I Ching, they gave it the mysterious name, After Completion. Its mystery is compounded further because it's paired with the 64th Gene Key, Before Completion. So we have the 63 - After Completion and the 64 - Before Completion, and of course the 64 is the final Gene Key, the final hexagram of the I Ching. There's a magic to the sequence of the 64 Gene Keys, and that the penultimate Gene Key is Truth, I find amusing. It would be much neater if the 64th was Truth; that would make such a tidy finale!

Yet here we see the universe at work, and it isn't all linear and it doesn't all fit neatly in a box, nor can it all be explained through logic. At its heart, life must always remain a mystery. And it's not a mystery to be solved, but a mystery to be lived. This is uncomfortable for the mind. This whole Gene Key is nothing but uncomfortable for the mind. The mind is amazing; it's such a beautiful instrument and is capable of perceiving and arranging an extraordinary range of frequencies, from number to colour and from concept to shape to pattern. The 63rd Gene Key specialises in patterns and loves nice neat shapes and geometries, perfect, sequential, logical, organisable data streams, giving meaning and purpose to our lives. It's about logical systems of thought, and that's the very Dilemma of this Gene Key, the logical mind itself.

The 63rd Shadow is what drives all this need for organised thinking. It is the Shadow of Doubt. It's the source of logic itself. Every scientific insight (I won't call them truths, because they aren't) has emerged out of someone's doubt. Science is born out of our mind's need to have an answer, and yet even when it has an answer and that answer appears to be proven as true, our mind still can't rest. The answer isn't complete; no logical answer

Shadow: Doubt **Gift:** Inquiry **Programming Partner:** Gene Key 64
Dilemma: Logic **Siddhi:** Truth **Codon Ring:** The Ring of Divinity

can be complete. Truth can only come after our mind has done its business; Truth can only come After Completion.

The 63rd Shadow gives us humans a really hard time. It's the left brain, and because of its nature it's deeply suspicious of its counterpart, the right brain! Isn't it funny that we're born divided. This is especially true for the male mind (and I don't mean men and women, but the male mind, which has to have an answer to its doubt). The left brain is suspicious of the right brain, and the right brain looks at the left brain as though its kind of….. Well, it's how women sometimes look at men, as though they're actually a bit stupid with all their theories and questions and their searching. At the Shadow frequency, we're always divided. Yin serves yang instead of the other way around, the natural way. Yin sees the big picture; the right brain is holistic. And Yang sees the parts, the details and how to take it all apart. One unifies and the other divides. It's like that joke about the perfect world ….

This is all about brain chemistry. It's about maintaining equilibrium in our chemistry. The Shadow frequency and its unconscious fears release some heavy hormones into our body and these upset our mental equilibrium. The more afraid we become, the more we move into doubt. The most horrendous doubt is self-doubt, in which we undermine ourself and actually disempower ourself at a chemical level. When we give way to self-doubt and collapse under it, our body literally loses all its energy. Its systems go offline, we get tired and become unable to function. It's a real horror story, and all because of self doubt. We're unable to love or be loved. We don't even allow ourself to be supported. It's a deadlock.

That's internal doubt taken to its extreme, and then we have external doubt, which is equally horrendous, and so goddam boring. This is doubt as suspicion, scepticism, cynicism. It isn't really scepticism in fact. I always love when I meet someone who considers himself a sceptic (they're usually men), because most of the time they're really a cynic masquerading as a sceptic. A true sceptic is sceptical of their scepticism. This isn't just a cute wordplay; it's true. Next time someone comes at you with this energy, challenge them and ask if that's a label they're wearing. The true sceptic is simply undecided. They are coming from the 63rd Gift in a process of inquiry and open-mindedness. So many people who claim to be scientific are not open-minded; they're simply opinionated and bigoted. They've already decided, and they aren't interested in inquiry. They're riddled with suspicion and all they've done is project their intense self-doubt onto the world around them. In fact, they're as insecure as hell and their bodies are usually deeply cancerous. Doubt can be a cancer if we set up a home for it to live inside us.

These cynics reinforce the fear of the Shadow field. They've lost touch with the feminine, the aspect of our chemistry that naturally perceives the whole, the right brain, the part of us that brings balance to the world we see. When the left brain sees a sunset, it hears only words. It's always thinking about something else, or about tomorrow, or what to say next to impress someone; it's always thinking or talking. When the right brain sees a sunset, it just absorbs its wordless beauty and is rendered speechless.

The other day I sat in a sushi restaurant in central London, and I was next to this couple. She was a beautiful woman, a really sweet essence, and he sat there throughout the whole meal talking incessantly about his work. He hardly even noticed her. I was agog, as I would have just sat there with a huge smile on my face, and let her talk through the whole meal so I could take in her beauty! It made me laugh. That's our logical left brain, which doesn't receive but only puts out. The 63rd Shadow is simply the mind working in the wrong order. It's an imbalance in our brain chemistry. First, we have to take in the beauty of the mystery, and only then can our mind begin to examine it, if, that is, we're still able to speak.

The 63rd Gift – Inquiry

So how the heck do we reroute this insane mind of ours and return to equilibrium, we may ask? Well, as always at the Gift frequency, it's about creativity. The Gift of Inquiry is about keeping an open mind and using the energy of logic rather than becoming a victim of it. This is such a powerful healing gift, this Gift of Inquiry. It's how all seekers begin. The doubt sets off on a journey to discover its source. In the beginning it may not know that this is what it's doing. Someone may use their logical mind to resolve a great problem in the world, and as long as they stay open-minded, the journey of logic can continue and the creativity never dries up. Creative logic only dries up when it tries to fix itself as truth.

There's no such thing as scientific truth. There you go, a bold statement from Mr. Rudd. There's no such thing as scientific truth. There's scientific discovery, scientific insight, but never truth. It's never fixed; inquiry has to always remain open. That's what the word means, and it's filled with energy. The moment the mind becomes fixed in a finite system or structure, we have dogma and opinion. The moment we have those, we have division once again. Remember, the Gift frequency is the frequency of the human heart, and it's about creativity and love.

Inquiry is about having the mind of a child; we're endlessly unravelling the mystery, but a part of us is really only playing. Our right brain holds the balance; it knows that any answer we come up with can only ever be a relative truth. This is a magical perspective and it means we're no longer a victim of logic or thinking, but can use it in service of the whole. That's heart expanding, as opposed to heart contracting.

The moment our mind gets fixed on anything external as truth, we have the dilemma of having to defend it. There will always be those who're willing to attack us, and only when we're truly open-minded and open-ended can we become indefensible, indivisible. So many of us become victims of the system, the mental organised thinking world, and we become serious and closed. The right brain always holds the vision. It knows that life is infinite and grasps the holographic nature of reality. This is what actually frees logic to fly. When we look through the 64th Gene Key, the source of the right brain, there's no inquiry. There's no question there; it's all just infinity, which is a great fear as well at the Shadow frequency. Logic that isn't self-obsessed or self-serving is logic that opens the heart.

The 63rd Gift has so much to offer the world, and it's constantly offering itself to the world. It makes life easier, more efficient, more organised. It creates technology that brings us together, and frees us from hunger and all manner of problems. Science is wonderful and logic is so beautiful, but only in the right hands. At the Gift frequency, logic is used to serve the whole. It serves the long term, big view, and aligns its insights with the knowing of the right brain. It brings great healing into the world. This is what the Gift of Inquiry does.

As I said earlier, the Transformational Way through this Gift sooner or later leads towards the source of the doubt itself. We begin to look inwards, and this is truly powerful. The outer world can really be a distraction; all outer inquiry eventually realises itself as self inquiry. Our open mindedness leads inwards, because inwards is where we can find the only thing we've really been longing for all along – truth, an end to the doubt and an end to the suffering we feel.

When that inner journey begins, the 63rd Gift can be used to our advantage. It's naturally drawn to systems of self-knowledge, to teachers who can guide the logical mind further into the great mystery. This 63rd Gene Key really represents the logical mind that likes to follow sequences and systems and needs answers. Yet, the 63rd Gift is not about answers; it's about questions. It's about going deeply into the doubt and the nature of our being. This is why I said at the beginning of this Gene Key that the journey to truth can only be lived. At a certain point, the Gift of Inquiry moves beyond the mind and into the heart, and the heart too is a great inquirer. What is love? asks our heart, and it asks over and over. Thus open-mindedness engenders open-heartedness.

At this stage, the doubt is not really experienced as doubt anymore; it's more the question mark of our being. When we do experience self doubt, it's simply allowed to move through and it passes by us and is transformed. At the higher reaches of the 63rd Gift we begin to enter into the paradox of our lives and our mind really becomes much softer and pliant. We see the limitations of logic and begin to leave it behind us. We begin to let go into the mystery… and then we dissolve into our search…

The 63rd Siddhi — Truth

Truth is only realised After Completion, when we've finished with logic and the mind. It's not that the mind is seen as useless; it'll always have its beauty, but it has no business with truth. Logic has no relationship to truth. They aren't of the same world or dimension. When logic sees its own futility, it's naturally transcended and will always defeat itself. The logical mind can only operate in a dualistic world. It requires space and time to lay out its patterns. So one day logic returns to its source. Often this Gene Key will give an individual an experience known as divine doubt. It's the final letting go of one's identity within space and time. We experience a void, a terrifying emptiness in which all the doubt is purged from our system and wiped from our DNA.

We emerge reborn. And at the siddhic level, we're always reborn. We emerge flawless, pristine, without doubt and without fear. It's simply gone, forever deleted from our hard drive, and there's no inquiry anymore either. Since there's no inquirer, there's no question mark, inquiry or movement within towards anything. There's just a resting in consciousness, in the truth of consciousness.

When we come to the Gene Keys, we're invited into a world of logical patterns woven from words. We're invited into the world of my inquiry, since this Gene Key is one of my primary Gifts. All around you'll find the fruits of my inquiry as I've transformed my doubt into something inspirational, something I hope you experience as beautiful. You'll also perhaps feel the playfulness of the Gene Keys as a logical system that doesn't take itself seriously and that frequently plays with paradox. Because I feel the truth beneath and between the words, I can't take this system seriously. I feel obliged to keep pointing this out to everyone who comes to this wisdom. Let's not get caught up in terminology, labels, profiles, and processes. Let's allow it all just to flow through. It's a transmission, a stream of truth that has nothing to do with the words and concepts. It's a structure in which the magic of transformation is invited to occur.

This is what makes life so interesting; Truth can't and won't ever be pinned down. No one will ever be able to put it into words. All the greatest teachings attest to this. The Tao Te Ching begins with the words, *The Tao that can be spoken of is not the true Tao.*

Don't you just love that? It undermines itself before it's even begun! There can be no mistake in this. Some people come to this teaching with a presupposition that it's claiming to be the truth, the only way. That's just habit, because that's what most people are claiming these days. Rare are teachings playful enough to undermine themselves from the very beginning.

GENE KEY 63

The 63rd Siddhi has planned this and created this game, because truth, that is, absolute truth, is collective. In order for truth to be realised, all human beings must realise it. One human being realising truth is an aspect of the whole truth, but they can't know the absolute truth. Each Siddhi holds a variation of the same truth, expressed differently through a unique genetic mechanism. Humanity is a single organism. We stand at a time in evolutionary history in which the process of truth is being triggered. One day all humanity will realise itself as truth. Truth must always come about through communion, through creative resonance, and only when the mind has been transcended. As humanity begins to open its heart in the epoch that lies before us, more and more layers of truth will be revealed. We've been through the Age of Outer Inquiry, and we're now passing into the Age of Inner Inquiry, in which more and more people will begin to turn naturally inwards and seek the source of their being. This is the natural Transformational Way of this Gene Key.

The 63rd Siddhi exists already, and has existed forever. We already know and are truth. After completion, the truth will stand revealed for us all to see. This is the only truth there is. At the same time we're moving through a hall of mirrors as we witness the unravelling of truth. For us as individuals, truth has some secrets to utter – that all is truth. Whatever we're experiencing at all times is truth. All is to be trusted. All is to be allowed. Our planet and all the people and creatures that populate it, living, dead and yet to be born, we're all aspects of a single truth, and we each contribute an essence into that truth. How beautiful and infinite is this world and endlessly, endlessly beautiful its paradoxes, gifts, and wonders. Yes, truth makes everything simple. It can't be proven, and that's its beauty. It's beyond our perception, and yet it's closer than a heartbeat. It's our nature and goal, to be an embodiment of truth, so that we too one day can say, 'I am the Way, the Truth, and the Light'.

… THE 64 WAYS

The 64th Way

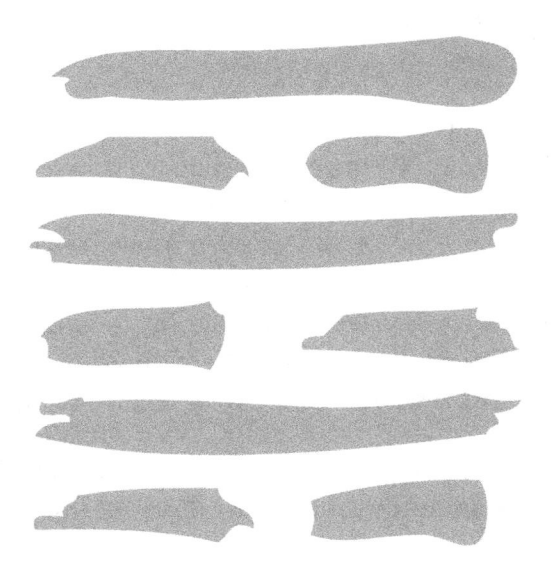

Gene Key 64

THE WAY OF IMAGINATION

The Transformational Way of the 64th Gene Key moves from Confusion to Illumination, and it's the Way of Imagination.

The 64th Gene Key, along with its Programming Partner the 63rd Gene Key, are such an extraordinary pairing. The whole I Ching can be reduced down to four Gene Keys – the 1 and 2 and the 63 and 64, the book ends which mystically contain all the others, the 64th being one of the most unusual of all. My own inner process of contemplation of the 64 Gene Keys and their Transformational Ways has taken me on a magical mystery tour. These codes are alive inside us, so when we enter into contemplation of them they're unconsciously activated in us and our life will reflect their qualities back to us. As long as we stay engaged with the process, eventually we'll receive an insight.

The whole process can be so confusing, and this is the 64th Shadow, Confusion. Here's the secret right up front - confusion needs time. That's all any of this needs - time to become clear on its own, according to a natural process. Of course at the Shadow frequency we never allow ourselves or our processes time, at least not enough time. We allow external or internal forces to pressure us into premature action or activity. Contemplation and digestion takes time in order that we can absorb and assimilate the nutrients and they can make sense to us. This is the path of moving from confusion to Illumination. It's what life is. This is what it means to find out who and what we really are.

The Programming Partner Gene Key 63 is Truth, so life is really about getting to the bottom of life, to answer the questions like: What is the truth? Who am I? And what is the meaning and purpose of it all? These are the questions we carry inside us at some deep level. Until we arrive at a point in our evolution that we're aware of these questions,

Shadow: Confusion   **Gift**: Imagination   **Programming Partner:** Gene Key 63
Dilemma: Consistency   **Siddhi**: Ilumination   **Codon Ring:** The Ring of Alchemy

---

we're really living in the shadowlands. Not that that's bad or wrong; it's just that we're asleep in the matrix. We're dreaming, and our dreams can even be great. We can have a fun life in there, but the Gene Keys are about awakening, and awakening can be uncomfortable. This is the state of confusion. We are confused about reality. This is what the root of that word really means, we're merged, fused, muddled in with creation. We're undistilled, unrefined and our true potential remains unrealised.

It's uncomfortable to realise we're asleep, and yet still be asleep. We have to return to the symbolism of alchemy to get to the bottom of this Gene Key; we're the massa confusa, the nigredo, the primal chaos, the potential, the raw material. Life is the laboratory and it puts us through a series of transformations in which our true nature is progressively revealed from within. In between those transformations we live our lives. Confusion only really arrives when a transformation comes around, because then we enter into the void state where all that we think we know about ourselves is questioned. And there are always transformations. They are catalysed by karmic forces acting out in our lives. Maybe someone robs our house, or we become quite sick, or our lover has an affair, or someone close to us dies. These are part of the drama of life and they all allow us the possibility of awakening something hidden in our nature. They invite us either to expand or contract in our hearts and minds.

The 64th Shadow is never far away; it always accompanies transformation, big or small. It's about entering into the not-knowing, into the mystery. To the mind, it's frightening and confusing. Our mind tries to find a way out in order to resolve the confusion. It wants to come up with a reason for the state we're in. Then it gets us to take some kind of action to resolve the confusion and make it go away. It tries to put things back in order, so we have the illusion of feeling safe again. The irony is that action arising out of confusion only creates more confusion. These are the times when humans are most tested, when we're doubtful and confused. Most of us aren't able or willing to stay that vulnerable, so we retreat into false order and control. We end up repressing the transformation that was inviting us to evolve our awareness in some way.

At the Shadow frequency people don't like change. They like consistency and order. The Shadow consciousness needs order to feel safe, so this is the Dilemma of the 64th Shadow. It doesn't like feeling incomplete, and confusion is a state of utter incompleteness. This 64th Gene Key was originally named 'Before Completion' because it refers to the transformational state. Unlike the 63rd Gene Key, the 64th isn't progressive or sequential; it specialises in sudden quantum leaps.

If we don't embrace the confusion, we never get the leap. Instead we stay with the safe, with the consistency of our life the way it is. As I said at the beginning, the key with this one is time. We just have to stay with the uncertainty and allow it time to reveal the mystery and the magic.

The 64th Gift – Imagination

When we do allow confusion some time and space, then magic comes in. This is the Gift of Imagination and imagination is about magic and surprises and the unexpected. These Gene Keys are powerful and they aren't just about dealing with challenging states - they're magical keys. When we enter into deep contemplation on the Gene Keys, we engage the hidden forces of evolution and involution. We begin to tempt magic back into our life. The word imagination comes from the same root as the word magic, and this little prefix 'ma' is all about influencing matter, mater, the mother, the Maya. It's about manipulating matter; that's what magic is, and that's what imagination is.

I was in France recently, driving through Paris, and I was thinking about the Eiffel Tower. Someone had an idea of 'I'll build a huge tower out of metal right in the middle of my city', and a decade later we have the Eiffel Tower, an iconic symbol for Paris and a part of the whole identity of a culture. Before, it wasn't there at all. It didn't even exist, and that's pretty weird when we really think about it. It's the power of the mind, of psychic energy, and this 64th Gene Key is all about psychic energy, about mind over matter. It's not about being psychic; it's about engaging the transformational forces of nature.

Every Gift has an inherent genius and the 64th has a gift of receiving the psychic energy of creativity right into their bones. This is a Gift of action; it's not enough to imagine something, we also have to enact and implement it. The 64th Shadow can have the vision, but it's too afraid to commit to it because it'll undoubtedly change everything in their safe little world. The 64th Gift is the genius of listening to the visions coming through the imagination and trusting them. At the Gift level, genius always contains boldness. It takes courage to surrender to the force of evolution inside us, because it's like riding a wild stallion – we can only guide it in a certain direction as long as it agrees with us!

When we hear that this is the Gift of Imagination, let's not make the mistake of just thinking that this is about thinking, dreaming, painting, problem solving or writing. We aren't just talking about what career we have; we're talking about moving through profound transformational periods and cycles. We're talking about grappling with universal archetypes that have real power to influence and shake up our life and the world. To fulfil this kind of genius we have to really allow deep change into our life. We can't afford to be married to consistency; genius abhors consistency. As Oscar Wilde once said: 'Constancy is the last refuge of the truly unimaginative'.

Genius thrives on quantum leaps. Imagination means to conjure something magical out of the mists of confusion. It also entails great patience. We can't rush the creative process or it will shut down on us the moment we jump into our mind and try and figure it out. I've learned a thing or two about this Gene Key over the years. In my own Profile, it's my Life's Work, one of my Prime Gifts, and the external expression of my work and creative genius in the world. When you look at the Gene Keys, you see the interplay of the 64th Gift grounded by the 63rd Gift - a body of wisdom that invites quantum leaps, but that's grounded in a logical, sequential system. I've been through intense periods in which my whole life gets elevated to a higher frequency, an old paradigm dies and a new vista opens up inside me. My journey has been all about this process, and it requires constant surrender. The moment I seem to have found an external stability, something happens to shake it all up again and in the process, a powerful creative current is born inside and through me.

We have to live through these Gifts. We have to trust in the impulses moving through our imagination, no matter who we are. It doesn't matter whether we have this in our Profile or not. The Gene Keys are a universal wisdom, each one of them is for everyone.

This 64th says, 'trust in your wildest dreams'. It says to listen and allow them to transform us, and they'll transform the world as they're born. The 64th Gift is illogical, poetic, wild and is about trusting in the spontaneous, the unacceptable, the unexpected. It's about embracing Heisenberg's Uncertainty Principle. To this Gift nothing is ever complete; it's always 'before completion'. There's always the possibility of a greater leap in consciousness and the possibility of a miracle. That's the true power of imagination.

The 64th Siddhi — Illumination

The 64th Siddhi is the crowning glory – Illumination. The moment we truly awaken, we're lit up from within and that which has lain hidden inside our DNA for so long, now blazes out from within every cell of our body. Some people who've awakened say it's a very ordinary thing and not about fireworks or displays of light or haloes or any of that stuff. Some people say that's all distracting propaganda that only serves to pull us off our path. For years I heard that and I always felt disappointed inside, because I really had this inner memory of the fireworks going off somewhere inside me. The good news is that both are true. When we come to the Siddhis, both sides are always true.

When awakening occurs through this Siddhi, it comes as inner light. Some Siddhis are just showy, while others seem completely inconsequential. It all depends on our genetics. Isn't that funny? Awakening is this vast timeless state of consciousness, and as long as we're inside one of these human vehicles, it's limited in its expression by the nature of the matter, the physical DNA.

This is where the Gene Keys are pretty interesting, because they show us the whole panoply of the various manifestations of the awakened state. They give us a glimmer of our 'style', because the Siddhi is the finale of our life process. It's like a cosmic drama, a soap opera for the gods – will we become a divine mother, an ecstatic dervish, a silent monk, a simple ordinary man, a tricky wizard, a world visionary, a paradigm smashing political leader, the source of a new teaching or religion…what will our drama be?

The Gene Keys are all about reading the drama and capturing the essence of the flavour of our awakening. When we look at our Prime Gifts and dive into our sequences along the Golden Path, we're uncovering the script of our awakening. This gives us a sense of our style, and that's so powerful because it draws us along the trajectory of our naturalness.

Even if the codes are incorrect, there will be certain ones that always feel like they resonate so deeply, and those will give us permission to trust in our own inner guidance.

The 64th Siddhi is one of those flashy ones, and it's part of the Codon Ring of Alchemy. All those inner transformations mapped out by the ancient alchemists describe the polishing of the inner essence, and they often represent the inner stages of awakening as colours. We begin with the nigredo, the black raw material. We heat it in the crucible, our belly, and it whitens or turns yellow or green, or coagulates or multiplies. There are all these wonderful metaphorical descriptions of the inner stages, and as we get towards the end, we get to what the medieval alchemists called the Rubedo. The Taoists called it the golden elixir, the red-gold fire. I forget the name given to it in the Vedas, but it's always resplendent, shining, and either diamantine or golden.

This is the stage of Absorption, attained at the higher reaches of the Gift frequency, or if we've read the 22nd Gene Key, the 4th and 5th Initiations. What happens is that our DNA vibrates at such a high frequency that it becomes very, very pure, and an essence begins to crystallise within the core of every molecule. The DNA spiral is like a vortex, and it creates an energetic spin throughout our being. This draws higher dimensional energy fields into play, fields that we call the higher subtle bodies, quantum bodies that interpenetrate deep space and cross over the boundaries of time. It's all about light, which is the key to Illumination and the purpose of alchemy. Light is everything, everywhere, and everything is woven from it, even darkness. Inner light is different from the light that we see. The light of consciousness, the pure light, is beyond our physical understanding of what light is. It's resplendent and shines out from its core. It's life and the life divine.

The 64th Siddhi will light a person up from within like a sun. It will be unmistakeable when we see it. The eyes will shine, the brow will radiate, the whole room around such a person will seem as though shimmering, as if we're standing in the presence of a god, which of course we are. We each are that god, and it'll trigger that same light inside us. It'll become such a reminder to us of who we really are. Such people only come into the world rarely, and after they've gone, legends and stories grow up around them. They become depicted as Saints or great masters; their Illumination can't be denied and they have such a profound impact on the world. They come to remind others that they're still unfinished; they're still 'before completion'.

After the process of absorption comes to a natural culmination, it's as though all the elements within a person's aura are sucked inwards into the core, into what we call the One Point, behind the navel. For a brief moment they stop shining, and the process of refinement hits a natural pause. It's a terrifying moment. It's when we die and the void claims us. It's when we feel as though we're being annihilated. Then all of a sudden, all that energy that's condensed inside us just explodes like a supernova, and after that moment, we're never the same. This is the 6th Initiation, which is when we finally become a fully embodied human being. Now we become our own torus, a source of perpetual inner light, without a single stain, purified eternally, all doubt and fear removed forever from our DNA. Everywhere we look there's light,. Now there's no You, only light streaming forth from within you. These kinds of things aren't easy to put into words. It takes a poet of the 64th Siddhi to do so… so here's what it felt like to the great mystical poet Kabir:

A million suns are ablaze with light.
The sea of blue spreads in the sky.
The fever of life is stilled
And all stains are washed away
when I sit in that world.
Hark to the unstruck bells and drums!
Take your delight in love.
Rains pour down without water
and the rivers are streams of light.
One love it is that pervades the whole world -
Few there are who know it fully.

THE 64 WAYS

Dilemmas of the Gene Keys

1 - Numbness
2 - Agenda
3 - Clinging
4 - Reasons
5 - Surrender
6 - Protection
7 - Boundaries
8 - Imitation
9 - Perspective
10 - Ease
11 - Belief
12 - Aloneness
13 - Pessimism
14 - Self-Belief
15 - Comfort
16 - Laziness
17 - Politics
18 - Flaws
19 - Heresy
20 - Self-Awareness
21 - Discipline
22 - Accountability
23 - Timing
24 - Gravity
25 - Anxiety
26 - Lack
27 - Consideration
28 - Avoidance
29 - Postponement
30 - Temptation
31 - Choice
32 - Panic

33 - Attention
34 - Trying
35 - Self-Indulgence
36 - Overwhelm
37 - Submission
38 - Habit
39 - Blockages
40 - Excess
41 - Planning
42 - Disappointment
43 - Knowing
44 - Hierarchy
45 - Insecurity
46 - Fortune
47 - Ownership
48 - Not-Knowing

49 - Needs
50 - Resignation
51 - Harshness
52 - Shallow Breathing
53 - Restlessness
54 - Egotism
55 - External Validation
56 - Pleasure/Pain
57 - Trust
58 - Rhythm
59 - Trauma
60 - Balance
61 - Knowledge
62 - Facts
63 - Logic
64 - Consistency